THE ELECTRIC VEGETARIAN

natural cooking the food processor way

Paula Szilard   Juliana J. Woo

Johnson Publishing Company: *Boulder*

Cover design and illustrations by Hanna West

LC Catalog Card No.: 80-83141

Distributed by
Ten Speed Press
Box 7123
Berkeley, California 94707

Printed in the United States of America by
Johnson Publishing Company
1880 South 57th Court
Boulder, Colorado 80301

Dedicated to

My mother Pansy, who guided me through the preparation and cooking of many meals, and to the memory of my father, Joel.

Julie

My parents, who have farmed or gardened organically as far back as I can remember, and who have taught me the simple pleasures of homegrown, homecooked food.

Paula

Contents

Foreword

Vegetarians in the United States are often misunderstood. The typical reaction which the vegetarian encounters in polite conversation is, how do you find anything to eat, or where do you get your protein? This is strange, indeed, because a sound vegetarian diet is invariably more diverse than that of the person who eats meat, and it also contains adequate protein. What this type of remark indicates is that Americans in general are uninformed about vegetarian cookery and nutrition.

There is a good reason for this, of course. While the number of vegetarians in the United States is steadily increasing, overall we remain a society of meat eaters. This approach to eating is sustained by a fallacy that dictates a meat-centered diet for adequate nutrition and equates meat eating with strength and endurance. This meat myth, however, no longer commands the respect that it once did. Most people continue to believe it, and I suspect that it will be many years before it is completely abandoned, yet it is obvious to anyone who takes the time to look that its unquestioned position of authority has undergone considerable erosion.

The most influential agent in this erosion has been Frances Moore Lappé, in her cogently argued and widely read book, *Diet For A Small Planet* (1971). She explained how various non-meat foods can be combined to supply protein (the bug-a-boo of the meat myth) that is as good or better than meat, but much cheaper. It was through this argument that the American public was first exposed to the concept of protein complementarity, and the meat myth suffered a setback from which it is unlikely to recover.

During the same period in which Lappé's approach to complementary protein vegetarian cooking began to gain acceptance, Americans were becoming more health conscious. At one level this change was reflected in the growth of the physical fitness movement, the increase in the number of health oriented publications, and the dramatic growth of the natural foods industry. At the same time, a concern developed over the presence of synthetic hormones in our meat, the use of pesticides on our crops, and the excess of fat and lack of fiber in the typical American diet.

At the institutional level this concern for the American diet found expression in reports and guidelines emanating from the United States government. *Dietary Goals of the United States*, prepared by the Select Committee on Nutrition and Human Needs of the United States Senate, appeared in 1977. It was followed in 1979 by *Healthy People: The Surgeon General's Report on Health Promotion and Disease Prevention*, and in the same year by The National Cancer Institute's *Statement on Diet, Nutrition and Cancer*. In early 1980, the Department of Agriculture and Department of Health, Education and Welfare jointly issued *Dietary Guidelines for Americans*. What these documents have in common is a concern for the over-consumption of dietary fat in the United States and the relative under-consumption of complex carbohydrates. To remedy this situation they recommended a reduction in fat intake, red meat being one of its principal sources, and an increase in the consumption of vegetables, whole grains, and fruits as sources of complex carbohydrates.

What appears more and more obvious, then, is that there seems to be a growing body of scientific opinion which suggests that the "vegetarian alternative" should be taken seriously. Thus, if one places a premium on good health, vegetarian eating may come closer to "the diet of choice" than the typical American diet, and may well prove to be the wave of the future as we learn more about our nutritional needs and how to realize them.

But, even if one were to accept this argument and decide to become a vegetarian, there would still remain the problem of preparation time. The manual chopping, slicing, grating, and other tedious tasks associated with vegetarian cooking are very time consuming. Until the advent of the food processor, the prospect of such tedium deterred many people in the United States from trying vegetarian cuisine and severely limited the creativity of those who were already vegetarians. This, I think, is where the authors have made their real contribution. They have blended the nutritional knowledge provided by Lappé and others with their own culinary experience, and applied a contemporary technology—the food processor—to reduce the time one needs to spend in the kitchen. This not only results in delicious food in less time, but may prove to be the optimal approach to vegetarian cooking for Americans who characteristically lead fast-paced lives which leave little time for meal preparation.

My opinion is that the food processor is going to be partially responsible for a vegetarian revolution in the United States and that *The Electric Vegetarian* will contribute significantly to this change. I whole-heartedly recommend this book to the aspiring or experienced vegetarian, the person who wants to reduce his meat intake, and anyone interested in good eating. *The Electric Vegetarian* is a synthesis of the best of the East and the West and is an idea whose time has come.

A. Manoharan, M.D., Dr. P.H.
Professor of International Health,
School of Public Health;
Professor of Community Medicine,
John A. Burns School of Medicine;
University of Hawaii.
July 1980
Presently Medical Director,
Harlem Hospital Center,
Clinical Professor of
Public Health Administration,
School of Public Health,
Columbia University.

Introduction

Traditional vegetarian cooking is as old as cooking itself. Modern Western vegetarian cooking has often tried to imitate it, but has not been overly successful. Both are time-consuming, and though the traditional has been both tasty and nutritious, the contemporary often has not been. Therefore, we consider this book a departure point for a new, less time-consuming style of vegetarian cooking—a style that maximizes taste, nutritional value, and ease of preparation. We emphasize taste because too often it has been neglected in the attempt to achieve nutritional soundness. We stress nutrition because it has frequently been disregarded in the pursuit of taste. And we underscore ease of preparation because the vegetarian cook has often had to sacrifice both nutritional value and taste to save time. With the advent of the food processor none of these values needs be slighted in an attempt to realize the others.

The food processor is without a doubt the most revolutionary kitchen appliance to appear in the last twenty years. In a vegetarian kitchen, where most cooking is done from scratch, it is nothing short of miraculous and has given us a sense of freedom we hope you will soon share. It has opened up a whole new world of good cooking and eating where the imagination is unconstrained by conventional techniques, and the dull, repetitive tasks no longer take up so much time that they inhibit our creativity. Chopping, slicing, shredding, grating, puréeing, mixing, and kneading take only seconds or minutes now. And the processor allows us to do things that were difficult, if not impossible, before, such as pulverizing chiles for enchilada sauce or grinding sesame seeds right into a crêpe batter.

Here are only a few of the tasks that can be performed by this modern miracle machine using each of the major basic blades or discs.

METAL BLADE
  Finely chopping onions and other vegetables
  Mincing parsley and mint for tabouli salad
  Making nut flours and nut butters
  Making mayonnaise
  Making pasta dough
  Mixing quick breads, cakes, and pancakes
  Mixing and kneading bread dough
  Making pastry doughs
  Making bread crumbs
  Puréeing garbanzos for hummus
  Making pesto sauce
  Grating hard cheeses

SLICING DISC
  Slicing vegetables and fruits
  Slicing cabbage for coleslaw
  Cutting vegetables into julienne strips
  Frenching beans

SHREDDING DISC
  Shredding carrots and other vegetables for salads
  Shredding potatoes for potato pancakes
  Shredding cheese

We adhere to the complementary protein approach to vegetarian cooking. Throughout the preparation of this book we have been inspired by Frances Moore Lappé's now classic work *Diet For A Small Planet*. From the beginning, we wanted to make this a cookbook with a real difference. We wanted to emphasize nutrition in a very concrete way and decided to do this chiefly by providing detailed information on the protein content of each dish. We focused on protein because the supposed lack of it is often viewed as an obstacle to proper nutrition in a meatless diet. You will notice that all of our main dishes (over 100) contain at least 10 grams of protein per serving.

We decided to include a chapter on the "Basics of Vegetarian Nutrition" to furnish a framework for interpreting our protein calculations. It contains information on protein and on other nutrients which are difficult to obtain in some vegetarian diets. We decided not to expand this chapter to include a discussion of all major nutrients as they relate to a vegetarian diet because this is primarily a cookbook with supplementary nutritional information—not a nutrition book containing a few recipes.

Although experienced vegetarians will find some new information here, the nutrition chapter may be most useful to those just starting out. It is, however, possible to use the recipes without reading the entire chapter. Simply follow the suggestions at the end of the chapter on "How to Get a Balanced Diet Using this Book" and familiarize yourself with the symbols for the various groups or families of complementary foods. It will then be easy for you to complement the major protein source served at every meal. Complementing without worrying about precise proportions is so simple that it will quickly become second nature to you.

Vegetarian cuisine has been dominated by what we euphemistically refer to as "the health food school of cooking," where a few foods are emphasized to the exclusion of others because they are viewed as "health promoting." Food is regarded as medicine, and questions of taste are largely irrelevant. Our orientation is quite different. We believe that nutritious food must taste delicious, and to insure this we have tried and tested all of our recipes with the food processor until we felt they were as good and tasty as possible.

Other than pleasing the palate, irresistible food can provide an incentive for family members to be at home when meals are served instead of grabbing a bite on the run. Good food also furnishes a pleasurable atmosphere for socializing with friends, and looking forward to a sandwich made with homemade bread for lunch certainly makes the work day pass a bit more quickly. So if you expected another volume of nondescript recipes, seemingly designed to be morally uplifting, rather than taste teasing, you will be pleasantly surprised.

You will also be surprised if you expect to be subjected to ethical arguments for becoming a vegetarian. Although there are some good ones, we do not make them here for two reasons. The first and most important is that this is a cookbook, not a philosophy text. Secondly, we believe the change to vegetarian eating is usually a long term process, barring some traumatic incident, which must come from within and not from without. We have observed that those individuals who remain vegetarians have made the transition gradually. They progressively eat less and less meat until they completely lose their taste for it. On the other hand, if the conversion involves the overnight "giving up" of meat, the new style of eating is usually short-lived because the resulting sacrifice and self-denial are difficult to sustain. We are not going to try to convince you to become a vegetarian, but if you are ready to make the change, this book will help you to do so.

Whether you are making the transition or have already made it, we can help you prepare pleasurable and nourishing meals in a reasonable length of time. Although our recipes are aimed chiefly at lacto-ovo-vegetarians, vegans (pure vegetarians) will be able to use a large number of them. Also, those committed to a natural style of eating will find that, whenever possible, we use unrefined or minimally processed foods. And those who, for economic or health reasons, are attempting to cut back on their meat intake will be pleased to discover that we include an extensive section of over 100 main dishes. In addition, our numerous recipes and detailed directions for making whole grain breads and pastas will be useful to all cooks who want to prepare these foods using only the most wholesome of ingredients.

Although all of our recipes use the food processor, we do not view the book as a basic manual on how to use these machines. There are a number of such books available already. Food processors differ slightly and directions for the basic procedures may vary a little, depending on the make of the machine. It is best to familiarize yourself thoroughly with the capabilities, directions for use, and safety precautions that come with your particular model.

We developed all of our recipes on a Cuisinart food processor, but the directions for preparation apply equally well to other machines. If you have not as yet purchased a machine, the best advice we can give you is to consider very carefully all of the tasks you will want it to perform. For bread making, for instance, it is wise to have a heavy base so your machine does not "wander" when it kneads the heavier whole grain bread doughs. A machine with direct drive is preferable to a belt-driven model because the belts may break under a heavy load. It is best to consult *Consumer Reports* for information about which machines are most proficient at performing the tasks you have in mind. Talking to food processor owners is also a good idea, but remember that the same features are not equally important to everyone.

Basics of Vegetarian Nutrition

Vegetarian Diets Can Be Healthful

Though much has been written about vegetarianism and vegetarian nutrition, not all of it is reliable. There are, for instance, a number of books based on principles totally foreign to sound nutrition, such as those advocating extreme macrobiotic diets. Numerous vegetarian cookbooks contain recipes for main dishes clearly without a major protein source. In 1974, anxiety about vegetarian diets had reached such a level, particularly among parents concerned about the health of their vegetarian offspring, that the Committee on Nutritional Misinformation of the Food and Nutrition Board in the National Research Council considered it necessary to issue a brief statement explaining that a well-planned vegetarian diet could be nutritionally adequate.[1]

A nutritionally sound diet can be attained by a balanced approach to vegetarian cooking such as we present in this book. However, a word of caution is in order for the new vegetarian. It is unwise to stop eating meat without changing dietary habits as a whole. When it comes to matters of health, we recommend a conservative stance. We have had friends who have briefly experimented with vegetarian diets without otherwise changing their eating habits. They suffered from health problems as a result, or returned to a meat-centered diet because it made them feel better. If you see yourself inching toward vegetarianism, it's best to do it right and eat a balanced diet! If you follow our suggestions and adhere to our recipes, you will find them healthful and no more demanding than the cooking that you do now.

Making the transition from a meat-centered diet to a vegetarian diet means examining all of your assumptions about what constitutes a balanced diet and an adequate protein source. People often think of different foods as being composed of, or representative of, major nutrient classes—carbohydrates, fats, or proteins—when in fact most unrefined foods contain two or all three. These misconceptions are due to established dietary habits in our culture. Meat, eggs, cheese, fish, and milk are thought of as providing the protein in our diet; grains and legumes are commonly thought of as starchy and as contributing only carbohydrate. Actually, meat and fish contain both protein and fat, and milk and cheese contain protein, carbohydrate, and fat. Grains and legumes also contain all three nutrient classes.

Natural Is Best

We are committed to foods which are as close to their original state as possible. It is true that most food is "natural," in the sense of coming from nature, but the important point is how much processing it has undergone, what percentage of the edible portion remains, what nutrients are left, and what additives have been introduced to make the food easier to process, more colorful, or longer lasting. Our preference is for unrefined whole grain cereals, fresh fruits and vegetables, naturally aged cheeses, and dried, not canned legumes. We use sugar and even honey conservatively.

The following are some reasons why natural foods are preferable to refined foods:

1. They taste better. Americans are used to poor tasting and denatured food because too much stress has been placed on convenience and increased shelf life. As a nation, our sense of taste has become perverted toward the artificial.

2. Whole grain foods, such as brown rice and

whole wheat flour, contain more protein and a better balance of amino acids than their refined counterparts. Vegetarians can ill afford such losses because of their dependence on plant protein sources.

3. Most whole foods are higher in vitamins and minerals than refined foods. Of all the nutrients removed in the refining process, only a few are replaced by enrichment. Checking any standard table of food values for vitamins and minerals contained in whole wheat flour vs. enriched white flour should convince even the most skeptical.

4. It's best to eat whole foods to insure obtaining nutrients which have not yet been identified. Since nutrition is a relatively young science, we really don't have any guarantee that all essential nutrients have been discovered. It makes sense to avoid highly refined foods from which many important, but as yet unknown, nutrients may have been removed.

5. Whole foods, especially grains, legumes, and vegetables, are much higher in dietary fiber than refined foods. Although some of the claims made for high fiber diets are as yet unsubstantiated, fiber has been shown useful in the prevention and treatment of constipation, diverticulosis, and the irritable bowel syndrome. Although some physicians still maintain that bowel movements at two to three day intervals are normal, Denis Burkitt and others[2] have demonstrated that the refined foods eaten in industrial societies are responsible for some of our digestive problems. Native peoples who eat a high-fiber diet have larger, heavier stools that absorb more water, and therefore pass without strain. In short, being normal in a constipated society means only that you are as constipated as everyone else.

What Is Protein?

The body needs a continuous supply of protein for growth, maintenance, and repair of tissues, as well as for the production of enzymes, hormones, and antibodies.

Protein is composed of twenty-two amino acids. These are literally the building blocks with which all plant and animal proteins are constructed—including those required by the human body.

Nine of these amino acids cannot be produced in the body and must be obtained in the food we eat. These are referred to as the essential amino acids. Not only must these be present in our food, but each must be available in the quantity the body needs and in the correct proportion to the others. The body is capable of utilizing only a certain limited "profile" of amino acids. If one of the nine essential amino acids is in short supply, it limits the extent to which

all of the others are used and is therefore called the limiting amino acid.

The protein quality, or usability, of a food is largely determined by its amino acid profile and its digestibility. The protein in the egg is generally considered the highest in quality because it closely resembles the amino acid pattern required by human beings. This is why the egg is frequently used as a standard for evaluating the quality of other proteins.

To Complement or Not to Complement?

The question of protein is generally uppermost in people's minds whenever vegetarianism is discussed. Of all the books published on the subject only a handful stand out: Frances Moore Lappé's now classic *Diet for a Small Planet*;[3] its companion volume, Ellen Ewald's *Recipes for a Small Planet*;[4] and the superbly well-produced and researched *Laurel's Kitchen: A Handbook for Vegetarian Cookery and Nutrition* by Laurel Robertson, Carol Flinders, and Bronwen Godfrey.[5]

All of these books provide highly reliable information. Yet Lappé and Ewald take a much more structured approach to protein nutrition than we think necessary—both recommend complementing proteins at each meal in rather precise proportions. The authors of *Laurel's Kitchen* emphasize a balanced diet but consider complementing proteins at each meal unnecessary. We are convinced that a middle course is best. It is not essential to approach complementing with Lappé's precision, but some complementing is necessary at each meal because the body can compensate only partially for poor quality proteins by recycling amino acids from within.

Too Much Protein?

Many Americans daily consume twice or more the recommended amount of protein. Most of this is animal protein, making the typical diet very high in saturated fat which has long been implicated as a possible factor in coronary heart disease. Unsaturated fat is somewhat superior, but even it requires caution since there is a correlation, though not necessarily a cause-effect relationship, between high total dietary fat intake and breast and colon cancer rates. Moreover, consuming excessive fat not only displaces other valuable nutrients, but can also lead to obesity, as can an excess of calories in either of the other nutrient classes. Remember that a gram of fat contains nine calories, while a gram of carbohydrate or protein contains about four calories.

Popular opinion has it that excess protein will not result in weight gain. This could not be farther from the truth. There is simply no way for the body to store protein as protein. If the body gets more than it needs, the excess is either broken down and used as an energy source, like the carbohydrates and fats, or it is stored in the adipose tissue as fat. To use protein as a source of energy is both expensive and extremely wasteful.

Where Do You Get Your Protein?

The following families or groups of foods serve as the major protein sources in a well-balanced vegetarian diet:

Legumes: Includes all dried beans, peas, lentils, soybeans, and soybean products such as tofu.

Grains: Includes all whole grain cereals and cereal products such as wheat, rye, triticale, oats, barley, millet, rice, buckwheat, and corn.

Seeds: Includes sesame, sunflower, and pumpkin seeds.

Nuts: This group is limited chiefly to those nuts which are not excessively high in fat content, such as peanuts and cashews, and nut butters made from these nuts. Other nuts, such as pistachios and black walnuts, are excluded only because they are now too expensive to serve as major protein sources for the vegetarian.

Milk and Milk Products: In addition to fluid milk, this group includes non-instant, non-fat dry milk and all cheese except very fatty cheeses, such as cream cheese.

Eggs: These should be used conservatively until the dietary cholesterol-heart disease controversy is resolved.

Vegetarians Do Not Live By Vegetables Alone

Although all plant foods contain all of the essential amino acids, legumes, nuts, seeds, and grains are the best sources of plant protein. Fruits and vegetables are generally not good sources because their total percentage of protein is quite low and their amino acid balance is frequently poor. There are, however, a few notable exceptions, such as potatoes and certain leafy green vegetables, which can constitute acceptable supplementary sources of protein, but they do not contain enough protein to be considered adequate sources by themselves. Vegetables and fruits are, of course, extremely good sources of vitamins and minerals and should be eaten in liberal quantities to satisfy our requirements for these nutrients.

We've done some calculating to illustrate the futility of trying to meet protein requirements by eating vegetables alone. Let's assume that you are the mythical American female between the ages of 19 and 50, and that you weigh 120 pounds. You need roughly 44 grams of high quality protein (around 75% usable) per day. If you should try to meet this need with cooked carrots alone, you must take into account that 100 grams (⅔ cup) provides less than one gram of protein, and that it is not of high quality. To make up for this, you would need to consume approximately 53 cups of carrots a day to obtain your required amount of high quality protein. For most people that would be a feat indeed—not to mention that it might change the color of your skin!

Contrast this with the amount of protein contained in grains and legumes. The same 120-pound woman can obtain her daily requirement for protein from 1⅙ small loaf of bread, if the bread is made of 3 cups of whole wheat flour per loaf. If she obtained all of her protein from cooked garbanzo beans alone, she would need roughly 3¾ cups of cooked beans. Either approach is much better than eating 53 cups of carrots.

These extreme examples illustrate the two major dimensions of our concern with protein intake—the percentage of protein in the food and its amino acid composition. While it is possible to live on foods which contain a very small percentage of protein and a relatively poor amino acid balance, we must consume them in large quantities to make up for these deficiencies.

The Tradition of Complementing

Foods vary widely in the amounts of essential amino acids they contain. Combining two or more foods in one dish, or at a single meal, allows them to complement one another, bringing the amount of each amino acid up to a higher level in relation to the others and results in a higher quality protein. Consequently, the number of protein grams the body can use is greater than when the foods are eaten separately.

This principle of protein complementarity was popularized and made comprehensible to the layperson by Frances Moore Lappé in *Diet For a Small Planet.* Although her major concerns were the world food supply and the wasteful consumption of meat in the wealthier countries, to her alone must go the credit for making millions of Americans aware that it is possible to eat a vegetarian diet without being deficient in protein. This was no simple feat because Americans have long been oversold on the value of a high animal protein diet.

Interestingly, most traditional cuisines have evolved some time-tested complementary dishes. Yet these evolved before there was any conceptual framework to hang them on. They were made up of the basic foods available to a large percentage of the population where meat was either in short supply or inequitably distributed. People used their imaginations to combine these foods in appetizing ways. In Mexico, the beans with rice and beans with corn (tortillas) combinations occur in a large number of staple dishes and meals. In India, dals (legumes of all types) are served with rice and chapatis, a whole grain bread. In Italy, numerous pasta dishes feature noodles and some type of cheese. Some Middle Eastern combinations are sesame, garbanzos, and wheat, found both in felafel and hummus with pita bread. In Switzerland, cheese fondue with bread is a national favorite. In China and Japan, tofu and other soy products are always eaten with rice.

What to Combine and Why

Animal proteins frequently contain a somewhat better amino acid balance and a higher percentage of protein than plant sources. Liquid foods like milk are an exception because they contain a great deal of water, and therefore a lower percentage of protein than solid foods, such as meat and cheese.

Amino acids in most foods are distributed in such a way that if we concern ourselves with supplying three or four of the essential amino acids, the others will automatically be present. This applies to animal and vegetable proteins alike.[6] Foods may be deficient (low in relation to the egg or other standard) in any of the following amino acids: tryptophan, isoleucine, lysine, and the combination of sulfur-containing amino acids, methionine and cystine.

Fortunately, however, amino acid strengths and weaknesses generally occur in patterns that apply to entire groups or families of foods. Most legumes (beans, peas, lentils, and soybeans) are generally deficient in tryptophan and the sulfur-containing amino acids. They are reasonably strong, on the other hand, in isoleucine and exceptionally strong in lysine. Most grains are deficient in isoleucine and lysine, but higher in tryptophan and the sulphur-containing amino acids. Combining the two foods in adequate proportions raises the level of the sulphur-containing amino acids and tryptophan and results in a larger percentage of usable protein by increasing the amounts of the limiting amino acids in the mixture. (See the appendix for a detailed discussion of amino acids.)

The following are some important general principles relating to the complementing of protein foods.

Combinations of Entire Food Families where most members combine interchangeably with other members:

1. *Milk or a milk product* with or in any dish complements all grains, legumes, seeds, nuts, and certain vegetables, such as potatoes. In other words, milk products complement all vegetable proteins.

2. *Legumes* in dried form, such as all beans, peas, lentils, soybeans, and soybean products complement grains such as rice, millet, wheat, rye, triticale, and corn as well as flours and other products made from these grains.

3. *Seeds*, such as sesame and sunflower seeds, complement legumes.

Combinations of Individual Foods which cannot be extended to other members of the family:

1. *Peanuts* with sunflower seeds
2. *Sesame seeds* with rice

Multiple Combinations used less frequently:

1. *Peanuts* with wheat and milk
2. *Soybeans or soybean products* with sesame seeds and wheat
3. *Soybeans or soybean products* with peanuts and sesame seeds
4. *Soybeans or soybean products* with peanuts and wheat

How Much Protein Is Enough?

As we have indicated, the amount of protein required varies considerably with the quality of the protein consumed. Populations living primarily on an animal protein diet require fewer grams of protein a day than populations consuming a diet of vegetable proteins. If a vegetarian diet is complemented in part by animal protein sources such as milk and milk products, its usable protein equivalent will be close or identical to the animal protein based diet.

A lacto-ovo-vegetarian diet relies to a considerable extent on animal protein sources, such as milk and milk products of all types. We estimate that its protein usability is somewhere in the neighborhood of 70-75%, using the egg as a standard.

Like the protein content in a diet, the protein requirements of an individual can be stated in two ways: in terms of usable protein grams per day or total protein grams per day. In *Diet for a Small Planet*, Frances Moore Lappé computed requirements in terms of usable protein grams. In our view, this is much more important in a pure vegetarian diet than in a lacto-ovo-vegetarian diet. Because our diet is so close to the national norm, we prefer to base our calculations on the number of total protein grams as expressed in the *Recommended Dietary Allowances* issued by the Food and Nutrition Board of the National Research Council.[7]

Since it is nitrogen that makes protein different from other nutrients, estimates of the amount of protein required for maintenance of the healthy adult are based on nitrogen balance studies. If the total amount of nitrogen (protein) consumed is equivalent to the amount eliminated in the feces and urine and lost through the hair, perspiration, etc., one is said to be in a state of nitrogen equilibrium. This means that no new protein tissues are being built, nor is the body forced to deplete muscle tissue to maintain vital organs, as in negative nitrogen balance. Growing children and pregnant women are said to be in positive nitrogen balance because they retain more nitrogen than they lose. All nitrogen (protein) lost from the body must be replaced, or nitrogen equilibrium cannot be maintained. These nitrogen losses are used by the Food and Nutrition Board as a basis for calculating the recommended dietary allowance for protein.

The adult allowance for protein is .8 grams per kilogram, or .36 grams per pound of body weight. This means that the average 154-pound man should be consuming about 56 grams of protein a day, and the average 120-pound woman around 44 grams.

This allowance is intended to keep most healthy individuals in the population in nitrogen balance. It is arrived at by totalling all known protein losses, adding a margin of safety to allow for individual differences, allowing for the reduced usability of protein when consumed at or near requirement levels, and then making adjustments for the protein quality of the typical American diet.

Nitrogen balance studies indicate that a man weighing 154 pounds sustains nitrogen losses roughly equivalent to 24 grams of protein a day. A woman weighing 120 pounds loses approximately 19 grams a day. These losses are equivalent to .34 grams per kilogram or .15 grams per pound of body weight. It cannot be overemphasized, however, that these are averages only, and that precise amounts vary a great deal from individual to individual. About half of the population loses more nitrogen daily, and half loses less. Since the Food and Nutrition Board is supposed to make recommendations that apply to almost all healthy people in the country, these amounts are increased to meet the needs of 97.5% of the population.

One of these increases takes into account the reduced usability of even high quality (egg) protein when intake approaches requirement levels. It is recognized that because of this reduced usability, an amount exceeding the required level is needed to maintain nitrogen balance.

The other increase allows for the protein quality or usability of our national diet. The mixed animal and vegetable protein diet of the United States is assumed to be 75% usable. If we lived in a country where plant protein diets were the norm, the usability of our diet would be approximately 55%.

It is true that the recommended allowances for protein exceed the needs of most normal individuals, but they are actually not high enough for the 2½% of the population with abnormally high needs. Even though it is possible to make statistical generalizations about the population as a whole, it is virtually impossible for a given individual to know what his or her particular needs are. When viewed in this light, the somewhat conservative approach taken by the Food and Nutrition Board makes a great deal of sense.

An individual's need for protein varies throughout the life cycle. During the first year of life an infant triples its body weight. Its increase in body protein is over 3 grams a day. This growth must be adequately provided for in a diet consisting only of milk. As children become older, less and less protein is needed for growth, and more is used for maintenance.

The protein allowance for pregnant women must be liberal enough to provide adequately for the growing fetus, the placenta and other support tissue, as well as meeting the mother's requirement for maintenance. No wonder it is set so high! During lactation the mother's protein intake must be high enough for maintenance and an adequate supply of milk for the infant, with some allowance for a loss of efficiency during the conversion process. (The table of recommended dietary allowances in the appendix contains detailed information on the protein requirements for infants, children, adolescents, and adults.)

Other Nutrients

It is outside the scope of this book to discuss each essential nutrient as it relates to a vegetarian diet. For a good discussion of all the major nutrients, see *Laurel's Kitchen*. Our concern in this section is to alert the reader to those vitamins and minerals which tend to be inadequately supplied in a vegetarian diet: namely, iron, zinc, calcium, and vitamin B-12.[8]

Iron: The recommended allowance for a woman in her child-bearing years is 18 milligrams per day. This is about twice the amount recommended for men, because iron is regularly lost in the menstrual flow. This allowance is inadequately supplied even by the typical American diet,[9] which is much higher in usable iron than a vegetarian diet. The iron intake of rapidly growing children and adolescents of both sexes may also be inadequate.

Until recently, it has been assumed that approximately 10% of all dietary iron is absorbed. Now that we have more data, we know that we must clearly differentiate between heme iron, a highly absorbable form derived from animal tissues, and nonheme iron, derived from both animals and plants.[10] An estimated 40% of the iron in animal tissues is heme iron, and this is absorbable in amounts ranging from 25-35%. Nonheme iron, the only source of iron in a vegetarian diet, is much more plentiful in all diets than heme iron, yet absorption may be as low as 2%. Its absorption in any particular meal is markedly influenced by the following factors:

1. The amount of animal tissue consumed, in other words, the amount of meat, fish, or fowl.

2. The level of vitamin C in the meal. This vitamin has the effect of reducing iron in the ferric state to ferrous iron, a much more absorbable form. Since vitamin C is destroyed by heat, the cooked food itself cannot be relied upon to provide a sufficient amount of this vitamin.

3. The iron status of the individual. The more limited the iron stores of an individual, the larger the fraction of dietary iron absorbed, and vice versa.

Since vegetarians do not have the option of consuming animal tissue, they must rely on other ways of increasing the amount of absorbed iron—for example, eating fresh vitamin C rich fruits and vegetables at the same meal with iron rich foods, such as dried beans, peas and lentils. It is assumed that 1 milligram of vitamin C promotes iron absorption as well as 1 gram of meat. This means that in terms of its enhancing effect, 100 milligrams of vitamin C should be equivalent to a typical 3½-ounce serving of meat. Absorption of iron in a meal containing only nonheme iron and minute amounts of vitamin C is calculated at roughly 3%, whereas the consumption of at least 90 milligrams of vitamin C increases absorption to approximately 8%.[11]

Another way of increasing the quantity of absorbed iron is to eat liberal amounts of yeast-raised bread. Much of the iron in wheat and other grains is bound up tightly in the form of a chemical substance known as phytate. While the dough is rising, the action of the yeast helps activate the phytase, an enzyme which breaks this bond, and releases the iron for absorption by the body.

Cooking foods in cast iron pots and pans has also been suggested as a way of increasing iron intake.[12] This practice results in some of the iron being leached out into the food. We only suggest this as a possible option. We don't do it ourselves because we don't like the taste of certain foods cooked in iron pots.

All of the above suggestions will help to bring the amount of absorbed iron to acceptable levels. It should be kept in mind, however, that individuals in groups which are likely to be deficient, such as women in their child-bearing years, should consider an iron supplement as the most reliable way of insuring an adequate intake.

Zinc: This mineral, which is an essential constituent of the hormone insulin and of enzymes involved in the metabolic process, is in short supply even in a conventional American diet. It is extremely scarce in a vegetarian diet. Recommended allowances are high because absorption is low. In vegetable sources absorption is limited because, like iron and calcium, this mineral is bound up in the form of phytate. Yeast raised breads are a good source. However, to meet the daily adult allowance, a vegetarian would have to eat an uncomfortably large quantity of certain foods (7½ cups of garbanzo beans, 1¾ loaves of whole wheat bread, 1¼ cups of wheat germ, 16⅔ cups milk, etc.). Supplementation is desirable.

Calcium: The equivalent of three glasses of milk per day is sufficient to meet the needs of most of the population. In a purely plant-based diet, though, this nutrient may be supplied in inadequate amounts and is inconsistently absorbed. Calcium in plants is frequently bound up in the form of phytate and oxalate, the same compounds that bind together other essential minerals. Phytate is chiefly found in whole grain cereals, while oxalate is found in certain vegetables, such as beet greens, spinach, rhubarb, chard, and soybeans. These compounds are thought to form insoluble salts in the intestines and are difficult or impossible to break down under ordinary circumstances. The extent to which these substances make calcium unavailable is still controversial.[13]

Other factors which are thought to decrease calcium absorption and retention are high levels of dietary protein—levels clearly exceeding twice the recommended allowance[14]—and high levels of phosphate.[15] Phosphates occur naturally in some foods, such as bran, whole wheat flour and unpolished rice, or may be introduced in the form of food additives.

It should be emphasized that calcium intake has virtually no effect on blood calcium levels, which remain relatively constant. The body simply withdraws what it needs from storage in the bones if dietary calcium is inadequate and redeposits it when blood levels begin to rise. If calcium is inadequate over a long period of time, these stores become depleted, resulting in porous, brittle bones. The whole system is a bit analogous to withdrawing from your savings account in time of financial crisis and then replenishing your savings when you have more income. Also, when calcium intake is high, less of it is absorbed, and as a result more is excreted in the feces.

An adequate intake of vitamin D or exposure to sunshine is essential for the absorption of calcium. Other substances which increase absorption are lactose (milk sugar) and certain amino acids, such as lysine.[16] All of these are contained in vitamin D fortified milk, making it the best possible source of this mineral. For the lactose intolerant, fermented milk products such as buttermilk and yogurt, which are low in lactose, may help. Or, lactase (the enzyme that breaks down lactose) may be purchased in tablet form and added to milk.

Vegetable foods which can make a small, but significant contribution toward meeting our daily allowance for calcium are corn tortillas made from corn soaked in calcium hydroxide, those types of tofu precipitated using calcium compounds, and green vegetables like broccoli, kale, and collard greens which do not contain significant amounts of oxalate. Sesame seeds are frequently thought of as a good source of calcium, but this calcium, unfortunately, is largely unavailable because most of it is bound up in the form of calcium oxalate in the outer husk of the seed. Calcium fortified soy milk is the best and most reliable source of this mineral for the pure vegetarian.

Vitamin B-12: This vitamin is found almost exclusively in foods of animal origin. As far as we know there are only a few significant vegetable sources. Large amounts are contained in tempeh, a fermented soybean cake common in Indonesia and increasingly available in the United States. A typical serving may contain more than the recommended allowance. Other soy foods containing this vitamin are miso, natto, and naturally fermented soy sauce.

A mixed vegetable and animal protein diet such as ours is adequate in this nutrient. Our major sources are eggs, milk, and cheese. Pure vegetarians must take care to eat generous amounts of the fermented soy foods mentioned above, or make liberal use of vitamin B-12 fortified soy milk. The only alternative is supplementation in moderate amounts.

How To Get a Balanced Diet Using This Book

Now that we have discussed requirements for protein and other critical nutrients, you may want to use the table of recommended allowances in the appendix to locate requirements for the major nutrients for your sex and age group. Adhering to the guidelines for a balanced diet outlined below should insure an adequate intake of protein as well as vitamins and minerals.

People sometimes exceed caloric requirements because they equate individual foods with single nutrients. An awareness that most foods are rich in several key nutrients will help to keep caloric intakes within reasonable limits. For example, most dark green leafy vegetables are not only good sources of vitamin A, but also contain substantial amounts of vitamin C, riboflavin, folacin, potassium and other minerals. Milk, in addition to being an excellent source of calcium and protein, is a good source of vitamin B-12, vitamin A, riboflavin, phosphorus, and zinc.

Major Protein Sources: Always include a major protein source and its complement at each meal. For the purposes of this book, a major protein source is defined as any single food, dish, or combination of foods containing approximately 10 grams of protein per serving. It can consist of legumes, grains, nuts, seeds, eggs, or milk and milk products. Because legumes are such excellent sources of major nutrients besides protein, try to include them in your diet as often as possible. They are excellent sources of thiamin, niacin, folacin, phosphorus, potassium, and magnesium and are good sources of zinc.

The major protein source will usually be in the form of a main dish and will generally include its own complement. If a dish does not contain a complement, follow the serving suggestions in the recipe or scan the list of combinations provided earlier in this chapter.

Each recipe containing a substantial amount of protein provides information on the total number of protein grams per serving. Our main dishes, by definition, have at least 10 protein grams per serving. Each recipe has symbols representing the groups or families of protein sources that are complementary. For example, our Bean and Raisin Enchiladas contain 16 grams of protein per serving, consisting of the following complementary protein combinations: corn plus beans, beans plus cheese.

Milk and Milk Products: Include an 8-ounce glass of milk or its equivalent three times a day, preferably at meals. Equivalents are: 1-1½ ounces cheese, 1 cup cottage cheese, yogurt, buttermilk, or calcium fortified soy milk. Concentrate on skim milk, nonfat dry milk, buttermilk, low fat yogurt, and the less fatty cheeses such as cottage cheese, mozzarella, Parmesan, and Swiss. Avoid cream, cream cheese, sour cream, and other very fatty dairy products.

If you have milk or cheese with or in your meal, you are accomplishing two things at once—providing a complement for any of the major families of vegetable proteins and contributing toward meeting your daily allowance of calcium and other nutrients. It is a fiction that adults don't need milk. They certainly can do without the fat contained in whole milk, but they do need the calcium! That's why we suggest using skim milk and low fat milk products whenever possible.

Major Nutrients Supplied:
    protein
    vitamins: vitamin A, riboflavin (vitamin B-2), vitamin B-12 (cobalamin), vitamin D
    minerals: calcium, phosphorus, zinc

Whole Grain Cereals: Include a whole grain cereal at each meal, preferably a whole grain yeast-raised bread. Yeast-raised breads are an important staple in any vegetarian diet because the action of the yeast helps make iron and other minerals more readily available to the body.

The whole grain cereal may be in the main dish or served as a complement to the main dish. If you are serving a whole grain pasta dish complemented with plenty of Parmesan cheese, you have provided for your major protein source and its complement, have contributed toward meeting your calcium requirement, and have provided for a whole grain cereal product at the same time. If you desire, you may serve a yeast-raised bread with this meal, but it is not essential if you have already had several servings of yeast-raised bread that day.

Major Nutrients Supplied:
    protein
    vitamins: thiamin (vitamin B-1), niacin (vitamin B-3), vitamin B-6 (pyridoxine), folacin (folic acid), vitamin E
    minerals: iron, magnesium, zinc, phosphorus (all more available in yeast-raised breads)

Vegetables: Include at least one serving of leafy green or dark yellow vegetables per day. The general rule is the darker, the better. This includes carrots, spinach, kale, hubbard or banana squash, winter squash, butternut squash, sweet potatoes, beet greens, turnip greens, chard, mustard greens, romaine, and other dark salad greens. When fresh papayas, mangoes, and cantaloupes are available, they may be substituted for these vegetables. Include one or more servings of other types of vegetables, such as green beans, fresh peas, beets, cabbage, celery, corn, alfalfa or mung bean sprouts, zucchini, tomatoes, broccoli, and bell peppers. We serve at least one fresh salad a day, preferably as an accompaniment to our evening meal. Good, fresh spinach is available so rarely in the markets, that when we succeed in finding some, we almost invariably use it in a fresh, green salad. Use iceberg lettuce as little as possible. Other salad greens have much more to offer nutritionally.

Major Nutrients Supplied:
    vitamins: vitamin A (leafy green and dark yellow vegetables only), riboflavin (vitamin B-2), vitamin B-6 (pyridoxine),folacin (folic acid), thiamin (vitamin B-1), vitamin C (raw or carefully cooked vegetables only)
    minerals: potassium, iron, and calcium (the latter two being largely unavailable to the body)

Fruit: Include three or more servings of fresh fruit per day, preferably with meals. If possible, try to include at least one generous serving of citrus fruit or juice, papaya, or guava when available. Berries and melons, such as watermelons, cantaloupes, and honeydew melons also count as fruit.

Major Nutrients Supplied:
    vitamins: vitamin C, folacin (folic acid)
    minerals: potassium

Following these suggestions means nothing more than applying the basic principles of a good diet to foods usually consumed by vegetarians. Basically, all we're suggesting is that you have an adequate amount of protein at each meal, that you try to complement this protein, that you serve plenty of whole grain foods, a sufficient amount of milk, and a lot of fresh fruits and vegetables.

NOTES

[1] National Research Council, Food and Nutrition Board, Committee on Nutritional Misinformation, *Vegetarian Diets* (Washington, D.C.: National Academy of Sciences, 1974). Also published in *Journal of the American Dietetic Association* 65 (1974): 121-22.

[2] D.P. Burkitt, A.R.P. Walker, and N.S. Painter, "Dietary Fiber and Disease," *Journal of the American Medical Association* 229 (1974): 1068-74. See also various articles in D.P. Burkitt and H. Trowell, eds., *Refined Carbohydrate Foods and Disease* (New York: Academic Press, 1975).

[3] Frances Moore Lappé, *Diet for a Small Planet*, 2nd ed. rev. (New York: Ballantine Books, 1975).

[4] Ellen Ewald, *Recipes for a Small Planet* (New York: Ballantine Books, 1973).

[5] Laurel Robertson, Carol Flinders, and Bronwen Godfrey, *Laurel's Kitchen: A Handbook for Vegetarian Cookery and Nutrition* (Berkeley: Nilgiri Press, 1976).

[6] Ross L. Hackler, "In Vitro Indices: Relationships to Estimating Protein Value for the Human," in *Evaluation of Proteins for Humans*, ed. C.E. Bodwell (Westport, Conn.: AVI, 1977), pp. 55-66.

[7] National Research Council, Food and Nutrition Board, *Recommended Dietary Allowances*, 9th ed. rev. (Washington, D.C.: National Academy of Sciences, 1980), pp. 39-51.

[8] Robert S. Goodhart, "Criteria for an Adequate Diet," in *Modern Nutrition in Health and Disease*, 6th ed., ed. Robert S. Goodhart and Maurice Shils (Philadelphia: Lea and Febiger, 1980), pp. 445-455.

[9] National Research Council, Food and Nutrition Board, *Recommended Dietary Allowances*, 8th ed. rev. (Washington, D.C.: National Academy of Sciences, 1974), p. 94.

[10] Elaine R. Monsen, et al., "Estimation of Available Dietary Iron," *American Journal of Clinical Nutrition* 31 (1978): 134-41.

[11] Ibid., p. 139.

[12] Robertson, et al., *Laurel's Kitchen*, p. 436.

[13] Louis McBean and Elwood W. Speckmann, "A Recognition of the Interrelationships of Calcium with Various Dietary Components," *American Journal of Clinical Nutrition* 27 (1974): 603-09.

[14] Ibid., p. 607.

[15] Louis V. Avioli, "Major Minerals: A. Calcium and Phosphorus," in *Modern Nutrition in Health and Disease*, 6th ed., Goodhart and Shils, eds., pp. 294-309.

[16] Ibid., p. 300.

Symbols For Major Protein Sources

 Milk, cheese, and yogurt

 Whole grain cereals and cereal products, such as wheat, rye, triticale, oats, barley, millet, rice, buckwheat, and corn

 Dried beans, peas, lentils, soybeans, and soybean products, such as tofu

 Sesame and sunflower seeds

 Nuts, chiefly cashews and peanuts, but also almonds and walnuts

 Potatoes

 Eggs

Major Complementary Combinations

 + or or or or or or

Because eggs are viewed by many nutritionists as the ideal protein, they are not considered as complementary in this book. Technically, they stand by themselves. Nevertheless, they do enhance the quality of all vegetable proteins eaten at the same meal.

Protein Calculations

The designation Protein g/s stands for protein grams per serving. Protein calculations are approximate and are for total rather than usable protein grams. They were arrived at using values obtained from *Food Values of Portions Commonly Used* by C. F. Church and H. N. Church and *Laurel's Kitchen: A Handbook For Vegetarian Cookery and Nutrition* by Laurel Robertson and others. A few values not contained in these sources were obtained from the producers. Most vegetables were not included in the calculations because their contributions to the protein content of a dish was considered insignificant. We made an exception in the case of fresh peas, fresh corn, and potatoes.

Keeping a Vegetarian Kitchen

In our grandmother's time it was common for women to spend a good part of the day preparing and cooking food. Today, either out of economic necessity or a desire to pursue a career, many women work outside the home. They have less time to devote to meal preparation and have become dependent on the "instant" foods which predominate in our supermarkets.

A generation or two of women are convinced that cooking from "scratch" is an impossible undertaking unless you have the greater part of the day to devote to it. We hope that in this chapter and throughout the entire book, we help to dispel this myth. What we want to convey is that you and your family can be properly nourished without your spending an entire day in the kitchen. All that is required is some time-saving equipment, a kitchen well stocked with staple foods, and a certain amount of advance planning and preparation.

Equipment

After food processors, which are discussed in the introduction, pressure cookers are the most valuable kitchen technology you can buy. They have been improved so much over the years and contain so many safety features that Consumers Union considers them entirely safe when used as directed. They can save considerable time and electricity, particularly in the preparation of beans and soups. For instance, most beans can be cooked in 10-15 minutes at 15 pounds pressure, if presoaked overnight. Contrast this with 1½-2 hours of cooking in a regular pot! Although some cookers can be set to cook at 5, 10, or 15 pounds of pressure, there seems little point in using the lower pressures when the highest pressure setting will cook food more quickly and just as safely.

Manufacturers of some cookers do not recommend their use for split peas or lentils because these legumes have a tendency to froth and clog the vent. Directions for others indicate that you may cook split peas or lentils provided that you fill the cooker no more than half full. Carefully follow the instructions for your particular cooker.

Pressure cookers come in a wide range of sizes. Because we cook large quantities of beans ahead of time for freezing, we prefer the 6 or 8 quart size. We've learned from past experience that it's smart to keep extra rubber gaskets and safety fuses on hand in case these parts deteriorate.

Another important piece of kitchen equipment is a scale. In recipes for the food processor, ingredients to be processed are frequently weighed instead of measured. Our preference is for a scale that registers both ounces and grams and has a bowl large enough for weighing dry ingredients such as beans.

Staple Foods to Have on Hand

Beans, Peas, and Lentils: Pinto beans, kidney beans, black turtle beans, garbanzo beans, lentils, yellow split peas, Great Northern, or navy beans (little white beans), and mung beans for sprouting if you sprout your own.

Shopping Hints: Obviously, the dry beans are preferable to the canned type. The latter are generally considered more convenient, but you can achieve a similar degree of convenience at considerably less expense by cooking large quantities in your pressure cooker and freezing them for later use.

Most beans, peas, and lentils can be purchased at your co-op or supermarket.

Storage: Store in tightly covered glass jars, preferably right out on the kitchen counter, where you can see when your supply needs replenishing. Most beans will keep at least a year when stored in this manner.

Tofu: If you observed that soybeans were conspicuously absent from the above list, it's because we're not really fond of them. We prefer to use tofu instead.

Shopping Hints: There are generally two types sold in the United States—the denser Chinese style, called doufu, and the traditional Japanese style tofu, which is medium firm. Both kinds are becoming increasingly available in large supermarkets, co-ops, and health food stores across the country. Tofu is generally sold in 24-ounce tubs (undrained weight). In Chinatown markets it is frequently available in smaller cakes. The truly enterprising among you may want to make your own. Kits are available in health food stores and co-ops.

Storage: Remove tofu from its container and put it in a bowl of fresh water. Cover, and store in the refrigerator. It will stay fresh for a week if the water is changed daily. A sour taste indicates that it's past its prime.

Grains, Flours, and Flour Products: Whole wheat flour, buckwheat flour, rye flour, soy flour, bulgur or cracked wheat, millet, brown rice, bran, wheat germ, non-instant rolled oats, and an assortment of whole wheat pastas to use when you don't have time to make your own.

Shopping Hints: We standardized all of our recipes using Gold Medal whole wheat flour. Any other 100% extraction flour is acceptable, although the amount of liquid needed will vary. Either purchase flour from a refrigerated case, or make sure your supermarket or co-op has a rapid turnover of this product. We are not convinced that all the nutritional claims made for stone ground whole wheat flours are true. Their coarseness alone does not make them more wholesome. The process of stone grinding itself produces lower temperatures than regular milling of flour, and may therefore better preserve a few of the vitamins which are affected by heat.

However, these gains are miniscule, considering that no one eats flour in the raw state. A loaf of bread must be baked. And during baking it will be exposed to much higher temperatures for a much longer time than during milling. Besides, a finely ground 100% extraction flour can be used for all baking and cooking, whereas the coarser 100%

extraction stone ground flours are used chiefly in yeast raised breads. What is more, they tend to cost more than regular whole wheat flours. When shopping for rye flour, keep in mind that both light and medium rye flours are less desirable than dark rye flour, which is much higher in protein and other nutrients.

Storage: Whole grain flours should never be stored in your kitchen cabinet unless used almost immediately. Either freeze or refrigerate them, or their natural oils will quickly become rancid. Remember to allow time to bring them to room temperature before using them in yeast-raised doughs. Wheat germ and grains which have been cracked must likewise be kept under refrigeration. Bran, rice, and millet may be stored for longer periods of time in tightly sealed glass jars at room temperature. Whole wheat pastas should not be stored at room temperature for longer than a few days. Home made pastas may either be frozen or dried and refrigerated.

Seeds: Sunflower seeds, sesame seeds, and alfalfa seeds, if you do your own sprouting.

Shopping Hints: Our recipes call for hulled sunflower and sesame seeds, both of which are available at your local co-op or health food store. We use the hulled sesame seeds because they are more digestible than the unhulled type. You can tell which ones are hulled because they are white and shiny in contrast to the pale brown color of the unhulled variety. Make certain that any seeds you buy for sprouting are intended specifically for that purpose. Some of the seeds intended for planting are treated with harmful chemicals.

Storage: Store sunflower seeds and sesame seeds in the refrigerator or freezer unless they will be used almost immediately. Store alfalfa and other seeds for sprouting in an airtight jar in a cool, dry place.

Nuts: Peanuts, cashew nuts, and some walnuts for baking.

Shopping Hints: Purchase raw nuts in bulk and roast them yourself in the oven at 325°F for roughly 35-45 minutes. Watch carefully so they don't become overdone. Peanuts with the skins on make very good peanut butter.

Storage: Refrigerate or freeze unless they will be used almost immediately.

Milk and Cheese: Non-fat dry milk, preferably non-instant, cottage cheese or ricotta cheese, and a selection of your preferred cured cheeses, such as natural white Cheddar, Monterey Jack, mozzarella, and Swiss cheese. Also skim milk, 2% milk, or buttermilk for cooking and drinking.

Shopping Hints: Non-instant, non-fat dry milk is best because it is highest in protein and lowest in fat. It is generally available at co-ops and health food stores. It is easily blended to a lump-free consistency using your food processor. Insert the metal blade, place the dry milk in the work bowl, and turn the machine on. Then slowly add the water. The yellowish-orange cheeses are to be avoided for obvious reasons: they contain artificial coloring, but this is generally not indicated on the label.

Storage: All milk and milk products should be refrigerated. Even dry milk will deteriorate in several weeks' time after the container is opened. It's best to place it in a tightly sealed plastic container and refrigerate it.

Eggs:

Shopping Hints: Buy eggs as fresh as possible, preferably those produced in your area. Buy only from stores which have refrigerated storage cases.

Storage: Refrigerate immediately. Eggs will keep in the refrigerator for approximately three weeks. They are less likely to absorb refrigerator odors if you store them in the original cardboard carton.

Sweeteners and Dried Fruit: Honey, brown sugar, blackstrap molasses, 100% maple syrup, and raisins.

Shopping Hints: Our preference is for honey and brown sugar, although excess sugar in any form is undesirable, and this unfortunately includes sweeteners such as honey. This is probably a good time to mention the differences between sugars. Nutritionally, there is little difference between white and brown sugar. The latter is only refined sugar with a little molasses added for color. So-called raw sugar is actually partly refined sugar. Real raw sugar is unavailable in this country. All honey is "natural," so a word like "natural" on the label tells you nothing. There is no law defining "natural." Buy unstrained, uncooked honey and don't worry if it has crystallized. It can be liquified again by placing the opened can or jar in a pan of simmering water and heating it until the crystals dissolve.

Storage: Honey may be stored for up to 18 months in your kitchen cabinet, molasses for two years, and all types of sugar for several years if you use glass containers. We refrigerate our maple syrup because we've had problems with mildew forming on the top. Raisins will keep for approximately six months at room temperature sealed in a glass jar.

Oils and Fats: A good quality vegetable oil, high in polyunsaturated fat, such as safflower or soy oil and safflower margarine or butter.

Shopping Hints: In order to understand the difference between vegetable oils, it is necessary to know how they are produced. Oil is either pressed out of the seeds or beans, or extracted by use of a petroleum solvent. Oils which are pressed are expeller pressed, which means that the seeds are cut into small flakes or pieces and pressed at high pressures to extract the oil. Oils labelled "cold-pressed" are actually pressed at temperatures ranging from 120°F-150°F. These are nutritionally superior to "hot-pressed" oils, which are pressed the same way, but at much higher temperatures. Oils which are solvent extracted undergo the greatest losses of vitamin E.

After the oil is extracted from the seeds, it may or may not be refined. If it remains unrefined, it is simply filtered and bottled. If it is refined, it may undergo up to five additional processes. In one of these, most of the vitamin E in the oil is removed for use in vitamin supplements. Many natural oils which are totally unrefined may be rich in vitamin E, but they are difficult or impossible to cook with because they have such strong flavors of their own. We have tried making mayonnaise from unrefined sesame and safflower oils. It had to be thrown out because it had too strong a taste. It's a trade-off. The less refined the oil, the more nutritious it is, but the less people are willing to eat it.

Do not purchase cottonseed oils. These may have higher than normal pesticide residues, because cotton is sprayed rather freely.

The best olive oils are labelled "virgin olive oil." The lesser quality olive oils, which bear the designation "pure olive oil," are pressed or solvent extracted from the pulp that remains after the "virgin olive oil" is made.

The best butter is made from sweet cream and bears that designation on the label. Commercially sold butter is often colored with artificial or natural coloring, yet this information never appears on the label. Therefore, you might consider making your own, especially if you can get heavy cream directly from your local dairy at a reasonable price. Butter is easily made by whipping the cream in your food processor or electric mixer until the fat separates. Pour off the fresh buttermilk and carefully rinse the butter with cold water. Compress it into small cakes and keep frozen until you're ready to use it.

Buy margarine made from polyunsaturated oil with the name of the oil listed first on the label. It should be colored only with beta carotene, a precursor of vitamin A, and should be free of artificial flavors and preservatives.

Storage: Refrigerate all oils and fats. You may freeze butter and margarine for long-term storage. Even though olive oil does not become rancid as rapidly as other oils, it should be refrigerated because it is usually purchased in large containers and is used up more slowly. It will become semi-solid under refrigeration. Simply bring it to room temperature before using.

Vegetables: Several packages of frozen spinach, a green pepper or two, canned tomato sauce and paste, canned tomatoes—stewed or plain. Also useful are lots of onions, both green and regular, potatoes, carrots, celery, romaine lettuce, and fresh tomatoes.

Shopping Hints: Canned tomato products are best purchased in large quantities when they are on sale. We shop for most of our vegetables at our co-op or our neighborhood supermarkets. We do appreciate the superior taste of home grown organic produce, yet under the present circumstances, the consumer who does not have a garden of his own has no guarantee that he is actually getting what he pays for. Because there is no legal definition of "organic," almost anything can be labelled "organic" by an unscrupulous manufacturer or dealer. Since there are no assurances about growing conditions or pesticide residues, we prefer to spend less and buy conventional produce—at the same time wishing that it tasted as good as the vegetables Paula's parents grow, using only horse manure as fertilizer.

Storage: Celery can be kept for two weeks, and carrots for several weeks sealed in a plastic bag in the vegetable crisper of your refrigerator. Potatoes will keep for two to three months in the vegetable crisper unwrapped. Green peppers, tomatoes, and romaine lettuce will keep approximately ten days sealed in an airtight container in the bottom of the refrigerator. Green onions stored in this manner will keep up to a week.

Seasonings: In addition to standard items like salt and pepper, you will need a good assortment of dried herbs and spices. Grow some of your own herbs, if possible, even if it's only on your window sill. Other useful items to have on hand are vegetable bouillon cubes, chicken-flavored vegetable seasoning, Vegit vegetable seasoning, Vegex vegetable soup seasoning, Dijon mustard, plenty of fresh garlic, Japanese rice vinegar, red wine vinegar, and malt vinegar.

Shopping Hints: Chemical analysis has revealed that sea salt is not nutritionally superior to plain iodized salt. Use it if you prefer the taste. Because the sodium content of the American diet is high, many people are making a conscious effort to cut down on their salt intake. A relatively new product called Morton's Lite Salt is used like ordinary table salt, but contains only one half the sodium chloride.

The rest is potassium chloride. Even this product should be used sparingly.

Storage: Certain vegetable bouillon cubes keep better when refrigerated. It's best to check the label. Dijon mustard should be refrigerated after opening. Garlic keeps well at room temperature, if air is allowed to circulate around it freely. Vinegars and dried herbs should be sealed tightly in glass jars. Spices are best when freshly ground.

The staples discussed above are basic items to have on hand regardless of the type of cooking you do. Those listed below are commonly-used foods you will need to prepare the many ethnic recipes in our book. The more perishable items are listed last.

Italian dishes: Basic Marinara Sauce (see index) from your freezer; frozen spinach; olive oil; Parmesan or Romano cheese; mozzarella cheese; ricotta or cottage cheese; basil, fresh if possible.

Greek and Middle Eastern dishes: Cooked garbanzo beans from your freezer; canned ripe olives; olive oil; Sesame Tahini (see index); lemons; feta cheese; eggplant.

Mexican dishes: Cooked pinto beans from your freezer; canned mild green chiles; canned black olives; an assortment of mild, dried red chiles; chili powder; ground cumin; masa harina and corn germ (if you make your own tortillas); frozen tortillas (in case you decide not to make your own); Monterey Jack cheese; natural white Cheddar cheese; avocados.

Japanese and Chinese dishes: Long grain brown rice; soy sauce, either regular or low-sodium; oriental sesame seed oil; fresh ginger; fresh mung bean sprouts; green onions; tofu.

Indian dishes: A variety of dals (e.g. split peas, lentils, garbanzos, and other beans); long grain brown rice; ground turmeric; ground coriander; ground cumin; ground cardamom; fresh ginger. If you cook a lot of Indian food, it may be useful for you to invest in a small electric food mill so you can roast and grind your own spices for *garam masala* from whole seeds. This is much more flavorful than using commercially ground spices.

Advance Planning and Preparation

Cooking Ahead

The key to efficient and time-saving vegetarian meals is cooking large quantities of staple items from scratch and always having them on hand in your freezer. We have found the weekend best for this. Always cook two or three times the basic ingredients you need for a meal and freeze the rest or save some in the refrigerator to prepare a different dish two or three days later. Here are some general suggestions on how you can best use this book to organize your cooking more efficiently.

1. Bread can be made any time you spend three continuous hours at home. Bake all of your bread for the week at once, freeze all but one loaf, and remove what you need from the freezer during the week. This is much more energy-efficient than baking several times because the oven is heated only once.

2. Pasta may be made ahead on the weekends. It may be frozen or dried and refrigerated in a plastic bag. If frozen, it should be put into boiling water for cooking without defrosting.

3. Our Basic Marinara Sauce makes approximately 14 cups of sauce. If you make the full recipe as suggested, you should have enough for the following dishes: Lasagna, Spinach Lasagna or Eggplant Lasagna; Zucchini or Eggplant Parmesan; Oven or Lentil Spaghetti; Whole Wheat Ravioli; and Pizza. Freeze the sauce in amounts you are most likely to use at one time, for example, 1½ cups for pizza, 3 cups for lasagne, etc. Just one recipe of this sauce will last you approximately five weeks if you serve one Italian dish per week.

4. Many of our recipes specify cooked beans or lentils. We cook ours with vegetable bouillon cubes for better flavor. Never prepare beans or lentils without preparing at least two or three times the amount you need for a particular recipe. For example, if you are cooking garbanzos for hummus, you will need only 1 cup dry, or two cups cooked beans. Consider making at least 4½ additional cups dry, or 9 cups cooked beans so you can have them on hand for making the following dishes over a month or two: Felafel, Arabic Musakka'a, Curried Garbanzo Beans, Four Bean Salad, Greek Chef's Salad, and Garbanzo Cheese Salad with Cumin Dressing. The same approach can be used with pinto beans. If you are making Bean and Raisin Enchiladas, consider making additional beans for our Mexican Chef's Salad, Refried Beans, Tamale Pie, and Vegetarian Tacos. Always check the major ingredient index to see what else you can do with a staple ingredient and then make the amount you will probably need for a month or two.

5. Our recipe for Enchilada Sauce makes enough for four or five batches of enchiladas. Freeze it in containers of 10-12 ounces. It can be used to make the following dishes: Mexican Black Bean Bake, Bean and Raisin Enchiladas, Sonora Style Enchiladas, Fresh Corn Enchiladas, and Enchiladas Coloradas.

6. When making crepes, consider making your crepe dough the night before and letting it stand in the refrigerator until ready to use. This will save you an hour of "standing time" just before dinner.

7. Always prepare twice as much rice as you think you can use in one meal. Refrigerate it and use it within four or five days to make the following: Chinese Style Fried Rice, Cheesy Green Rice, Moussaka, and Mexican Rice Crust Pizza.

8. Prepare salad dressing ahead of time. Vinegar and oil dressings are much better if allowed to stand for a day or two before using. They may be refrigerated for several weeks without adverse effects. Milk, egg, or cheese based dressings will keep up to four or five days.

Planning Your Menus

Give careful consideration to the rules for a balanced diet outlined in the chapter on the "Basics of Vegetarian Nutrition" when planning your weekly menu. Be realistic and also consider the time you have available for cooking. When you are especially short on time, consider the following possibilities:

1. Serve a quickly prepared, stir fried tofu dish at least once a week.

2. Prepare a chef's salad or a quickly prepared main dish salad once or twice a week—any salad that has approximately 10 grams of protein per serving.

3. Cook quantities of main dishes on the weekends, and serve the left-overs once or twice a week.

4. Scan our main dish recipes, make a note of those which are particularly fast to prepare, and develop a repertoire of those your family likes.

Shopping

If you do most of your shopping at a supermarket, scan the specials and then plan your menu for the week using the major ingredient index at the back of the book. If you do most of your shopping at a co-op, there will be few or no specials to take advantage of, so plan your menu around seasonal items. Allow yourself enough flexibility to take advantage of especially good buys that you discover while shopping. Keep a continuous list of staples you are low on, so you know what items need replenishing when specials are offered. We use small note cards attached to the refrigerator door with a magnet.

We hope that you will use the above short-cuts and advice for keeping a vegetarian kitchen and in due time develop some of your own. In this chapter we've tried to show that you can prepare nutritious and appetizing meals without spending an undue amount of time in the kitchen. If you have found that most of what we have said is new to you, we suggest that you go about following our suggestions incrementally.

Appetizers

Chile and Olive Turnovers

4 dozen turnovers

These tasty morsels may be prepared in advance, cooled and refrigerated. Reheat uncovered in a 350° oven about 10 minutes or until heated through. A tortilla press speeds up the preparation time.

Pastry

2¼ cups whole wheat flour, measured scoop and level
½ teaspoon salt
¾ cup butter or margarine, well-chilled, cut into 1-inch pieces
5-6 tablespoons ice water

METAL BLADE: Add flour, butter and salt to work bowl. Process 8-10 seconds or until mixture has consistency of coarse meal. With processor running, pour ice water through feed tube in a steady stream. Stop processing as soon as dough begins to form a ball. Turn out onto wax paper and shape into a flattened disc. Wrap well and refrigerate while preparing filling.

Filling

6 ounces Monterey Jack cheese, well-chilled
3-4 canned green chiles, rinsed and seeded
1 can pitted black olives (6 ounces drained weight)
½ teaspoon dry leaf oregano, crumbled
⅛ teaspoon salt, pepper

SHREDDING DISC: Cut Monterey Jack cheese to fit feed tube. Shred with moderate pressure. Remove cheese from bowl and set aside.

METAL BLADE: Add chiles to work bowl and pulse on/off to finely mince. Add to cheese. Add drained olives to work bowl. Pulse on/off to finely chop and add to cheese. Toss cheese, chiles, olives, oregano, salt and pepper together to mix.

Divide dough into quarters. Work with one quarter at a time, keeping remaining portions of dough refrigerated. Divide the quarter into 12 pieces, cover. Pat a piece of dough 2 or 3 times to partially flatten and place on a tortilla press, a bit back of center, inside a folded sheet of wax paper. Close the lid and press. Remove the dough round from the press and peel off the wax paper. If you don't have a press, roll out dough 1/16-inch thick between two sheets of wax paper. Cut into 3-inch rounds.

Preheat oven to 375°.

Place one rounded teaspoonful filling on one half of each circle, leaving a small margin. Run a wet finger over margin and fold dough over to cover; press gently to seal well. Prick three times with fork.

Place turnovers on a baking sheet. Bake 15-18 minutes or until golden. Cool slightly before serving.

Preparation: 1-1½ hours
Baking: 15-18 minutes
Chilling: chill dough while preparing filling
Protein g/s: 1.5 per piece

Alice's Super Layers

Serves 10-12

Alice and Julie are running partners and usually exchange stories to take their minds off the "chore." During one particular run neither had a story, but Alice had this delicious recipe in reserve. Scoop up the layers with homemade tortilla chips or spoon into pita halves.

2 *cups plain low-fat yogurt*
1 *recipe Guacamole (see index)*
1 *teaspoon chili powder*
2 *cups cooked kidney beans (⅔ cup dry), reserve*
   some of the cooking liquid
2 *7-ounce cans whole green chiles, rinsed, seeded*
12 *ounces sharp Cheddar cheese*
2 *cans pitted black olives (drained weight 6 ounces)*
4-6 *green onions*
3 *medium tomatoes*
⅓ to ½ *cup green taco sauce (optional)*

Have ready a large flat serving dish with a rim and assemble as the ingredients are processed. Spread yogurt over the bottom of the dish in an even layer and spoon on guacamole. Sprinkle on chili powder.

METAL BLADE: Add cooked kidney beans and process until of spreading consistency, adding cooking liquid as needed. Spread purée of beans over previous layers. Add green chiles, coarsely chop, and sprinkle over beans.

SHREDDING DISC: Cut Cheddar cheese to fit feed tube and shred. Distribute evenly over green chiles.

METAL BLADE: Add drained olives to work bowl, pulse on/off until coarsely chopped and scatter over cheese. Cut green onions into 1-inch lengths, add to work bowl; pulse on/off to finely chop and sprinkle over cheese. Cut tomatoes into wedges, add to work bowl; pulse on/off to coarsely chop and spread on top of layers. Pour on green taco sauce, if used.

Preparation: 10-15 minutes
Cooking: allow time to cook beans
Protein g/s: 10 servings—13
              12 servings—10.5

Carrot Filled Zucchini

30 appetizers

Make these early in the day and refrigerate until serving time.

6-7 *narrow zucchini, about 8-inches long*
10 *medium carrots, peeled, about 1½ pounds*
3 *tablespoons butter or margarine*
3 *tablespoons peanut butter*

Place whole zucchini in boiling water. Cook over medium heat 8 minutes, then plunge in cold water to stop cooking. Place in colander to drain well.

SLICING DISC: Cut carrots to fit feed tube vertically; stack and slice. Steam carrot slices until fork tender, about 17-20 minutes.

METAL BLADE: Add steamed carrots, butter and peanut butter to work bowl. Process until smooth.

ASSEMBLY: Cut zucchini into 1½-inch lengths. Using a small knife, remove pulp and reserve for another use. Place zucchini lengths, cut side down, on paper towels to drain. Fill with puréed carrot mixture. Serve warm or refrigerate several hours to chill.

Preparation: 15 minutes
Cooking: 20-25 minutes

Parmesan Herb Dip

2 cups, 8 ¼-cup servings

Serve with cauliflowerets, green pepper wedges, zucchini or cherry tomatoes.

2 *ounces Parmesan cheese, room temperature*
2 *large cloves garlic*
⅓ *cup parsley sprigs*
1 *teaspoon dry leaf basil*
¾ *teaspoon salt*
½ *teaspoon fresh ground pepper*
2 *eggs*
3 *tablespoons lemon juice*
1 *cup mild flavored oil*

METAL BLADE: Add Parmesan cheese, cut into 1-inch pieces, to work bowl. Process until finely grated. Add garlic, parsley, basil, salt and pepper. Pulse on/off until garlic and parsley are finely minced.

Add eggs, lemon juice and 1 tablespoon oil to work bowl. Process 30 seconds. With machine running, add remaining oil very slowly through the feed tube until you can see the mixture has thickened. Remaining oil can be added a little faster. This is similar to making mayonnaise. Process until the dip is thick. Remove to serving bowl. Cover and chill 1 hour.

Preparation: 10 minutes
Chilling: 1 hour
Protein g/s: 4

Divide dough in half and form each portion into a roll 6 inches long. Wrap in plastic wrap or wax paper. Place in freezer 1 hour or in refrigerator until well-chilled and firm, about 4 hours. Dough may be kept in the refrigerator up to a week.

Preheat oven to 375°. Cover a cookie sheet with aluminum foil. Slice roll into ⅛ to ¼-inch slices and arrange about ½ inch apart on the foil. Bake 7-9 minutes or until edges are golden.

Remove from cookie sheet. Cool on wire rack and store in airtight container.

Preparation: 10 minutes
Baking: 7-9 minutes
Chilling: allow time for dough to chill well
Protein g/s: 1 per piece.

Swiss Crispies

7 dozen appetizers

Serve these delicate crispies with wine or sliced apples.

8 ounces Swiss cheese, well-chilled
2-3 ounces Parmesan cheese, room temperature
¾ cup whole wheat flour, measured scoop and level
½ cup cornmeal
⅛ teaspoon salt (optional)
½ cup butter, cut into 1-inch pieces
1 tablespoon Dijon mustard
2 tablespoons water

SHREDDING DISC: Cut Swiss cheese to fit feed tube; shred using medium pressure. Remove from bowl and set aside.

METAL BLADE: Add Parmesan cheese, cut into 1-inch pieces, to work bowl. Process until finely grated Stop machine, remove work bowl cover and add flour, cornmeal, salt and butter. Pulse on/off until mixture resembles coarse meal. Add mustard, water and Swiss cheese. Process until well-blended and smooth. Stop machine and scrape down sides of bowl if necessary.

Cucumber Dip

2½ cups, 10 servings

Served with a variety of raw vegetables or pita wedges, this dip will be welcomed at any party.

1 clove garlic
2 large cucumbers, pared
2 cups thick yogurt
¾-1 teaspoon salt
¼ teaspoon pepper

METAL BLADE: Add garlic and pulse on/off until finely minced. Remove to a medium mixing bowl. Stir in yogurt, salt and pepper.

SHREDDING DISC: Cut cucumbers to fit feed tube vertically. Shred. Place half the cucumber in a tea towel and squeeze to remove as much moisture as possible. Repeat with remaining cucumber. Add to yogurt and stir gently to mix. Cover and refrigerate 1 hour.

Preparation: 10 minutes
Chilling: 1 hour
Protein g/s: 1.5

Mushroom Broccoli Tartlets

18 tartlets

Make these bite-size tartlets a day in advance and refrigerate. Bake uncovered in a 350° oven about 10 minutes to reheat.

Pastry

1¾ cups whole wheat flour, measured scoop and
    level
2 ounces Parmesan cheese, room temperature, cut
    into 1-inch pieces
6 tablespoons butter or margarine, cut into 1-inch
    pieces
1 egg
2-3 tablespoons ice water

METAL BLADE: Add Parmesan cheese to work bowl and process until finely grated. Add flour, pulse on/off to mix. Add butter, pulse on/off until mixture resembles coarse meal. With machine running, add egg and enough ice water to form a soft ball of dough. Stop machine as soon as the ball forms. Remove ball to wax paper. Flatten slightly wrap well and refrigerate while making filling.

Filling

2 green onions, cut into 1-inch lengths
4 ounces fresh mushrooms
8 ounces broccoli, trimmed, cut into 1-inch pieces
2 tablespoons oil
1 teaspoon dry leaf thyme
1 tablespoon lemon juice
½ teaspoon salt
4 ounces Swiss cheese
2 tablespoons oil

METAL BLADE: Add green onions to work bowl; process to mince. Add mushrooms; pulse on/off to coarsely chop mushrooms.

Heat 2 tablespoons in a large skillet over medium-high heat. Add onion/mushroom mixture and cook 2 minutes.

METAL BLADE: Add broccoli to work bowl; pulse on/off until finely chopped. Add broccoli, thyme, lemon juice and salt to mushrooms. Stir to mix. Cover and cook over low heat until broccoli is tender and liquid has evaporated, about 10-15 minutes. Stir to avoid sticking. Remove from heat and set aside.

SHREDDING DISC: Cut Swiss cheese to fit feed tube. Shred with light pressure.

Divide pastry dough into 18 pieces. Press each portion of dough into a muffin cup or 2½-inch tart pan. Divide mushroom/broccoli mixture among muffin cups, about 1 tablespoon each. Top with Swiss cheese.

Preheat oven to 400°.

Custard

4 eggs
1 cup half & half or milk
¼ cup dry white wine or vermouth (or ¼ cup addi-
    tional half & half)
¼ teaspoon ground nutmeg
⅛ teaspoon ground white pepper
¼ teaspoon salt

METAL BLADE: Add 4 eggs to work bowl; with machine running, pour in half & half, white wine, nutmeg, salt and ground white pepper. Process until well-blended. Carefully spoon custard over filling.

Place muffin pans on middle rack in the oven. Turn temperature down to 375°. Bake 25-30 minutes until custard is set and tops are lightly browned and puffed.

Cool in pans 10 minutes. Serve warm or tip out onto wire racks to cool completely.

Preparation: 30 minutes
Baking: 25 minutes
Standing: 10 minutes
Protein g/s: 6.5

Baba Ghannouj (Eggplant Dip)

This Middle Eastern salad is a good dip to serve with raw vegetables, taco chips, or wedges of pita or chapatis.

1-2 eggplants, about 1½ pounds
4-5 tablespoons sesame tahini
3 large garlic cloves
¼-½ teaspoon salt
juice of 1 lemon
3 sprigs parsley
1 tomato

Line a baking pan with foil, lightly oiled. Place eggplant on baking pan and bake at 400° for 30-40 minutes or until very soft. Cool slightly, peel off skin and cut pulp into 2-inch pieces.

METAL BLADE: Add garlic cloves to work bowl, and pulse on/off to mince fine. Add eggplant pieces; process until smooth. Add tahini, salt and lemon juice. Process until well-blended.

Pour dip into a small bowl and garnish with parsley. Arrange tomato wedges around the edge of the bowl.

Preparation: 10 minutes
Baking: 30-40 minutes to bake eggplant

Swiss & Cottage Cheese Turnovers

4 dozen turnovers

A tortilla press makes the preparation of these tasty bite-size treats quick and simple. Make these ahead of time; cool; refrigerate and reheat in a 350° oven 10 minutes or until heated through.

Pastry
2¼ cups whole wheat flour, measured scoop and
      level
½ teaspoon salt
¾ cup butter or margarine, well-chilled, cut into
      1-inch pieces
5-6 tablespoons ice water

METAL BLADE: Add flour, butter and salt to work bowl. Process 8-10 seconds or until mixture has consistency of coarse meal. With processor running, pour ice water through feed tube in a steady stream. Stop processing as soon as dough begins to form a ball. Turn out onto wax paper and shape into a flattened disc. Wrap well and refrigerate while preparing filling.

Filling
1 cup cottage cheese, drained
6 ounces Swiss cheese
1 egg
2 tablespoons whole wheat flour
⅛ teaspoon salt, pepper
½ teaspoon dry leaf thyme

Place 1 cup cottage cheese in a colander; set aside to drain.

SHREDDING DISC: Cut Swiss cheese to fit feed tube. Shred using moderate pressure. Remove cheese and set aside.

METAL BLADE: Add cottage cheese, egg, whole wheat flour, salt, pepper and thyme to work bowl. Process until well-mixed. With machine off, add Swiss cheese. Pulse on/off until just mixed.

Divide pastry dough into quarters. Work with one quarter at a time, refrigerating remaining portions. Divide the quarter into 12 pieces. Cover to prevent dough from drying out. Pat a piece of dough 2-3 times to partially flatten and place on a tortilla press, a bit back of center, inside a folded sheet of wax paper. Close the lid and press. Remove the dough round from the press and peel off the wax paper. If you don't have a press, roll out dough between two sheets of wax paper to 1/16 inch thick; cut into 12 3-inch rounds.

Preheat oven to 375°.

Place one rounded teaspoonful filling on one half of each circle, leaving a small margin. Run a wet finger over margin and fold dough over to cover; press gently to seal well. Prick three times with a fork. Place turnovers on a baking sheet. Bake 15-18 minutes or until golden. Cool slightly before serving.

Preparation: 1-1½ hours
Baking: 15-18 minutes
Chilling: chill pastry dough while preparing filling
Protein g/s: 2.5 per turnover

Guacamole

Serves 4-6

Served on a bed of alfalfa sprouts, garnished with crisp toasted corn tortillas, this tasty dish makes an excellent salad. Traditionally, guacamole is served as a dip accompanied by chips. Make your own chips by cutting corn tortillas into wedges and frying in a small amount of oil or toasting in the oven.

2 large, very ripe avocados, 1½ pounds
2-3 green onions, cut into 2-inch lengths
½ green pepper, cut into small pieces
1 small tomato, quartered
3 tablespoons fresh squeezed lemon juice
½ teaspoon salt
⅛ teaspoon ground black pepper
pinch cayenne pepper
2 tablespoons Vinaigrette Herb Dressing (see index)
    or similar oil and vinegar dressing

Scoop out avocado with a spoon.

METAL BLADE: Add green onions, green pepper, tomato, avocado, lemon juice, salt, pepper, cayenne pepper and dressing to work bowl. Pulse on/off until ingredients are finely chopped. Do not process to make a smooth purée.

Preparation: 10 minutes

Green Chile Dip

1½ cups, 6 servings

This is a spicy dip. Serve with a variety of raw vegetables, pita wedges or toasted tortilla wedges.

1 4-ounce can *whole* green *chiles, rinsed, seeded*
½ *cup pitted black olives*
1 *cup yogurt*
¼ *cup mayonnaise*
¼ *teaspoon salt*
½-¾ *teaspoon chili powder*

In a small bowl, stir together yogurt, mayonnaise, salt and chili powder.

METAL BLADE: Add chiles to work bowl, pulse on/off until finely chopped. Add to yogurt. Add olives to work bowl, pulse on/off until finely chopped. Add to yogurt. Stir to mix. Cover and refrigerate 30-60 minutes.

Preparation: 10 minutes
Chilling: 30-60 minutes
Protein g/s: 1.5

Soups

Vegetarian Chili

Serves 8-10

Beans, cashews and cheese are good complementary protein sources when combined in this tasty chili. Serve with whole grain bread or whole wheat flour tortillas.

3   cups dry kidney beans, rinsed
2   vegetable bouillon cubes
1   bay leaf
1   teaspoon Vegit seasoning
3   large cloves garlic
2   medium onions
2-3   stalks celery
1   large green pepper, halved and seeded
3   tablespoons oil
2   28-ounce cans tomatoes
½   cup raisins
¼   cup vinegar
¼   cup dry red wine
1   tablespoon chili powder
1   teaspoon salt
1½   teaspoons dry leaf oregano
1½   teaspoons dry leaf basil or 6-8 fresh basil leaves, minced
1½   teaspoons ground cumin
1   teaspoon ground allspice
¼   teaspoon ground black pepper
¼   teaspoon Tabasco sauce
2   sprigs parsley
1   cup beer
1   cup cashew nuts, lightly roasted
4-5   ounces Monterey Jack cheese, well-chilled, ½ ounce per serving

Soak beans in 9 cups water at room temperature overnight. In a large pot or pressure cooker, combine beans, soaking water, bouillon cubes, bay leaf and Vegit. Simmer over the range until beans are just tender, about 2 hours, or pressure cook at 15 pounds pressure, 15 minutes. Allow pressure to drop of its own accord.

METAL BLADE: Add garlic cloves to work bowl; pulse on/off until finely minced. Add onions, cut into 1-inch pieces, pulse on/off until chopped medium-fine. In a skillet, heat oil over medium-high heat. Add garlic and onions; sauté 2-3 minutes.

SLICING DISC: Cut celery to fit feed tube vertically; slice. Add to onions and sauté 1 minute. Quarter each green pepper half, wedge into feed tube vertically; slice. Add to skillet and sauté one minute. Stir into beans. Drain liquid from tomatoes into the pot. Quarter tomatoes and add to beans.

METAL BLADE: In a dry work bowl, add parsley; pulse on/off until coarsely chopped. Add to beans along with raisins, vinegar, wine, chili powder, salt, oregano, basil, cumin, allspice, pepper and Tabasco sauce. Bring to a boil and simmer, covered, about 1 hour. Stir in beer and continue cooking 15-25 minutes to thicken. Add cashews just before serving.

SHREDDING DISC: Cut Monterey Jack cheese to fit feed tube, shred. To serve, ladle chili into bowls and top with a generous handful of cheese.

Preparation: 15 minutes
Cooking: 1¾ hours, pressure cooking
         3¾ hours over the range
Protein g/s: 8 servings—22.5
             10 servings—18.5

Minestrone

Serves 10-14

This recipe yields 10-14 servings so you'll need a 10-15 quart pot. We like to serve this soup with whole grain bread and herb butter. The soup freezes well, making it an ideal make-ahead meal.

1 *pound dry cranberry or kidney beans, rinsed*
6 *quarts water, total*
3 *vegetable bouillon cubes*
2-4 *teaspoons Vegit seasoning*
1 *teaspoon salt, to taste*
2 *large onions*
3 *medium leeks*
2-3 *tablespoons oil*
2-3 *large carrots, peeled*
2 *large stalks celery, trimmed*
2-3 *large potatoes, peeled*
8 *ounces green beans, cut into ½-inch lengths*
½ *cup whole wheat elbow macaroni, uncooked*
½ *small head cabbage*
4 *small zucchini, scrubbed*
2-3 *large cloves garlic*
¼ *cup fresh basil or*
   2 tablespoons dry leaf basil
½ *teaspoon dry leaf oregano*
1 *16-ounce can whole tomatoes*
2 *cups parsley leaves*
salt and pepper to taste
grated Parmesan cheese, 2 tablespoons (½ ounce)
   per serving

Soak beans in 2 quarts water at room temperature overnight. Combine beans, soaking water, 2 quarts additional water, vegetable bouillon cubes, Vegit and salt and cook until beans are tender. Pressure cook at 15 pounds of pressure, about 15 minutes. Allow pressure to drop of its own accord, or cook in a pot over the range about 2 hours.

Wash leeks thoroughly to remove grit collected between the leaves. Discard the tough upper portions of the tops.

METAL BLADE: Add onions and leeks, cut into 1-inch pieces, to work bowl. Pulse on/off until chopped medium-fine.

In a skillet, heat oil over medium-high heat. Add onions and leeks; sauté until soft, 3-4 minutes.

SLICING DISC: Cut carrots in half lengthwise then into lengths to fit feed tube vertically; slice. Cut celery to fit feed tube vertically, slice. Add to skillet with onions. Sauté until tender-crisp, about 5 minutes Stir into beans along with the remaining 2 quarts water. Boil for 10 minutes over medium heat. Quarter potatoes and cut into lengths to fit feed tube vertically, slice. Sauté potatoes and green beans until partially softened. Stir into beans along with macaroni. Cut cabbage and zucchini to fit feed tube vertically, slice and add to pot. Wipe work bowl dry.

METAL BLADE: Add garlic to work bowl; pulse on/off until finely minced. Add fresh basil leaves; pulse on/off until finely minced. Stir into soup along with oregano. Cook soup until potatoes are tender, 20 minutes. Add tomatoes and liquid to work bowl. Process until coarsely chopped. When vegetables are tender, stir in chopped tomatoes. Add parsley to a dry work bowl; pulse on/off until finely minced.

To serve, top soup with parsley and Parmesan cheese.

Preparation: 20 minutes
Cooking: 1 hour, pressure cooking
        2½ hours over the range
Protein g/s: 10 servings—17.5
       12 servings—15.5
       14 servings—14

Lentil Soup

Serves 8

When served with our Whole Wheat French Bread (see index) and cheese, this soup makes a hearty main dish.

3 *cups dry lentils, rinsed*
2½ *quarts water*
2 *vegetable bouillon cubes*
2 *teaspoons Vegit seasoning*
3 *medium or large onions*
2 *stalks celery*
3 *medium carrots, peeled*
2-3 *tablespoons oil*
1 *8-ounce can tomato sauce*
1-2 *tablespoons molasses*
2 *tablespoons lemon juice*
vinegar to taste
salt and pepper to taste

In a large pot, combine lentils, water, bouillon cubes and Vegit seasoning. Simmer until lentils are tender, but not mushy, 1-1½ hours.

METAL BLADE: Add onions, cut into 1-inch pieces, to work bowl. Pulse on/off until chopped medium-fine. Remove metal blade; insert slicing disc.

SLICING DISC: Cut celery and carrots to fit feed tube vertically; slice.

In a skillet, heat oil over medium-high heat. Add onions, celery and carrots. Sauté until tender-crisp, approximately 5 minutes. Stir into lentils and continue cooking until vegetables are tender, 30-45 minutes. Stir in tomato sauce, molasses, lemon juice, vinegar, salt and pepper. Adjust seasonings to taste.

Preparation: 10 minutes
Cooking: 1½-2 hours
Protein g/s: 17.5

Black Bean Soup

Serves 8

A generous serving of whole grain bread makes this a hearty main dish. It's especially attractive when garnished with a dollop of yogurt surrounded with lemon slices.

2½ cups dry black turtle beans, rinsed
8 cups water
2 large onions
1 lemon, cut into 8 wedges
2 vegetable bouillon cubes
2-3 tablespoons olive oil
8 cloves
1 teaspoon Vegex vegetable soup seasoning or
    1 tablespoon Worcestershire sauce
½ teaspoon nutmeg
⅛ teaspoon ground allspice
⅛ teaspoon ground pepper
1 teaspoon salt
1 tablespoon plus 1 teaspoon molasses
2 cups additional water
1 teaspoon Japanese rice vinegar
¼ cup dry sherry, optional
yogurt
several sprigs of parsley
lemon slices

Soak beans in 8 cups water at room temperature overnight.

METAL BLADE: Add onions, cut into 1-inch pieces, to work bowl. Pulse on/off until finely chopped.

In a large pot or pressure cooker, heat oil over medium-high heat. Add onions and sauté until soft and transparent. Add beans, soaking water, lemon wedges, bouillon cubes, cloves, Vegex, nutmeg, allspice, pepper, salt, molasses and 2 cups additional water to pot.

Simmer in pot on range for approximately 2 hours. Or pressure cook soaked beans at 15 pounds pressure for 10-15 minutes. Allow pressure to drop of its own accord. Or pressure cook unsoaked beans at 15 pounds pressure for 45 minutes. Allow pressure to drop of its own accord. When beans are cooked, remove lemon wedges and drain. Reserve liquid.

METAL BLADE: Add parsley sprigs to work bowl. Pulse on/off until minced. Remove from bowl and set aside. Add half the beans to work bowl; process until puréed. Return to pot with liquid. Repeat with remaining beans. Stir in vinegar and sherry. To serve, ladle soup into a bowl, top with a dollop of yogurt, surround with 2 lemon slices and sprinkle on parsley.

Preparation: 15 minutes
Cooking: 20-40 minutes, pressure cooking
            2 hours over the range
Protein g/s: 14

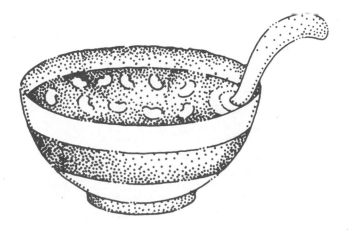

Garden Vegetable Tofu Soup

Serves 6-8

This tasty soup is ready in 15 minutes with the help of a pressure cooker. Serve with a whole grain bread and cheese. Fresh fruit for dessert is a nice way to end this light meal.

1 *large onion*
2 *tablespoons oil*
1 *pound carrots, peeled*
1 *pound celery, including leaves*
1 *medium zucchini, scrubbed*
8 *ounces green beans, cut into 2-inch lengths*
1 *small head cabbage*
2-3 *sprigs parsley*
4 *ripe tomatoes or*
    1 *16-ounce can tomatoes*
2 *tablespoons Spike vegetable seasoning or to taste*
pinch *brown sugar*
1 *bay leaf*
1 *tablespoon soy sauce*
2 *tablespoons pearl barley*
6 *cups water*
1 *block tofu, 22 ounces, drained, cut into 1-inch cubes*

SLICING DISC: Cut onion to fit feed tube; slice. In a large pot or 6-quart pressure cooker, heat oil over medium-high heat. Add onion slices and cook until transparent, but not browned. Cut carrots, celery and zucchini to fit feed tube vertically; slice. Add vegetables to pot. Stir in green beans. Cut cabbage to fit feed tube; slice. Remove from bowl and set aside.

METAL BLADE: Add tomatoes, cut into wedges, and parsley to work bowl. Pulse on/off until coarsely chopped. If using canned tomatoes, add to work bowl with liquid; process until coarsely chopped.

Add to pot along with Spike seasoning, brown sugar, bay leaf, soy sauce, pearl barley and water. Cook at 15 pounds of pressure 10 minutes. Cool cooker immediately. Remove cover and gently stir in tofu cubes.

Or cook soup in a pot over the range until vegetables are just tender, about 30 minutes. Add tofu cubes during the last 5 minutes of cooking. To serve, place a handful of cabbage in soup bowl and ladle in hot soup.

Preparation: 5-8 minutes
Cooking: 15 minutes, pressure cooking
          35 minutes, over the range
Protein g/s: 6 servings—6.5
             8 servings—5

Salads and Dressings

Carrot and Zucchini Slices with Curry Dressing

Serves 8

This non-wilt salad is perfect for a picnic or pot-luck.

3 green onions
4 medium zucchini, scrubbed
8 medium carrots, peeled
2 tablespoons lemon juice
⅓ cup oil
¾-1 teaspoon curry powder
pinch salt
¼ teaspoon freshly ground white pepper
3 tablespoons yogurt

METAL BLADE: Add green onions, cut into 1-inch lengths, to work bowl. Pulse on/off until finely minced. Remove metal blade and insert slicing disc.

THIN or MEDIUM SLICING DISC: Cut zucchini and carrots to fit feed tube vertically; slice. When using the medium slicing disc, process using a light pressure to obtain thin slices. Remove to a glass or ceramic mixing bowl.

In a measuring cup, whisk together the lemon juice, oil, curry powder, salt, pepper and yogurt. Pour over vegetables, toss to mix well. Cover and refrigerate 3-4 hours to allow flavors to blend.

Preparation: 10 minutes
Chilling: 3-4 hours

Carrot Coconut Orange Salad

Serves 8

Freshly grated carrots and coconut combine with orange segments for this refreshing salad. Do not substitute sweetened shredded baking coconut.

6 medium carrots, peeled
meat of ⅓-½ fresh coconut*
3 sweet oranges or 4 fresh mandarin oranges or
   1 11-ounce can mandarin oranges, drained
4-5 tablespoons mayonnaise

SHREDDING DISC:** Cut carrots to fit feed tube vertically; shred. Cut coconut to fit feed tube; shred. Remove shredding disc and carefully insert metal blade.

METAL BLADE: Pulse on/off until carrots and coconut are finely grated.

Pare oranges with a knife to remove the rind; section and remove membrane. Cut into chunks and add to the mixing bowl. When using fresh mandarin oranges, peel, section and remove membrane. Cut into chunks and add to mixing bowl. Add mayonnaise, toss gently to mix. Serve immediately or cover and refrigerate until serving time.

*See index for Coconut Milk recipe on how to prepare coconut.

**Use FINE SHREDDING DISC if available. Omit grating with metal blade. Remove carrots and coconut to a mixing bowl.

Preparation: 20 minutes

Carrot Raisin Salad

Serves 6

Here's an old standby quickly made with your food processor.

6 medium carrots, peeled
5-6 tablespoons mayonnaise
½ cup raisins or currants
⅛ teaspoon salt

SHREDDING DISC: Cut carrots to fit feed tube vertically; shred. For more finely grated carrots, remove shredding disc and carefully insert METAL BLADE. Pulse on/off until finely grated, or use the FINE SHREDDING DISC, if available, and omit the second step.

In a mixing bowl, combine carrots, mayonnaise, raisins and salt. Toss gently to mix. Serve immediately or cover and refrigerate until serving time.

Preparation: 10 minutes

Cauliflower with Creamy Parmesan Dressing

Serves 6

Both the vegetables and dressing can be prepared in advance, refrigerated and combined just before serving.

1 medium head cauliflower
2 green onions
2 ounces radishes
1 cup whole milk yogurt
1 tablespoon finely grated Parmesan cheese
½ clove garlic, crushed
juice of ½ lemon
2 tablespoons olive oil
½ teaspoon salt
⅛ teaspoon freshly ground white pepper

Trim cauliflower and divide into flowerets.

METAL BLADE: Add onions, cut into 2-inch lengths, to work bowl. Pulse on/off until finely minced.

SLICING DISC or FINE SLICING DISC: Arrange cauliflower in feed tube, alternating heads and stems. Slice using light pressure. Stack radishes in feed tube; slice using light pressure. Remove to a mixing bowl, cover and chill until serving time.

In a small dish, stir together yogurt, Parmesan cheese, garlic, lemon juice, oil, salt and pepper. Cover and refrigerate.

At serving time, pour dressing over salad mixture and toss to mix. Spoon onto lettuce-lined salad bowls.

Preparation: 15 minutes
Chilling: variable
Protein g/s: 1.5

Tabouli Salad

Serves 4

A perfect salad to take along on a picnic or serve at a buffet because it won't wilt. Rather than boiling the bulgur, which results in a sticky mess, we soften it in hot water. Serve with beans, lentils or a milk product. Try the variation with soy grits, too.

1 cup bulgur or cracked wheat
3 cups boiling water
2 bunches parsley, 2 ounces
2 bunches fresh mint, 2 ounces
3-4 green onions
1 large or 2 small ripe firm tomatoes
2-4 tablespoons olive oil
5 tablespoons fresh lemon juice
1 large clove garlic, pressed
½ teaspoon salt

Variation

½ cup cooked soy grits
1 tablespoon additional lemon juice
1 tablespoon additional olive oil
salt to taste

Cover bulgur or cracked wheat with water, let stand 1 hour. Drain, wrap in cheese cloth and squeeze out excess water. Place in a mixing bowl.

METAL BLADE: Pinch off leaves from parsley and mint and add to work bowl along with green onions, cut into 2-inch lengths. Pulse on/off until finely minced. Combine with wheat, oil, lemon juice, garlic and salt. Chill, covered, until ready to serve, at least 45 minutes. Quarter tomato(es) and add to work bowl; pulse on/off until coarsely chopped. Drain off excess liquid, place in a small dish and refrigerate, covered.

At serving time, gently mix in tomatoes and mound wheat mixture into a shallow bowl or individual serving dishes.

VARIATION: Add soy grits, lemon juice, olive oil and salt; refrigerate as directed.

Preparation: 10 minutes
Standing: 1 hour
Chilling: 45 minutes
Protein g/s: 5; with soy grits, 8

 or

White Bean Salad Vinaigrette

Serves 4-8

This is an excellent summer main dish when complemented by grains or milk. Although we use whichever white bean is available, there is little doubt that Kentucky Wonders have the best flavor, followed by Great Northerns and navy or little white beans.

3 cups cooked white beans, chilled (1 cup dry)
4 medium carrots, peeled
2-3 stalks celery, trimmed
2 tablespoons oil
1 teaspoon Vegit seasoning
½ cup Vinaigrette Herb Dressing (see index) or
   similar oil and vinegar dressing
½ teaspoon dry leaf thyme
salt and pepper to taste
tops from 2-3 green onions

SLICING DISC: Cut carrots and celery to fit feed tube vertically; slice.

In a skillet, heat oil over medium-high heat. Add carrots and celery; sauté until tender-crisp, 5-7 minutes. Remove from heat, add Vegit seasoning and allow to cool slightly. In a large bowl, combine beans, vegetables, dressing, thyme, salt and pepper. Allow to stand at room temperature or refrigerate 30-60 minutes.

By hand, cut onions into ¼-inch pieces. If you are not concerned with evenly cut onions, process in the work bowl with the metal blade in place until finely

minced. At serving time, add onions, stir to mix well. This salad may be served at room temperature or chilled.

Preparation: 10 minutes
Cooking: allow time to cook beans, plus 5-7 minutes
Standing: 30-60 minutes
Chilling: allow time to chill beans
Protein g/s: 4 servings—11
        6 servings—7.5
        8 servings—5.5

Cheese Radish Salad

Serves 4

This high-protein salad is especially good when served with a whole grain rye bread. It's ideal for lunch or a light supper.

2 hard-cooked eggs, chilled and sliced
1 small bunch chives
1 bunch radishes, about 12 ounces, trimmed
6 ounces Swiss cheese, cut into julienne strips
2 sprigs parsley
bib lettuce leaves to line salad bowl
1 teaspoon Dijon mustard
6 tablespoons oil
2 tablespoons cider vinegar
½ teaspoon brown sugar
salt and pepper to taste

METAL BLADE: Add chives, cut into 1-inch lengths, to work bowl, pulse on/off until finely minced. Remove metal blade.

SLICING DISC: Stack radishes into feed tube; slice. Line a salad bowl with lettuce leaves. Combine radishes, cheese, eggs and chives in a mixing bowl. Mound into lettuce-lined salad bowl.

METAL BLADE: Add Dijon mustard, oil, vinegar, brown sugar, salt and pepper to work bowl. Process until well-mixed. Pour evenly over salad and garnish with parsley. Toss gently to mix and serve.

Preparation: 15 minutes
Protein g/s: 14

Celery Root Herb Salad

Serves 4

A good winter salad. By peeling and slicing the root, we shorten its cooking time.

1 celery root, 4-4½-inches diameter, *washed and*
    peeled
1½ *lemons*
1 *teaspoon brown sugar*
¾ *teaspoon salt*
3-4 *sprigs parsley*
6 *green onions*
1 *large clove garlic*
3 *tablespoons olive oil*
1 *teaspoon vinegar*
¾ *teaspoon dry leaf thyme*
¼ *teaspoon freshly ground pepper*

SLICING DISC: Cut celery root into 8 wedges. Stack into feed tube, vertically; slice.

Place celery root in a shallow pan and add water to just cover. Add juice of half a lemon, ½ teaspoon brown sugar, and ½ teaspoon salt. Bring to a boil; reduce heat to medium and cook until just tender, 6-10 minutes. Drain and place in a medium bowl.

METAL BLADE: Add parsley to work bowl; pulse on/off until finely chopped. Remove from bowl and add to celery root. Add onions, cut into 2-inch lengths, to work bowl. Pulse on/off until finely minced. Remove from bowl and add to celery root. Add garlic clove to work bowl; pulse on/off to mince. Add oil, juice of 1 lemon, vinegar, thyme, pepper and remaining sugar and salt. Process until well-mixed.

Pour over celery mixture; toss well to mix. Cover and refrigerate at least 40 minutes to allow flavors to blend.

Preparation: 10 minutes
Cooking: 10 minutes
Chilling: 40 minutes

Red and White Coleslaw

Serves 8

Radishes contribute a bit of piquancy to this delightful variation of a traditional favorite. One pound of cabbage yields about 6 cups cut.

¼ *pound red cabbage*
½ *pound white cabbage*
4 *4-inch stalks celery*
6 *radishes, trimmed*
½ *cup Aioli Mayonnaise (see index)*
2 *teaspoons malt vinegar*
1 *tablespoon lemon juice*
2 *heaping teaspoons brown sugar*

SLICING DISC: Cut cabbage vertically into wedges. Core and cut into sections to fit feed tube. Wedge cabbage pieces upright in the feed tube; slice using moderate to light pressure. Place celery in feed tube vertically; slice.

SHREDDING DISC: Stack radishes in feed tube; shred. Remove vegetables to a large bowl. In a small dish, stir together mayonnaise, vinegar, lemon juice and brown sugar. Pour over cabbage mixture; toss gently to mix. Refrigerate, covered, until serving time.

Preparation: 10 minutes

Peanut Sunflower Waldorf Salad

Serves 6-8

Peanuts and sunflower seeds are a good complementary protein combination. Serve on lettuce leaves.

3 *medium Red Delicious apples*
2 *stalks celery, trimmed*
⅔ *cup roasted, unsalted peanuts*
¾ *cup unroasted sunflower seeds*
¼ *cup raisins*
juice of ½ lemon
4-6 *tablespoons mayonnaise*

SLICING DISC: Core apples; cut into 8 wedges. Stack into feed tube vertically; slice. Cut celery to fit feed tube vertically, slice.

In a large bowl, combine apples, celery, peanuts, sunflower seeds, raisins, lemon juice and mayonnaise. Stir gently to mix well. Spoon into lettuce-lined salad bowl or individual serving dishes.

Preparation: 10 minutes
Protein g/s: 6 servings—8.5
            8 servings—6.5

Hot German Potato Salad

Serves 8

Authentic in flavor and aroma but without the bacon. Complement the salad with a milk product.

2½ pounds salad potatoes
2 medium onions
3 tablespoons oil
2 vegetable bouillon cubes
1 cup boiling water
½ teaspoon Dijon mustard
1 tablespoon brown sugar
5 tablespoons cider vinegar
dash pepper
1 tablespoon Aioli Mayonnaise (see index)
1 bunch chives
1 bunch radishes, optional
parsley for garnish.
salt and pepper to taste

Cook the potatoes until just done yet still firm, 20-25 minutes. Drain and allow to cool enough to handle, then peel. Cut into slices ¼-inch thick and about 1-inch across. Place in a large bowl.

METAL BLADE: Add onions, cut into 1-inch pieces, to work bowl. Pulse on/off until chopped medium-fine.

In a skillet, heat oil over medium-high heat. Sauté onions until soft and lightly browned. Add onions and excess oil to potatoes; stir gently to mix. Dissolve bouillon cubes in boiling water. Stir in mustard, sugar, vinegar and pepper. Pour into potatoes. Add mayonnaise and mix well with a wooden spoon. Season with salt and additional pepper.

METAL BLADE: Add chives, cut into 1-inch lengths, to a dry work bowl. Pulse on/off until finely minced. Add to potatoes. If you plan to reheat potato salad for later use, do not add radishes.

SLICING DISC: Stack radishes in feed tube; slice and add to salad. If the salad has cooled during preparation, heat briefly in a hot oven. Garnish with parsley and serve hot.

Preparation: 15 minutes
Cooking: 20-25 minutes
Protein g/s: 3

Korean Bean Sprout Salad

Serves 6

This traditional Korean salad is highly seasoned with soy sauce, sesame oil, garlic and cayenne pepper. We've developed a variation that enhances both the amount and quality of the protein in the salad.

1 pound fresh mung bean sprouts
4-5 cups boiling water
tops from 5-6 green onions
½ red or green pepper
2-3 tablespoons oriental sesame oil
4 tablespoons low-sodium soy sauce, less when
     using regular soy sauce
1-2 large cloves garlic, pressed
¼ teaspoon salt, optional
pinch teaspoon cayenne pepper
4 tablespoons hulled sesame seeds

Variation
½ block tofu, drained
1-2 teaspoons soy sauce
1-2 teaspoons oriental sesame oil

Rinse bean sprouts and place in a colander. Pour in boiling water. Allow to drain and remove to a large bowl.

METAL BLADE: Add green onions, cut into 2-inch lengths, to work bowl. Pulse on/off until finely minced. Remove from bowl and add to sprouts. Add green pepper to work bowl; pulse on/off until coarsely chopped.

Combine green peppers with sprouts. Add sesame oil, soy sauce, garlic, salt and cayenne. Toss gently to mix. Toast sesame seeds in a non-stick pan over medium heat until they are light brown. Add to salad. Refrigerate, covered, at least 30 minutes to allow flavors to blend.

VARIATION: Cut tofu into small cubes and add to salad along with additional sesame oil and soy sauce. Toss gently to mix; refrigerate.

Preparation: 15 minutes
Chilling: 30 minutes
Protein g/s: 3; with tofu, 9

Swiss Cheese Salad

Serves 6-8

Served with a thick slice of whole grain bread and fresh fruit, this salad is sure to bring on the compliments.

1   medium head iceberg lettuce
8   ounces Swiss cheese, well-chilled
1   cucumber, unpeeled
2   stalks celery, trimmed
1   medium green pepper, halved and seeded
1   can pitted black olives (drained weight 6 ounces)
2   green onions
2   tablespoons red wine vinegar
½   cup oil
1   tablespoon Dijon mustard
pinch salt and pepper

SLICING DISC: Cut lettuce vertically into quarters. Core and cut into smaller pieces to fit feed tube. Wedge lettuce pieces upright in the feed tube; slice. Remove to a large salad bowl.

SHREDDING DISC: Cut Swiss cheese to fit feed tube; shred using light pressure. Add to lettuce.

SLICING DISC: Cut cucumber in half lengthwise; scoop out seeds. Cut into lengths to fit feed tube vertically; slice. Cut celery and green pepper to fit feed tube vertically; slice. Place olives in feed tube; slice. Remove and add to lettuce. Wipe work bowl dry with paper towel.

METAL BLADE: Add onions, cut into 2-inch lengths, to work bowl. Pulse on/off until finely minced. Add to salad bowl. In a small jar, combine vinegar, oil, mustard, salt and pepper. Shake well to mix. Pour over salad; toss gently to mix and serve immediately.

Preparation: 15 minutes
Protein g/s: 6 servings—10.5
              8 servings—8

Mexican Chef's Salad

Serves 1

Assemble this tasty, colorful, meal-in-itself salad on a dinner plate. The quantities listed are for one serving. Corn or flour tortillas are a nice accompaniment.

3-4   romaine lettuce leaves
½   tomato, chopped
¼-½   avocado, cubed
⅛-¼   mild medium onion
½-1   cup cooked kidney beans, chilled
1   ounce Cheddar cheese, well-chilled
Honey French Dressing (see index)
Tabasco sauce, optional
taco chips

Arrange lettuce leaves, torn into bite-size pieces, over the bottom of a dinner plate.

METAL BLADE: Add onion, cut into 1-inch pieces, to work bowl; pulse on/off until finely chopped. Sprinkle about half of the onions over lettuce; top with beans and remaining onions.

SHREDDING DISC: Cut Cheddar cheese to fit feed tube; shred. Arrange over salad. Top salad with chopped tomato and avocado. Pour over several tablespoons salad dressing and a few drops of Tabasco sauce. Garnish with taco chips.

Preparation: 15 minutes
Cooking: allow time to cook kidney beans
Chilling: allow time to chill kidney beans
Protein g/s: 14-21

Sweet and Sour Spinach Salad

Serves 6-8

Red shreds of beets and the green of fresh spinach combine to make this an attractive and delicious salad. Cook the beets and eggs earlier in the day and refrigerate several hours to chill.

4   medium beets, ¾ pound, cleaned
2   hard-cooked eggs
1   pound fresh spinach
2   large cloves garlic
⅓   cup oil
4   tablespoons English or Canadian malt vinegar
1   tablespoon brown sugar
½   teaspoon dry leaf thyme
½   teaspoon dry leaf marjoram
⅛   teaspoon salt
¼   teaspoon freshly ground pepper

Boil beets in water to cover until tender, 35-40 minutes. Drain and allow to cool enough to handle. Peel and refrigerate.

SHREDDING DISC or SQUARE JULIENNE BLADE: Halve beets vertically and cut into pieces to fit feed tube; shred. Remove from bowl and set aside. Wipe work bowl clean and dry. Halve the eggs. Scoop out the yolks and mash slightly with a fork. Set aside.

METAL BLADE: Add egg white to work bowl; pulse on/off until finely chopped. Remove from bowl and set aside. Add garlic; pulse on/off until finely minced. Add vinegar, brown sugar, thyme, marjoram, salt and pepper and process until well-mixed.

Wash and dry spinach leaves. Tear into bite-size pieces and place in a large bowl. Add egg whites and dressing; toss to mix. Make a well and spoon in beets. Sprinkle in egg yolks and serve.

Preparation: 10 minutes
Cooking: 35-40 minutes
Chilling: 2-3 hours to chill beets and eggs
Protein g/s: 6 servings—2.5
           8 servings—2

Dilled Egg Salad

Serves 8-10

This is a good recipe for a large group. The eggs can be cooked ahead of time and chilled in the refrigerator.

10 hard-cooked eggs, chilled or cooled to room
     temperature
3 medium dill pickles
2 stalks celery, trimmed
½ medium green pepper, quartered
½ small onion
2 sprigs parsley
½ cup plain or Aioli Mayonnaise (see index)
2 teaspoons dry dill weed
salt and pepper to taste
radishes for garnish

METAL BLADE: Add 5 eggs, cut in half, to work bowl. Pulse on/off until coarsely chopped. Remove to a large mixing bowl. Repeat with remaining 5 eggs. Add pickles, cut into 1-inch pieces, to work bowl; pulse on/off until finely chopped. Remove to

mixing bowl. Cut celery into 1-inch pieces and add to work bowl; pulse on/off until finely chopped. Remove to mixing bowl. Add green pepper to work bowl; pulse on/off until finely chopped. Add to egg mixture. Add onion, cut into 1-inch pieces, and parsley to work bowl; pulse on/off until finely chopped. Add to mixing bowl along with mayonnaise, dill weed, salt and pepper. Toss gently to mix.

Cover and refrigerate about 1 hour to allow flavors to blend. Cut radishes into flowers by making multiple incisions on four sides; open with your fingers. Arrange on top of the salad.

Preparation: 10 minutes
Cooking: allow time to cook eggs
Chilling: 1 hour
Protein g/s: 8 servings—8.5
              10 servings—7

Greek Chef's Salad

Serves 1

Since it's easier to make individual salad plates, the quantities listed are for 1 serving. Rinse the Feta cheese and olives with water to remove some of the excess salt.

3-4 large romaine lettuce leaves
½ cup cooked garbanzo beans (¼ cup dry) chilled
¼ small red onion
½ small ripe firm tomato
1-2 ounces Danish Feta cheese, cut into small
     pieces
½ cup black olives
Tart Greek Salad or Olive Oil Lemon Dressing (see
     index)

Line salad bowl with lettuce leaves, torn into bite-size pieces. Spoon in garbanzo beans.

SLICING DISC: Place onion in feed tube; slice. Place tomato in feed tube; slice. Arrange over garbanzo beans. Top with Feta cheese and olives. Pour on 2-3 tablespoons dressing.

Preparation: 10 minutes
Protein g/s: 16-22

Mexican Salad

Serves 6-8

Assemble the salad ahead of time, cover and refrigerate. Just before serving, add the avocado slices, pour on the dressing and toss gently.

2 medium potatoes
1 medium head romaine lettuce
1 small onion
1 medium green pepper, halved and seeded
2 stalks celery
1 can pitted black olives (6 ounces drained weight)
1 medium avocado
lemon or lime juice
⅓ cup oil
3 tablespoons red wine vinegar
¾ teaspoon chili powder
½ teaspoon dry leaf oregano, crumbled
pinch salt
pinch freshly ground pepper

Early in the day, or the night before, cook potatoes. peel if desired and chill. Tear lettuce leaves into bite-size pieces and line a large salad bowl.

SLICING DISC: Cut potatoes into quarters lengthwise, place in feed tube vertically and slice. Cut onion into wedges to fit feed tube; slice with light pressure. Cut celery to fit feed tube vertically, slice. Wedge green pepper into feed tube; slice. Stack olives in feed tube; slice.

Remove sliced vegetables to the prepared salad bowl. Cover and refrigerate until serving time. Cut avocado to fit feed tube; slice. Sprinkle with lemon or lime juice. Remove to a small bowl; cover and refrigerate. In a small jar, combine oil, vinegar, chili powder, oregano, salt and pepper. Refrigerate at least 30 minutes to allow flavors to blend.

Shake well to combine; pour into salad bowl. Toss gently to mix.

Preparation: 15 minutes
Cooking: 20-25 minutes
Chilling: allow time for potatoes to chill
           30 minutes to chill dressing

Potato Salad Plus

Serves 6-8

Fresh dill flavors this distinctive salad. Cottage cheese and yogurt greatly increase the quantity and quality of the protein.

2½ pounds salad potatoes
½ bunch, about 1 ounce, fresh chives
1 bunch, about 1 ounce, fresh dill or
    1 tablespoon dry dill weed
1 small or medium onion
1 cup cottage cheese
⅓ cup mayonnaise
⅓-½ cup yogurt
½ teaspoon salt
½ teaspoon pepper
1-1½ teaspoon Japanese rice vinegar, or other mild
       vinegar
fresh lemon juice to taste
parsley for garnish

Cook potatoes in water to cover until tender yet still firm, 20-25 minutes. Drain and allow to cool enough to handle, then peel. Cut into slices ¼-inch thick and 1-inch across. Place in a large bowl; cool to room temperature. May be done early in the day, covered and refrigerated.

METAL BLADE: Cut the tough stems off the dill. Add dill and chives, cut into 2-inch lengths, to work bowl. Pulse on/off until chopped medium-fine. Remove from bowl and add to potatoes. Add onion, cut into 1-inch pieces, to work bowl; pulse on/off until finely minced; add to potatoes.

METAL BLADE: Add cottage cheese to work bowl. Process until just smooth. With machine off, add mayonnaise, yogurt, salt and pepper. Combine with 2-3 on/off pulses. Add to potatoes along with vinegar and lemon juice. Using a wooden spoon, stir gently to mix. Garnish with parsley. Cover and refrigerate about 1 hour or until serving time.

Preparation: 15 minutes
Cooking: 20-25 minutes
Chilling: allow time for potatoes to cool
           allow about 1 hour to chill salad
Protein g/s: 6 servings—10
              8 servings—7.5

Garbanzo Cheese Salad with Cumin Dressing

Serves 6-8

A good contribution to a pot-luck or picnic. The flavor is enhanced with chilling.

4 cups cooked garbanzo beans (about 2 cups dry) chilled
2 sprigs fresh parsley
2 firm ripe tomatoes
1 small cucumber, seeded
4 ounces sharp Cheddar cheese, well-chilled
4 tablespoons olive oil
¼-⅓ cup lemon juice
¾ teaspoon ground cumin
½ teaspoon salt
¼ teaspoon freshly ground white pepper

Place garbánzo beans into a medium mixing bowl and add remaining ingredients as they are processed.

METAL BLADE: Add parsley to work bowl; pulse on/off until finely minced; remove. Quarter tomatoes and add to work bowl; pulse on/off until chopped medium-fine; remove. Add cucumber, cut into 1-inch pieces; pulse on/off until chopped medium-fine.

SLICING DISC: Cut cheese into strips, wedge into feed tube vertically and slice to make small cubes, remove.

METAL BLADE: Add olive oil, lemon juice, cumin, salt and pepper to work bowl. Process until well-mixed. Pour over bean mixture, stir to mix.

Cover and refrigerate at least 30 minutes.

Preparation: 7-10 minutes
Cooking: allow time to cook beans
Chilling: 30 minutes
Protein g/s: 6 servings—18.5
            8 servings—14

Four Bean Salad

Serves 5-6

Even people who say they don't like beans enjoy this nutritious salad. An excellent luncheon dish when complemented by grains or milk.

1 cup cooked garbanzo beans (½ cup dry) cooled to room temperature or chilled
1 cup cooked kidney beans (⅓ cup dry) cooled to room temperature or chilled
1 cup cooked fresh or frozen lima beans, cooled to room temperature or chilled
1 cup cooked fresh or frozen yellow wax beans, cooled to room temperature or chilled
½ medium red onion
½ cup olive oil
2 tablespoons plus 1 teaspoon Japanese rice vinegar
½ teaspoon Vegex vegetable soup seasoning or Worcestershire sauce
½ teaspoon salt
1 teaspoon dry tarragon
2 tablespoons lemon juice
1 tablespoon plus 1 teaspoon honey
¼ teaspoon freshly ground pepper
tops from green onions for garnish, optional

Combine beans in a large bowl.

METAL BLADE: Add onion, cut into 1-inch pieces, to work bowl. Pulse on/off until finely chopped.

Add to beans.

Add oil, vinegar, Vegex, salt, tarragon, lemon juice, honey and pepper. Combine with several on/off pulses. Pour over beans, stir to mix well. Cover and refrigerate for at least 20 minutes to allow flavors to blend. Garnish with green onions.

Preparation: 10 minutes
Cooking: allow time to cook beans
Chilling: 20 minutes or more
Protein g/s: 5 servings—10
            6 servings—8

Mayonnaise

1½ cups

There is just no comparison between freshly made mayonnaise and the bottled product. Instructions for making mayonnaise may vary with each machine so review your manual and adapt them accordingly. Lemon or lime juice may be substituted for the vinegar.

1　egg
1　tablespoon Japanese rice vinegar or
　　your choice of vinegar, lemon or lime juice
1　rounded teaspoon Dijon mustard
1　tablespoon oil
¼-½　teaspoon salt
1¼-1⅓　cups mild-flavored oil

METAL BLADE: Add egg, vinegar, mustard, 1 tablespoon oil and salt to an absolutely dry work bowl. Process for 60 seconds. With machine running, pour in oil very slowly, almost drop by drop until you can see the mixture has thickened. The remaining oil can be added a little faster. Process until thick. The longer you run the machine, the thicker the mayonnaise will become.

A feature found in some machines is a small hole at the bottom of the pusher. The egg, vinegar, mustard, 1 tablespoon oil and salt are processed for 60 seconds. Then ¼ cup oil is poured into the pusher and allowed to dribble through the hole. The remaining oil is added gradually through the feed tube. Finish mayonnaise as above. Keep in a covered container in the refrigerator up to a week.

Preparation: 5 minutes

Aioli Mayonnaise

1½ cups

A simple cheese, sprout and avocado sandwich becomes a gourmet treat with this variation of the basic mayonnaise.

1　recipe Mayonnaise
2　large cloves garlic, pressed

When mayonnaise is thick, add pressed garlic and continue processing until blended.

Preparation: 5 minutes

Honey French Dressing

1⅓ cups

You'll get compliments when you serve this delicious creamy French dressing over a green or vegetable salad!

2　large cloves garlic
¾　cup oil
5　tablespoons Japanese rice vinegar
¼　cup tomato paste
2　tablespoons honey
¾-1　teaspoon salt
½　teaspoon pepper
½　teaspoon paprika
1-2　drops Tabasco sauce, optional

METAL BLADE: Add garlic to work bowl; pulse on/off until finely minced. With machine running, pour in oil, vinegar, tomato paste, honey, salt, pepper, paprika, and Tabasco sauce. Process until well-mixed and creamy, about 15 seconds. Pour into a container, cover and refrigerate until serving time.

Preparation: 3-5 minutes

Vinaigrette Herb Dressing

1¼ cups

A delicious sweet-sour, salt-free dressing. A few drained capers may be added for a nice variation.

1　large or 2 small cloves garlic
1　cup oil
¼　cup Japanese rice vinegar or
　　malt vinegar
1　teaspoon dry leaf thyme or
　　1 tablespoon fresh thyme
1　teaspoon dry leaf marjoram or
　　1 tablespoon fresh marjoram
1-2　teaspoons brown sugar
¼　teaspoon salt, optional

METAL BLADE: Add garlic to work bowl; process until finely minced. With machine running, pour in oil and vinegar. Add thyme, marjoram, sugar and salt (if used). Process until well-blended. Let stand in a covered container 30 minutes to allow flavors to blend. Store in the refrigerator until serving time.

Preparation: 2-3 minutes
Standing: 30 minutes

Bleu Cheese Dressing

1¼ cups or 5 servings

Low in fat but not low in flavor! To further decrease the fat content, omit the mayonnaise and increase the yogurt to 1 cup.

4 ounces bleu cheese
½ cup mayonnaise
½ cup yogurt
1 clove garlic, pressed
¼-½ teaspoon freshly ground pepper
pinch salt

METAL BLADE: Add bleu cheese, cut into small pieces, to work bowl. Process until smooth. With machine off, add mayonnaise, yogurt, garlic, pepper and salt. Combine with 2-3 on/off pulses until just mixed. Store in covered container in the refrigerator.

Preparation: 2 minutes
Protein g/s: 5.5

Creamy Dijon Dressing

1 cup or 4 servings

A simple tossed green salad becomes a taste delight when this dressing is added.

3 rounded teaspoons Dijon mustard
1 tablespoon oil
1 tablespoon Japanese rice vinegar
½ cup oil
3 cloves garlic, pressed
pinch salt
pinch pepper
⅓ cup buttermilk

METAL BLADE: Add mustard, 1 tablespoon oil and vinegar to work bowl; process until mixture begins to thicken, about 40 seconds. With machine running, pour in oil very slowly, almost drop by drop, until the mixture has thickened like mayonnaise. Turn off machine, add garlic, salt and pepper. Pulse on/off until just mixed. With machine running, slowly pour in buttermilk. Process only to mix. Remove to a covered container and refrigerate.

Preparation: 5 minutes

Green Horseradish Dressing

2 cups or 8 servings

The spiciness of this dressing is controlled by the amount of horseradish used. Start with the smaller amount and increase to taste.

¼ cup cottage cheese
1 cup yogurt
¼ cup buttermilk
¼ cup oil
tops from 4-5 green onions, cut into 1-inch lengths
2-5 teaspoons prepared horseradish
1-2 teaspoons dry dill weed
½ teaspoon salt
¼ teaspoon pepper

METAL BLADE: Add cottage cheese and yogurt to work bowl. Process until smooth. Stop machine to scrape down sides of bowl as needed. Add buttermilk, oil, onions, horseradish, dill, salt and pepper. Process until well-mixed and onion is puréed. Scrape down sides of bowl occasionally. Remove to covered container and refrigerate until serving time.

Preparation: 5 minutes
Protein g/s: 2

Tart Greek Salad Dressing

1⅓ cups

The essential ingredient in the traditional Greek salad of lettuce, tomatoes, onions, Feta cheese and black olives.

2 large cloves garlic
3 tablespoons red wine vinegar
3 tablespoons lemon juice
1 cup olive oil
½ teaspoon salt
½ teaspoon freshly ground pepper

METAL BLADE: Add garlic to work bowl; process until finely minced. With machine running, pour in vinegar, lemon juice, oil, salt and pepper. Process until well-blended. Let stand in a covered container 30 minutes to allow flavors to blend. Store in the refrigerator until serving time.

Preparation: 3 minutes
Standing: 30 minutes

Yogurt Herb Dressing

1 cup or 5 servings

Yogurt keeps this dressing low in fat and calories.

¾ ounce Parmesan or Romano cheese, room temperature (3 tablespoons)
2 cloves garlic
12 fresh basil leaves
⅓ bunch fresh chives, about 1 ounce, cut into 2-inch lengths
1-2 sprigs parsley, torn into small pieces
¼ teaspoon freshly ground pepper
juice of 1 small lime
1 cup yogurt

METAL BLADE: Add Parmesan cheese, cut into small pieces, to work bowl. Process until finely grated. Add garlic cloves and continue processing until finely minced. Stop machine, add basil, chives, and parsley. Pulse on/off until herbs are finely minced. Add lime juice and yogurt; combine with 2-3 on/off pulses. Refrigerate in a covered container until serving time.

Preparation: 5 minutes
Protein g/s: 3

Olive Oil Lemon Dressing

⅔ cup

This is milder than our Tart Greek Salad Dressing (see index). We enjoy this dressing on our Greek Chef's Salad or any simple green salad featuring Feta cheese and olives.

1 large clove garlic
½ cup olive oil
3 tablespoons lemon juice
½-1 teaspoon brown sugar
¼ teaspoon salt
¼ teaspoon pepper
1 teaspoon Japanese rice vinegar or other mild vinegar
1 teaspoon dry leaf oregano, crumbled

METAL BLADE: Add garlic to work bowl and process until finely minced. With machine running, pour in oil and lemon juice. Add sugar, salt, pepper, vinegar and oregano. Process until well-blended.

Pour into a covered container and refrigerate until serving time. The flavors are enhanced when the dressing is allowed to stand about 30 minutes after mixing.

Preparation: 3 minutes
Standing: 30 minutes

Main Dishes

Grains and Legumes

Tamale Pie

Serves 6

Corn germ in the crust brings back the authentic corn-like flavor and nutrients removed from masa. Serve with our Whole Wheat Flour Tortillas and a tossed green salad.

2 cups cooked pinto beans (⅞ cup dry)
1 medium onion
½ medium green pepper
2 canned whole green chiles, rinsed and seeded
2 tablespoons oil
1 16-ounce can tomatoes, drained
1 can pitted black olives (6 ounces drained weight)
2 tablespoons tomato sauce
1 large clove garlic, pressed
1 cup fresh or frozen corn, defrosted, uncooked
2 teaspoons chili powder
½ teaspoon salt
4-6 ounces mild Cheddar or Monterey Jack cheese
¾ cup Quaker Oats Masa Harina
½ cup corn germ
1 tablespoon oil
¾ cup plus 2 tablespoons water

METAL BLADE: Add onion, cut into 1-inch pieces, to work bowl; pulse on/off until coarsely chopped. Add green pepper, cut into 1-inch pieces, to work bowl; pulse on/off until pepper is coarsely chopped. Dry chiles with paper towel; add to bowl and process until just chopped. Do not overprocess. At this point, the onion and green pepper should be chopped medium-fine.

In a 3 or 4-quart pot, heat oil over medium-high heat. Add onion mixture and sauté until onions are soft and transparent, 3-5 minutes.

SLICING DISC: Stack olives in feed tube; slice. Remove from bowl, reserving a few for garnish, and add to onions.

METAL BLADE: Add tomatoes to work bowl; pulse on/off until coarsely chopped. Add to pot along with tomato sauce, garlic, corn, chili powder, salt and beans. Stir to mix well. Cook over medium heat until thickened, 8-10 minutes. Preheat oven to 350°.

Wipe work bowl dry. Add masa and corn germ to work bowl. Process until corn germ is finely ground. With machine running, pour in oil and water. Process until well-mixed. Press evenly over the bottom and up sides of a well-greased 10-inch Pyrex pie plate. Pour in filling.

SHREDDING DISC: Cut cheese to fit feed tube; shred. Sprinkle evenly over the filling. Bake, uncovered, for 30 minutes. Sprinkle on reserved olives; cut into wedges and serve.

Preparation: 10-15 minutes
Cooking/Baking: allow time to cook beans
                                 plus 35 minutes

Protein g/s: 14

Lentil-Sunflower Burgers

Serves 3, 2 patties per serving

A quick meal when lentils are prepared ahead. Serve with or without a whole wheat bun and your choice of condiments. These burgers go well with a tossed green salad.

1 cup cooked lentils, drained (⅓ cup dry)
⅔ cup raw sunflower seeds
1 small onion
2 eggs, lightly beaten
1-2 cloves garlic, pressed
1 teaspoon soy sauce or
   ½ teaspoon Vegex vegetable soup seasoning
¼ teaspoon salt
2 teaspoons ketchup
oil

METAL BLADE: Add sunflower seeds to work bowl; pulse on/off until chopped medium-fine. Remove to a mixing bowl and combine with the lentils. Add onion, cut into 1-inch pieces, to work bowl; pulse on/off until finely chopped. Add to bowl along with eggs, garlic, soy sauce, salt and ketchup. Using a wooden spoon, stir to mix well.

Heat a teflon-coated or similar non-stick pan over medium heat. Add 1-2 tablespoons oil. Using a ⅓ cup measure, spoon lentil mixture into the hot pan; flatten slightly with the back of a spoon. Cook until burger is brown on one side and firm, about 5 minutes. Turn and brown the other side.

Preparation: 10 minutes
Cooking: 10-20 minutes
         allow time to cook lentils
Protein g/s: 17.5

Mexican Black Bean Bake

Serves 8

A complete, protein-rich meal in one dish. Since green chiles vary in their degree of "hotness," sample them first before you add them to the Bake. Use a pair of kitchen shears or a pasta machine to cut the tortillas into strips.

4 cups cooked black turtle beans, drained (2 cups dry)
2 cloves garlic
2 medium onions
2-4 canned whole green chiles, rinsed and seeded
6 tablespoons oil
¾ teaspoon chili powder
½-1 teaspoon salt
12 corn tortillas, cut into ¼-inch strips
8 ounces Cheddar cheese
½ cup pitted black olives, drained
½ red bell pepper
⅔ cup Enchilada Sauce (see index)

METAL BLADE: Add garlic to work bowl; process until finely minced. Add onions, cut into 1-inch pieces, to work bowl; pulse on/off until coarsely chopped. Dry chiles with paper towel and add to onions. Pulse on/off until coarsely chopped.

In a 10-12-inch frying pan, heat 2 tablespoons of oil over medium-high heat. Add onions and chiles; sauté until onions are soft and transparent but not browned, 3-5 minutes. In a large bowl, combine onion mixture with chili powder, beans and salt. Set aside.

In a clean frying pan, heat remaining 4 tablespoons oil over medium heat. Fry tortilla strips until they start to blister; do not allow to crisp. This takes only a few moments. Remove and drain on paper towels.

SHREDDING DISC: Cut Cheddar cheese to fit feed tube; shred. Remove from bowl and set aside.

SLICING DISC: Place bell pepper in feed tube vertically; slice. Remove from bowl and set aside. Stack olives in feed tube; slice.

In a large, deep, greased baking dish layer ingredients as follows: half the tortilla strips; half the enchilada sauce; half the cheese; half the olives and all of the beans. Repeat with the remaining tortilla strips, sauce, cheese and olives. Arrange bell pepper over the top. Bake, uncovered, in a 350° oven for 25-30 minutes or until hot and bubbly.

Preparation: 15 minutes
Cooking/Baking: allow time to cook black beans
               plus 40 minutes
Protein g/s: 20.5

Felafel

54 balls or 12 servings

Fill pita bread halves with four or more felafel balls, top with chopped cucumbers, tomatoes and a generous spoon of Taratour Sauce (see index). A nice appetizer served with taratour sauce for dipping.

8　ounces garbanzo beans, soaked in water at least
　　12 hours
4　tablespoons bulgur
3　cloves garlic
1　teaspoon salt
1　tablespoon flour
1½　teaspoons ground cumin
¼　teaspoon ground coriander
¼-½　teaspoon crushed red pepper
1　egg
oil for deep frying
whole wheat pita bread, purchased or homemade
　　(see index)

Soak bulgur in 1 cup hot water for about 1 hour, drain. Drain garbanzo beans.

METAL BLADE: Add about half of the beans to the work bowl; pulse on/off until coarsely chopped. Add remaining beans, bulgur, garlic, salt, flour, spices and egg. Pulse on/off until finely ground but not puréed.

Form into balls, using about 1½ tablespoons of the mixture. Fry in oil until golden brown, about 5 minutes. Drain slightly on paper towels, serve hot. To reheat, wrap in foil and place in a 300-325° oven for 20-30 minutes.

Preparation: 15 minutes
Cooking: 20 minutes
Protein g/s: 11.5, served with ½ pita
　　　　　　　and one tablespoon sauce

Vegetarian Tacos

Serves 6, 2 tacos per serving

Our version of this traditional favorite is quick and easy to prepare when the beans are cooked in advance.

1　medium onion
½　small green pepper, seeded
1-2　canned whole green chiles, rinsed and seeded
2-3　tablespoons oil
1　large clove garlic, pressed
3　cups cooked pinto beans, drained (1¼ cups dry)
1　8-ounce can tomato sauce
1½　teaspoons chili powder
½　teaspoon salt
¼　teaspoon ground cumin
½　small head iceberg lettuce
6　ounces Cheddar cheese, well-chilled
2　medium tomatoes
12　taco shells
taco sauce

METAL BLADE: Add onion, cut into 1-inch pieces, to work bowl; pulse on/off until coarsely chopped. Add green pepper, cut into 1-inch pieces; pulse on/off until coarsely chopped. Pat chiles dry with paper towel. Add to work bowl; pulse on/off until coarsely chopped.

In a large saucepan, heat oil over medium-high heat. Add onion mixture and sauté until onions are soft, 3-5 minutes. Stir in garlic, beans, tomato sauce, chili powder, salt and cumin. Cover and simmer until very thick, 5-10 minutes. Wipe work bowl dry with paper towel.

SLICING DISC: Cut lettuce in wedges to fit feed tube vertically; slice. Heat taco shells in a 350° oven about 5 minutes.

SHREDDING DISC: Cut Cheddar cheese to fit feed tube, shred. Remove from bowl and set aside.

METAL BLADE: Add tomatoes, cut into quarters, to work bowl; pulse on/off until coarsely chopped. Remove from work bowl and set aside.

To serve, place ¼ cup bean mixture into the taco shell; top with chopped tomato, lettuce, cheese, and taco sauce to taste.

Preparation: 10 minutes
Cooking/Baking: allow time to cook beans
　　　　　　　　　plus 20 minutes
Protein g/s: 17.5

Split Pea and Spinach Curry

Serves 6

A Sri Lankan friend, Chitra Stuiver, prepares a split pea and spinach curry. She says this is one way mothers tempt their children to eat spinach. This is our adaptation of her recipe. Good with rice or Chapatis (see index).

1 piece fresh ginger root, 1 x ¼-inch
1 large clove garlic
1 medium or large onion
2-3 tablespoons oil
1 teaspoon ground cumin
¾ teaspoon ground turmeric
1 teaspoon ground coriander
⅛ teaspoon cayenne pepper
1½ cups yellow split peas, rinsed, unsoaked
4-5 cups water
1 12-ounce can frozen coconut milk, defrosted or
    1½ cups Coconut Milk (see index)
½ teaspoon salt
¾-1 pound fresh spinach, rinsed and stems discarded or
      1 10-ounce package frozen leaf spinach, defrosted, uncooked
additional salt to taste

METAL BLADE: Cut ginger into 8 pieces. Start the processor and drop ginger through the feed tube. Let the processor run until finely grated. Remove from bowl and set aside. Add garlic to work bowl; pulse on/off until finely minced. Add onion, cut into 1-inch pieces; pulse on/off until coarsely chopped.

In a large dutch oven, heat oil over medium-high heat. Add onion and garlic and sauté until soft and transparent, 3-5 minutes. Add ginger; sauté 30 seconds. Add cumin, turmeric, coriander and cayenne pepper; sauté 1 minute. Stir constantly to avoid burning. Add split peas, water, coconut milk and salt. Cover and simmer 20-25 minutes or until peas are tender.

METAL BLADE: Add spinach to work bowl; pulse on/off until coarsely chopped. Stir into peas and continue cooking for 10 minutes. Add a small amount of water if mixture is too thick.

Preparation: 10 minutes
Cooking: 35-40 minutes
Protein g/s: 12

Curried Kidney Beans (Rajma Dal)

Serves 6-8

Serve with Yellow Rice Pilaf and Chapatis (see index). For a spicier curry, increase the amount of cayenne pepper.

3 tablespoons oil
6 cups cooked kidney beans (2 cups dry)
1 piece fresh ginger root, 1 x ¼-inch
1 large clove garlic
1 large onion
1 teaspoon turmeric
2 teaspoons ground coriander
1 teaspoon ground cumin
1 teaspoon garam masala* or
¼ teaspoon ground cloves
¼ teaspoon ground cinnamon
¼ teaspoon ground cardamom
¼ teaspoon ground coriander
pinch ground black pepper
pinch cayenne pepper
1 15-ounce can stewed tomatoes
salt to taste

METAL BLADE: Cut ginger into 8 pieces. Start the processor and drop the ginger through the feed tube. Let processor run until finely grated. Remove from bowl and set aside.

Add garlic to work bowl; process until finely minced. Add onion, cut into 1-inch pieces, to work bowl; pulse on/off until chopped.

In a 6-quart dutch oven, heat oil over medium heat. Add garlic and onions and sauté until soft and transparent, 3-5 minutes. Add ginger and continue cooking 30 seconds. Stir in spices and cook 2 minutes, stirring constantly to avoid burning. Add beans, tomatoes and salt. Cover and simmer 15 minutes to allow flavors to blend.

Preparation: 5 minutes
Cooking: allow time to cook kidney beans
          plus 20-25 minutes
Protein g/s: 6 servings—14
             8 servings—10.5

*Instructions for making garam masala are with recipe for Curried Garbanzo Beans (see index).

Curried Garbanzo Beans (Chana Dal)

Serves 4-6

Yellow Rice Pilaf and Chapatis (see index) make nice accompaniments as well as complementary protein sources.

4 cups cooked garbanzo beans (2 cups dry) plus
    ¾-1 cup cooking liquid
3 tablespoons oil
½ teaspoon cumin seeds
1 large onion
1 piece fresh ginger root, 1 x ¼-inch
1 large clove garlic, pressed
¾ teaspoon ground turmeric
½ teaspoon ground cumin
¾ teaspoon garam masala* or
    ⅛-¼ teaspoon ground cloves
    ¼ teaspoon ground cinnamon
    ¼ teaspoon ground cardamom
    ¼ teaspoon ground coriander
    pinch ground black pepper
⅛ teaspoon cayenne pepper
leaves from 2-3 sprigs fresh coriander for garnish

In a 3-4 quart pot, heat oil over medium heat. Roast cumin seeds for one minute to bring out the flavor. Be careful not to let them burn.

METAL BLADE: Add onion, cut into 1-inch pieces, to work bowl. Pulse on/off until finely chopped. Add to the pot and sauté about 3 minutes. Cut ginger into small pieces. Turn on machine and drop in ginger pieces through feed tube. Process until finely grated. Add ginger and garlic to pot and continue to cook, stirring constantly. Add turmeric, ground cumin, garam masala (or substitute) and cayenne. Sauté for 1 minute being careful not to burn spices. Stir in garbanzo beans and cooking liquid. Cover and cook for 15 minutes or until sauce has thickened and flavors are blended. Garnish with coriander leaves.

Preparation: 8-10 minutes
Cooking: allow time to cook garbanzo beans
            plus 20 minutes
Protein g/s: 4 servings—20.5
            6 servings—13.5

*Garam masala is a blend of spices which varies from region to region in India. Make your own by toasting spices in a 200° oven for 30 minutes. Use a spice grinder or blender to make a fine powder. DO NOT USE THE FOOD PROCESSOR AS DAMAGE MAY RESULT.

1 part whole coriander seeds
1-1½ parts whole black peppercorns
2 parts whole cumin seeds
2 parts whole cloves
4 parts whole cardamom pods or 2 parts cardamom
    seeds
1 part cinnamon stick, broken into small pieces

Coconut Milk

1¾ cups

Contrary to popular belief, coconut milk is strictly non-dairy. It's the juice that's pressed out of the coconut meat. Shake the nut before you purchase it. A splashing sound indicates that the coconut is fresh. Coconuts sold are conveniently husked.

2 large coconuts, 4-4½ inches in diameter
⅓ cup boiling water

With a clean screwdriver, ice pick or similar implement, poke out the three eyes on top to drain out the liquid. Discard the liquid or save it for cooking.

Place the whole coconuts on a foil-lined baking sheet and bake in a 350° oven about 30 minutes or until they crack in several places. Remove from oven and allow to cool enough to handle. Gently loosen the chunks of meat with a knife. Peel off the brown covering, using either a paring knife or vegetable peeler. Cut coconut in pieces approximately 1-inch square.

METAL BLADE: Add coconut pieces and process until finely grated but not puréed, about 1-2 minutes. Pour in boiling water and allow to stand for 15 minutes. Turn machine on and process for 10 seconds. Squeeze through several thicknesses of cheesecloth to remove as much of the milk as possible. Discard the pulp. Coconut milk is ready to use or freeze.

Preparation: 15 minutes
Baking: 30 minutes
Standing: 15 minutes

Rice and Vegetable Torte

Serves 8

A slice of this torte reveals a layer of herbed vegetables between two layers of brown rice. The filling can be made the night before. Refrigerate until you are ready to assemble the torte.

4 *cups cooked brown rice (about 1½ cups raw)*
5 *ounces Parmesan cheese, room temperature*
8 *ounces mozzarella cheese, well-chilled*
1 *clove garlic*
1 *medium onion*
1 *pound eggplant, unpeeled*
12 *ounces zucchini, scrubbed (about 2 medium)*
¾ *teaspoon dry leaf basil*
1½ *teaspoons dry leaf oregano*
½ *teaspoon salt*
¼ *teaspoon freshly ground white pepper*
12 *ounces tomatoes (about 2 medium)*
2 *eggs*
paprika

METAL BLADE: Add Parmesan, cut into 1-inch pieces, to work bowl. Process until finely grated. Remove from bowl and set aside.

SHREDDING DISC: Cut mozzarella cheese to fit feed tube, shred using light pressure. Remove from bowl and set aside.

METAL BLADE: Add garlic and onion, cut into 1-inch pieces, to work bowl. Pulse on/off until finely chopped. In a 3-quart dutch oven or large frying pan, heat 3 tablespoons oil. Add onion and sauté 2 minutes.

THIN or MEDIUM SLICING DISC: Cut eggplant into quarters to fit feed tube, slice. Add to dutch oven. Cook over medium heat, stirring often, until vegetables are soft, about 10 minutes. Cut zucchini to fit feed tube vertically, slice. Add to dutch oven. Add basil, oregano, salt and pepper. Continue to cook, stirring often, until zucchini is soft, about 6 minutes.

METAL BLADE: Add tomatoes, cut into wedges, to work bowl. Pulse on/off until coarsely chopped. Remove to a colander and allow to drain.

Add to skillet and simmer rapidly until all liquid has evaporated, about 15 minutes. Stir often. Remove from heat and allow to cool. In a large mixing bowl, combine brown rice, 1 egg, 1 cup Parmesan and half the mozzarella cheese. Press half the rice mixture into the bottom of a well-oiled 9-inch springform pan. Preheat oven to 350°F.

Add 1 egg and remaining ¼ cup Parmesan to vegetable mixture. Spoon over rice. Top with remaining rice mixture; press to form an even layer. Scatter remaining mozzarella cheese over top and sprinkle on paprika generously. Bake 1 hour. Remove from oven and allow to stand 10 minutes before removing sides of the pan. Cut into wedges and serve.

Preparation: 15 minutes
Cooking/Baking: 1½ hours
Standing: 10 minutes
Protein g/s: 17.5

Chile Rice Bake

Serves 8

This can be assembled earlier in the day and refrigerated until baking time. It's a spicy dish and goes well with a refreshing fruit salad.

3 *cups cooked brown rice (1 cup raw)*
1⅓ *cups cooked black turtle beans (½ cup dry)*
2 *cloves garlic*
1 *small onion*
1 *tablespoon oil*
1 *4-ounce can whole green chiles, rinsed and seeded*
1 *cup low-fat cottage cheese*
8 *ounces Monterey Jack cheese, well-chilled*
2 *ounces Cheddar cheese, well-chilled*

METAL BLADE: Add garlic and onion, cut into 1-inch pieces, to work bowl. Pulse on/off until finely chopped. In a small skillet, heat oil over medium heat. Add onions and sauté until soft and transparent, 3-5 minutes. Remove from heat and set aside. Dry chiles on a paper towel. Add to work bowl, pulse on/off until coarsely chopped. In a mixing bowl, combine rice, beans, onions and chiles. Wipe work bowl dry with paper towels.

SHREDDING DISC: Cut Monterey Jack cheese to fit feed tube, shred. Remove from bowl and set aside. Cut Cheddar cheese to fit feed tube, shred. Remove from bowl and set aside.

In an oiled 8x8-inch baking dish make layers of ⅓ rice mixture, cottage cheese, ⅓ rice mixture, Monterey Jack cheese, ⅓ rice mixture. Bake, covered, in a 350° oven 30 minutes. Remove cover and sprinkle on Cheddar cheese. Return to oven, uncovered, to bake 10 minutes or until cheese is melted.

Preparation: 10 minutes
Cooking/Baking: 50 minutes
            allow time to cook rice and beans
Protein g/s: 18

Boston Baked Beans

Serves 8

A tossed green salad and a grain or milk product are perfect accompaniments to this classic bean dish. Soak the beans in 6 cups of water overnight and pressure cook at 15 pounds of pressure for about 15 minutes, allowing pressure to drop of its own accord. Cooking in a pot over the range will take about 2 hours. Add 2 vegetable bouillon cubes to the cooking water to enhance the flavor.

6 cups cooked Great Northern or navy beans
  (2 cups dry)
1 large onion
2 tablespoons oil
1 teaspoon salt
3 tablespoons molasses
2 tablespoons honey
6 tablespoons tomato sauce
1 tablespoon tomato ketchup
1 tablespoon prepared mustard
¼ teaspoon vinegar

METAL BLADE: Add onion, cut into 1-inch pieces, to work bowl. Pulse on/off until finely chopped.

In a skillet, heat oil over medium-high heat. Add onions and sauté until soft and transparent but not browned, 5-8 minutes. In a large mixing bowl, combine beans, onions, salt, molasses, honey, tomato sauce, tomato ketchup, mustard and vinegar. Grease a large baking dish, approximately 10-inches in diameter and 3-inches high, or any similar size dish. Pour in bean mixture, cover with foil and bake at 350° for 30 minutes. Uncover and bake an additional 30 minutes.

Preparation: 10 minutes
Cooking/Baking: 1 hour; allow time to cook beans
Protein g/s: 11.5

Double Decker Tortilla Bake

Serves 8-10

Assemble ahead, refrigerate and bake just before serving for a quick and easy main dish. This is perfect for a crowd or "pot-luck" dinner.

3 cups cooked brown rice (about 1 cup raw)
2 cups cooked pinto beans (about ¾ cup dry)
1½ pounds Monterey Jack cheese, well-chilled
1 dozen corn tortillas, purchased or homemade
2 cups thick low-fat yogurt

Sauce
1 14-ounce can Mexican tomatillos, drained
1 small onion
2 cloves garlic
1 7-ounce can whole green chiles, rinsed and seeded
1 bunch fresh coriander
1 teaspoon salt
½ teaspoon brown sugar
½ teaspoon crushed red pepper

Combine cooked rice and beans, set aside.

SHREDDING DISC: Cut Monterey Jack cheese to fit feed tube; shred using medium pressure. Remove from work bowl and set aside.

METAL BLADE: Add onion, cut into 1-inch pieces, and garlic to work bowl. Pulse on/off until finely chopped. Add tomatillos, green chiles, coriander, salt and sugar. Process until smooth and well-blended. Stop machine, stir in crushed red pepper. Generously grease or oil the bottom and sides of a 9 x 13-inch baking pan. Cover the bottom of the pan with 6 tortillas, each cut into 6 wedges. Press in half of the rice/bean mixture. Top with half of the green chile sauce, about 1 cup. Spoon on 1 cup yogurt. Sprinkle on half of the Monterey Jack cheese. Repeat layering with remaining tortilla wedges, rice/bean mixture, sauce, yogurt and cheese.

Cover pan with foil and refrigerate as long as overnight. Bake, covered, in a 350° oven for 40 minutes, 45-55 minutes if refrigerated. Remove foil and continue baking 10 minutes or until cheese is bubbly and lightly browned. Cut into squares and serve.

Preparation: 15-20 minutes
Cooking/Baking: 45-60 minutes
            allow time to cook beans and rice
Protein g/s: 8 servings—28.5
          10 servings—22.5

Taratour Sauce

1 cup or 12 servings

Top hot felafel balls with this tasty sauce.

2 cloves garlic
½ cup sesame Tahini (see index) or purchased
¼ cup fresh lemon juice
½ teaspoon salt
¼ cup plus 1 tablespoon cold water
pinch cayenne pepper, optional

METAL BLADE: Add garlic to work bowl. Process until finely minced. Add sesame tahini, lemon juice and salt. Process to mix well. Turn machine off and scrape down sides of bowl. With machine running, pour in water in a steady stream. Process until well-mixed. Store in a covered container and refrigerate.

Preparation: 5 minutes
Protein g/s: 2

Cheesy Green Rice

Serves 6

We enjoy this family and company favorite with a tossed green salad and whole grain bread.

3 cups cooked brown rice, cooled (1 cup raw)
1 ounce Parmesan cheese, room temperature
6 ounces Monterey Jack cheese, well-chilled
⅓ cup parsley leaves
1 10-ounce package frozen spinach, defrosted, squeezed dry
⅓ cup green onion bottoms
2 tablespoons oil
2 eggs
1 cup milk
½-1 teaspoon Vegex vegetable soup seasoning or 1 tablespoon Worcestershire sauce
salt and pepper to taste

Preheat oven to 325°.

METAL BLADE: Add Parmesan cheese, cut into small pieces, to work bowl. Process until finely grated.

SHREDDING DISC: Cut Monterey Jack cheese to fit feed tube; shred using light pressure. Combine rice and cheeses in a large mixing bowl. Set aside.

METAL BLADE: Add parsley and spinach to work bowl. Pulse on/off until finely chopped but not puréed. Remove from work bowl and add to rice. Cut green onion bottoms into 1-inch pieces; add to work bowl and pulse on/off until finely chopped.

In a small skillet, heat 1 tablespoon oil over medium-high heat. Add onions and sauté 3-5 minutes. Add to rice mixture.

METAL BLADE: Add eggs to work bowl. With machine running, pour in remaining 1 tablespoon oil, milk, Worcestershire sauce or Vegex seasoning, salt and pepper. Process until well-mixed. Pour into rice mixture. Stir to mix well.

Spread mixture evenly over the bottom of a greased 9x12-inch or similar size baking dish. Bake 30-35 minutes or until firm. Remove from oven and let stand 10 minutes. Cut into squares and serve.

Preparation: 10-15 minutes
Cooking/Baking: 35-40 minutes
                        allow time to cook rice
Standing: 10 minutes
Protein g/s: 15

Arabic Musakka'a

Serves 6

Ordinary ingredients—eggplant, tomato and the garbanzo bean—are combined in this traditional dish with a not so ordinary flavor! Serve with pita bread and a Greek salad topped with Feta cheese and olives.

2 medium eggplants, about 1 pound each, unpeeled
olive oil
2 large onions
2 28-ounce cans whole tomatoes, drained, liquid reserved
3 cups cooked garbanzo beans (1½ cups dry)
1½ teaspoons salt
½ cup reserved tomato liquid

Quarter eggplants and with a sharp knife, cut into large cubes, about 2 x 2 inches. In a heavy skillet, heat about ¼-inch olive oil over medium-high heat. Add eggplant pieces and cook until all sides are golden brown. Watch carefully to avoid burning. Add additional oil as needed. Remove from skillet and allow to drain on paper towels.

SLICING DISC: Cut onions into quarters, insert into feed tube vertically; slice.

In the same skillet, heat 1-2 tablespoons olive oil over medium-high heat. Add onions and sauté until golden brown, 3-5 minutes. Remove skillet from heat. Preheat oven to 350°.

Pour reserved tomato liquid through a sieve to remove seeds. Measure out ½ cup, set aside.

METAL BLADE: Add tomatoes to work bowl; pulse on/off until coarsely chopped. In a large casserole or dutch oven, layer ingredients as follows: all the eggplant, ½ teaspoon salt, all the onions, garbanzo beans, ½ teaspoon salt, and tomatoes. Pour in ½ cup tomato liquid and sprinkle with remaining ½ teaspoon salt. Cover with foil and bake for 40 minutes.

Preparation: 10 minutes
Cooking/Baking: 1-1¼ hours
Protein g/s: 10

Curried Lentils

Serves 4

Serve with Yellow Rice Pilaf, Chapatis (see index) or millet.

3 cups cooked lentils (1 cup dry) plus about ½ cup cooking liquid
1 piece fresh ginger root, 1 x ¼-inch
1 large clove garlic
1 large onion
2-3 tablespoons oil
¾ teaspoon turmeric
½ teaspoon ground cumin
¼ teaspoon ground coriander
¾-1 teaspoon garam masala* or
        ⅛-¼ teaspoon ground cloves
        ¼ teaspoon ground cinnamon
        ¼ teaspoon ground cardamom
        ¼ teaspoon ground coriander
        pinch ground black pepper
pinch cayenne pepper, optional
¼ teaspoon salt

METAL BLADE: Cut ginger into 8 pieces. Start the processor and drop the ginger through the feed tube. Let processor run until finely grated. Remove from bowl and set aside.

Add garlic to work bowl, process until finely minced. Add onion, cut into 1-inch pieces, to work bowl; pulse on/off until chopped.

In a large pot, heat oil over medium heat. Add garlic and onion; sauté until soft and transparent, 3-5 minutes. Add ginger and sauté 30 seconds. Stir in spices and continue to cook 1 minute. Stir constantly to avoid burning. Add the lentils and cooking liquid, cayenne pepper and salt. Cook for about 5 minutes or until the liquid is cooked down. Taste and adjust seasonings.

Preparation: 5 minutes
Cooking: 10-15 minutes
            allow time to cook lentils
Protein g/s: 12

*Instructions for making garam masala are with recipe for Curried Garbanzo Beans (see index).

Lentils Burgundy

Serves 8

A hearty main dish when complemented by a thick slice of whole grain bread. The aroma of the lentils during cooking will bring your family to the table without coaxing.

2½ cups dry lentils
6 cups water
1 bay leaf
2 vegetable bouillon cubes
2 large onions
2-3 tablespoons oil
3 large carrots, peeled
2 large leeks
1 large clove garlic, pressed
½-1 teaspoon dry leaf thyme
1½ cups Burgundy wine
salt and pepper to taste

Rinse lentils and soak overnight in 5 cups of water at room temperature. Combine lentils, soaking water, 1 cup additional water, bay leaf, and bouillon cubes in a large pot. Bring to a boil, reduce heat to medium and cook until lentils are done, about 30 minutes.

METAL BLADE: Add onions, cut into 1-inch pieces, to work bowl; pulse on/off until coarsely chopped.

SLICING DISC: Cut carrots to fit feed tube vertically; slice. In a skillet, heat oil over medium-high heat. Add onions and carrots; saute until tender-crisp, 5-8 minutes. Stir into lentils.

Wash leeks thoroughly, removing all of the grit accumulated between the leaves. Discard the upper, tough portion of the tops. Slice into ¼-inch pieces and sauté in about 1 tablespoon oil until soft. Add to lentils. (If you are not concerned with evenly cut leeks, coarsely mince in your food processor with the metal blade in place.)

When vegetables and lentils are tender, stir in garlic, thyme and Burgundy wine. Cook for 25-30 minutes over medium heat to thicken. Taste and adjust seasonings.

Preparation: 10 minutes
Cooking: 1 hour
Protein g/s: 15

Cracked Wheat Chili

Serves 6

Serve this well-seasoned but not too hot chili over a scoop of brown rice, topped with shredded cheese.

1 cup dry pinto beans, rinsed
3 cups water
2 cloves garlic
1 small onion
1 7-ounce can whole green chiles, rinsed and seeded
1 tablespoon oil
1 14- or 15-ounce can whole tomatoes
½ tablespoon honey
½ teaspoon ground cumin
½ teaspoon dry leaf oregano
½ teaspoon dry leaf basil
½ teaspoon salt
⅛ teaspoon ground coriander
⅓ cup cracked wheat
½ cup water
6 ounces Cheddar cheese, well-chilled

Soak beans in 3 cups water overnight. In a pressure cooker at 15 pounds pressure, cook beans in soaking water for 10 minutes. Let pressure drop of its own accord, or cook in a pot over the range about 2 hours or until beans are tender.

METAL BLADE: Add garlic and onion, cut into 1-inch pieces, to work bowl. Pulse on/off until coarsely chopped. Pat chiles dry with paper towels; cut into thirds; add to work bowl. Pulse on/off until chopped medium-fine. In a skillet, heat 1 tablespoon oil over medium-high heat. Add onion mixture and sauté until soft, 4-6 minutes. Remove from heat. Add tomatoes and liquid, honey, cumin, oregano, basil, salt and ground coriander to work bowl. Process until smooth.

Stir cracked wheat and ½ cup water into beans. Bring to a boil; stir in onion and tomato mixture. Bring to a boil; lower heat, cover and simmer 30-45 minutes or until thick. Stir occasionally to keep chili from sticking to the bottom of the pot.

SHREDDING DISC: Cut cheese to fit feed tube; shred. Serve chili over brown rice; top each serving with 1 ounce shredded cheese.

Preparation: 10 minutes
Cooking: 55 minutes using the pressure cooker
2½ hours cooking over the range
Protein g/s: 15

Eggs, Milk, and Cheese

Broccoli Rice Bake

Serves 6

Have the cooked rice ready ahead of time and dinner will be ready before you know it. Reheat leftovers, covered, in a 350° oven 20-25 minutes.

1½ cups cooked brown rice, cooled (about ½ cup raw)
1 pound broccoli, untrimmed
6 ounces sharp Cheddar cheese
1 small onion
2 tablespoons butter or margarine
1 teaspoon salt
¼ teaspoon pepper
3 eggs
1 cup skim milk

Trim broccoli and break into flowerets. Cut stalks into 1-inch pieces. Steam until tender but crisp; set aside.

SHREDDING DISC: Cut cheese to fit feed tube, shred. Remove to large mixing bowl.

METAL BLADE: Add onion, cut into pieces, to work bowl. Pulse on/off until finely chopped. In a small skillet, heat 2 tablespoons butter over medium-high heat. Add onions and sauté until soft; add salt and pepper. Preheat oven to 350°. Add broccoli to work bowl. Pulse on/off until coarsely chopped. Combine rice, broccoli and onion in mixing bowl with cheese. Toss to mix. Add eggs to work bowl; process 5 seconds. With machine running, pour in milk. Stop machine as soon as the milk is added. Pour into the broccoli mixture. Stir gently to mix.

Pour into a greased 8 x 8-inch baking pan. Bake, uncovered, 35-40 minutes or until custard is set. Let stand 10 minutes; cut into squares to serve.

Preparation: 15-20 minutes
Cooking/Baking: allow time to cook rice
plus 35-40 minutes
Standing: 10 minutes
Protein g/s: 13

Cheddar Scalloped Carrots with Walnuts

Serves 6-8

Serve with a grain or bread and a tossed green salad.

8 ounces Cheddar cheese
2 pounds carrots, pared
2 small onions
4 tablespoons butter or margarine
4 tablespoons whole wheat flour
2 teaspoons Vegit seasoning
1¾ cups hot milk
tops from 6 green onions, cut into ½-inch lengths
4 ounces walnuts, lightly roasted

SHREDDING DISC: Cut Cheddar cheese to fit feed tube, shred. Remove from bowl and set aside.

SLICING DISC: Cut carrots to fit feed tube vertically, slice. Steam until tender-crisp, 7-10 minutes. Remove from heat and set aside.

METAL BLADE: Add onions, cut into 1-inch pieces, to work bowl. Pulse on/off until finely chopped.

In a saucepan, melt butter over medium heat. Sauté onions until soft and transparent. Remove from heat; gradually stir in flour and Vegit seasoning. Replace pan on burner. Gradually pour in hot milk, stirring constantly until mixture has thickened. Slowly add cheese, a handful at a time. Cook over low heat until cheese is melted and smooth, stirring constantly. Add green onions.

Preheat oven to 350°. Arrange carrots over the bottom of a greased shallow baking dish. Top with sauce. Bake, uncovered, for 15 minutes. Top with walnuts and continue baking 15 minutes.

Preparation: 15 minutes
Cooking/Baking: 45-50 minutes
Protein g/s: 6 servings—15
8 servings—11

Cauliflower Basil Mushroom Bake

Serves 4-6

1 *small cauliflower (1 pound) broken into small*
   flowerets
2 *tablespoons oil*
6 *ounces sharp Cheddar cheese*
1 *clove garlic*
1 *small onion*
8 *ounces fresh mushrooms*
1 *slice whole wheat bread*
¼ *teaspoon salt*
¼ *teaspoon dry leaf basil, crumbled*
3 *eggs*
½ *cup skim milk*

Steam cauliflower until tender but crisp. Remove from heat and set aside.

SHREDDING DISC: Cut Cheddar cheese to fit feed tube. Shred using light pressure. Remove from bowl and set aside.

METAL BLADE: Add garlic clove, pulse on/off until finely minced. Add onion, cut into 1-inch pieces. Pulse on/off until finely chopped. In a large skillet, heat 2 tablespoons oil over medium-high heat. Sauté onions and garlic until soft, about 5 minutes.

SLICING DISC: Stack mushrooms in feed tube; slice with firm pressure. Add mushrooms to skillet and continue cooking until mushrooms are soft and liquid is evaporated, about 5 minutes. Remove from heat and set aside.

METAL BLADE: Add bread, torn into pieces. Process to make fine crumbs. Add salt, basil, eggs and milk. Pulse on/off to mix well. Stop machine, add 1 cup cheese. Pulse on/off until just mixed. Stir into skillet.

Arrange cauliflower in a single layer in a lightly oiled 8 x 8-inch baking dish. Spread mushroom onion mixture over cauliflower. Top with remaining ½ cup cheese. Bake, uncovered, in a preheated 350° oven for 20-25 minutes or until set. Cut into squares and serve.

Preparation: 15 minutes
Cooking/Baking: 25 minutes
Protein g/s: 4 servings—18
                6 servings—12

Moussaka

Serves 8

This tastes surprisingly authentic even without the lamb. Serve with a tossed green salad made with lettuce, olives, tomatoes, sliced red onions, small cubes of Feta cheese and Tart Greek Salad Dressing (see index).

Tomato Sauce

3 *medium onions*
2 *cloves garlic, pressed*
2 *tablespoons olive oil*
leaves from 2-3 sprigs fresh mint or
   1 *tablespoon dry leaf mint*
2 *sprigs fresh parsley*
1-2 *teaspoons honey*
½ *teaspoon salt*
½ *teaspoon pepper*
2 *8-ounce cans tomato sauce*
¼ *teaspoon dry leaf rosemary*

METAL BLADE: Add onions, cut into 1-inch pieces, to work bowl. Pulse on/off until finely chopped. In a saucepan, heat 2 tablespoons olive oil over medium heat. Add onions and garlic, sauté until soft and transparent, 5-8 minutes. Wipe work bowl with a paper towel.

METAL BLADE: Add mint leaves and parsley to work bowl. Pulse on/off to finely mince. Add to onions along with honey, salt, pepper, tomato sauce and rosemary. Cover and simmer 30 minutes.

Eggplant-Rice Base

1½ *pounds eggplant*
2-2½ *cups cooked brown rice, cooled (¾ cup raw)*
½-¾ *teaspoon ground nutmeg*
½-¾ *teaspoon ground cinnamon*
½-¾ *teaspoon ground allspice*
olive oil for oiling baking pans

SLICING DISC: Preheat oven to 400°. Cut eggplant to fit feed tube; slice. Place slices on a well-oiled baking sheet. Bake for 15 minutes or until slices are tender. Remove from oven and set aside. Reduce heat to 375°.

Custard Topping

2 *ounces Parmesan cheese, at room temperature*
4 *large eggs*
1 *cup ricotta cheese*
1 *cup milk*
¼ *teaspoon ground nutmeg*
additional nutmeg for topping

METAL BLADE: Add Parmesan cheese, cut into 1-inch pieces, to a dry work bowl. Process until finely grated. Add eggs, ricotta cheese, milk and nutmeg. Combine with 2-3 on/off pulses. Stop machine, scrape down sides of bowl. Process until mixed.

ASSEMBLY: Arrange the eggplant over the bottom of a well-greased baking dish, approximately 9 x 13-inches. Sprinkle with half of the nutmeg, cinnamon and allspice. Spread rice over eggplant; press down gently to form an even layer. Sprinkle with remaining nutmeg, cinnamon and allspice. Spoon on tomato sauce. Pour custard over tomato sauce. Sprinkle with additional nutmeg. Bake at 375° for 40-45 minutes.

Preparation: 20 minutes
Cooking/Baking: 1½ hours
                    allow time for rice to cook
Protein g/s: 11

Cheese Filled Tortillas

Serves 6

A perfect make-ahead dish for a crowd.

1 bunch parsley
1 medium onion
1½ pounds Monterey Jack cheese, well-chilled
¼ teaspoon pepper
6 tablespoons butter or margarine
1 dozen 8-inch Whole Wheat Flour Tortillas (see index) or purchased

METAL BLADE: Add parsley to work bowl and pulse on/off until finely minced. Remove from bowl and set aside. Add onion, cut into 1-inch pieces. Pulse on/off until finely chopped. In a 10-inch frying pan with a non-stick surface, melt 4 tablespoons butter over medium-high heat. Sauté onions until soft. Remove from heat.

SHREDDING DISC: Cut cheese to fit feed tube; shred. Add to onions along with parsley and pepper. Stir to mix. Place about ½ cup firmly packed cheese mixture in a line just off center on each tortilla. Roll tortillas firmly around the filling and place, seam-side down, in a shallow greased or oiled baking pan. Cover and refrigerate if made ahead.

Melt remaining 2 tablespoons butter and brush on all exposed tortillas. Bake, uncovered, in a 375° oven for 15-20 minutes or until tortillas are lightly browned and cheese is melted.

Preparation: 15 minutes
Cooking/Baking: 15-20 minutes
Protein g/s: 17

Egg Fu Yung Omelet

Serves 3

This dish is ideal when you want a meal in a hurry.

1 medium onion
2-3 stalks celery
2 tablespoons oil
2 cups fresh mung bean sprouts
1 clove garlic, pressed
1 tablespoon soy sauce
6 eggs
minced chives or green onions for garnish

SLICING DISC: Cut onion in half to fit feed tube; slice with light pressure. Cut celery to fit feed tube vertically; slice.

In a small skillet, heat 2 tablespoons oil over medium-high heat. Add onions and celery, sauté 3-5 minutes. Add bean sprouts and garlic; cook about 1 minute or until sprouts are limp. Add soy sauce and sauté until the liquid has evaporated. Do not overcook the vegetables; they should be somewhat crisp.

PLASTIC MIXING BLADE or METAL BLADE. Add 2 eggs to work bowl. Process until beaten. Pour into a lightly oiled 8-inch non-stick pan and cook over medium heat until eggs are done to your liking. Spoon ⅓ of the filling down the center; fold and slip onto a serving plate. Repeat with remaining eggs. Garnish with chives or green onions.

Preparation: 5 minutes
Cooking: 10 minutes
Protein g/s: 16.5

Green Chile and Pepper Bake

Serves 6

This has a soufflé-like consistency . . . light and spicy.

4 ounces Monterey Jack cheese
4 ounces sharp Cheddar cheese
1 small onion
1 medium green pepper
1 4-ounce can whole green chiles, rinsed, seeded
4 eggs
½ cup low-fat yogurt
½ cup cottage cheese
¼ teaspoon salt
¼ teaspoon chili powder
dash pepper
1 tablespoon butter or oil

Preheat oven to 350°.

SHREDDING DISC: Cut Monterey Jack and Cheddar cheese to fit feed tube, shred. Remove to a medium mixing bowl. Toss to mix and set aside.

METAL BLADE: Add onion, cut into 1-inch pieces; green pepper, cut into 1-inch pieces; and green chiles to work bowl. Pulse on/off until coarsely chopped.

In a skillet, heat 1 tablespoon butter over medium-high heat. Add onion mixture and sauté 3-5 minutes or until vegetables are soft and liquid has evaporated. Remove from heat and allow to cool slightly.

METAL BLADE: Add eggs, yogurt, cottage cheese, salt, chili powder and pepper to work bowl. Process 5 seconds. Stop machine, remove cover and scrape down sides of bowl. Process 10 seconds or until smooth.

Combine cheese, cooked vegetables and egg mixture in the medium mixing bowl. Pour into an oiled 8 x 8-inch baking dish. Bake, uncovered, for 35-40 minutes or until custard is set. Allow to cool 10 minutes, then cut into squares to serve.

Preparation: 15 minutes
Cooking/Baking: 35-40 minutes
Standing: 10 minutes
Protein g/s: 17.5

Zucchini Lasagna

Serves 6

Crisp steamed zucchini slices are the "noodles" in this quick-to-assemble entrée.

2 slices whole wheat bread, toasted
2 pounds zucchini, scrubbed
6 ounces mozzarella cheese, well-chilled
2 cups low-fat cottage cheese
2 eggs
1 tablespoon dry parsley flakes
1 clove garlic, pressed
1 8-ounce can tomato sauce
½ teaspoon salt
½ teaspoon dry leaf oregano
¼ teaspoon dry leaf basil
pinch rosemary

Preheat oven to 350°.

METAL BLADE: Add bread, torn into pieces, to work bowl. Process to make fine crumbs. Remove from bowl and set aside.

SLICING DISC: Cut zucchini into the largest size that will fit horizontally into the feed tube, slice. Steam until tender-crisp, 3-5 minutes. Remove from heat and allow to drain.

SHREDDING DISC: Cut mozzarella cheese to fit feed tube, shred using light pressure. Remove from bowl and set aside.

METAL BLADE: Add cottage cheese and eggs. Combine with 3-4 on/off pulses. Add parsley, process to mix. In a bowl, stir together garlic, tomato sauce, oregano and basil.

ASSEMBLY: In a greased 8 x 8-inch baking dish layer ingredients as follows: half the zucchini, half the bread crumbs, half the cottage cheese mixture, half the tomato sauce and half of the mozzarella cheese. Repeat layering with remaining zucchini, bread crumbs, cottage cheese and tomato sauce. Reserve remaining cheese.
Bake, uncovered, 25 minutes. Sprinkle with reserved cheese. Return to oven and bake until cheese melts, 4-6 minutes. Let stand 10 minutes. Cut into squares to serve.

Preparation: 20 minutes
Cooking/Baking: 35 minutes
Standing: 10 minutes
Protein g/s: 21

Vegetable Tortilla Bake

Serves 6

A fresh fruit salad is a nice accompaniment to this spicy dish.

1 *7-ounce can whole green chiles, rinsed, seeded*
1 *small onion*
2 *medium zucchini, about ½ pound, scrubbed*
1 *small eggplant, about ½ pound, unpeeled*
1 *green pepper*
¼ *teaspoon salt*
⅛ *teaspoon pepper*
½ *teaspoon ground cumin*
1 *cup low-fat cottage cheese, drained*
1 *egg*
6 *ounces sharp Cheddar cheese, well-chilled*
6 *ounces Monterey Jack cheese, well-chilled*
6 *corn tortillas, each cut into 6 wedges*
3 *tablespoons oil*

Preheat oven to 350°.

METAL BLADE: Add green chiles to work bowl; pulse on/off to coarsely chop. Remove to medium mixing bowl. Add onion, cut into 1-inch pieces, to work bowl. Pulse on/off until finely chopped. In a 12-inch skillet, heat 3 tablespoons oil over medium-high heat. Add onions and cook 2 minutes until clear but not brown.

SLICING DISC: Cut zucchini to fit feed tube vertically, slice. Cut eggplant to fit feed tube, slice. Quarter and seed green pepper, stack into feed tube, slice. Add vegetables to onions. Cook until vegetables are just tender, about 5 minutes. Add salt, pepper and cumin. Remove from heat and cool slightly.

SHREDDING DISC: Cut Cheddar and Monterey Jack cheeses to fit feed tube, shred. Remove from bowl and set aside.

METAL BLADE: Add cottage cheese and egg to bowl; process until mixed. Remove to bowl with chiles; stir to mix.

ASSEMBLY: Arrange half the tortilla wedges evenly in the bottom of a lightly oiled 8 x 8-inch baking pan. Spoon on half the vegetable mixture, half the cottage cheese and sprinkle with half the shredded cheese. Repeat layers of tortilla wedges, vegetables, cottage cheese and shredded cheese. Bake, uncovered, 30-35 minutes or until bubbly. Cut into squares to serve.

Preparation: 20 minutes
Cooking/Baking: 40-45 minutes
Protein g/s: 22

Chiles Rellenos

Serves 6

These chiles have a puffy egg coating. Serve topped with taco sauce accompanied by Spanish Rice and Refried Beans (see index).

6 *ounces Monterey Jack cheese, well-chilled*
1 *7-ounce can whole green chiles*
3 *eggs, separated*
1 *tablespoon water*
⅛ *teaspoon salt*
3 *tablespoons whole wheat flour*
additional flour for dusting chiles
oil for frying
taco sauce

SHREDDING DISC: Cut cheese to fit feed tube, shred. Remove from bowl and set aside. Carefully slit chiles and remove any seeds found inside. Rinse and pat dry with paper towels.

METAL BLADE: Add egg yolks, water and salt to work bowl. Combine with 2-3 on/off pulses. Stop machine, remove work bowl cover, scrape down sides of bowl. With machine running, add flour. Process until just mixed. Remove to medium mixing bowl.

Using an electric or hand beater, beat egg whites until stiff. Fold into egg yolk mixture. Divide cheese evenly among whole chiles. Place cheese inside each chile, folding chile over to enclose cheese. Dust with flour and dip into egg mixture.

Heat ¼-inch oil in a frying pan over medium-high heat. Fry chiles rellenos 3-4 minutes on each side or until golden brown. Drain on paper towels. Spoon on taco sauce and serve.

Preparation: 10 minutes
Cooking: 20 minutes
Protein g/s: 11

Stuffed Eggplant

Serves 4

Eggplants may be stuffed ahead of time. If refrigerated, add 10-15 minutes to the baking time. These also freeze well.

2 small round eggplants, about 8 ounces each
2 ounces Parmesan cheese, at room temperature
2 slices whole wheat bread
3 sprigs parsley
½ teaspoon dry leaf basil
3 ounces Swiss cheese
3 cloves garlic
1 small onion
2 tablespoons olive oil
⅛ teaspoon crushed red pepper
¼ teaspoon salt
juice of ½ lemon
1 large tomato
dry leaf oregano

METAL BLADE: Add Parmesan cheese, cut into 1-inch pieces, to work bowl. Process until finely grated. Add whole wheat bread, torn into pieces, and process to make coarse crumbs. Add parsley and basil. Process until parsley is finely minced. Remove mixture from bowl and set aside.

SHREDDING DISC: Cut Swiss cheese to fit feed tube, shred. Remove from bowl and set aside. Reserve ¼ cup for topping. Cut the eggplants in half and scoop out the pulp, leaving a shell about ¼-inch thick. Reserve pulp for filling.

METAL BLADE: Add garlic cloves and onion, quartered, to the bowl. Pulse on/off until finely chopped. In a skillet, heat 2 tablespoons olive oil over medium-high heat. Add onions, sauté about 2 minutes. Add eggplant pulp to work bowl, pulse on/off until finely chopped.

Add chopped eggplant to onions, continue cooking 2 minutes. Remove from heat. Add bread crumb mixture, crushed red pepper, salt, lemon juice and ½ cup Swiss cheese. Stir to mix well. Fill the eggplant shells, mounding in the center.

SLICING DISC: Cut tomato to fit feed tube, slice with firm pressure. Top each filled shell with tomato slices, overlapping slightly. Sprinkle on remaining Swiss cheese and a pinch of oregano. Place in a lightly oiled baking dish. Cover and bake at 375° 40-50 minutes until hot and eggplant is tender.

Preparation: 15 minutes
Cooking/Baking: 40-50 minutes
Protein g/s: 11.5

Nut Cheese Loaf

Serves 8

Serve with a tossed green salad and steamed green vegetables.

1½ cups cooked brown rice (about ½ cup raw)
¼ cup parsley
1½ cups walnuts
16 ounces sharp Cheddar cheese, well-chilled
1 small onion
1 clove garlic
4 ounces fresh mushrooms
4 eggs
1 recipe Two-in-One Tomato Sauce (see index)
   or similar sauce

Preheat oven to 350°. Place cooked rice in a large mixing bowl.

METAL BLADE: To maintain the individual textures, process remaining ingredients separately and add to the bowl with the rice. Toss to mix. Pulse on/off to: finely mince parsley, coarsely chop nuts, finely chop garlic and onions, coarsely chop mushrooms.

SHREDDING DISC: Cut cheese to fit feed tube, shred. Add to rice mixture.

METAL BLADE: Add eggs to work bowl. Process until well-blended. Pour into rice mixture and mix.

Butter a 9 x 5-inch loaf pan and line with cooking parchment or buttered wax paper. Spoon rice mixture into prepared pan. Bake 1 hour. Let stand 10 minutes before unmolding. Serve slices topped with Two-in-One Tomato Sauce.

Preparation: 15-20 minutes
Cooking/Baking: 1 hour to bake loaf
                allow time to cook rice
Standing: 10 minutes
Protein g/s: 22

Cheese and Broccoli Bake

Serves 4

This dish is light in texture and taste. Serve with steamed carrots and a tossed green salad.

1 pound broccoli
4 ounces sharp Cheddar cheese
2 cups low-fat cottage cheese
2 eggs
½ teaspoon dry dill weed
1 tablespoon lemon juice
2 tablespoons whole wheat flour
2 tablespoons bran
salt and pepper to taste

Trim broccoli; break into flowerets and steam until just done. Broccoli should be crisp.

SHREDDING DISC: Cut cheese to fit feed tube, shred. Remove to medium mixing bowl and set aside.

METAL BLADE: Add broccoli to work bowl. Pulse on/off until coarsely chopped. Remove from bowl and add to cheese. Add cottage cheese, eggs, dill weed, lemon juice, flour and bran to bowl. Combine with 2-3 on/off pulses. Scrape down sides of bowl and process until smooth. Pour into mixing bowl. Stir gently to mix.

Turn broccoli mixture into a lightly oiled 1-quart casserole. Bake, uncovered, in a 350° oven for 35-40 minutes or until set. Allow to stand 5-10 minutes and cut into squares to serve.

Preparation: 20 minutes
Cooking/Baking: 35-45 minutes
Standing: 5-10 minutes
Protein g/s: 26.5

Broccoli Mushroom Layers

Serves 6

This is a light main dish. Serve with a baked potato or vegetable salad.

1½ pounds broccoli
3 ounces Parmesan cheese, at room temperature
8 ounces Monterey Jack cheese, well-chilled
3 green onions
8 ounces fresh mushrooms
4 eggs
¼ cup skim milk
½ teaspoon dry leaf thyme
½ teaspoon dry leaf basil
¼ teaspoon salt
1 tablespoon oil

Trim broccoli, cut into 1-inch lengths. Steam until tender but crisp. Remove from heat; set aside.

METAL BLADE: Add Parmesan cheese, cut into 1-inch pieces, to work bowl. Process until finely grated. Remove from bowl and set aside.

SHREDDING DISC: Cut Monterey Jack cheese to fit feed tube. Shred using light pressure. Remove from bowl and set aside.

METAL BLADE: Add green onions, cut into 2-inch lengths. Pulse on/off until finely minced. Remove from bowl and set aside.

SLICING DISC: Stack mushrooms in feed tube; slice with firm pressure. In a skillet, heat 1 tablespoon oil over medium-high heat. Add green onions, sauté 30 seconds. Add mushrooms, cook 3-4 minutes or until mushrooms are soft and liquid has evaporated. Remove from heat. Preheat oven to 375°.

METAL BLADE: Add broccoli to the bowl. Pulse on/off until coarsely chopped. Remove to large mixing bowl. Add cooked mushroom mixture to broccoli, toss to mix. Add eggs, milk, Parmesan cheese, salt, thyme and basil to work bowl. Process until well-mixed. Pour into broccoli mixture, stir to combine.

Spread half the vegetable mixture on bottom of a lightly oiled 8 x 8-inch baking pan. Top with half the Monterey Jack cheese. Make a second layer using the remaining vegetable mixture and cheese. Bake, uncovered, 30 minutes. Cut into squares to serve.

Preparation: 15 minutes
Cooking/Baking: 35 minutes
Protein g/s: 19

Zucchini and Mushroom Cheese Custard

Serves 6

Swiss and cottage cheeses are mixed with eggs to make a custard that tops a layer of fresh mushrooms.

1 *slice whole wheat bread, toasted*
1 *medium onion*
1 *pound fresh mushrooms*
2 *medium zucchini, about 12 ounces, scrubbed*
4 *ounces Monterey Jack cheese, well-chilled*
4 *ounces Swiss cheese, well-chilled*
1 *cup cottage cheese, drained slightly*
6 *eggs*
½ *teaspoon salt*
½ *teaspoon pepper*
¼ *teaspoon ground nutmeg*
1 *tablespoon oil*
2 *tablespoons butter*

Preheat oven to 350°.

METAL BLADE: Add whole wheat bread, torn into pieces, to work bowl. Process to make fine crumbs. Remove from bowl and set aside. Add onion, cut into 1-inch pieces, to work bowl. Pulse on/off to finely chop. In a large skillet, heat oil and butter over medium-high heat. Add onions and sauté 1-2 minutes.

SLICING DISC: Stack mushrooms in feed tube. Slice with firm pressure. Add to skillet and continue cooking until mushrooms are soft and liquid has evaporated, 5-7 minutes. Remove from heat.

SHREDDING DISC: Cut zucchini to fit feed tube horizontally; shred. Squeeze out excess liquid. Transfer to medium mixing bowl. Cut cheeses to fit feed tube, shred. Add to zucchini.
METAL BLADE: Add cottage cheese, eggs, and bread crumbs to work bowl. Process until well-mixed. Pour over zucchini cheese mixture. Stir in salt, pepper and nutmeg. Mix well. Spread mushroom onion mixture over the bottom of an oiled 8 x 8-inch baking pan. Spoon on custard topping. Bake, uncovered, 40-45 minutes or until custard is firm, puffy and lightly browned. Remove from oven; let stand 10 minutes. Cut into squares and serve.

Preparation: 15 minutes
Cooking/Baking: 50-55 minutes
Standing: 10 minutes
Protein g/s: 22.5

Cheese Scalloped Potatoes with Mushrooms

Serves 6-8

Serve this hearty family favorite with a tossed green salad and freshly baked rolls. Using a clear Pyrex baking dish results in an overly brown bottom.

1 *bunch green onions*
2 *tablespoons oil*
1 *pound fresh mushrooms*
¼-½ *teaspoon salt*
8 *ounces Cheddar or Monterey Jack cheese, well-chilled*
3 *pounds potatoes*
¼-½ *teaspoon salt, as needed*
2 *tablespoons butter or margarine*
1¼ *cups hot milk*

METAL BLADE: Add green onions, cut into 2-inch lengths, to work bowl. Pulse on/off to mince. In a skillet, heat 2 tablespoons oil over medium-high heat. Add green onions, sauté 1-2 minutes.

SLICING DISC: Stack mushrooms into feed tube, slice. Add to skillet and sauté until soft and liquid has evaporated. Stir in ¼-½ teaspoon salt. Remove from heat.

SHREDDING DISC: Cut cheese to fit feed tube, shred. Remove from bowl and set aside.

SLICING DISC or THIN SLICING DISC: Cut peeled potatoes to fit feed tube, slice.

Use about 1 tablespoon butter to grease a 9 x 13-inch or similar size baking pan. Arrange half the potatoes over the bottom of the pan. Sprinkle with a few pinches of salt. Cover with half the cheese and all of the mushroom mixture. Finish layering with remaining potatoes, a pinch or two of salt, and cheese. Carefully pour in the hot milk and dot with remaining butter. Bake at 375°, covered, for 40 minutes. Remove cover and continue baking for 20 minutes or until potatoes are tender.

Preparation: 20 minutes
Baking: 60-70 minutes
Protein g/s: 6 servings—16
　　　　　　8 servings—12

Swiss 'n' Broccoli Bake

Serves 4

1 bunch broccoli, about 12 ounces
4 ounces Swiss cheese
1 small onion
2 tablespoons oil
1 slice whole wheat bread
2 sprigs fresh parsley
¼ teaspoon salt
⅛ teaspoon freshly ground white pepper
½ teaspoon dry leaf oregano
4 eggs
¼ cup skim milk

Preheat oven to 375°. Trim broccoli, break into flowerets. Steam broccoli until tender but crisp. Do not overcook. Remove from heat and set aside.

SHREDDING DISC: Cut cheese to fit feed tube, shred with light pressure. Remove to large mixing bowl and set aside.

METAL BLADE: Add onion, cut into 1-inch pieces, to work bowl. Pulse on/off until finely minced. In a small skillet, heat 2 tablespoons oil over medium heat. Add onions and sauté until soft, 3-5 minutes. Add broccoli to work bowl. Pulse on/off to coarsely chop. Combine broccoli and onions with cheese in mixing bowl. Wipe work bowl with paper towel. Add bread, torn into pieces. Process to make fine crumbs. Add parsley, salt, pepper and oregano. Process to finely chop parsley. Stop the machine and add eggs. Combine with 3 on/off pulses. With machine running, pour in milk. Turn off machine as soon as all the milk has been added.

Pour into vegetable mixture, mix gently. Turn into a lightly oiled 1½-quart baking dish. Bake 40 minutes or until custard is firm and lightly browned. Let stand 10 minutes before serving.

Preparation: 10-15 minutes
Cooking/Baking: 55 minutes
Standing: 10 minutes
Protein g/s: 16

Parmesan Topped Zucchini Trio Bake

Serves 6

Assemble earlier in the day and bake just before serving.

2 ounces Parmesan cheese, at room temperature
2 pounds zucchini, scrubbed
whole wheat flour
8 ounces mozzarella cheese, well-chilled
1 medium onion
2 firm tomatoes
½ teaspoon dry mixed herbs
freshly ground pepper

Preheat oven to 400°.

METAL BLADE: Add Parmesan cheese, cut into 1-inch pieces, to work bowl. Process until finely grated. Remove from bowl and set aside.

SLICING DISC: Cut zucchini to fit feed tube horizontally, slice. Shake zucchini slices with about ½ cup flour in a paper bag to coat. Lightly oil 2 baking sheets. Arrange slices in a single layer and bake 10 minutes. Turn slices and bake an additional 10 minutes. Remove pans from oven and set aside. Reduce oven temperature to 350°.

SHREDDING DISC: Cut mozzarella cheese to fit feed tube, shred. Remove from bowl and set aside.

SLICING DISC or THIN SLICING DISC: Cut onion and tomatoes to fit feed tube, slice. Lightly oil a 2-quart baking dish. Arrange a single layer of one-third of the zucchini, half the onions, and half the tomatoes. Sprinkle on ¼ teaspoon herbs, small amount of ground pepper, and half of the mozzarella cheese. Continue layering with another one-third of the zucchini, the remaining tomato and onion slices, herbs, pepper and mozzarella cheese. Top with remaining one-third zucchini slices and sprinkle on Parmesan cheese. Cover the dish and bake for 1 hour (add 15-20 minutes if refrigerated). Remove the cover and bake 10 minutes or until cheese is lightly browned.

Preparation: 20 minutes
Baking: 1 hour 10 minutes
Protein g/s: 13.5

German Potato Pancakes

Serves 4, 2 pancakes per serving

The addition of non-fat milk powder increases the protein power of our version of this traditional recipe. Serve with Red Cabbage and Apples (see index) and a slice or two of rye bread.

½ *bunch fresh parsley*
1 *medium onion*
1 *pound potatoes*
2 *eggs*
½ *cup non-instant, non-fat milk powder*
4 *tablespoons whole wheat flour*
2 *tablespoons sour cream or yogurt*
½ *teaspoon salt*
oil for frying
yogurt and chives for garnish, optional

METAL BLADE: Add parsley to work bowl. Pulse on/off until finely minced. Remove to medium mixing bowl. Add onion, cut into 1-inch pieces, to work bowl. Pulse on/off until finely chopped. Drain off excess liquid; add to parsley.

SHREDDING DISC: Cut peeled potatoes to fit feed tube; shred. Remove to wax paper.

METAL BLADE: Add shredded potatoes to work bowl. Process until finely chopped or puréed. In Germany the potatoes are so finely shredded that they resemble a purée. Add potatoes to onions. Stir together milk powder and flour. Add eggs to work bowl. Process 5 seconds. Scrape down sides of bowl. With machine running, add milk powder and flour mixture, sour cream, and salt. Process until smooth. Pour into mixing bowl; stir to mix well.

In a non-stick pan, heat 1-2 tablespoons oil over medium-high heat. Drop the batter from a ⅓ cup measure into the hot pan. Brown the pancakes on one side, about 5 minutes; turn and brown the other side, 5 minutes. Serve with yogurt and chives or a dab of applesauce.

Preparation: 15 minutes
Cooking: 30 minutes
Protein g/s: 12.5

Zucchini Frittata

Serves 4

Drain the zucchini ahead of time to cut the preparation time of this recipe. Your kitchen will be filled with the aroma of herbs as the frittata is baking.

1 *tablespoon salt*
2 *pounds zucchini, scrubbed*
2 *ounces Parmesan cheese, room temperature*
1 *slice whole wheat bread*
1 *teaspoon dry parsley flakes or*
    1 *tablespoon fresh, minced*
1 *teaspoon dry leaf oregano*
4 *eggs*
½ *cup skim milk*
2 *tablespoons melted butter*

An hour before baking time, prepare zucchini. This can be done the night before. Wrap and refrigerate until ready to use.

SHREDDING DISC: Cut zucchini to fit feed tube vertically; shred. Remove to a colander, sprinkle with 1 tablespoon salt and let stand at least 1 hour. Drain zucchini, put in a tea towel and squeeze out the excess moisture. Preheat oven to 375°.

METAL BLADE: Add Parmesan cheese, cut into 1-inch pieces, to work bowl. Process until finely grated. Add whole wheat bread, torn into pieces. Process to make fine crumbs. Add parsley and oregano, pulse on/off to mix. Add eggs, milk and butter, process until well-mixed. Stop machine, remove work bowl cover and add zucchini. Combine with 2-3 on/off pulses until just mixed. Do not overprocess.

Pour into a greased 1-quart baking dish. Bake 35-40 minutes or until puffy and center is firm. Let stand 5 minutes; cut into squares and serve.

Preparation: 10 minutes
Cooking/Baking: 35-40 minutes
Standing: allow 1 hour for zucchini to drain;
            5 minutes after baking
Protein g/s: 13.5

Mushroom Olive Bake

Serves 6

Serve with brown rice and a tossed green salad. This dish is definitely for mushroom lovers! To clean mushrooms, wipe with a damp paper towel. Do not soak in water.

3 *slices whole wheat bread, toasted*
8 *ounces Monterey Jack cheese, well-chilled*
1 *pound fresh mushrooms*
1 *can pitted black olives (6-ounces drained weight)*
¼ *cup milk*

Preheat oven to 350°.

METAL BLADE: Add bread, torn into pieces, to work bowl. Process to crumb. Remove from bowl and set aside.

SHREDDING DISC: Cut cheese to fit feed tube, shred. Remove from bowl and set aside.

SLICING DISC: Stack mushrooms in feed tube; slice with firm pressure. Remove from bowl and set aside. Add drained olives to feed tube, slice.

Lightly grease or oil an 8 x 8-inch baking dish. Sprinkle ¼ cup bread crumbs evenly over the bottom of the pan. Layer half the mushrooms, half the remaining crumbs, half the sliced olives and half the cheese. Repeat layers of mushrooms, crumbs, olives and cheese. Add milk. Bake 35-40 minutes. Allow to cool 5-10 minutes. Cut into squares and serve.

Preparation: 8-10 minutes
Baking: 35-40 minutes
Standing: 5-10 minutes
Protein g/s: 11.5

Tomato and Mozzarella Pie

Serves 4-6

A layer of cooked shredded potatoes holds a tasty tomato and mozzarella filling. Cook the potatoes the night before or earlier in the day.

2 *pounds White Rose or red potatoes*
2 *sprigs fresh parsley*
2 *tablespoons butter or margarine*
2½ *ounces Parmesan cheese, at room temperature*
8 *ounces mozzarella cheese, well-chilled*
3 *tomatoes*
1 *teaspoon dry leaf oregano*
butter
flour

Earlier in the day, cook potatoes until just tender and refrigerate. Preheat oven to 425°. Lightly butter and flour an 8 x 8-inch baking dish.

METAL BLADE: Add parsley sprigs to work bowl. Pulse on/off until finely minced. Remove from bowl and set aside. Add Parmesan cheese, cut into 1-inch pieces, to work bowl. Process until finely grated. Remove from bowl and set aside.

SHREDDING DISC: Cut chilled unpeeled potatoes to fit feed tube, shred with firm pressure. Toss with parsley. Spread potatoes evenly over the bottom of the prepared baking dish. Press in lightly. Dot with 2 tablespoons butter. Cut mozzarella cheese to fit feed tube, shred. Spread half the cheese over the potatoes. Reserve remaining half.

SLICING DISC: Cut tomatoes to fit feed tube, slice with firm pressure. Arrange the tomatoes in a single layer over cheese. Crumble oregano between fingertips and sprinkle over tomatoes. Top with remaining mozzarella and Parmesan cheeses. Bake 25 minutes, until cheese is melted and lightly browned. Cut into squares and serve.

Preparation: 10 minutes
Cooking/Baking: 25 minutes
          allow time to cook potatoes
Protein g/s: 4 servings—26
          6 servings—17

Monterey Jack Chile Bake

Serves 6

By the time the oven is preheated, this dish will be ready to bake.

8 ounces Monterey Jack cheese, well-chilled
1 7-ounce can whole green chiles, rinsed, seeded
6 eggs
¼ cup whole wheat flour, measured scoop and
   level
½ teaspoon baking powder
½ teaspoon salt
1 cup low-fat, small curd cottage cheese
2 tablespoons melted butter

Preheat oven to 350°.

SHREDDING DISC: Cut Monterey Jack cheese to fit feed tube, shred. Remove to medium mixing bowl and set aside.

METAL BLADE: Dry chiles on paper towel and add to work bowl. Pulse on/off until coarsely chopped. Remove from bowl and add to cheese. Add eggs, flour, baking powder, salt and cottage cheese to work bowl. Process 5 seconds. Stop machine, remove work bowl cover and scrape down sides of bowl. Continue processing until blended. Stop machine to add cheese and chiles. Pulse on/off only until just mixed.

Pour mixture into a well-greased 8 x 8-inch baking pan. Bake 35 minutes or until center is firm and top is lightly browned. Allow to stand 5-10 minutes. Cut into squares and serve.

Preparation: 10 minutes
Baking: 35 minutes
Standing: 5-10 minutes
Protein g/s: 22

Cheese Soufflé

Serves 4-6

The ingredients for this elegant dish are usually available in any well-stocked kitchen. Although it can be prepared quickly, it is not suitable for large groups as it needs special care and last minute attention.

8 ounces Cheddar or Monterey Jack cheese
4 tablespoons butter or margarine
4 tablespoons whole wheat flour
1 cup hot milk
4 eggs separated
salt to taste
butter or margarine to grease soufflé dish

SHREDDING DISC: Cut cheese to fit feed tube, shred. In a 2-quart saucepan, melt butter over medium heat. Slowly stir in flour and cook until mixture becomes a smooth paste, 1-2 minutes. Gradually stir in milk. Continue cooking and stirring until sauce is thick. Add cheese by the handful and cook, stirring constantly, until cheese is melted. Remove from heat and allow to cool to room temperature, 15 minutes.

METAL BLADE: Add egg yolks to work bowl. Process until well-blended. Slowly stir into the cooled sauce. Using an electric or hand beater, beat egg whites until stiff. Carefully fold into cheese mixture. Pour into a well-greased soufflé dish, measuring 6½ inches across and 3 inches high. Bake at 375° 30-35 minutes. The soufflé will rise about 2 inches above the rim of the dish. Serve immediately; it will begin to fall rather quickly.

Preparation: 10 minutes
Standing: allow 15 minutes for sauce to cool
Cooking/Baking: 40-45 minutes
Protein g/s: 4 servings—24
              6 servings—16

Pastas and Sauces

Americans have begun to appreciate the taste of homemade pasta. But making it by hand is a difficult and very time-consuming craft and is only for connoisseurs who value the subtle differences in texture produced by hand kneading, rolling, and stretching the dough. The use of a food processor and pasta machine requires less time and experience and makes an excellent tasting pasta.

Our pasta dough is prepared instantaneously in the food processor. It is then rolled into thin, narrow sheets and cut into ribbons by a pasta machine. The taste is exceptional, and the ingredients—whole grain flours and fresh eggs—make it nutritionally superior to anything you can buy. Pasta easily serves as the focal point of a meal when served with any of our sauces and topped with Parmesan or Romano cheese. You will find that there is no limit to the ingredients you can use for a good sauce—a little olive oil, onion, garlic, and whatever fresh vegetables are available.

Pasta Machines

Ours is a simple, hand-cranked machine which can produce noodles of two different widths. Manual machines are available with detachable cutting rollers, allowing a larger choice of noodle widths. Electric machines are a temptation because they are easier to use, and some people think the pasta produced has a better (rougher) texture. But they are more expensive, sometimes work too fast to keep up with, and are insufferably noisy.

Basic Techniques

Mixing the Dough: The metal blade of your food processor does an excellent job of mixing and kneading the dough to the right consistency. We make three types of noodle doughs: doughs made of flour and eggs, without water or oil; those made with flour, eggs, water and possibly oil; and those containing spinach or other vegetables or herbs. The techniques for each of these doughs differ slightly.

Flour/Eggs: Place the flour, salt, and any other dry ingredients in the work bowl. The amount of flour is approximate because the precise amount is determined by the size of the eggs. Add the eggs and process the dough until it forms a ball. To produce a firm, but elastic ball of dough, it may be necessary for you to add 1-4 tablespoons of flour.

Flour/Eggs/Water or Oil and Water: Put the flour and any other dry ingredients in the work bowl. With this type of dough, the amount of flour is fixed, because desired changes in the consistency are made by adjusting the amount of water. Add the eggs and the oil, if used. Process until the mixture resembles coarse meal. With the machine running, gradually add water in small amounts according to the directions in the individual recipe until the dough begins to form a ball. Stop adding water and process until ball is firm and elastic.

Flour/Eggs/Spinach or Other Vegetables or Herbs: Vegetables should be cooked and squeezed totally dry. Herbs, such as parsley or basil, are best left raw. Both must first be processed with the metal blade until they are puréed or very finely chopped. The flour, salt, and eggs are then added. At this point, directions for individual recipes vary, with some requiring the addition of flour, and some the addition of water to produce a ball of dough of the right consistency. Carefully follow the directions in the recipe you are using.

Problems: If the ball seems too "loose," it contains too much liquid. With the machine running, add flour by the tablespoonful until the dough is firm but still elastic. A ball which is too "tight," is an indication that too much flour has been worked into it. It will usually crumble when run through the pasta machine. When this happens, break it into small pieces and put it back into the work bowl. With the machine running, slowly add water by the teaspoonful until the dough has the right consistency. When dough made from fresh herbs comes apart when run through the pasta machine, it usually means that you did not chop or purée the herbs fine enough, or that you failed to work a sufficient amount of flour into the dough. In the former case, just put the ball back into the machine and process it until the herbs are more finely chopped. In the latter, put the ball back into the machine and process, slowly adding flour by the tablespoonful until the ball of dough is the right consistency.

Pasta Machine Technique: The instructions that come with the machine will be useless to most Americans as they are in Italian, and the English translation provided is usually incomprehensible. Most pasta machines have an adjustable roller mechanism with settings for rolling flat sheets of dough of different thicknesses. Usually, setting number one is the widest and setting number six is the narrowest and makes the thinnest noodles.

1. *Rolling the Dough:* Divide the dough into 8 pieces. Form it into balls and flour well. Do not use cornstarch because it will eventually gum up the cutting rollers, and it's extremely difficult to remove. Our machine techniques do not require a resting time to relax the gluten to make the dough more stretchy, but if you are rolling the dough by hand, allow it to rest for 15-20 minutes. Place the dough in a plastic bag to keep it from drying out and remove one ball of dough at a time, flour it, flatten it with the ball of your hand, and pass it through the roller mechanism lengthwise as follows, flouring as necessary:

1st Setting: Pass through the rollers. Fold dough into thirds and pass through two more times.
2nd Setting: Fold dough into thirds and pass through once.
3rd-5th Setting: Pass through each setting once without folding.
6th Setting: Use only if you like your pasta very thin.

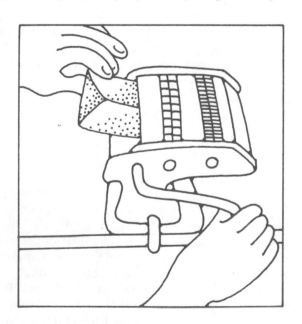

2. *Drying:* The dough must be partially dried, or the noodles will stick together when they are cut. Drying time depends both on the amount of humidity in the air and on the amount of flouring you have done. It may take anywhere from 15-35 minutes. You can drape the sheets of dough over chairbacks covered with kitchen towels, or place them on a specially designed pasta rack. If you purchase a pasta rack, be sure it holds at least 8 sheets of dough. If you want the dough to dry quickly, set it near a sunny window. Be careful not to dry it so long that the dough becomes brittle and cracks when run through the cutting rollers.

3. *Cutting the Noodles:* Flour the partially dried sheets of dough and feed them through the cutting roller of your choice, making sure to catch them as they come out the other side. Hang the noodles to dry until you are ready to use them. Some machines have optional attachments for making lasagna noodles, but they are hardly worth the expense since these large noodles are so easy to cut by hand. An interesting "square cut" can be achieved by stopping at the fourth setting and then cutting the noodles on the narrow cutting roller.

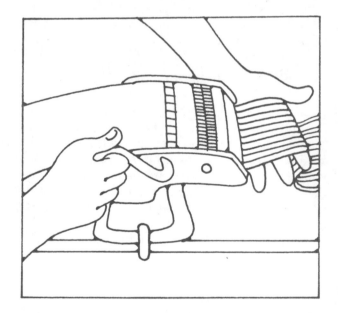

Manual Rolling and Cutting: Mix the dough in the processor as directed above. Divide it into four pieces. Flour well and allow it to rest for 15-20 minutes to relax the gluten for easier stretching and handling. Keep the pieces in a plastic bag to prevent drying out. Remove one ball of dough at a time, flatten it with the ball of your hand, and roll it into a circle 12″ in diameter and 1/16″ thick, or thinner, with a rolling pin or a pasta dowel. This is a real art and takes considerable practice. For more detailed directions refer to Marcella Hazan's *More Classic Italian Cooking* (New York: Knopf, 1978, pp. 154-72). Allow the dough to dry as above. Flour well, roll up jelly-roll fashion, and cut thin slices with a sharp knife. Unroll and hang up or lay flat on a floured board until ready to use.

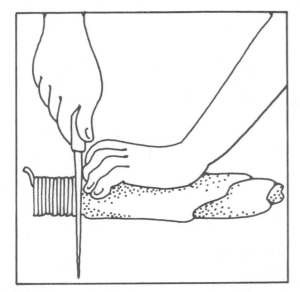

Storage: If you will be using the noodles the same day, just leave them out to dry until you need them. If you do not use the noodles the same day, you have two options—freezing them while they are still moist, or allowing them to dry out completely and refrigerating them in a tightly sealed plastic bag.

Cooking: Bring a large pot of water to a boil. Add salt and 2 tablespoons oil. The oil prevents the noodles from sticking. Add noodles and boil for 4-7 minutes. To cook frozen noodles, remove directly from the freezer and drop into the boiling water. Do not allow them to thaw or they will stick together. Cook the pasta until there is slight resistance to the bite. This is referred to as cooking al dente. The cooking time varies with the degree of dryness or thickness of the noodles. Moist, freshly made noodles cook in the shortest time. It's best to test them several times to avoid overcooking. Let individual preference be your guide. Remove the pasta with a pasta rake or drain in a colander. Rinsing is not recommended as nutrients are washed away.

Rich Egg Noodles

Serves 4-8

This is our best plain egg noodle recipe. It's unusual because it has no oil or water. The total amount of flour used is determined by the size of the eggs.

1⅞ cups *whole wheat flour, measured scoop and level*
½ *teaspoon salt*
3 *large eggs*
1-4 *tablespoons additional flour as needed*

METAL BLADE: Add flour and salt to work bowl; pulse on/off until well-mixed. With machine off, pour in eggs all at once. Turn machine on; process until dough forms into a solid ball. Stop machine and feel dough. It should be firm and elastic. Add additional flour as needed. Remove dough from work bowl; flour well. Proceed as in the basic directions for making pasta at the beginning of this chapter.

Preparation: 45-55 minutes
Protein: g/s: 4 servings—11
          6 servings—7.5
          8 servings—5.5

Wheat Germ Noodles

Serves 4-8

This is a nutritious variation of our basic recipe.

1½ cups *whole wheat flour, measured scoop and level*
½ *cup wheat germ*
½ *teaspoon salt*
2 *eggs*
5-9 *teaspoons water, as needed*

METAL BLADE: Add flour, wheat germ, and salt to work bowl. Pulse on/off to mix. Add eggs and process until the mixture resembles coarse meal, 3-4 seconds. With machine running, slowly pour in water by the teaspoonful until dough begins to gather into a ball. Stop adding water and continue processing until the ball of dough is firm and elastic. Remove dough from work bowl; flour well. Proceed as in the basic directions for making pasta at the beginning of this chapter.

Preparation: 45-55 minutes
Protein g/s: 4 servings—12.5
          6 servings—8
          8 servings—6

Whole Wheat Soy Noodles

Serves 4-6

Soy flour enhances the protein quality of these noodles but the taste is definitely that of the wheat.

1¼ cups whole wheat flour, measured scoop and
   level
¼ cup soy flour, measured scoop and level
½ teaspoon salt
2 eggs
1 teaspoon oil
1-9 teaspoons water, as needed

METAL BLADE: Add wheat flour, soy flour and salt to work bowl. Pulse on/off to mix. Add eggs and oil; process until mixture resembles coarse meal, 3-4 seconds. With machine running, slowly pour in water by the teaspoonful until dough begins to gather into a ball. Stop adding water and continue processing until the ball of dough is firm and elastic. Remove dough from work bowl; flour well. Proceed as in the basic directions for making pasta at the beginning of this chapter.

Preparation: 45-55 minutes
Protein g/s: 4 servings—10
             6 servings—6.5

Whole Wheat Egg Noodles

Serves 4-6

A good basic recipe for those wanting to decrease eggs.

1½ cups whole wheat flour, measured scoop and
   level
2 eggs
1 teaspoon oil
½ teaspoon salt
1-9 teaspoons water as needed

METAL BLADE: Add flour, eggs, oil and salt to work bowl. Pulse on/off until mixture has consistency of coarse meal, 3-4 seconds. With machine running, slowly pour in water by the teaspoonful until dough begins to gather into a ball. Stop adding water and continue processing until the ball of dough is firm

and elastic. Remove dough from work bowl; flour well. Proceed as in the basic directions for making pasta at the beginning of this chapter.

Preparation: 45-55 minutes
Protein g/s: 4 servings—9.5
             6 servings—6.5

Carrot Noodles

Serves 6-8

Top these orange-yellow noodles with Cacciatore Sauce (see index) and you'll be in for both a visual and taste treat.

12 ounces carrots, peeled
1 cup water
1 tablespoon oil
½ teaspoon salt
2¼ cups whole wheat flour, measured scoop and
   level
¼ cup non-instant, non-fat milk powder
1 egg
1-5 tablespoons whole wheat flour, as needed

SLICING DISC or THIN SLICING DISC: Cut carrots to fit feed tube vertically; slice with light pressure to produce extra thin slices. Combine carrots, water, oil and salt in a small saucepan. Bring water to a boil and cook, covered, until carrots are tender. Drain well and allow to cool slightly.

METAL BLADE: Add carrots to work bowl; process until puréed. Stop machine and scrape down sides of bowl as needed. Add flour, milk and egg. Process until dough forms a firm, elastic ball, adding flour as needed. Remove dough from work bowl; flour well. Proceed as in the basic directions for making pasta at the beginning of this chapter.

Preparation: 1 hour
Protein g/s: 6 servings—9
             8 servings—6.5

Spinach Noodles (Pasta Verde)

Serves 6-8

These noodles are a beautiful grass green when served fresh. Top the noodles with our Basic Marinara Sauce or use when making Baked Green Fettucine (see index).

1 10-ounce package frozen leaf spinach, cooked or
⅔ cup cooked fresh spinach leaves, packed
2¼ cups whole wheat flour, measured scoop and
level
½ teaspoon salt
2 eggs
1-4 tablespoons whole wheat flour, as needed

Allow cooked spinach to cool enough to handle. Placed in several thicknesses of cheesecloth and squeeze out as much excess liquid as possible.

METAL BLADE: Place spinach, cooled to room temperature, in work bowl. Pulse on/off until finely chopped. It will resemble a purée. With machine off, add flour, salt and eggs. Process until dough forms a firm, elastic ball, adding flour as needed. The dough will be slightly sticky. Remove dough from work bowl; flour well. Proceed as in the basic directions for making pasta at the beginning of this chapter.

Preparation: 55-60 minutes
Protein g/s: 6 servings—8.5
8 servings—6.5

Dark Buckwheat Noodles

Serves 4-6

These are best when cut very narrow.

1 cup whole wheat flour, measured scoop and level
½ cup dark buckwheat flour, measured scoop and
level
¼ cup non-instant, non-fat milk powder
½ teaspoon salt
2 eggs
1-6 teaspoons water, as needed

METAL BLADE: Add wheat flour, buckwheat flour, milk powder and salt to work bowl. Pulse on/off until mixed. Add eggs and process until mixture resembles coarse meal, 3-4 seconds. With machine running, slowly pour in water by the teaspoonful until the dough begins to gather into a ball. Stop adding water and continue processing until the ball of dough is firm and elastic. Remove dough from work bowl; flour well. The dough will be sticky. Proceed as in the basic directions for making pasta at the beginning of this chapter.

Preparation: 45-55 minutes
Protein g/s: 4 servings—11.5
6 servings—8

Parsley Noodles

Serves 4-6

Fresh parsley leaves are used in this simple recipe. To measure, pinch off the leaves, discard the stems and pack tightly to make 1 cup.

1 cup parsley leaves, packed tightly
1¾ cups whole wheat flour, measured scoop and
level
½ teaspoon salt
2 eggs
1-3 teaspoons water

Wash and dry parsley leaves.

METAL BLADE: Add parsley leaves to the work bowl. Pulse on/off until consistency is so fine that it is almost a purée. Stop machine; add flour, salt and eggs. Pulse on/off until mixture has the texture of coarse meal. With machine running, slowly pour in water by the teaspoonful until dough begins to gather into a ball. Stop adding water and continue processing until the ball of dough is firm and elastic. Remove dough from work bowl; flour well. Proceed as in the basic directions for making pasta at the beginning of this chapter.

Preparation: 45-55 minutes
Protein g/s: 4 servings—10.5
6 servings—7

Eggplant or Zucchini Parmesan

Serves 6-8

Whole grain bread and a tossed green salad make this a delightful meal.

2 medium to large eggplants, 2-2½ pounds, un-
      peeled or
    2 or 3 zucchini, 2-2½ pounds
2 eggs, beaten
½-⅔ cup whole wheat flour
salt to taste
oil for frying
1½ ounces Parmesan cheese, room temperature
8 ounces mozzarella cheese, well-chilled
2-2½ cups Basic Marinara Sauce (see index) or
      similar tomato-based sauce

With a sharp knife, cut eggplant into ¼-inch thick slices. Place eggs and flour into two separate shallow dishes. Dip eggplant slices into beaten eggs then into flour. Salt slices lightly. In a teflon-coated or similar non-stick surface pan, heat 1-2 teaspoons oil over medium-high heat. Fry eggplant slices until golden brown on both sides. As the slices are browned, place on paper towels to absorb excess oil.

METAL BLADE: Add Parmesan cheese, cut into 1-inch pieces, to work bowl; process until finely grated. Remove from bowl and set aside.

SHREDDING DISC: Cut mozzarella cheese to fit feed tube; shred using light pressure. Preheat oven to 375°. Place overlapping slices of eggplant over the bottom of a greased 8½ x 13½-inch or similar size baking dish. Spoon on marinara sauce, top with mozzarella cheese and sprinkle on Parmesan cheese. Bake, uncovered, 20-30 minutes or until hot and cheese is bubbly.

Preparation: 10 minutes
Cooking/Baking: 50 minutes
Protein g/s: 6 servings—15.5
             8 servings—11.5

Chinese Style Stir-Fried Noodles

Serves 6

Tofu turns this tasty noodle dish into a complementary main course. Excellent when served with Stir-Fried Vegetables and Cashews (see index).

1 recipe Whole Wheat Egg Noodles (see index) or
    ¾ recipe Rich Egg Noodles (dry or freeze excess)
    or 8-10 ounces purchased noodles
1 large carrot, peeled
2-3 medium stalks celery, trimmed
3-4 tablespoons oriental sesame oil
1 piece fresh ginger root, 1 x ¼-inch
1 large clove garlic, pressed
3-4 tablespoons low sodium soy sauce or
      2-3 tablespoons regular soy sauce
1½ cups fresh mung bean sprouts
4 green onions, cut into 1-inch lengths
½ teaspoon brown sugar
½ block tofu, drained, cut into 1-inch cubes

Bring a large pot of water to a boil. Add 2 tablespoons oil and a pinch or two of salt. Boil noodles until cooked al dente, 4-7 minutes for fresh noodles, 8-14 minutes for dry noodles. Drain, set aside and keep warm.

SHREDDING DISC: Cut carrot to fit feed tube horizontally, shred.

SLICING DISC: Cut celery to fit feed tube vertically, slice. In a large skillet, heat 2 tablespoons sesame oil over medium heat. Stir-fry carrots and celery 1 minute. Wipe work bowl completely dry.

METAL BLADE: Cut ginger into 8 pieces. Start the processor and drop the ginger through the feed tube. Let processor run until finely grated. Add ginger and garlic to skillet and stir-fry 1 minute. Add soy sauce, bean sprouts, green onions, brown sugar, tofu and remaining sesame oil as needed. Stir gently to mix and cook until tofu is hot and bean sprouts are just cooked. Do not overcook; the vegetables should remain crisp. Season to taste with soy sauce. Spoon over warm cooked noodles.

Preparation: 5-10 minutes plus time to prepare
                noodles
Cooking: 15-25 minutes
Protein g/s: 10

Stuffed Whole Wheat Shells with Mushroom Parmesan Sauce

Serves 4-5

Shells may be stuffed earlier in the day, covered and refrigerated. Add 10-15 minutes to the baking time.

20 *jumbo whole wheat shells, cooked according to directions, drained*

Sauce
3 *ounces Parmesan cheese, room temperature*
½ *small onion*
8 *ounces fresh mushrooms*
2 *tablespoons butter or oil*
2 *tablespoons whole wheat flour*
2 *cups skim milk*
½ *teaspoon salt*
dash pepper

METAL BLADE: Add Parmesan cheese, cut into 1-inch pieces, to work bowl. Pulse on/off until finely grated. Remove from bowl and set aside. Add onion, cut into 1-inch pieces, to work bowl. Pulse on/off until finely chopped. In a 2 or 3-quart saucepan, heat butter over medium-high heat. Add onions; sauté 1 minute.

SLICING DISC: Stack mushrooms in feed tube; slice using firm pressure. Add to onions and continue cooking until mushrooms are soft, 3-5 minutes. Stir in 2 tablespoons flour and cook 1 minute. Gradually stir in milk. Add salt and pepper. Cook, stirring constantly, until sauce is smooth and thickened, about 5 minutes. Remove from heat; stir in Parmesan cheese. Set aside.

Filling
1 *slice whole wheat bread*
2 *sprigs fresh parsley*
2 *cups cottage cheese*
1 *egg*

Preheat oven to 375°.

METAL BLADE: Add bread torn into pieces, to work bowl. Process to make fine crumbs. Add parsley; pulse on/off until finely chopped. Stop the machine and add cottage cheese and egg. Combine with 3-4 on/off pulses.

Stuff each shell with about 1 heaping teaspoon filling. Spread about half the sauce on the bottom of a lightly oiled 9 x 9-inch baking pan. Arrange shells in a single layer. Top with remaining sauce. Bake, uncovered, 25-30 minutes or until hot and bubbly.

Preparation: 20 minutes
Cooking/Baking: 45 minutes
Protein g/s: 4 servings—33
          5 servings—26.5

Lasagna

Serves 8

The food processor takes the work out of shredding and grating the cheese for this classic dish.

1 *recipe Whole Wheat Egg Noodles (see index) or*
  ½ *to ¾ recipe Rich Egg Noodles (see index) or*
  8 *ounces purchased whole wheat lasagna noodles*
2 *ounces Parmesan cheese, room temperature*
8 *ounces mozzarella cheese, well-chilled*
3 *cups Basic Marinara Sauce (see index) or*
  other similar tomato-based sauce
16 *ounces ricotta cheese*

Prepare pasta dough according to directions. Do not allow to dry. Cut by hand into 2 x 14-inch strips. Bring a large pot of water to boil. Add 1-2 tablespoons oil and a pinch or two of salt. Cook noodles in vigorously boiling water until done, 4-8 minutes. Drain and set aside. Cook purchased noodles according to package directions; drain. Preheat oven to 350°.

METAL BLADE: Add Parmesan cheese, cut into 1-inch pieces, to work bowl. Process until finely grated. Remove from bowl and set aside.

SHREDDING DISC: Cut mozzarella cheese to fit feed tube, shred using light pressure. In a greased 9 x 13-inch or similar size baking dish, layer half the noodles, 1 cup sauce, all of the ricotta cheese, half the mozzarella cheese, 1 cup sauce, remaining noodles, sauce and mozzarella cheese. Top with grated Parmesan. Bake, covered, 25-30 minutes or until hot and cheese is bubbly.

Preparation: 10-15 minutes
        allow time to prepare noodles
Cooking/Baking: 40-55 minutes
Protein g/s: 22

Cheese and Spinach Noodle Bake

Serves 6-8

A layer of cottage cheese, delicately seasoned with fresh herbs, between layers of homemade noodles and a spinach sauce makes this Bake an elegant dish. Rennetless, cultured cottage cheese is an excellent substitute for the taste of sour cream . . . low in fat and high in protein.

1 recipe Whole Wheat Egg Noodles (see index) or
   Rich Egg Noodles (see index) or
   10 ounces purchased whole wheat noodles

Filling
1 pound rennetless cottage cheese cultured with
   acidophilus or regular cottage cheese
leaves from ½ bunch fresh parsley
1 small bunch chives, cut into 1½-inch lengths
leaves from 6-8 sprigs fresh mint, do not substitute
   dry leaf mint
¼ teaspoon freshly ground black pepper
¼ teaspoon salt

Spinach Sauce
1 10-ounce package frozen leaf spinach, defrosted,
   uncooked or
   ¾-1 pound fresh spinach leaves, well-rinsed
1-2 large cloves garlic, pressed
1 medium onion
3 tablespoons butter or margarine
3 tablespoons whole wheat flour
2 vegetable bouillon cubes
1½ cups boiling water
¼ teaspoon salt
½ teaspoon nutmeg
paprika

Bring a large pot of water to boil, add 2 tablespoons oil and a pinch or two salt. Boil noodles 4-7 minutes, or until cooked al dente. Cook purchased noodles according to directions, 8-14 minutes. Drain. Spread noodles evenly over the bottom of a buttered 9 x 13-inch or similar size baking dish. Set aside.

METAL BLADE: Add cottage cheese to work bowl; process until just smooth. Add parsley, chives, mint, pepper and salt. Process until herbs are chopped medium-fine. Stop machine and scrape down sides of bowl as needed. Spread cheese over noodles to make an even layer. Reserve a bit for garnish.

Rinse fresh spinach thoroughly. Place fresh or frozen spinach in a pot and cook 1-2 minutes. The water clinging to the leaves will usually be enough liquid. Add garlic and cook, uncovered, until moisture has evaporated, 3-5 minutes. Remove from heat and set aside. Wash and dry work bowl.

METAL BLADE: Add onion, cut into 1-inch pieces, to work bowl; pulse on/off until chopped medium-fine. Remove from bowl. Add spinach; pulse on/off until minced fine. Dissolve bouillon cubes in boiling water, set aside.

Preheat oven to 350°. In a 2-quart saucepan, heat butter over medium-high heat. Add onions and sauté until soft, 3-5 minutes. Sprinkle in flour and cook to make a paste, stir constantly, 3 minutes. Gradually stir in vegetable broth. Continue cooking over medium heat, stirring constantly, until thick and smooth, 3-5 minutes. Stir in spinach and nutmeg. Taste and add salt, as needed.

Spoon on spinach sauce evenly over the cheese layer. Top with dabs of reserved cheese mixture and generously sprinkle on paprika. Cover with foil and bake 20-25 minutes. Cut into squares or spoon out with a large serving spoon.

Preparation: 10-15 minutes
Cooking/Baking: 40-45 minutes plus time to prepare
                and cook noodles
Protein g/s: 6 servings—16.5
              8 servings—12.5

Lentil Spaghetti

Serves 6

Having plenty of cooked lentils and marinara sauce in the freezer speeds up the preparation of dishes like this. Good when served with our whole wheat french bread and a tossed green salad.

1½ cups cooked lentils (½ cup dry)
4½ cups Basic Marinara Sauce (see index) or
     similar tomato-based sauce
½ cup burgundy
1 recipe Whole Wheat Egg Noodles (see index) or
   Rich Egg Noodles, cut to spaghetti noodle thickness or
   8-12 ounces purchased whole wheat spaghetti
2 tablespoons oil
salt
2 ounces Parmesan cheese, room temperature
4 ounces mozzarella cheese, well-chilled

In a large saucepan, combine lentils, marinara sauce and burgundy. Simmer 5 minutes or until heated through. Keep hot until noodles are ready. Bring a large pot of water to a boil. Add oil and a pinch or two of salt. Boil noodles 4-7 minutes or until cooked al dente. When using purchased noodles, cook according to package directions, 10-15 minutes. Drain.

METAL BLADE: Add Parmesan cheese, cut into 1-inch pieces, to work bowl. Process until finely grated. Remove from bowl and set aside.

SHREDDING DISC: Cut mozzarella cheese to fit feed tube; shred using light pressure. To serve, place spaghetti on individual dinner plates, top with sauce and generous sprinklings of mozzarella and Parmesan cheese.

Preparation: 10 minutes
        allow time to prepare noodles
Cooking: 15-20 minutes
Protein g/s: 18.5

Spinach Lasagna

Serves 8

This variation of our basic Lasagna (see index) has been popular with both friends and family.

as listed for Lasagna
1 10-12 ounce package frozen leaf spinach or leaves from ¾-1 pound fresh spinach

Cook spinach in a small amount of water. Drain in a colander and allow to cool slightly. Place spinach in several layers of cheese cloth and squeeze to remove as much excess liquid as possible.

METAL BLADE: Add ricotta cheese and spinach to work bowl. Process until spinach is finely chopped. Stop machine and scrape down sides of bowl as needed. The mixture should be smooth. Proceed as directed in Lasagna recipe.

Preparation: 10-15 minutes
        allow time to prepare noodles
Cooking/Baking: 45-60 minutes
Protein g/s: 22

Pasta With Mushrooms and Asparagus

Serves 6-8

Select an olive oil that has a mild flavor for this delicately seasoned dish. Preparing the noodles in advance will shorten the preparation time.

1 recipe Rich Egg Noodles, cut ¼-inch (see index) or 12 ounces purchased whole wheat noodles
2 tablespoons oil
salt
1½ pounds fresh asparagus
4 ounces Parmesan cheese, room temperature
1 pound fresh mushrooms
1 tablespoon butter or margarine
3 tablespoons olive oil
3 large cloves garlic, pressed
¼-½ teaspoon salt
¼ teaspoon freshly ground pepper

Bring a large pot of water to a boil. Add 2 tablespoons oil and a pinch or two of salt. Boil noodles until cooked al dente, 4-7 minutes. Drain and set aside. When using purchased noodles, cook according to package directions; drain and set aside. Snap off the lower tough portion of the asparagus stalks and discard. Cut into 1½-inch diagonal slices. Steam until tender-crisp, 3-5 minutes. Remove from heat to prevent further cooking and set aside.

METAL BLADE: Add Parmesan cheese, cut into 1-inch pieces, to work bowl. Pulse on/off until finely grated. Remove from bowl and set aside.

SLICING DISC: Stack mushrooms into feed tube; slice with firm pressure. In a large frying pan, wok or dutch oven, heat butter and olive oil over medium-high heat. Add mushrooms and sauté until soft and most of the liquid has evaporated, 5-7 minutes. Gently stir in asparagus and garlic and continue cooking 2-3 minutes. Add noodles, salt, pepper and Parmesan. Toss gently to mix well.

Preparation: 10 minutes
        allow time to prepare noodles
Cooking: 20-35 minutes
Protein g/s: 6 servings—13.5
          8 servings—10

Pasta Topped Eggplant

Serves 8

Tender slices of eggplant are topped with whole wheat vegetable elbow macaroni, fresh tomatoes and mozzarella cheese. This dish may be assembled ahead of time, refrigerated and baked just before serving.

8 *ounces whole wheat vegetable elbow macaroni,*
  cooked according to directions, drained
2 *eggplants, about 1 pound each*
salt
oil
2½ *ounces Parmesan cheese, room temperature*
6 *ounces mozzarella cheese, well-chilled*
1 *small onion*
1 *clove garlic*
3 *medium tomatoes, about 1 pound*
2 *teaspoons dry leaf basil or*
  2 tablespoons chopped fresh basil
salt and pepper to taste

With a sharp knife, cut eggplants crosswise into ½-inch slices. Sprinkle with salt and allow to drain for 30 minutes. Pat dry with paper towels. Brush slices with oil and arrange in a single layer in an oiled baking pan. Bake in a 450° oven 10-15 minutes or until tender.

METAL BLADE: Add Parmesan cheese, cut into 1-inch pieces, to work bowl. Process until finely grated. Remove from bowl and set aside.

SHREDDING DISC: Cut mozzarella cheese to fit feed tube; shred using light pressure. Remove to a large mixing bowl; set aside.

METAL BLADE: Add garlic and onion, cut into 1-inch pieces, to work bowl. Pulse on/off until finely minced. In a large skillet, heat 2 tablespoons oil over medium-high heat. Add onions and sauté until soft and transparent, 3-5 minutes.

METAL BLADE: Add tomatoes, cut into wedges, to work bowl; pulse on/off until coarsely chopped. Drain slightly and add to skillet. Continue cooking over medium-high heat, stirring to prevent sticking, until most of the liquid has evaporated. Stir in basil. Cover and cook for 5 minutes on low heat. Taste and adjust seasonings. Preheat oven to 375°. Combine cooked macaroni, mozzarella cheese, ¼ cup Parmesan cheese and tomato mixture.

Arrange eggplant, overlapping slightly, over the bottom of an 8 x 12-inch or similar size baking dish. Top with cheese-macaroni-tomato mixture. Sprinkle on remaining Parmesan cheese. Bake, uncovered, 25 minutes or until hot and cheese has melted. Cut into squares to serve.

Preparation: 15 minutes
Standing: 30 minutes
Cooking/Baking: 50-55 minutes
Protein g/s: 12.5

Two-In-One Tomato Sauce

2½ cups

This tomato-based sauce is an excellent topping for pizza. Thin the sauce with an 8-ounce can of tomato sauce for Whole Wheat Stuffed Shells (see index) or whole wheat noodles. Make up a large quantity and freeze in small portions for later use.

1 *medium onion*
3 *tablespoons olive oil*
2 *large cloves garlic*
1 *16-ounce can whole tomatoes*
1 *6-ounce can tomato paste*
1½ *teaspoon dry leaf basil*
1 *tablespoon dry leaf oregano*
2 *teaspoons brown sugar, lightly packed*
1 *teaspoon salt*
dash pepper
1 *bay leaf*
½ *teaspoon crushed red pepper*

METAL BLADE: Add onion, cut into 1-inch pieces, to work bowl. Pulse on/off until chopped medium-fine. In a saucepan or dutch oven, heat oil over medium-high heat. Add onions and sauté until soft and transparent, but not browned. Add garlic; pulse on/off until finely minced. Add tomatoes with liquid, tomato paste, basil, oregano, brown sugar, salt and pepper. Process until smooth. Pour into the saucepan. Add bay leaf and stir in crushed red pepper. Cover and simmer for 1½ hours.

VARIATION: For spaghetti sauce consistency, add one 8-ounce can of tomato sauce with the bay leaf.

Peparation: 10 minutes
Cooking: 1½ hours

Whole Wheat Stuffed Shells with Tomato Sauce

Serves 4-6

Make the sauce ahead and this dish can be assembled quickly. It's a perfect entree for a crowd or potluck.

24 *jumbo whole wheat shells, cooked according to*
    directions, drained
1 *recipe Two-in-One Sauce (variation, see index)*
2 *ounces Parmesan cheese, room temperature*
1 *slice whole wheat bread*
4 *ounces mozzarella cheese, well-chilled*
2 *cups cottage cheese*
1 *egg*
1 *tablespoon parsley flakes*
½ *teaspoon salt*
¼ *teaspoon pepper*

Preheat oven to 350°.

METAL BLADE: Add Parmesan cheese, cut into 1-inch pieces, to work bowl. Process until finely grated. Remove from bowl and set aside. Add bread, torn into pieces, to work bowl. Process to make fine crumbs.

SHREDDING DISC: Cut mozzarella cheese to fit feed tube; shred.

METAL BLADE: Add cottage cheese, egg, parsley flakes, salt and pepper to work bowl with bread crumbs and mozzarella cheese. Combine with 3-4 on/off pulses.

Stuff each shell with about 1 heaping teaspoon filling. Spread half the tomato sauce, about 1½ cups, over the bottom of a 9 x 13-inch baking pan. Arrange filled shells in a single layer. Top with remaining sauce; sprinkle with Parmesan cheese. Bake, uncovered, 25-30 minutes or until heated through.

Preparation: 10 minutes
Cooking/Baking: 25-30 minutes
            allow time to cook shells
Protein g/s: 4 servings—30.5
            6 servings—20.5

Pesto Sauce Over Pasta

Serves 4-6

This is a great dish to make when your garden abounds with fresh basil. Increase the amount of olive oil by 2-3 tablespoons and the sauce will be thinner.

1 *recipe Rich Egg Noodles or Whole Wheat Egg*
    Noodles (see index) or
    10-12 *ounces purchased noodles*
2 *tablespoons oil*
salt
3 *ounces Parmesan cheese, room temperature*
2 *ounces Romano cheese, room temperature*
4 *cups fresh basil leaves, firmly packed*
½-⅔ *cup olive oil*
2-4 *large cloves garlic, pressed*
⅓ *cup shelled pine nuts, optional*

Make noodles according to directions. Cook after the sauce is prepared.

METAL BLADE: Add Parmesan and Romano cheeses, cut into 1-inch pieces, to work bowl. Process until finely grated. Pat basil leaves with paper towels or spin in a lettuce dryer to dry. Add about 2 cups basil to work bowl with cheese. Turn machine on and gradually add remaining basil. Process until mixture has the consistency of a purée. Add garlic and with machine running, quickly pour in oil. Add pine nuts if used. Process until sauce is smooth.

Bring a large pot of water to a boil. Add 2 tablespoons oil and a pinch or two of salt. Boil noodles until al dente, 4-7 minutes. Drain. Dry noodles will take a bit longer to cook. Cook purchased noodles according to directions, drain. Place noodles in a large shallow dish, top with sauce and toss to mix. Noodles may also be placed on individual dinner plates. Pass the sauce and let each person top and toss their own serving.

Preparation: 10 minutes
            allow time to prepare noodles
Protein g/s: 4 servings—20.5
            6 servings—14

Lasagna With Eggplant-Mushroom Sauce

Serves 12

This is a convenient make-ahead dish. Make the sauce one or two days ahead. You do not need to reheat sauce before assembling the dish.

4   ounces Parmesan cheese, room temperature
12   ounces mozzarella cheese, well-chilled
1   medium onion
2   tablespoons oil
1   eggplant, about 1 pound unpeeled
¾-1   pound fresh mushrooms
1   16-ounce can whole tomatoes
1   12-ounce can tomato paste
1   teaspoon dry leaf basil, crumbled
1   tablespoon dry leaf oregano, crumbled
pinch dry leaf rosemary
1   teaspoon brown sugar
salt and pepper to taste
8   ounces purchased whole wheat lasagna
1½   pounds ricotta cheese
2   eggs

METAL BLADE: Add Parmesan cheese, cut into 1-inch pieces, to work bowl. Process until finely grated. Remove from bowl and set aside.

SHREDDING DISC: Cut mozzarella cheese to fit feed tube; shred using light pressure. Remove from bowl and set aside.

METAL BLADE: Add onion, cut into 1-inch pieces, to work bowl; pulse on/off until finely chopped. In a 3 or 4-quart saucepan, heat oil over medium-high heat. Add onions and sauté until soft, 3-5 minutes.

SLICING DISC: Quarter eggplant lengthwise; cut into pieces to fit tube vertically; slice. Wedge mushrooms into feed tube; slice with firm pressure. Add to onions and continue cooking 2-3 minutes.

METAL BLADE: Add tomatoes with liquid, tomato paste, basil, oregano, rosemary and brown sugar to work bowl. Process until smooth. Pour into saucepan; stir to mix. Cover and simmer about 1 hour or until thickened. Taste and adjust seasonings.

While sauce is cooking, cook noodles according to directions until al dente. Drain and set aside. Preheat oven to 350°. In a small mixing bowl, combine ricotta cheese and eggs. Spread ⅓ of the sauce over the bottom of an ungreased 9 x 13-inch or similar size baking dish. Layer ½ the noodles and spread over all the ricotta filling. Continue layering with ½ of the mozzarella cheese, ⅓ of sauce, remaining noodles, sauce and mozzarella cheese. Top with Parmesan cheese. Bake, covered, 25-30 minutes or until hot and cheese is bubbly. Let stand 5 minutes; cut into squares and serve.

Note: If planning to reheat to serve later, bake only 15 minutes and refrigerate. To reheat, bake in preheated 350° oven about 30-40 minutes or until hot.

Preparation: 15-20 minutes
Cooking/Baking: 1¾-2 hours
Standing: 5 minutes
Protein g/s: 20.5

Cacciatore Sauce Over Noodles

Serves 4-6

This has been a favorite with guests and family. When using a vegetable bouillon select the kind with a delicate vegetable flavor rather than a beefy one.

2-4   ounces Parmesan cheese, room temperature
2   medium or large onions
1   pound carrots, peeled
¾   pound celery stalks, trimmed
4   tablespoons olive oil
½   teaspoon salt
3   tablespoons chicken-flavored vegetable seasoning or 2 vegetable bouillon cubes
¼   cup boiling water
4   tablespoons tomato paste
1¾-2   cups dry sherry
salt and pepper to taste
1   recipe Whole Wheat Egg Noodles (see index) or 10-12 ounces purchased ¼-inch wide whole wheat noodles or
     ¾   recipe Rich Egg Noodles (freeze or dry excess for later use) or
     ½   recipe Carrot Noodles (freeze or dry excess for later use)

METAL BLADE: Add Parmesan cheese, cut into 1-inch pieces, to work bowl. Process until finely grated. Remove from bowl and set aside. Add onions, cut into 1-inch pieces, to work bowl. Pulse on/off until chopped medium-fine.

SLICING DISC: Cut carrots to fit feed tube vertically; slice. Cut celery to fit feed tube vertically; slice.

In a 3 or 4-quart sauce pan, heat oil over medium-high heat. Add onions and vegetables and sauté until tender, 5-8 minutes. Add ½ teaspoon salt. Dissolve chicken-flavored seasoning in boiling water. Stir into pan along with tomato paste and 1 cup sherry. Cover and simmer 15 minutes to allow the sauce to thicken. Add the remaining sherry and continue to simmer for 10 minutes. Stir in salt and pepper to taste. Meanwhile, bring a large pot of water to boil, add 2 tablespoons oil and salt to taste. Boil noodles 4-7 minutes, or until cooked al dente. Drain. Serve sauce over hot noodles. Sprinkle on 2 tablespoons Parmesan cheese per serving.

Preparation: 10 minutes
Cooking: 35 minutes for the sauce
        allow time to cook noodles
Protein g/s: 4 servings—14
        6 servings—11

Whole Wheat Ravioli

Serves 6

Your pasta machine will roll sheets of dough thin enough for ravioli. With a lot of elbow grease, the dough can be rolled, by hand, to ¹/₁₆-inch or thinner. When rolling by hand, let the dough rest, covered, momentarily during the process to relax the gluten. Follow the directions at the beginning of this chapter.

1 recipe dough for Whole Wheat Egg Noodles or
    Rich Egg Noodles (see index)
1 10-ounce package frozen leaf spinach, defrosted
3 ounces Parmesan cheese, room temperature
1 cup ricotta cheese
¼ teaspoon nutmeg
2 tablespoons minced fresh basil or
    1 tablespoon dry leaf basil
2 eggs
4 cups Basic Marinara Sauce (see index)
additional Parmesan cheese for topping, optional

Make noodle dough according to directions. Place in a plastic bag and allow to rest while making the filling. Wipe work bowl dry. Place defrosted spinach between several layers of cheese cloth and squeeze out all excess liquid. Set aside.

METAL BLADE: Add Parmesan cheese, cut into 1-inch pieces, to work bowl. Process until finely grated. Add spinach, ricotta cheese, nutmeg, basil and eggs. Pulse on/off until spinach is finely chopped.

Divide the dough into four pieces. Remove one piece at a time and shape into a ball. Keep remaining pieces in the plastic bag to prevent drying. Flour ball well, flatten and feed through the roller mechanism of your pasta machine as follows, flouring as necessary:

> 1st Setting: Pass through the rollers. Fold dough into thirds and pass through two more times, once horizontally and once vertically.
> 2nd setting: Fold dough into thirds and pass through once, vertically.
> 3rd-4th Setting: Pass through each setting once without folding.
> Cut dough in half, making two equally long wide pieces; flour.
> 5th Setting: Pass each piece through once without folding.

Take care not to allow the dough to dry during rolling or filling as dry dough does not seal well. The pieces will be ¹/₁₆-¹/₃₂ inch thick. Place one sheet on a floured board and dot with 1 teaspoon of filling at 1½-inch intervals, allowing a border around the edges. Place second sheet of dough over filling. With your fingertips, press down between the filling mounds; cut into squares with a fluted pastry wheel. To be sure the edges are well-sealed, trace again with the pastry wheel along the outer edge. Set ravioli aside on a floured surface until you are ready to cook.

Repeat with remaining two sheets of dough. Bring a large pot of water to a boil. Add 2-3 tablespoons oil and salt to taste. Cook ravioli about 10-15 minutes. Heat marinara sauce. Drain ravioli; place on serving plates and top with marinara sauce and a sprinkling of Parmesan.

Preparation: 2 hours, excluding marinara sauce
Cooking: 15 minutes
Protein g/s: 17.5

Pasta Rustica

Serves 6

The beans, noodles and cheese are complementary in this hearty pasta dish with vegetables. Serve with a tossed green salad and hot whole grain bread.

1 recipe Whole Wheat Egg Noodles (see index) or 10-12 ounces purchased *whole wheat noodles*, ¼-inch wide
1-2 tablespoons oil
salt
2 ounces Parmesan cheese, room temperature
2 small carrots, peeled
1 medium turnip, about 4 ounces, peeled
1 large or 2 small leeks
2-3 tablespoons oil
¼ cup fresh parsley leaves
¼ cup fresh basil leaves or
1 teaspoon dry leaf basil
3 cups Basic Marinara Sauce (see index)
½ small head cabbage, about 8 ounces
3 small zucchini, scrubbed
2 cups cooked kidney beans, well-drained (⅔ cup dry)
salt and pepper to taste

Bring a large pot of water to boil. Add 1-2 tablespoons oil and a pinch or two of salt. Boil noodles until cooked al dente, 4-7 minutes. Drain and set aside. When using purchased noodles, cook according to package directions. Drain and set aside.

METAL BLADE: Add Parmesan cheese, cut into 1-inch pieces, to work bowl. Process until finely grated. Remove from bowl and set aside.

SLICING DISC: Cut carrots to fit feed tube vertically, slice. Remove from bowl. Cut turnip into 8 wedges. Place in feed tube vertically, slice.

Wash leek(s) thoroughly to remove grit collected between the leaves. Discard the tough, upper portions of the tops. With a sharp knife, cut into ¼-inch pieces. In a 3 or 4-quart saucepan or dutch oven, heat 2-3 tablespoons oil over medium-high heat. Add carrots, sauté 1-2 minutes; add leeks and sauté about 30 seconds; add turnips and continue to cook 3-4 minutes.

METAL BLADE: Add parsley and fresh basil to work bowl; pulse on/off until finely minced. Add to saucepan and stir in marinara sauce. Bring sauce almost to a boil, reduce heat and allow to simmer while you prepare the remainder of the vegetables.

SLICING DISC: Cut cabbage into wedges to fit feed tube; slice. Cut zucchini to fit feed tube vertically, slice. Stir into marinara sauce. Continue cooking 3-5 minutes or until zucchini is just crisp-tender.

Carefully stir in noodles and beans. Cover and cook 2 minutes to allow flavors to blend. To serve, top individual portions with a sprinkling of Parmesan cheese.

Preparation: 15 minutes
Cooking: 20 minutes when noodles, beans and sauce are prepared ahead of time
Protein g/s: 14

Eggplant Pastitsio

Serves 8

Here is our version of a classic Greek dish. The "meat" layer—eggplant, delicately seasoned with allspice, cinnamon and nutmeg—bakes between layers of whole wheat macaroni, Parmesan and a custard sauce. It's the Greek vegetarian's answer to lasagna.

5 ounces Parmesan cheese, room temperature
2 medium eggplants, about 1 pound each, unpeeled
6 tablespoons olive oil
2 medium or large onions
2 8-ounce cans tomato sauce
½ teaspoon salt
1-2 teaspoons honey
2-3 large cloves garlic, pressed
½ teaspoon ground allspice
½-1 teaspoon ground cinnamon
½ teaspoon ground nutmeg
pinch dry leaf rosemary
leaves from 3-4 sprigs fresh mint, minced
12 ounces whole wheat macaroni
3 tablespoons butter or margarine
3 tablespoons whole wheat flour, measured scoop and level
1½ cups milk
salt and pepper to taste
4 eggs

METAL BLADE: Add Parmesan cheese, cut into 1-inch pieces, to work bowl. Process until finely grated. Remove from bowl and set aside.

SLICING DISC: Cut eggplant to fit feed tube vertically; slice using medium pressure. Generously oil 2 baking pans with several tablespoons of olive oil. Arrange eggplant over the bottom of the pans and bake at 400° until soft, 15 minutes. Turn slices once or twice during baking. Remove from oven and place on paper towels to drain excess oil.

METAL BLADE: Add onions, cut into 1-inch pieces, to work bowl; pulse on/off until finely chopped. In 5-quart dutch oven, heat about 2 tablespoons olive oil over medium-high heat. Add onions and sauté until soft and transparent but not browned. Stir in tomato sauce, salt, honey, garlic, allspice, cinnamon, ¼ teaspoon nutmeg, rosemary and mint. Reduce heat to medium, cover and cook 15-25 minutes to allow sauce to thicken and flavors to blend. Stir in eggplant and continue cooking about 10 minutes, or until mixture is thick. While the mixture is cooking, cook macaroni until al dente. Drain and set aside.

To make custard sauce, melt butter in a saucepan. Add flour, stirring with a wire whip. Gradually add milk, stirring constantly over medium heat. Add salt, pepper and ¼ teaspoon nutmeg. Cook, stirring constantly until thickened and bubbly. Remove from heat. In a small bowl, beat 2 eggs. Using a wire whip, gradually stir in about 4 tablespoons of hot sauce into eggs; blend well. Return egg mixture to remaining sauce, stirring rapidly.

In a large mixing bowl, beat remaining 2 eggs. Add macaroni and stir to mix well. Preheat oven to 350°.

Spread half of the macaroni mixture on the bottom of a greased 9 x 13-inch or similar size baking pan. Sprinkle with ¼ of the grated Parmesan; spread with half of the sauce and another sprinkle of ¼ of the grated Parmesan. Cover evenly with the eggplant mixture; sprinkle on ¼ of the grated Parmesan and cover with remaining sauce. Top with last ¼ of grated Parmesan and sprinkle very delicately with a few pinches of nutmeg.

Bake 30-40 minutes or until top is golden brown and dish is hot. Remove from oven, allow to stand about 5 minutes; cut into squares and serve.

Preparation: 15 minutes
Cooking/Baking: 1¾ hours
Standing: 5 minutes
Protein g/s: 16.5

Eggplant Lasagna

Serves 8

A welcome change for lasagna lovers. Marinara Sauce is layered between eggplant instead of noodles.

2 ounces Parmesan cheese, room temperature
8 ounces mozzarella cheese, well-chilled
2 large or 3 medium eggplants, 2½ pounds, unpeeled
2 eggs beaten
½-¾ cup whole wheat flour
oil for frying
3 cups Basic Marinara Sauce (see index) or similar tomato-based sauce
16 ounces ricotta cheese

METAL BLADE: Add Parmesan cheese, cut into 1-inch pieces, to work bowl. Process until finely grated. Remove from bowl and set aside.

SHREDDING DISC: Cut mozzarella cheese to fit feed tube; shred using light pressure. With a sharp knife, cut eggplant into ¼-inch thick slices. Place eggs and flour into two separate shallow dishes. Dip eggplant slices into beaten eggs then into flour.

In a teflon-coated or similar non-stick surface frying pan, heat 1-2 teaspoons oil over medium-high heat. Fry eggplant slices until golden brown on both sides. Do not overcook. Eggplant should be just done and not too soft or it may break apart when removed from the pan.

Preheat oven to 350°. In a greased 9 x 13-inch or similar size baking dish, layer half of the eggplant, 1 cup sauce, all of the ricotta cheese, half the mozzarella cheese, 1 cup sauce, remaining eggplant slices, sauce and mozzarella cheese. Top with grated Parmesan. Bake, covered, 25-30 minutes or until hot and cheese is bubbly. Cut into squares and serve.

Preparation: 10-15 minutes
Cooking/Baking: 50 minutes
Protein g/s: 17

Noodles Romanoff With Mushrooms

Serves 8

Rennetless cottage cheese, cultured with acidophilus, provides the flavor boost to this elegant noodle bake. It's generally available at co-ops and health food stores. Regular cottage cheese can be substituted in a pinch, but for best results use the rennetless type.

1 recipe Whole Wheat Egg Noodles (see index) or
   Rich Egg Noodles (see index) cut ¼-inch wide or
   10 ounces purchased whole wheat noodles
2-3 tablespoons oil
1 pound fresh mushrooms
2-3 tablespoons butter or margarine
4 green onions
1 tablespoon oil
5 ounces Cheddar cheese
2 cups rennetless cottage cheese, cultured with
   acidophilus
1 teaspoon Worcestershire sauce or
   ½ teaspoon Vegex vegetable soup seasoning
¼ teaspoon salt
4 drops Tabasco sauce
2-3 sprigs fresh parsley

Bring a large pot of water to a boil. Add 2-3 tablespoons oil and a pinch or two of salt. Boil noodles until cooked al dente, about 5 minutes. Drain and set aside. When using purchased noodles, cook according to directions on package; drain and set aside.

SLICING DISC: Stack mushrooms in feed tube; slice with firm pressure. In a skillet, heat butter over medium-high heat. Add mushrooms and sauté until soft and most of the liquid has evaporated, 5-7 minutes. Remove to a large mixing bowl.

METAL BLADE: Add onions, cut into 1-inch lengths, to work bowl; pulse on/off until finely minced. In the same skillet, heat 1 tablespoon oil over medium-high heat. Add onions and sauté 1 minute. Add to mushrooms. Preheat oven to 350°.

SHREDDING DISC: Cut Cheddar cheese to fit feed tube; shred. Push cheese to one side of the work bowl and carefully insert metal blade.

METAL BLADE: Add cottage cheese, Worcestershire sauce or Vegex, salt and Tabasco sauce to the work bowl. Process until just smooth. Turn off machine and scrape down sides of bowl. Add

parsley; pulse on/off until chopped medium-fine. Stir into mushroom mixture.

Spread noodles evenly over the bottom of a buttered 9 x 13-inch or similar size baking dish. Spread mushroom-cheese mixture over noodles. Cover and bake 20-25 minutes or until hot. Cut into squares and serve.

Preparation: 15 minutes
               allow time to prepare noodles
Cooking/Baking: 40-45 minutes
Protein g/s: 16.5

Hungarian Paprika Noodles

Serves 6

Homemade noodles are transformed into something special when topped with this delightful sauce. While the taste is authentic, it's higher in protein and lower in fat than the traditional version. Rennetless cottage cheese, cultured with acidophilus, provides the taste, but not the fat, of sour cream. If it's not readily available, regular cottage cheese may be substituted. The final product will be a bit less flavorful but nonetheless acceptable.

1 recipe Whole Wheat Noodles (see index) or
   noodles of your choice
4 medium or large onions
3-4 tablespoons oil
2-3 tablespoons paprika
2 vegetable bouillon cubes dissolved in ¾ cup boiling water
1-1¼ pound fresh mushrooms
1 teaspoon Vegex vegetable soup seasoning
1 teaspoon salt
⅓-½ cup dry sherry
¼-⅓ cup additional water as needed
2 cups rennetless cottage cheese or
   2 cups regular cottage cheese
½ cup sour cream

METAL BLADE: Add onions, cut into 1-inch pieces, to work bowl; pulse on/off until finely chopped. Heat 3 tablespoons oil in a large saucepan over medium-high heat. Add onions and sauté until soft, 5-8 minutes. Stir in paprika and sauté 1 minute; watch carefully so paprika does not burn. Remove from heat.

SLICING DISC: Wedge mushrooms in feed tube; slice. In a skillet, heat about 1 tablespoon oil over medium-high heat. Cook mushrooms until tender and most of the liquid has evaporated. Add to saucepan with onions. Stir in bouillon, Vegex, salt and sherry. Return saucepan to heat and continue cooking, over medium heat, 5 minutes to allow flavors to blend. Add additional water only if mixture begins to dry. Remove from heat.

METAL BLADE: Add cottage cheese and sour cream to work bowl. Process until just smooth, 30-60 seconds. Do not overprocess. Stir the cottage cheese mixture into the saucepan. Cover and place in a warm oven until ready to serve. Do not allow the mixture to come to a boil after the cottage cheese has been added or it will curdle. Cook noodles according to directions, drain. Top with sauce and serve.

Preparation: 15 minutes
Cooking: 20 minutes plus time to cook noodles
Protein g/s: 17

Oven Spaghetti

Serves 4-6

A brief baking melts the cheese and allows the flavors to blend in this quick main dish. Overbaking results in stringy cheese.

1 recipe Whole Wheat Egg Noodles (see index) or
    Rich Egg Noodles (see index) cut narrow or
    12 ounces purchased whole wheat spaghetti
1-2 tablespoons oil
salt
3 ounces Parmesan cheese, room temperature
4 ounces mozzarella cheese, well-chilled
3 cups Basic Marinara Sauce (see index) or
    similar tomato-based sauce

Bring a large pot of water to a boil. Add 1-2 tablespoons oil and a pinch or two of salt. Cook spaghetti until al dente, 4-7 minutes. Drain. When using purchased spaghetti, cook according to package directions, drain. Preheat oven to 350°.

METAL BLADE: Add Parmesan cheese, cut into 1-inch pieces, to work bowl. Process until finely grated. Remove from bowl and set aside.

SHREDDING DISC: Cut mozzarella cheese to fit feed tube; shred using light pressure. Spread spaghetti over the bottom of a well-buttered baking dish, about 3-quart size. Top with mozzarella cheese and cover with marinara sauce. Sprinkle on Parmesan. Cover with foil and bake 10-12 minutes or until noodles are hot and cheese is melted.

Preparation: 10 minutes when noodles and
                sauce are prepared in advance
Cooking/Baking: 20-30 minutes
Protein g/s: 4 servings—17.5
                6 servings—12

Basic Marinara Sauce

14 cups

This multipurpose sauce is used in a number of our recipes. This recipe makes a large amount but it freezes well. Freeze in 1 or 2 cup containers.

3-5 large onions
1 green pepper, halved and seeded
4-5 tablespoons oil
4 15-ounce cans tomato sauce
3 6-ounce cans tomato paste
2½ cups water
¼ teaspoon dry rosemary
¼ teaspoon dry leaf oregano
1 bay leaf
½ teaspoon dry leaf thyme
½ teaspoon dry leaf marjoram
3 whole cloves
2 teaspoons brown sugar
1 teaspoon Vegit seasoning
salt to taste
½ cup burgundy wine, optional

METAL BLADE: Add onions, cut into 1-inch pieces, to work bowl. Pulse on/off until chopped medium-fine. In a large dutch oven, heat oil over medium-high heat. Add onions and sauté 1-2 minutes. Meanwhile, add green pepper, cut into 1-inch pieces, to work bowl. Pulse on-off until chopped medium-fine. Add to onions and continue cooking until onions are soft and transparent. Stir in tomato sauce, tomato paste, water, rosemary, oregano, bay leaf, thyme, marjoram, cloves and brown sugar. Simmer, covered for 1½-2 hours. This can be cooked in a 5½-quart slow cooker, about 4 hours. Stir in Vegit and salt to taste. Pour in burgundy, simmer 5-10 minutes to allow flavors to blend.

Preparation: 10 minutes
Cooking: 1½-2 hours over the range
            4 hours in a slow cooker

Cashew Noodle Crunch

Serves 8

Cashews make this noodle dish a special treat.

1 cup raw cashews, roasted at 350° for 15-20 minutes
8 ounces Cheddar cheese, well-chilled
1 medium onion
2 stalks celery, trimmed
1 medium green pepper, halved and seeded
3-4 tablespoons oil
3 green onions, cut into 1-inch lengths
2 teaspoons Vegit seasoning
¼-½ teaspoon salt
3 tablespoons whole wheat flour
2 cups milk
1½ teaspoons Dijon mustard
1 recipe Whole Wheat Egg Noodles (see index) or
   ¾ recipe Rich Egg Noodles (freeze or dry excess for later use) or
   10-12 ounces purchased noodles
paprika

SHREDDING DISC: Cut Cheddar cheese to fit feed tube; shred. Remove from bowl and set aside.

METAL BLADE: Add onion, cut into 1-inch pieces, to work bowl; pulse on/off until chopped medium-fine.

SLICING DISC: Cut celery to fit feed tube vertically; slice. Quarter each green pepper half, wedge into feed tube vertically; slice.

In a saucepan, heat oil over medium-high heat. Add vegetables and sauté until tender, 8-10 minutes. Add green onions, Vegit and salt. Stir gently to mix. Sprinkle in flour and toss to mix. Gradually stir in milk and simmer until smooth and thickened. Add mustard. Stir in cheese and cook until melted and sauce is smooth. Turn off heat.

Bring a large pot of water to boil, add 2 tablespoons oil and a pinch or two of salt. Boil noodles 4-7 minutes, or until cooked al dente. Cook purchased noodles according to directions, 8-14 minutes. Drain.

Preheat oven to 350°. Pour noodles into a greased 9 x 13-inch or similar size baking dish. Pour in sauce and toss to mix well. Top with cashews and a generous sprinkle of paprika. Bake 25-30 minutes or until hot and bubbly.

Preparation: 10 minutes
Cooking/Baking: 50-60 minutes
Protein g/s: 17

Baked Green Fettucine

Serves 6-8

We owe this garlic lover's delight to our friend, Ann Williams. When the noodles are made in advance, it's a dish that's quickly prepared. The recipe can easily be cut in half. Freeze or dry the excess noodles for later use.

1 recipe Spinach Noodles, cut ¼-inch wide (see index) or
   1 pound purchased whole wheat spinach noodles
12 ounces Parmesan cheese, room temperature
3-4 tablespoons butter or margarine
4-8 large cloves garlic, pressed
2 sprigs flat-leaf parsley

METAL BLADE: Add Parmesan cheese, cut into 1-inch cubes, to work bowl. Process until finely grated. Wipe work bowl completely dry and prepare noodles, if not prepared in advance.

Bring a large pot of water to boil. Add 2 tablespoons oil and a pinch or two of salt. Boil noodles until cooked al dente, about 4 minutes for fresh noodles, longer for dry noodles. Drain.

Preheat oven to 350°. Layer ¼ of the noodles over the bottom of a large, greased baking dish. Dot with butter and garlic and sprinkle with ¼ of the Parmesan cheese. Repeat layering, ending with a sprinkling of cheese.

METAL BLADE: Add parsley to work bowl; pulse on/off until finely chopped. Set aside for garnish. Bake about 20 minutes or until the garlic aroma permeates the kitchen. Sprinkle on parsley.

Preparation: 10 minutes when noodles are prepared in advance
Baking: 20 minutes
Protein g/s: 6 servings—28
           8 servings—21

Parmesan Zucchini-Basil Sauce Over Pasta

3 cups or 4 servings

A quickly prepared sauce when you want a meal in a hurry. It's especially delicious over homemade pasta.

1 recipe Whole Wheat Egg Noodles or Rich Egg
   Noodles (see index) or
   8-12 ounces purchased whole wheat noodles,
   prepared according to directions
3 ounces Parmesan cheese, room temperature
1 pound zucchini, scrubbed
1 tablespoon oil
2 tablespoons butter or margarine
2 tablespoons oil
1 tablespoon whole wheat flour
1 cup skim milk
6-8 fresh basil leaves, cut into small pieces or
     1 teaspoon dry leaf basil
¼ teaspoon salt

Prepare noodles if making from scratch. Do not cook until sauce is just about done. When using purchased noodles, cook and keep warm.

METAL BLADE: Add Parmesan cheese, cut into 1-inch pieces, to work bowl. Process until finely grated. Remove from bowl and set aside.

SLICING DISC: Cut zucchini to fit feed tube horizontally; slice. Remove the slices. Insert the pusher into the feed tube, leaving a space at the bottom. Hold the cover sideways and wedge the stack of sliced zucchini in horizontally with the cut sides at right angles to the cover. Slice again to produce julienne strips.

In a 10-inch skillet, heat 1 tablespoon oil over medium-high heat. Cook zucchini until golden brown, about 5 minutes. Remove zucchini from skillet. Heat 2 tablespoons oil and 2 tablespoons butter over medium heat. Stir in flour and cook 1 minute. Gradually pour in milk stirring constantly with a wire whisk to keep the sauce smooth. Cook until thickened, about 1 minute. Stir in zucchini, Parmesan, basil and salt. Toss until Parmesan is melted and sauce is smooth. Serve immediately over hot cooked pasta.

Preparation: 15 minutes
Cooking: 10 minutes
Protein g/s: 18.5 using homemade noodles

Gnocchi Verdi

28 dumplings or 4-6 servings

Topped with our Basic Marinara Sauce (see index), these spinach dumplings make an elegant main dish. Serve with slices of hot whole wheat french bread and a tossed green salad.

1 10-ounce package frozen leaf spinach, defrosted,
   squeezed dry or
   ¾ cup cooked fresh spinach, packed firmly into
   measuring cup, squeezed dry
2 tablespoons butter or margarine
½ cup ricotta cheese
dash pepper
½ teaspoon nutmeg
2 eggs
3 ounces Parmesan cheese, room temperature
½ cup whole wheat flour, measured scoop and
   level
½ cup fresh basil leaves (do not substitute dry leaf
   basil)
salt to taste

In a skillet, heat butter over medium heat. Add spinach and sauté until traces of moisture have evaporated, 4-6 minutes. Stir in ricotta cheese, pepper and nutmeg. Continue cooking, 5 minutes, stirring constantly. Remove from heat and allow to cool to room temperature, 10 minutes.

METAL BLADE: Add Parmesan cheese, cut into 1-inch pieces, to work bowl. Process until finely grated. With machine off, add spinach mixture, eggs, flour and basil leaves. Pulse on/off until spinach and basil are finely chopped and mixture is well mixed.

Season to taste with salt. Remove from bowl and place in a mixing bowl; cover and refrigerate at least 1 hour. Bring a large pot of water to a boil. Add a pinch or two of salt. For each gnocchi, shape about 1 teaspoon spinach mixture into a ball. Flour and drop into boiling water; stir once or twice to prevent sticking. Simmer 8-10 minutes. Drain and serve.

Preparation: 20 minutes
Cooking: 20-25 minutes
Standing: 10 minutes
Chilling: 1 hour
Protein g/s: 4 servings—15.5
            6 servings—10.5

Pizzas and Turnovers

Mini Pita Pizzas

Serves 1

Whole wheat pita bread is used for the crust of this "pizza". Serve with a tossed green salad for a quick and simple dinner.

1 6-7-inch Pita (see index) or purchased
2 tablespoons Basic Marinara Sauce (see index)
⅛ teaspoon dry leaf oregano
2 ounces mozzarella cheese, well-chilled
⅛ medium onion
1 ounce fresh mushrooms
¼ medium green pepper

Preheat oven to 400°. Spread sauce on pita; sprinkle with oregano.

SHREDDING DISC: Cut mozzarella cheese to fit feed tube; using light pressure, shred. Sprinkle over sauce.

METAL BLADE: Add onion; pulse on/off to chop. Squeeze out excess liquid; sprinkle over cheese.

SLICING DISC: Stack mushrooms in feed tube; slice. Cut pepper into 4 pieces, stack in feed tube vertically and slice. Place mushrooms and green pepper evenly over onions. Place pita pizza on a cookie sheet; bake 15-20 minutes or until cheese is melted and bubbly.

Preparation: 10 minutes
Baking: 15-20 minutes
Protein g/s: 20.5

Whole Wheat Buttermilk Pizza Crust

Serves 8

You determine the crispness of the crust by the size of the pans used. The thinner the crust, the crisper.

1 tablespoon active dry yeast
⅓ cup warm water (105°-115°)
1 tablespoon oil
1 teaspoon honey
2½ cups whole wheat flour, measured scoop and level
½ teaspoon salt
½ cup buttermilk, room temperature
1-3 tablespoons water, as needed

In a measuring cup, sprinkle yeast over ⅓ cup warm water. Let stand in a warm place about 5 minutes until it dissolves or puffs. Add oil and honey.

METAL BLADE: Add whole wheat flour and salt to work bowl. Pulse on/off to mix. With machine running, pour yeast mixture through feed tube. Pour in buttermilk in a steady stream, only as fast as the flour absorbs it. Process to form a ball of dough, adding more water as needed. Process the ball of dough 20 seconds. Stop the machine and feel the dough. It should be elastic, sticky and wet. If not, process 10 seconds longer. Sprinkle dough with an additional 1-2 tablespoons flour. Pulse machine on/off to coat dough for easy removal from work bowl.

Transfer dough to an oiled bowl and turn so entire surface is oiled. Cover with plastic wrap or damp cloth and let rise in a warm place, free from drafts until doubled in bulk, about 1 hour. Punch down dough and knead for 30 seconds to press out the bubbles. Shape into a ball, let rest, covered 5 minutes. Preheat oven to 400°. Roll dough out to 1 large 14-15-inch circle approximately ½-inch thick or 2 small 9-inch circles. Place dough on greased pan(s). Pinch edges up to form a rim. Spread sauce over dough and sprinkle on toppings. Bake 20-25 minutes or until cheese is melted and bubbly.

Preparation: 10 minutes
Baking: 20-25 minutes
Standing: allow 1 hour for dough to rise
Protein g/s: 5.5

Mexican Rice Crust Pizza

Serves 10-12

Substitute your favorite enchilada sauce (about 2 cups) for a nice variation.

3 cups cooked brown rice (about 1 cup raw)
1 cup cooked pinto beans (about ½ cup dry)
6 ounces mozzarella cheese, well-chilled
8 ounces Monterey Jack cheese, well-chilled
2 eggs, slightly beaten

Sauce
1 14-ounce can Mexican tomatillos drained
1 small onion, cut into 1-inch pieces
2 cloves garlic
1 7-ounce can whole green chiles, rinsed and
   seeded
1 bunch fresh coriander
½ teaspoon salt
½ teaspoon brown sugar
¼-½ teaspoon crushed red pepper, optional

choice of toppings: sliced green peppers, mushrooms, black olives

Preheat oven to 375°.

SHREDDING DISC: Cut mozzarella cheese to fit feed tube; using light pressure, shred. Remove from bowl and set aside. Cut Monterey Jack cheese to fit feed tube, shred. Remove from bowl and set aside.

In a large mixing bowl, combine cooked brown rice, 1 cup shredded mozzarella cheese and 2 eggs. Toss to mix. Oil a 9x13-inch baking pan. Spread the rice mixture on the bottom of the pan; press lightly to form an even layer.

METAL BLADE: Add pinto beans to work bowl; pulse on/off to chop coarsely. Sprinkle chopped beans over rice mixture. Add tomatillos, onion, garlic, green chiles, coriander, salt and brown sugar to work bowl. Process until onion is finely chopped and sauce is smooth. Stop machine; stir in crushed red pepper.

Spread sauce evenly over beans. Top with remaining mozzarella cheese and all the Montery Jack cheese. Sprinkle on your choice of additional toppings. Bake 40 minutes. Cut into squares and serve.

Preparation: 15-20 minutes
Cooking/Baking: 40 minutes
        allow time to cook rice and beans

Chilling: allow time for rice and beans to cool or
            cook the day before, and refrigerate until
            ready to assemble pizza
Protein g/s: 10 servings—15.5
              12 servings—12.5

Cottage Cheese Oil Pizza Crust

Serves 8

This high protein baking powder crust is quick to prepare. The taste is surprisingly similar to a yeast-risen crust. It is based on a dough developed by the Dr. Oetker test kitchens in Bielefeld, Germany.

1¾ cups whole wheat flour, measured scoop and
     level
½ teaspoon salt
2½ teaspoons baking powder
½ cup cottage cheese, well-drained
4 tablespoons oil
3-5 tablespoons milk
additional flour for rolling out dough

Preheat oven to 400°.

METAL BLADE: Add flour, salt and baking powder to work bowl. Pulse on/off to mix. Remove cover of work bowl and add cottage cheese and oil. Process until well-mixed. With machine running, add the milk by tablespoonfuls until the dough forms a ball. Stop the machine as soon as the ball is formed.

If dough is sticky, sprinkle with flour before placing it on a floured board. Using a rolling pin, roll out the dough to a circle measuring 14 to 15-inches in diameter. If it is difficult to work dough, let it "relax" for a few minutes and then continue shaping.

Place circle on a well-greased pizza pan. Pinch up edge to form a slight ridge. Spread on your favorite sauce and toppings. Bake 20-25 minutes.

Preparation: 6-8 minutes
Baking: 20-25 minutes
Protein g/s: Crust only—5.5

Pizza

Serves 6-8

One rising of the dough produces a crisp thin crust.

1 tablespoon active dry yeast
⅔ cup warm water (105-115°)
2 tablespoons oil
2 cups whole wheat flour, measured scoop and
     level
½ teaspoon salt
12 ounces mozzarella cheese, well-chilled
other garnishes as desired: fresh mushrooms, green
peppers, zucchini, olives
1 cup Two-in-One Tomato Sauce (see index)

In a measuring cup, sprinkle yeast over ⅔ cup warm water. Let stand in a warm place about 5 minutes until it dissolves or puffs. Add oil.

METAL BLADE: Add flour and salt to work bowl. With machine running, pour in yeast mixture. After the liquid has been absorbed, let the processor run for 20 seconds. Stop the machine and feel the dough. It should be elastic, sticky and wet. If not, process 10 seconds longer.

Transfer dough to an oiled bowl and turn so entire surface is oiled. Cover with plastic wrap or damp cloth and let rise in a warm place, free from drafts until doubled in bulk. Do not punch down dough. Place dough on a greased 14-inch pizza pan. Pat dough to fit pan. Pinch the edge to form a rim. Let rest 10 minutes while oven is preheating to 400°.

SHREDDING DISC: Cut mozzarella cheese to fit feed tube; shred. Set aside.

SLICING DISC: Slice garnishes, set aside. Spread tomato sauce evenly over the dough. Sprinkle with cheese and garnishes. Bake for 25 minutes.

Preparation: 20 minutes
Baking: 25 minutes
Standing: allow 1 hour for dough to rise
Protein g/s: 15.5

Sicilian Pizza

Serves 6

1 tablespoon active dry yeast
¼ cup warm water (105°-115°)
2½ cups whole wheat flour, measured scoop and
     level
¾ teaspoon salt
¾ cup water, as needed
2 tablespoons olive oil
cornmeal
2 ounces Parmesan cheese, room temperature
8 ounces mozzarella cheese, well-chilled
1 cup Two-in-One Tomato Sauce (see index)
choice of toppings: fresh sliced mushrooms, olives,
green pepper, zucchini

In a measuring cup, sprinkle yeast over ¼ cup warm water. Let stand in warm place about 5 minutes until it dissolves or puffs.

METAL BLADE: Add Parmesan cheese, cut into 1-inch pieces, to work bowl; process until finely grated. Remove from bowl and set aside. Add flour and salt to work bowl. Pulse on/off to mix. With machine running, pour in yeast mixture. Pour in remaining water in a steady stream, only as fast as the flour absorbs it. All the water may not be needed to form a soft ball of dough. Process ball of dough for 20 seconds. Pour in olive oil and process 10 seconds. Place dough in a plastic bag and let rest for 25 minutes.

SHREDDING DISC: Cut mozzarella cheese to fit feed tube; using light pressure, shred. Set aside.

SLICING DISC: Slice toppings of your choice. Lightly grease a 14x10-inch (or similar size) baking pan. Dust with cornmeal. Pat the dough to fit the pan. Cover with plastic and let rise in warm place, free from drafts until almost double in bulk, about 25 minutes. Brush top lightly with olive oil. Bake in a preheated 400° oven about 5 minutes or just until crust begins to set. Remove from oven. Spread 1 cup sauce evenly over crust. Top with mozzarella and Parmesan cheeses and sliced toppings or your choice. Continue baking at 400° 20-25 minutes until crust is golden brown and cheese is bubbly.

Preparation: 15-20 minutes
Standing: allow 1-1½ hours for dough to rise
Baking: 25-30 minutes
Protein g/s: 20

Crusty Turnovers with Eggplant Cheese Filling

Serves 6

Looking for a new picnic idea? Make these the night before; reheat, uncovered, in a 350° oven 15-20 minutes until hot; wrap in foil and pack in an insulated bag. You don't have to wait for a picnic though; these turnovers will make any meal a treat.

Crust
1½ *tablespoons active dry yeast*
¼ *cup warm water (105°-115°)*
2 *tablespoons oil*
1 *teaspoon honey*
2¾ *cups whole wheat flour, measured scoop and level*
½ *teaspoon salt*
scant ½ *cup warm water*

In a measuring cup, sprinkle yeast over ¼ cup warm water. Let stand in warm place about 5 minutes until it dissolves or puffs. Add oil and honey.

METAL BLADE: Add flour and salt to work bowl. Pulse on/off to mix. With machine running, pour in yeast mixture and enough of the remaining warm water to form a soft ball of dough. Pour in the liquid in a steady stream to allow flour to absorb liquid. Process the ball of dough 20 seconds. Turn off machine and feel dough. It should be elastic, sticky and wet. If not, process 10 seconds longer. Add an additional tablespoon of flour; pulse on/off to coat dough for easy removal. Place dough in a plastic bag and let rest 20 minutes. Preheat oven to 475°. Punch down dough and divide into 6 portions. Form each portion into a ball and allow it to rest, covered for 5 minutes. On a lightly floured board, roll out each ball to a 7-inch circle. Brush each circle lightly with oil.

Filling
3 *ounces Parmesan cheese at room temperature*
8 *ounces mozzarella cheese, well-chilled*
1 *clove garlic*
1 *small onion*
1 *eggplant, about 1 pound*
8 *ounces mushrooms*
1 *small green pepper*
1 *can pitted whole black olives (6 ounces drained weight)*
1 *teaspoon dry leaf basil*
2 *teaspoons dry leaf oregano*
1 *6-ounce can tomato paste*
⅛ *teaspoon crushed red pepper*
salt and pepper to taste
2 *tablespoons oil*

Wipe work bowl dry with paper towel.

METAL BLADE: Add Parmesan cheese, cut into 1-inch pieces, to work bowl. Process until finely grated.

SHREDDING DISC: Cut mozzarella cheese to fit feed tube; shred with light pressure. Remove Parmesan and mozzarella cheeses from bowl and set aside.

METAL BLADE: Add garlic and onion, cut into pieces, to work bowl; process until finely chopped. In a large skillet, heat 2 tablespoons oil over medium-high heat. Add chopped onions and garlic. Cook until soft, about 3 minutes.

SLICING DISC: Cut eggplant into quarters, lengthwise. Place in feed tube and slice. Cut green pepper into quarters lengthwise, remove seeds; place in feed tube and slice. Stack mushrooms in feed tube; slice.

Add sliced eggplant, green pepper and mushrooms to skillet with onions. Cook over medium heat until vegetables are soft and liquid is evaporated, about 5-8 minutes. Watch carefully and stir to prevent sticking to the pan.

SLICING DISC: Add drained olives to feed tube; slice. Add olives to the skillet along with tomato paste, oregano, basil, crushed red pepper, salt and pepper. Stir gently to mix. Simmer, covered, 5 minutes. Remove from heat and allow to cool slightly. Stir in cheeses. Makes about 6 cups filling. Filling may be made ahead, covered and refrigerated. Remove from refrigerator and allow to warm to room temperature while you make the crust.

ASSEMBLY: Spread 1 cup filling over half of each circle, leaving a ½-inch border. Fold plain half over filling; press edges together to seal well. Roll ½-inch edge up and over, pinch to seal. Place turnovers on a baking sheet that has been greased and dusted with cornmeal. Prick tops well and brush lightly with oil. Bake 15-20 minutes or until golden brown.

Preparation: 10 minutes to prepare dough
           10 minutes to prepare filling
Cooking/Baking: 25-30 minutes
Standing: allow 30 minutes for dough to rest
       25-30 minutes to shape and fill
Protein g/s: 22

Onion Mushroom Pizza

Serves 8

A tossed green salad is perfect with this dish.

1 *Whole Wheat Buttermilk Pizza Crust or Cottage*
   Cheese Oil Crust (see index)
1¼-1½ *cups Basic Marinara Sauce (see index)*
½ *teaspoon dry leaf oregano*
8 *ounces mozzarella cheese, well-chilled*
1 *medium onion*
4 *ounces fresh mushrooms*
½ *medium green pepper*

Preheat oven to 400°. Spread sauce over pizza crust.

SHREDDING DISC: Cut mozzarella cheese to fit feed tube; using light pressure, shred. Spread cheese over sauce. Sprinkle on oregano.

METAL BLADE: Add onion, cut into 8 wedges, to work bowl. Pulse on/off to coarsely chop. Remove excess moisture by squeezing in paper towels. Arrange in an even layer over cheese.

SLICING DISC: Stack mushrooms in feed tube; slice. Cut green pepper into vertical strips, stack in feed tube and slice. Top pizza with sliced mushrooms and green pepper. Bake 20-25 minutes or until cheese is melted and bubbly.

Preparation: 10 minutes
Baking: 20-25 minutes
Protein g/s: Yeast Crust—13
              Cottage Cheese Oil Crust—13.5

Quiches, Pies, and Tarts

Whole Wheat Quiche Shell

1 shell

The egg white to glaze the shell is borrowed from the custard of the quiche. Return the unused portion to the custard.

1 cup whole wheat flour, measured scoop and level
⅛ teaspoon salt
¼ cup butter, well-chilled
1 egg
½ tablespoon lemon juice or ice water

METAL BLADE: Add flour and salt to work bowl, pulse on/off to mix. Add butter, cut into 1-inch pieces, pulse on/off until mixture resembles coarse meal. With machine running, add egg and lemon juice. Stop processing as soon as dough begins to form a ball.

Flatten dough into an 8-inch round circle and dust lightly with flour. Place between two sheets of wax paper. Using a rolling pin, roll from the center outward in all directions. Carefully peel off top sheet of wax paper to release dough, replace paper and turn over. Repeat with second side. Continue rolling out dough, lifting off wax paper and turning until a circle 11-inches in diameter is formed.

Roll the dough over the lightly floured rolling pin and gently lift over a 9-inch quiche pan with removable bottom. Unroll the dough into position and gently press into place. Trim excess by rolling the pin across the top of the pan.

Prick entire surface of the shell with a fork. To seal the dough against moisture and prevent it from becoming soggy, brush with slightly beaten egg white. Let dry uncovered in the refrigerator for about 1 hour. Glaze may also be set by placing the shell in a preheated 450° oven 2-3 minutes. Remove to rack and allow to cool before filling.

Preparation: 5 minutes
Standing: allow 1 hour for egg white glaze to dry in
     refrigerator or for heated shell to cool
Protein g/s: 4

Parmesan Quiche Shell

1 shell

We borrow part of an egg white from the custard of the quiche recipe to glaze the shell. Return unused portion to the custard.

1 ounce Parmesan cheese at room temperature
1 cup whole wheat flour, measured scoop and level
¼ cup butter, well-chilled
⅛ teaspoon salt
1 egg
½ tablespoon ice water

METAL BLADE: Add Parmesan cheese, cut into 1-inch pieces, to work bowl. Process until finely grated. Add flour and salt, pulse on/off to mix. Cut butter into 1-inch pieces, add to bowl. Pulse on/off until mixture has the consistency of coarse meal. With machine running, add egg and ice water. Stop processing as soon as dough begins to form a ball.

Flatten dough into an 8-inch round circle and dust lightly with flour. Place between two sheets of wax paper. Using a rolling pin, roll from the center outward in all directions. Carefully peel off top sheet of wax paper to release dough, replace paper and turn over. Repeat with second side. Continue rolling out dough, lifting off wax paper and turning until a circle 11-inches in diameter is formed.

Roll the dough over the lightly floured rolling pin and gently place over a 9-inch quiche pan with removable bottom. Unroll the dough into position and gently press into place. Trim excess by rolling the pin across the top of the pan.

Prick entire surface of the shell with a fork. To seal the dough against moisture and prevent it from becoming soggy, brush with slightly beaten egg white. Let dry uncovered in the refrigerator for about 1 hour. Glaze may also be set by placing the shell in a preheated 450° oven 2-3 minutes. Remove to rack and allow to cool before filling.

Preparation: 5 minutes
Standing: allow 1 hour for egg white glaze to dry in
     refrigerator or for heated shell to cool.
Protein g/s: 5.5

Sesame Seed Oil Crust

1 shell

It's difficult to make an oil crust that's as flaky as one made with solid fat. We think we've come close with this one. The whole sesame seeds add an interesting texture.

1¼ cups whole wheat flour, measured scoop and
　　level
¼ cup hulled white sesame seeds
½ teaspoon salt
5 tablespoons oil
6 tablespoons ice water
1-2 additional tablespoons ice water as needed

METAL BLADE: Add flour, sesame seeds and salt to work bowl. Pulse on/off to mix. In a measuring cup, stir together oil and ice water. With machine running, pour liquid through feed tube in a steady stream. Slowly sprinkle in additional water as needed to form a ball of dough. Stop processing as soon as dough begins to form a ball.

Flatten dough into an 8-inch round circle and dust lightly with flour. Place between two sheets of wax paper. Using a rolling pin, roll from the center outward in all directions. Carefully peel off top sheet of wax paper to release dough, replace paper and turn over. Repeat with second side. Continue rolling out dough, lifting off wax paper and turning until the circle is ⅛-inch thick and 2 inches larger than 9-inch pie plate.

Shaping for 9-inch pie plate: Grease a pie plate. Roll the dough onto the floured rolling pin and gently lift over plate and unroll it into position. Press gently into place. Do not stretch. Trim edge; leaving a 1-inch overhang. Fold edge under to build up all around; flute. Prick entire surface of the shell evenly with a fork. Refrigerate pastry 10-15 minutes. Meanwhile, preheat oven to 400°. Bake 10-12 minutes or until golden. Cool completely on wire rack.

Shaping for 9-inch quiche pan: Roll the dough onto the floured rolling pin and gently lift over pan and unroll it into position. Press into place. Trim excess by rolling the pin over the top of the pan. Prick the bottom of the crust evenly with a fork. Brush with slightly beaten egg white and allow to dry, uncovered, in the refrigerator for 1 hour. Glaze may also be set by placing the shell in a preheated 450° oven 2-3 minutes. Cool completely on wire rack.

Shaping for a 9-inch springform: Reserve ⅓ of the dough for the sides. Roll out remaining portion as directed above to fit the bottom of the pan. Press into place. Divide remaining dough into 4 pieces. Roll each into 6-6½ inch strips. Press into the sides of the pan to form an edge about 1-inch high. Join seams well. Glaze with egg white or bake as directed above.

Preparation: 10-15 minutes
Baking: 10-12 minutes
Chilling: 10-15 minutes with pie pan
　　　　　　 1 hour with quiche pan
Protein g/s: 3.5

Whole Wheat Oil Crust

1 shell, serves 8

If you are cutting down on your intake of butter, this is a good crust to substitute for our whole wheat quiche shell. It's a pliable dough and easy to work.

1¼ cups whole wheat flour, measured scoop and
　　level
½ teaspoon salt
⅓ cup oil
6 tablespoons cold milk

Pour the oil and milk into a measuring cup; do not stir.

METAL BLADE: Add flour and salt to work bowl. Pulse on/off to mix. With machine running, pour in liquid mixture. Stop machine as soon as all the liquid has been added. The dough will be crumbly and will not form into a ball. Carefully remove metal blade. Gather crumbs of dough into a ball and flatten into a 6-inch circle. Place between two sheets of wax paper and let rest 5 minutes.

With a rolling pin, roll from the center outward in all directions to form a 12-inch circle. Peel off top sheet of wax paper. Fold pastry in half and unfold carefully in pan. When using pie plate, fold edge under to build up all around; flute. If using quiche pan, trim excess by rolling the pin across the top of the pan. Prick entire surface of pie crust evenly with a fork to prevent crust from puffing.

BAKED CRUST: Refrigerate crust while preheating oven to 400°. Bake 12-15 minutes or until just brown. Remove to rack and allow to cool.

PARTIALLY BAKED CRUST: Refrigerate crust while preheating oven to 400°. Bake 8-10 minutes. Remove to rack and allow to cool.

GLAZED CRUST, unbaked: Brush surface of crust with slightly beaten egg white. Let dry uncovered in the refrigerator for about 1 hour. Glaze may also be set by placing the crust in a preheated 450° oven 2-3 minutes. Remove to rack and allow to cool.

Preparation: 10 minutes
Standing: 5 minutes
Baking: 8-15 minutes
Chilling: 15 minutes while preheating oven
Protein g/s: 3

Whole Wheat Filo Dough

16 sheets

Our fondness for spanakopita prompted us to develop this whole wheat version. While it is not as thin as machine-made filo sheets, it is a workable alternative for the nutrition conscious cook. Good results are achieved using a food processor for the dough and an Italian pasta machine to obtain thin sheets. The only draw-back is that the width of the dough is determined by the width of the pasta machine. For many uses it is not mandatory to have large sheets.

1¾ cups whole wheat flour, measured scoop and
    level
1 egg
2 teaspoons oil (olive oil is preferred, but not man-
    datory)
½ cup lukewarm water
1-5 tablespoons cornstarch
additional cornstarch for flouring

METAL BLADE: Place flour, egg and oil into the work bowl. Turn machine on and slowly pour in water. Continue processing until the dough forms a ball. This usually takes no more than 2-3 seconds after you have added the water. With the machine running, add the cornstarch one tablespoon at a time. Usually 2-3 are enough to make the dough smooth and elastic. The ball will break up and reform each time you add cornstarch. You will know that you have added enough when the dough is silky-smooth, moderately firm, but still very elastic. Another sure sign is a clean work bowl when you remove the dough. Coat with cornstarch.

Allow the dough to rest for about 10 minutes in a plastic bag. Divide into 8 pieces, kneading each one by hand for 30 seconds. Roll in cornstarch. Keep pieces in the plastic bag before working on them one at a time. Flatten dough with the ball of your hand and insert into the roller mechanism as follows, flouring with cornstarch as necessary.

1st Setting: Pass through once. Fold into thirds, and pass through again lengthwise. By now the piece should measure roughly 2 x 6 inches. Fold into thirds and pass through again lengthwise.

2nd Setting: Fold into thirds and pass through horizontally. Stretch by hand to make the piece as nearly square as possible.

3rd-5th Setting: Pass through each setting vertically without further folding. At this point, the dough should measure roughly 5 x 15 inches. Cut into 2 7½-inch long pieces and flour well.

6th Setting: Pass each piece through once without folding. Now each piece should measure roughly 5½ x 15 inches.

Now do a little horizontal stretching with the tips of your fingers, working out from the center to increase the width by 1½-2 inches. Flour well with cornstarch and place between sheets of wax paper until ready to use. Sheets should be used almost immediately because they dry out rapidly. They freeze well if layered between sheets of wax paper and sealed in a plastic bag.

Preparation: 40 minutes
Protein g/s: 4.5

Whole Wheat Pâte Brisée Crust

1 shell

This is the whole wheat version of a recipe originally developed by Cuisinarts, Inc. It makes an excellent shell for quiche or fruit pies because it does not absorb moisture easily. The dough may be used immediately or chilled if desired. If chilled, allow to stand at room temperature to soften slightly.

1⅓ cups whole wheat flour, measured scoop and
    level
½ teaspoon salt (less if salted butter is used)
½ cup butter, well-chilled
4 tablespoons ice water
1-2 tablespoons additional ice water as needed

METAL BLADE: Add flour and salt to work bowl. Pulse on/off to mix. Add butter, cut into 1-inch pieces. Pulse on/off until mixture resembles coarse meal. With machine running, pour ice water through feed tube in a steady stream. Stop processing as soon as dough begins to form a ball. Add additional water only as needed.

Flatten dough into an 8-inch round circle and dust lightly with flour. Place between two sheets of wax paper. Using a rolling pin, roll from the center outward in all directions. Carefully peel off top sheet of wax paper to release dough, replace paper and turn over. Repeat with second side. Continue rolling out dough, lifting off wax paper and turning until the circle is ⅛-inch thick and 2 inches larger than the pie plate or pan.

Roll the dough onto the rolling pin and gently lift over pan and unroll it into position. Press into place and trim edges.

For a 10¾-inch quiche pan, trim excess dough by rolling the pin across the top of the pan.

For a 9- or 10-inch pie plate, trim edge, leaving a 1-inch overhang. Fold edge under to build up all around; flute.

For a 9-inch springform pan, reserve ⅓ of dough. Roll remainder to a circle to fit the bottom of the pan. Divide the reserved dough into 4 pieces. Roll each into a 6-6½-inch strip. Press into the sides to form an edge about 1-inch high. Join seams well.

Prick entire surface of the shell evenly with a fork. Refrigerate pastry 10-15 minutes. Meanwhile, pre-

heat oven to 400°. Bake 12-15 minutes until golden. For a partially baked crust, bake for 7-10 minutes.

Preparation: 10-15 minutes
Baking: 12-15 minutes
Chilling: 10-15 minutes
Protein g/s: 2.5

Zucchini Tomato Quiche

Serves 6

Start this quiche 1 hour before baking time. Zucchini can be drained the night before to shorten preparation time.

1 9-inch Whole Wheat Quiche Shell, glazed with
    egg white, cooled
1 ounce Parmesan cheese at room temperature
¼ teaspoon salt
¼ teaspoon dry leaf oregano
pinch pepper
8 ounces zucchini, scrubbed
½ small onion
1 clove garlic
1½ teaspoons oil
4 ounces Swiss cheese, well-chilled
1 ounce sharp Cheddar cheese, well-chilled
1 firm tomato
2 eggs
1 cup half & half or milk
dash cayenne pepper

METAL BLADE: Add Parmesan cheese, cut into small pieces, to work bowl. Process until finely grated. Add salt, oregano and a few grindings of pepper. Pulse on/off to mix. Remove from bowl and set aside.

SLICING DISC: Cut zucchini to fit feed tube vertically, slice. Transfer to colander, sprinkle with 1½ teaspoons salt and allow to stand 1 hour. Drain zucchini, put in a tea towel and squeeze out the excess moisture.

METAL BLADE: Add garlic and onion, cut into 1-inch pieces, to work bowl. Pulse on/off until finely minced. In a skillet, heat 1½ teaspoons oil over medium heat, sauté onion and garlic until soft, 2-3 minutes. Remove from heat and allow to cool slightly. Preheat oven to 375°. Wipe bowl dry with paper towel.

SHREDDING DISC: Cut Swiss cheese to fit feed tube, shred. Remove and set aside. Cut Cheddar cheese to fit feed tube, shred. Remove and set aside.

SLICING DISC: Cut tomato to fit feed tube, slice using medium pressure.

METAL BLADE: Add eggs and dash of cayenne pepper to work bowl. With machine running, pour in half & half. Process until blended.

Spread Swiss cheese over the bottom of the pastry shell. Cover with zucchini, tomato slices and onions. Sprinkle with Parmesan mixture and top with Cheddar cheese. Place pastry shell on cookie sheet. Carefully pour in custard mixture. Bake on the center rack 30-35 minutes or until custard is firm, puffy and lightly browned. Remove from oven; slide onto a wire rack and allow to cool for 10 minutes. Cut into wedges and serve.

Preparation: 10 minutes
Baking: 30-35 minutes
Standing: 1 hour to drain zucchini
          10 minutes after baking
Protein g/s: 14

Harvest Vegetable Quiche

Serves 6

1 9-inch Whole Wheat Quiche Shell, glazed with
   egg white, cooled
4 ounces Swiss cheese, well-chilled
1 clove garlic
1 small onion
1 small zucchini, scrubbed
1 small carrot, pared
8 ounces fresh mushrooms
1 tablespoon oil
1 tablespoon butter
3 eggs
1 cup half & half or milk
½ teaspoon salt
½ teaspoon dry leaf thyme
pinch freshly ground white pepper

Preheat oven to 375°.

SHREDDING DISC: Cut cheese to fit feed tube, shred using light pressure. Spread evenly over the bottom of the pastry shell.

METAL BLADE: Add garlic and onion, cut into 1-inch pieces, to the work bowl. Pulse on/off until finely chopped. In a 10-inch skillet, heat 1 tablespoon oil over medium heat. Add garlic and onions, sauté until soft, 4-6 minutes.

SHREDDING DISC (or ¼-inch square julienne disc): Cut zucchini and carrot to fit feed tube horizontally, shred using moderate to firm pressure. Add vegetables to the skillet and sauté 3-5 minutes. Remove to a small bowl and set aside.

SLICING DISC: Stack mushrooms sideways in the feed tube, slice with firm pressure. In the same skillet, melt 1 tablespoon butter. Sauté mushrooms 5 minutes or until soft and liquid has evaporated.

METAL BLADE: Add eggs, salt, thyme and pepper to the work bowl. With machine running, pour in half & half. Process until blended. Spread onion/zucchini/carrot mixture over cheese. Top with mushrooms. Place pastry shell on a cookie sheet and carefully pour in custard. Bake on the center shelf 35-40 minutes or until custard is firm, puffy and lightly browned. Remove from the oven; slide onto a wire rack and allow to cool for 10 minutes. Cut into wedges and serve.

Preparation: 5-8 minutes
Cooking/Baking: 50-55 minutes
Standing: 10 minutes
Protein g/s: 14

Asparagus Quiche

Serves 6

As with all our quiches this goes well with a tossed green salad and thick slice of whole grain bread. Chill the trimmed portion of the asparagus and add to the salad.

1　9-inch Parmesan Quiche Shell, glazed with egg white and cooled
　　(When making the crust, process an additional ¾ ounce Parmesan cheese. Remove 3 tablespoons of the grated cheese from the work bowl and set aside for the filling.)
1　dozen fresh asparagus spears
4　ounces mild Cheddar cheese
¼　cup non-instant, non-fat milk powder
¾　cup milk
3　eggs
¼　teaspoon salt
pinch nutmeg

Steam asparagus until tender but crisp. Trim to 4½-inch lengths, set aside to drain and cool. Preheat oven to 375°.

SHREDDING DISC.: Cut Cheddar cheese to fit feed tube, shred. Spread over the bottom of the pastry shell. Wipe work bowl dry with paper towel.

METAL BLADE: Add milk powder to the dry work bowl. With machine running, pour in the milk through the feed tube in a slow steady stream. Add eggs and salt. Process until smooth. Stop machine and scrape down sides of bowl as needed.

Sprinkle Parmesan over the Cheddar cheese. Arrange asparagus spears in a pattern resembling the spokes of a wheel, with the tips toward the center. Place pastry shell on a cookie sheet and carefully pour in custard. Sprinkle on nutmeg. Bake on the center shelf for 5 minutes. Reduce the heat to 350° and continue baking 30-35 minutes or until custard is firm, puffy and lightly browned. Remove from the oven; slide onto a wire rack and allow to cool for 10 minutes. Cut into wedges and serve.

Preparation: 15 minutes
Cooking/Baking: 40-45 minutes
Standing: 10 minutes
Protein g/s: 17

Eggplant Quiche

Serves 6

1　9-inch Parmesan Quiche Shell, glazed with egg white, cooled
1　small onion
1　small green pepper
1　small eggplant, about 8 ounces
2-3　tablespoons olive or vegetable oil
¼　teaspoon salt
⅛　teaspoon freshly ground white pepper
½　teaspoon dry leaf oregano
2　teaspoons minced fresh basil or ½ teaspoon dry leaf basil
2　ounces Swiss cheese, well-chilled
3　eggs
¼　cup milk
pinch nutmeg

METAL BLADE: Add onion, cut into 1-inch pieces, to work bowl. Pulse on/off until finely minced. In a large skillet, heat oil over medium-high heat. Add onions and sauté 2-3 minutes. Preheat oven to 400°.

SLICING DISC: Seed and quarter green pepper. Stack into tube vertically, slice. Quarter eggplant lengthwise, stack into feed tube vertically, slice. Add green pepper and eggplant to the skillet. Sauté until vegetables are soft, lightly browned and liquid has evaporated, about 10 minutes. Add salt, pepper, oregano and basil. Stir gently to mix. Remove from heat and allow to cool slightly. Wipe work bowl dry with paper towel.

SHREDDING DISC: Cut Swiss cheese to fit feed tube, shred using moderate pressure. Spread evenly over the bottom of the quiche shell.

METAL BLADE: Add eggs to work bowl. With machine running, pour in ¼ cup milk and pinch nutmeg. Process until blended. Stir into eggplant mixture. Set pastry shell on a cookie sheet and carefully spoon in filling. Place on the center shelf of oven, turn temperature down to 375° and bake 25-30 minutes or until custard is firm and lightly browned. Remove from the oven; slide onto a wire rack and allow to cool for 10 minutes. Cut into wedges and serve.

Preparation: 15-20 minutes
Cooking/Baking: 40-45 minutes
Standing: 10 minutes
Protein g/s: 11.5

Mushroom Quiche

Serves 6

1 9-inch Whole Wheat Quiche Shell, glazed with
   egg white, cooled
1 ounce Parmesan cheese at room temperature
3 green onions
3 tablespoons butter or margarine
12 ounces fresh mushrooms
1 tablespoon fresh lemon juice
2 tablespoons Madeira
¼ teaspoon salt
3 eggs
2 tablespoons dry white wine or vermouth
1 cup half & half or milk
pinch salt, nutmeg, freshly ground white pepper

METAL BLADE: Add Parmesan cheese, cut into
1-inch pieces, to work bowl. Process until finely
grated. Remove from bowl and set aside. Add green
onions, cut into 2-inch lengths, to work bowl. Pulse
on/off until finely minced. Scrape down sides of
bowl as needed. In a medium skillet, heat butter
over medium-high heat. Add green onions and
sauté until soft, 3 minutes.

SLICING DISC: Stack mushrooms sideways in the
feed tube. Slice with firm pressure. Add mushrooms to the skillet and sauté about 2 minutes.
Add lemon juice, Madeira and salt. Cover the skillet
and simmer about 5 minutes. Uncover, turn the heat
to medium-high and cook to evaporate the liquid.
Stir mushrooms occasionally to prevent sticking.
Cook until mushrooms are lightly browned. Preheat
oven to 375°. Pour white wine into a 1-cup measure
and add enough half & half to make 1 cup liquid.

METAL BLADE: Add eggs to work bowl. With
machine running, pour in half & half, salt, nutmeg
and pepper. Process until blended. Sprinkle Parmesan cheese evenly over the bottom of the shell. Top
with mushroom mixture. Place shell on a cookie
sheet and carefully pour in custard. Bake on the
center shelf 35-40 minutes or until custard is firm,
puffy and lightly browned. Remove from oven; slide
onto a wire rack and allow to cool for 10 minutes.
Cut into wedges and serve.

Preparation: 5 minutes
Cooking/Baking: 45-50 minutes
Standing: 10 minutes
Protein g/s: 10

Cheese and Onion Quiche

Serves 6

Swiss cheese or Cheddar cheese may be used in this
quiche. Try it both ways!

1 9-inch Whole Wheat Quiche Shell, glazed with
   egg white, cooled
6 ounces sharp Cheddar or Swiss cheese, well-
   chilled
8 ounces onions
¼ teaspoon salt
pinch freshly ground white pepper
3 tablespoons butter or margarine
3 eggs
2 tablespoons white wine or vermouth
1 cup half & half or milk
pinch salt
freshly ground white pepper
pinch nutmeg

Preheat oven to 400°.

SHREDDING DISC: Cut cheese to fit feed tube,
shred. Remove from bowl and set aside.

SLICING DISC: Cut onions to fit feed tube; slice with
light pressure. In a skillet, heat butter over medium-
high heat. Add the onions and sauté until soft and
golden, 5-7 minutes. Add salt and pepper.

METAL BLADE: Add eggs to work bowl. With
machine running, pour in wine, half & half, salt,
pepper and nutmeg. Process until blended.

Spread half the cheese over the bottom of the pastry
shell. Spread onions over cheese. Top with remaining cheese. Set the pastry shell on a cookie sheet and
carefully pour in custard. Bake on the center shelf 5
minutes. Reduce the heat to 375° and continue baking 30-35 minutes or until custard is firm, puffy and
lightly browned. Remove from the oven; slide onto a
wire rack and allow to cool for 10 minutes. Cut into
wedges and serve.

Preparation: 10 minutes
Standing: 10 minutes
Cooking/Baking: 35-40 minutes
Protein g/s: 15.5

Garden Vegetable Quiche

Serves 6

By varying the vegetables, you can bake a different quiche each time you use this basic recipe. Keep the amount of onions constant and do not exceed the total amount of vegetables.

1 9-inch Parmesan Quiche Shell, glazed with egg white, cooled
tops from ½ bunch green onions
1 stalk celery
1 medium carrot, pared
2-3 ounces cauliflower flowerets
⅓ cup green peas
2 tablespoons oil
1 teaspoon Vegit vegetable seasoning
⅛-¼ teaspoon salt
4 ounces mild Cheddar cheese, well-chilled
¼ cup non-instant, non-fat dry milk
¾ cup milk
3 eggs

Preheat oven to 375°.

METAL BLADE: Add green onions, cut into 2-inch lengths, to the work bowl. Pulse on/off until finely minced. In a 10-inch skillet, heat oil over medium-high heat. Add green onions and sauté a minute or two.

SLICING DISC: Cut celery to fit feed tube vertically, slice. Cut carrot to fit feed tube vertically, slice. Stack cauliflower in feed tube, slice. Add vegetables to skillet and sauté 2-3 minutes. Add peas and continue cooking until vegetables are tender but crisp. Add Vegit and salt, stir gently to mix. Remove from heat and allow to cool slightly. Spoon vegetables into the pastry shell.

SHREDDING DISC: Cut cheese to fit feed tube, shred. Sprinkle over vegetables. Wipe work bowl dry with paper towel.

METAL BLADE: Add milk powder to dry work bowl. With machine running, pour in milk through the feed tube in a slow, steady stream. Add eggs. Process until smooth. Place pastry shell on a cookie sheet and carefully pour in custard. Place on center rack; reduce heat to 350°; bake 30-35 minutes or until custard is firm, puffy and lightly browned. Remove from the oven; slide onto a wire rack and allow to cool 10 minutes. Cut into wedges and serve.

Preparation: 15 minutes
Cooking/Baking: 40-45 minutes
Standing: 10 minutes
Protein g/s: 14.5

Pepper Olive Quiche

Serves 6

1 9-inch Whole Wheat Quiche Shell, glazed with egg white, cooled
1 medium green pepper, halved and seeded
1 teaspoon oil
6 ounces sharp Cheddar cheese, well-chilled
2 canned whole green chiles, rinsed and seeded
1 can pitted ripe olives, 6 ounces drained weight
3 eggs
1 cup half & half or milk
pinch salt, nutmeg, freshly ground white pepper

SLICING DISC: Wedge green pepper into feed tube, slice. In a small skillet, heat 1 teaspoon oil over medium heat. Cook green pepper until soft, 5 minutes. Remove from heat and allow to cool slightly. Preheat oven to 375°.

SHREDDING DISC: Cut Cheddar cheese to fit feed tube, slice. Remove from bowl and set aside.

METAL BLADE: Pat chiles dry with paper towel and add to work bowl. Pulse on/off until coarsely chopped.

SLICING DISC: Add drained olives to feed tube, slice. Spread half the Cheddar cheese over the bottom of the pastry shell. Top with chopped chiles, olives, green peppers and remaining cheese.

METAL BLADE: Add eggs, salt, nutmeg and pepper to work bowl. With machine running, pour in half & half. Process until blended. Place pastry shell on cookie sheet and carefully pour in custard. Bake on the center rack 30-35 minutes or until custard is firm, puffy and lightly browned. Remove from the oven; slide onto a wire rack and allow to cool 10 minutes. Cut into wedges and serve.

Preparation: 10 minutes
Cooking/Baking: 35-40 minutes
Standing: 10 minutes
Protein g/s: 16

Cauliflower Quiche

Serves 6

Curry powder flavors this spicy quiche.

1 9-inch Whole Wheat Quiche Shell, glazed with
   egg white, cooled
1 small head cauliflower, broken into flowerets
1 medium onion
1 large firm tomato
2 tablespoons oil
2 teaspoons curry powder
¼ teaspoon crushed red pepper (optional if you
   like it spicy!)
3 eggs
1 cup plain yogurt
¼ cup non-instant, non-fat milk powder
1 tablespoon whole wheat flour

Preheat oven to 375°.

SLICING DISC: Stack cauliflower flowerets in feed tube, slice. Steam the cauliflower until just tender. Remove from heat and allow to cool slightly.

METAL BLADE: Add onion, cut into 1-inch pieces, to work bowl. Pulse on/off until coarsely chopped. In a skillet, heat 2 tablespoons oil over medium heat. Add curry powder, cook 30 seconds. Watch carefully so curry does not burn. Add onions and sauté 3-5 minutes. Add tomato, cut into pieces, to work bowl. Pulse on/off to coarsely chop. Add to skillet and cook until soft and liquid has evaporated, 5-7 minutes. Remove from heat. Stir in crushed red pepper. Wipe work bowl dry with a paper towel. Add milk powder, yogurt and eggs to work bowl. Process 5 seconds. Stop machine, remove cover and scrape sides of bowl. Process 10-15 seconds until smooth.

Sprinkle 1 tablespoon flour over the bottom of the pastry shell. Arrange cauliflower slices in an even layer. Top with onion/tomato mixture. Place pastry shell on a cookie sheet and carefully pour in yogurt mixture. Bake on the center shelf 5 minutes. Reduce heat to 350° and continue baking 30-35 minutes or until custard is firm, puffy and lightly browned. Remove from the oven; slide onto a wire rack and allow to cool for 10 minutes. Cut into wedges and serve.

Preparation: 15 minutes
Chilling: cook cauliflower ahead and allow to cool
Cooking/Baking: 35-40 minutes
Standing: 10 minutes
Protein g/s: 10.5

Mexican Quiche

Serves 6

Serve with Spanish Rice (see index), tortillas and a salad.

1 9-inch Whole Wheat Quiche Shell, glazed with
   egg white, cooled
4 ounces Cheddar cheese, well-chilled
1 small onion
1 small red bell pepper, halved and seeded, may
   substitute green bell pepper
2-4 canned whole green chiles, rinsed and seeded
⅔ cup stewed tomato chunks, well-drained
½ teaspoon salt
1½ teaspoons chili powder
¼ cup non-instant, non-fat milk powder
1 cup milk
3 eggs
pinch cayenne pepper

SHREDDING DISC: Cut Cheddar cheese to fit feed tube, shred. Remove from bowl and set aside.

SLICING DISC: Cut onion in half to fit feed tube, slice. In a skillet, heat 2 tablespoons oil over medium-high heat. Add the onions and cook until soft, about 3 minutes. Stack bell pepper in feed tube, slice. Add pepper, tomato chunks, chili powder and salt to skillet. Stir gently to mix. Add green chiles, cut into ¼ inch strips, and continue to cook, stirring often, until vegetables are soft and liquid has evaporated, 5 minutes. Remove from heat and allow to cool. Preheat oven to 400°. Wipe work bowl dry with paper towel.

METAL BLADE: Add milk powder to the dry work bowl. With machine running, slowly pour in milk. Add eggs, salt and cayenne. Process until smooth, 3-5 seconds. Spread vegetable mixture evenly over the bottom of the pastry shell. Top with Cheddar cheese. Place the pastry shell on a cookie sheet and carefully pour in custard.

Bake on the center shelf 5 minutes. Reduce heat to 375° and continue baking 30-35 minutes or until custard is firm, puffy and lightly browned. Remove from the oven; slide onto a wire rack and allow to cool for 10 minutes. Cut into wedges and serve.

Preparation: 15 minutes
Cooking/Baking: 35-40 minutes
Standing: 10 minutes
Protein g/s: 15

Mozzarella Cheese Quiche

Serves 6

No cooking is required to prepare the filling for this quiche. It's simple and fast!

1   9-inch Whole Wheat Quiche Shell, glazed with
       egg white, cooled
2½ ounces Parmesan cheese at room temperature
2   sprigs fresh parsley
8   ounces mozzarella cheese, well-chilled
¼   teaspoon salt
pinch freshly ground white pepper
3   eggs
1   cup half & half or milk
pinch salt and pepper
⅛   teaspoon nutmeg

Preheat oven to 375°.

METAL BLADE: Add Parmesan cheese, cut into 1-inch pieces, to work bowl. Process until finely grated. Add parsley and process until finely minced.

SHREDDING DISC: Cut mozzarella cheese to fit feed tube, shred with light pressure. Remove the mozzarella cheese, parsley and Parmesan to a bowl and set aside. Add pinch ground pepper and ¼ teaspoon salt. Toss gently to mix.

METAL BLADE: Add eggs to work bowl. With machine running, pour in half & half, salt, pepper and nutmeg. Process until blended.

Spread cheese mixture over the bottom of the pastry shell. Place the pastry shell on a cookie sheet and carefully pour in custard. Bake on the center shelf 30-35 minutes or until custard is firm, puffy and lightly browned. Remove from the oven; carefully slide onto a wire rack and allow to cool for 10 minutes. Cut into wedges and serve.

Preparation: 10 minutes
Standing: 10 minutes
Cooking/Baking: 30-35 minutes
Protein g/s: 19

Sprout Quiche

Serves 6

1   9-inch Whole Wheat Quiche Shell, glazed with
       egg white, cooled
6   ounces sharp Cheddar cheese, well-chilled
1   small onion
1-2 stalks celery
8   ounces mung bean sprouts
1   teaspoon dry leaf thyme
1   tablespoon whole wheat flour
¼   teaspoon salt
3   eggs
1   cup half & half or milk
pinch freshly ground white pepper
pinch salt
pinch nutmeg
1-2 tablespoons oil

Preheat oven to 400°.

SHREDDING DISC: Cut cheese to fit feed tube, shred. Remove from bowl and spread evenly over the bottom of the pastry shell.

SLICING DISC: Cut onion and celery to fit feed tube vertically, slice. In a skillet, heat 1-2 tablespoons oil over medium-high heat. Add onion and celery. Cook until onion is soft, 3-5 minutes. Add sprouts and cook until just limp. Remove from heat, drain off excess liquid. Add salt and thyme. Sprinkle in flour, toss to mix.

METAL BLADE: Add eggs to work bowl. With machine running, pour in half & half, pepper, salt and nutmeg. Process until blended. Place pastry shell on a cookie sheet. Spread sprout mixture over bottom of pastry and carefully pour in custard.

Bake on the center shelf 5 minutes. Reduce heat to 375° and continue baking 30-35 minutes or until custard is firm, puffy and lightly browned. Remove from the oven; slide onto a wire rack and allow to cool for 10 minutes. Cut into wedges and serve.

Preparation: 10 minutes
Cooking/Baking: 40-45 minutes
Standing: 10 minutes
Protein g/s: 16.5

Zucchini and Green Chile Quiche

Serves 6

This quiche can be quickly assembled and put into the oven if the zucchini is drained the night before or earlier in the day.

1 9-inch *Whole Wheat Quiche Shell, glazed with egg white, cooled*
¾ *pound zucchini, scrubbed*
4 *ounces Cheddar cheese, well-chilled*
2 *ounces Monterey Jack cheese, well-chilled*
½ *small onion*
2 *canned whole green chiles, rinsed and seeded*
1 *tablespoon whole wheat flour*
1 *tablespoon oil*
3 *eggs*
1 *cup half & half or milk*
pinch *salt and freshly ground white pepper*

SHREDDING DISC: Cut zucchini to fit feed tube vertically, shred. Remove to a colander, sprinkle with ½ tablespoon salt and let stand 30 minutes. Drain, put in a tea towel and squeeze out the excess moisture. Wipe the bowl dry with paper towels. Cut the cheeses to fit feed tube, shred using light pressure. Remove to a small bowl, toss to mix. Set aside.

SLICING DISC: Cut onion to fit feed tube, slice using light pressure. In a skillet, heat 1 tablespoon oil over medium heat. Sauté onions until soft, 3-5 minutes. Stir in zucchini and cook for several minutes. Sprinkle in flour. Stir to mix. Remove from heat. Preheat oven to 400°.

METAL BLADE: Dry chiles with paper towels and add to work bowl. Pulse on/off until coarsely chopped. Spread half the cheese over the bottom of the pastry shell. Top with zucchini/onion mixture. Sprinkle on the chiles and the remaining cheese. Add eggs to work bowl. With machine running, pour in half & half, salt and pepper. Process until blended.

Place pastry shell on a cookie sheet and carefully pour in custard. Bake on the center shelf 15 minutes. Reduce the heat to 350° and continue baking 20 minutes or until custard is firm, puffy and lightly browned. Remove from the oven; slide onto a wire rack and allow to cool for 10 minutes. Cut into wedges and serve.

Preparation: 15 minutes

Cooking/Baking: 40-45 minutes
Standing: 30 minutes to drain zucchini
10 minutes to cool
Protein g/s: 16

Parmesan Rice Crust Pie

Serves 6

If you have reserved green chile sauce from the Double-Decker Tortilla Bake, use it in place of green taco sauce.

1½ *cups cooked brown rice, slightly cooled (about ⅔ cup raw)*
1 *egg*
2 *ounces Parmesan cheese, at room temperature*
3 *ounces sharp Cheddar cheese, well-chilled*
3 *ounces Monterey Jack cheese, well-chilled*
1 *small zucchini, scrubbed*
1 *can pitted black olives, drained weight 6 ounces*
¼ *cup green taco sauce or any enchilada-type sauce*
cornmeal *for dusting pie plate*

Preheat oven to 375°.

METAL BLADE: Add Parmesan cheese, cut into 1-inch pieces, to work bowl. Process until finely grated. In a medium mixing bowl, combine rice, Parmesan cheese and egg. Stir to mix well. Lightly oil a 9-inch Pyrex pie plate; dust with cornmeal. Press rice mixture firmly into the bottom and sides of the plate to form a crust. Bake 15 minutes.

SHREDDING DISC: Cut Cheddar and Monterey Jack cheeses to fit feed tube, shred. Remove from bowl and set aside.

SLICING DISC: Cut zucchini to fit feed tube vertically, slice. Stack drained olives in feed tube, slice. Spread the taco sauce over the hot crust. Sprinkle on about ¾ of the cheese and all the zucchini and olives. Top with remaining cheese. Bake 20 minutes longer or until cheese is bubbly and zucchini is tender. Cut into wedges and serve. This may be baked ahead and reheated, covered, in a 350° oven 15-20 minutes.

Preparation: 15 minutes
Cooking/Baking: 35 minutes
allow time to cook rice
Protein g/s: 13

Bean and Chile Cheese Pie

Serves 8

The filling can be prepared ahead of time. Spoon into the crust just before baking.

1 *Whole Wheat Oil Crust, unbaked; fit into a 9-inch pie plate. Refrigerate crust while making filling.*
1 *medium onion*
1 *small green pepper*
1 *4-ounce can whole green chiles, rinsed and seeded*
1½ *cups cooked kidney beans, cold (¾ cup dry)*
½ *cup corn*
2 *teaspoons dry leaf oregano*
¾ *teaspoon ground cumin*
¾ *teaspoon chili powder*
¼ *teaspoon salt*
dash cayenne pepper
6 *ounces Monterey Jack cheese, well-chilled*
4 *ounces sharp Cheddar cheese, well-chilled*
1 *egg*
¼ *cup milk*
1 *medium tomato, sliced into thin rounds*
oil for cooking vegetables

Preheat oven to 350°.

METAL BLADE: Add onion, cut into 1-inch pieces, to work bowl. Pulse on/off until finely chopped. Remove from bowl and set aside. Add green pepper, cut into 1-inch pieces, to work bowl. Pulse on/off until finely chopped. Remove from bowl and add to onions. Dry the chiles with paper towels; add to work bowl; pulse on/off until coarsely chopped. Add to vegetables.

In a 2 or 3-quart saucepan, heat 1 tablespoon oil over medium-high heat. Add onions, pepper and chiles and sauté until soft, 3-4 minutes. Stir in oregano, cumin, chili powder, salt and pepper. Remove from heat.

METAL BLADE: Add kidney beans to work bowl. Pulse on/off until coarsely chopped. Add beans and corn to cooked vegetables. Stir gently to mix.

SHREDDING DISC: Cut Monterey Jack and Cheddar cheese to fit feed tube; shred. Remove from work bowl and set aside. Toss to mix.

METAL BLADE: Add egg to work bowl. With machine running, pour in milk. Stop machine as soon as all the milk has been added. Stir into bean mixture along with ⅓ of the cheese. Spread ⅓ of the cheese over the bottom of the crust. Spoon in filling, gently press down. Arrange sliced tomatoes over top and sprinkle with remaining cheese. Bake, uncovered, 35-40 minutes or until filling is firm and top is lightly browned. Remove from the oven; slide onto a rack and allow to cool 10 minutes. Cut into wedges and serve.

Preparation: 15 minutes
Cooking/Baking: 40-45 minutes
        allow time to cook and cool beans
Standing: 10 minutes
Protein g/s: 15.5

Pie Valaisan

Serves 8

This double crust pie with a filling of Swiss cheese, leeks, potatoes and apples is an elegant company dish.

2 *recipes Whole Wheat Pâte Brisée Crust (see index), refrigerated until ready for use*
4 *medium potatoes*
1 *pound Swiss, Gruyere or Emmenthal cheese*
1 *pound leeks*
2-3 *tablespoons oil*
salt
pepper
paprika
18 *large fresh basil leaves or 1½ teaspoons dry leaf basil*
2-3 *tart apples, Pippin, Granny Smith or Newtons*
Glaze: 1 egg beaten with ¼ cup water

Scrub potatoes, cook in water to cover until tender. Cool and peel.

SHREDDING DISC: Cut cheese to fit feed tube, shred. Remove from bowl and set aside. Wash leeks taking care to remove all the grit between the leaves. Cut into 2-inch lengths. In a skillet, heat oil over medium heat. Add leeks and sauté until soft but not browned, 8-10 minutes. Season to taste with pepper, salt and paprika. Remove from heat and set aside.

Roll out ⅔ of the pastry dough into a circle ⅛-inch thick and 14-15 inches in diameter. Fit into a well-greased 9½-inch springform pan. The edges will hang over the sides. Prick the bottom evenly with a fork and brush with oil. Slice potatoes thinly and layer in the bottom of the pan. Sprinkle on paprika, salt and pepper.

METAL BLADE: Add basil leaves to work bowl. Pulse on/off until finely chopped. Sprinkle ⅓ of the basil over the potatoes. Top with cheese and season with another ⅓ of the basil and paprika. Peel, core and quarter apples.

SLICING DISC: Add apple quarters to feed tube, slice. Arrange over cheese. Season with remaining basil, salt and pepper. Roll out remaining pastry and cover top of pie. Trim and roll under overhang. Pinch edges together and flute. Brush with egg glaze. Prick entire surface to allow steam to escape. Decorate with leftover pastry dough if desired. Bake at 350° for 30-40 minutes or until lightly browned.

Preparation: 30 minutes
            allow time to cook and cool potatoes
Cooking/Baking: 1-1¼ hours
Protein g/s: 22

South-of-the-Border Tortilla Pie

Serves 6

Flour tortillas make a thin but sturdy shell for this quick-to-assemble pie. The preparation of the filling takes full advantage of your processor.

vegetable shortening to grease pan
3 8-inch flour tortillas, room temperature, purchased or freshly made
oil
1 large clove garlic
4 green onions
1 7-ounce can whole green chiles, rinsed and seeded
1½ cups cooked garbanzo beans, cooled (about ¾ cup dry or 1 15-ounce can, drained)
6 ounces Monterey Jack cheese, well-chilled
2 eggs
⅔ cup low-fat yogurt
¼ teaspoon paprika
½ teaspoon chili powder
½ teaspoon salt
¼ teaspoon pepper
avocado slices, garnish, optional

Preheat oven to 400°. Grease a 9-inch pie plate. Cut 2 tortillas in half and arrange in pan to form the sides of the "crust" (as illustrated). Place remaining tortilla in the center. Brush with oil and bake 5-7 minutes or until lightly browned. Remove shell from oven; reduce temperature to 325°.

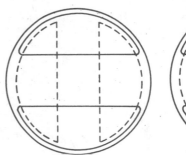 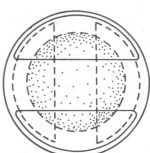

METAL BLADE: Add garlic and onions, cut into 2-inch lengths, to the work bowl. Pulse on/off until finely minced. Remove to a large mixing bowl. Pat chiles dry with paper towels; add to work bowl. Pulse on/off until coarsely chopped. Add to onions. Add garbanzo beans to work bowl. Pulse on/off until coarsely chopped. Add to onions.

SHREDDING DISC: Cut cheese to fit feed tube; shred. Add to mixing bowl with beans and toss to mix.

METAL BLADE: Add eggs to work bowl and process until well-beaten. Pour over bean mixture. Stir in yogurt, paprika, chili powder, salt and pepper. Mix gently. Pour into the tortilla shell. Bake on the center shelf 45-50 minutes or until filling is firm and lightly browned. Remove to a wire rack and allow to cool 10 minutes. Cut into wedges; garnish with avocado slices and serve.

Preparation: 15 minutes
Cooking/Baking: 50-55 minutes
            allow time to cook garbanzo beans
Standing: 10 minutes
Chilling: allow time to cool garbanzo beans
Protein g/s: 16.5

Spanakopita

Serves 8

Our own whole wheat dough makes this one of our most requested company dishes. Prepare the filling and refrigerate before proceeding with the dough. We use Danish Feta because it is less salty. If you use Bulgarian or Greek Feta, add a bit more ricotta cheese to reduce the salty taste.

2 10-ounce packages frozen spinach or 2 pounds fresh spinach leaves, cooked and squeezed dry
1 large onion
3 tablespoons olive oil
1 pound Danish Feta cheese
16 ounces ricotta cheese or well-drained cottage cheese
4 eggs
⅛ teaspoon pepper
1 teaspoon dry dill weed
¾ cup butter or margarine
1 recipe Whole Wheat Filo Dough (see index) or 1 pound purchased filo dough
1 teaspoon anise seeds
additional butter if using purchased dough

METAL BLADE: Add onion, cut into 1-inch pieces, to work bowl. Pulse on/off until finely chopped.

In a skillet, heat oil over medium heat. Add onions and sauté until limp and transparent. Do not let the onions brown. Remove from heat and set aside. Rinse Feta cheese under cold water to remove some of the salt. Pat dry with paper towel.

METAL BLADE: Add Feta, broken into 2-inch pieces, to work bowl and process with ricotta cheese to break Feta into small chunks. Add eggs, pepper and dill. Process until blended. Remove to a large bowl. Add spinach to work bowl. Pulse on/off until finely chopped, but not puréed. Add spinach and onions to cheese mixture. Stir to mix well. Cover and refrigerate while making filo dough.

Preheat oven to 375°. In a saucepan, melt butter over low heat. Butter an 8¾ x 13¼-inch Pyrex baking dish. Layer one half of the filo sheets on the bottom of the dish, brushing the top of each sheet with butter. Since the sheets don't fit the size of the pan, overlap and alternate as necessary. Spoon on all the spinach mixture and continue layering until all the sheets are used. Generously butter the top filo layer. Sprinkle with anise seeds. Bake, uncovered, 25-35 minutes or until golden.

Preparation: 1 hour, allow an additional hour if making filo dough
Cooking/Baking: 25-35 minutes
Protein g/s: 25.5

Mushroom Cheese Tart

Serves 6

1 Whole Wheat Pâte Brisée Crust, partially baked in a 9½-inch springform pan (see index)
12 ounces fresh mushrooms
2 tablespoons butter or margarine
1½ cups ricotta cheese
¼ cup sour cream
¼ cup yogurt
2 eggs
¼ teaspoon nutmeg
salt and pepper to taste

Preheat oven to 350°.

SLICING DISC: Wipe mushrooms with a damp paper towel. Stack sideways into the feed tube; slice using firm pressure. In a skillet, heat butter over medium-high heat. Add mushrooms and sauté until cooked and liquid has evaporated. Remove from heat and allow to cool slightly.

METAL BLADE: Add ricotta cheese, sour cream, yogurt, eggs, salt and pepper to the work bowl. Combine with 2-3 on/off pulses. Stop machine, scrape down sides of bowl and continue to process until smooth and well-blended.

Reserve a spoon or two of the mushrooms for garnish. Combine remaining mushrooms and cheese mixture in a mixing bowl. Spoon into pastry shell. Top with reserved mushrooms. Place on a cookie sheet and bake 30-40 minutes or until custard is firm, puffy and lightly browned. Remove from the oven; slide onto a wire rack and allow to cool for 10 minutes. Cut into wedges and serve.

Preparation: 15 minutes
Cooking/Baking: 40-50 minutes
Standing: 10 minutes
Protein g/s: 12.5

Cottage Cheese and Onion Tart

Serves 6

For years we made this recipe using ricotta cheese and sour cream. In an effort to cut down on fat intake, we switched to cottage cheese and yogurt. We leave the choice up to you.

1 9-inch *Whole Wheat Pâte Brisée Crust, glazed with egg white and cooled*
2 ounces Parmesan cheese, at room temperature
4 medium onions
3 tablespoons oil
1 cup cottage cheese or ricotta cheese
½ cup yogurt or sour cream
2 eggs
¼ teaspoon nutmeg
½ teaspoon salt
pepper
additional nutmeg for sprinkling on the top

Preheat oven to 350°.

METAL BLADE: Add Parmesan cheese, cut into 1-inch pieces, to the work bowl. Process until finely grated. Remove from bowl and set aside. Add onions, cut into 1-inch pieces, to work bowl. Pulse on/off until coarsely chopped.

In a skillet, heat oil over medium-high heat. Add onions and sauté until limp and dry. Remove from heat and allow to cool slightly.

METAL BLADE: Add cottage cheese (ricotta) to work bowl. Process 30-45 seconds or until smooth. Stop machine and scrape down sides of bowl occasionally. Add yogurt (sour cream), eggs, nutmeg, salt, pepper, and Parmesan cheese. Combine with 3-4 on/off pulses. Stop machine, remove work bowl cover and add ⅔ of the onions. Pulse on/off just to mix in. Spoon in the pastry shell. Top with reserved onions. Bake 30-45 minutes or until lightly browned. Remove from oven; slide onto a wire rack and allow to cool for 10 minutes. Cut into wedges and serve.

Preparation: 10 minutes
Standing: 10 minutes
Cooking/Baking: 40-55 minutes
Protein g/s: 14.5

Danish Feta and Spinach Tart

Serves 6

We use Danish Feta as it is less salty than the Bulgarian or Greek variety.

1 *Whole Wheat Pâte Brisée Crust, partially baked in a 9½-inch springform pan (see index)*
3 ounces *Cheddar cheese, well-chilled*
1 medium onion
2 tablespoons oil
8 ounces *Danish Feta cheese, rinsed in cold water*
10 ounces *low-fat cottage cheese*
2 eggs
1 10-ounce package *frozen spinach or leaves from 1 pound fresh spinach, cooked, squeezed dry*
5 tablespoons *sour cream, optional*
paprika

SHREDDING DISC: Cut Cheddar cheese to fit feed tube, shred. Remove from bowl and set aside.

METAL BLADE: Add onion, cut into 1-inch pieces, to the work bowl. Pulse on/off until finely chopped. In a skillet, heat oil over medium-high heat. Add onions and sauté until soft and transparent. Remove from heat and allow to cool. Preheat oven to 350°. Add Feta, cottage cheese, and eggs to the work bowl. Process until smooth. Add the spinach, pulse on/off only until just mixed. Do not overprocess to purée the spinach.

Carefully remove the metal blade from the work bowl. Add onions to the work bowl and mix with a wooden spoon. Spoon into the pastry shell. Dot with sour cream, if used. Sprinkle generously with paprika and top with Cheddar cheese. Bake on the center shelf 30-35 minutes or until filling is firm.

Remove from the oven; slide onto a wire rack and allow to cool for 10 minutes. Cut into wedges and serve.

Preparation: 10 minutes
Cooking/Baking: 35-40 minutes
Standing: 10 minutes
Protein g/s: 19.5

Crêpes and Enchiladas

Whole Wheat Crêpes

9 crêpes

Crêpe batters can be made the night before and refrigerated, covered. Should the batter become too thick, thin with a bit of milk. We bake the crêpes in a well-seasoned 7-8-inch crêpe pan or in a SilverStone non-stick pan.

1½ *cups skim milk*
2 *tablespoons oil*
½ *teaspoon salt*
2 *eggs*
1 *cup whole wheat pastry flour or*
  whole wheat flour, measured scoop and level
additional oil for baking

In a large measuring cup, combine milk, oil, salt and eggs.

METAL BLADE: Add flour to work bowl. With machine running, pour in liquid in a slow, steady stream. Process until well-blended. Pour batter into a mixing bowl, cover and refrigerate at least 1 hour so that the milk and flour will be well-combined.

Pour about 1 tablespoon of oil in the pan and heat until it is hot. Tip out the oil. Return pan to a moderately high heat. Pour about 3 tablespoons batter in the pan and roll it around quickly until the bottom of the pan is completely covered. Tip out excess batter. The crêpe should be as thin as possible. When the batter appears dull and the edges begin to brown, flip it onto the other side. Continue to cook until second side is lightly browned. Remove the crêpe from the pan and discard. The first crêpe absorbs the oil from the pan.

It is not necessary to add any more oil to the pan after the first crêpe is made. The oil in the batter will prevent the crêpe from sticking. As each crêpe is baked, stack on a clean tea towel. The side of the crêpe that cooks first is the outside because it usually looks more attractive.

Preparation: 5 minutes
Standing: 1 hour
Cooking: 20-30 minutes
Protein g/s: 4.5

Cornmeal Crêpes

18 crêpes

Directions are given for a 6-inch crêpe pan. Adjust amount of batter when using a larger pan.

1½ *cups skim milk*
3 *eggs*
2 *tablespoons melted butter or margarine*
¼ *teaspoon salt*
½ *cup whole wheat flour, measured scoop and level*
½ *cup cornmeal, measured scoop and level*
additional oil for baking

In a large measuring cup, combine milk, eggs, butter and salt.

METAL BLADE: Add whole wheat flour and cornmeal to work bowl. Pulse on/off to mix. With machine running, pour in liquid in a slow, steady stream. Process until well-blended. Pour batter into a mixing bowl, cover and refrigerate at least 1 hour so that the milk and flour will be well-combined.

Pour about 1 tablespoon of oil in the pan and heat until it is hot. Tip out the oil. Return pan to a moderately high heat. Pour about 2 tablespoons batter in the pan and roll it around quickly until the bottom of the pan is completely covered. Tip out excess batter. The crêpes should be as thin as possible. When the batter appears dull and the edges begin to brown, flip it onto the other side. Continue to cook until second side is lightly browned. Remove the crêpe from the pan and discard. The first crêpe absorbs the oil from the pan.

It is not necessary to add any more oil to the pan after the first crêpe is made. The butter in the batter will prevent the crêpe from sticking. As each crêpe is baked, stack on a clean tea towel. The side of the crêpe that cooks first is the outside because it usually looks more attractive.

Preparation: 5 minutes
Standing: 1 hour
Cooking: 20-30 minutes
Protein g/s: 2.5

Herb Crêpes

18 crêpes

Fresh herbs flavor this whole wheat crêpe. Directions are given for a 6-inch crêpe pan. Adjust the amount of batter when using a larger pan.

1½ cups skim milk
2 eggs
2 tablespoons melted butter or margarine
1 cup whole wheat flour, measured scoop and level
1 tablespoon fresh chives
1 tablespoon fresh parsley
generous pinch dry leaf basil or 1 fresh basil leaf
generous pinch dry leaf oregano
¼ teaspoon salt
additional oil for baking

In a large measuring cup, combine milk, eggs and butter.

METAL BLADE: Add flour, chives, parsley, basil, oregano and salt to work bowl. Pulse on/off until herbs are finely chopped. With machine running, pour in liquid in a slow, steady stream. Process until well-blended. Pour batter into a mixing bowl, cover and refrigerate at least 1 hour so that the milk and flour will be well-combined.

Pour about 1 tablespoon of oil in the pan and heat until it is hot. Tip out the oil. Return pan to a moderately high heat. Pour about 2 tablespoons batter in the pan and roll it around quickly until the bottom of the pan is completely covered. Tip out excess batter. The crêpe should be as thin as possible. When the batter appears dull and edges begin to brown, flip it onto the other side. Continue to cook until second side is lightly browned. Remove the crêpe from the pan and discard. The first crêpe absorbs the oil from the pan.

It is not necessary to add any more oil to the pan after the first crêpe is made. The oil in the batter will prevent the crêpe from sticking. As each crêpe is baked, stack on a clean tea towel. The side of the crêpe that cooks first is the outside because it usually looks more attractive.

Preparation: 5 minutes
Standing: 1 hour
Cooking: 20-30 minutes
Protein g/s: 2.5

Buckwheat Crêpes

18 crêpes

Directions are given for a 6-inch crêpe pan. When using a larger pan, add more batter.

1 cup skim milk
2 eggs
¼ teaspoon salt
2 tablespoons melted butter or margarine
1 cup minus 2 tablespoons buckwheat flour, measured scoop and level
additional oil for baking

In a large measuring cup, combine milk, eggs, salt and butter.

METAL BLADE: Add flour to work bowl. With machine running, pour in liquid in a slow, steady stream. Process until well-blended. Pour batter into a mixing bowl, cover and refrigerate at least 1 hour so that the milk and flour will be well-combined.

Pour about 1 tablespoon of oil in the pan and heat until it is hot. Tip out the oil. Return pan to a moderately high heat. Pour about 2 tablespoons batter in the pan and roll it around quickly until the bottom of the pan is completely covered. Tip out excess batter. The crêpe should be as thin as possible. When the batter appears dull and the edges begin to brown, flip it onto the other side. Continue to cook until second side is lightly browned. Remove the crêpe from the pan and discard. The first crêpe absorbs the oil from the pan.

It is not necessary to add any more oil to the pan after the first crêpe is made. The oil in the batter will prevent the crêpe from sticking. As each crêpe is baked, stack on a clean tea towel. The side of the crêpe that cooks first is the outside because it usually looks more attractive.

Preparation: 5 minutes
Standing: 1 hour
Cooking: 20-30 minutes
Protein g/s: 2

Whole Wheat Sesame Crêpes

9-10 crêpes

Sesame seeds, ground into a fine flour, add a slightly nutty flavor to these crêpes. Directions are given for a 7-8-inch pan.

1 cup whole wheat pastry flour or
   whole wheat flour, measured scoop and level
½ cup hulled white sesame seeds
1⅓ cups skim milk
½ teaspoon salt
2 eggs
2 tablespoons oil
additional oil for baking

In a large measuring cup, combine milk, salt, eggs and oil.

METAL BLADE: Add flour and sesame seeds to work bowl; process until the sesame seeds are finely ground, 2-3 minutes. With machine running, pour in liquid in a slow, steady stream. Process until well-blended. Pour batter into a mixing bowl, cover and refrigerate at least 1 hour so that the milk and flour will be well-combined.

Pour 1 tablespoon of oil in the pan and heat until it is hot. Tip out the oil. Return pan to a moderately high heat. Pour about 3 tablespoons batter in the pan and roll it around quickly until the bottom of the pan is completely covered. Tip out excess batter. The crêpes should be as thin as possible. When the batter appears dull and the edges begin to brown, flip it onto the other side. Continue to cook until second side is lightly browned. Remove the crêpe from the pan and discard. The first crêpe absorbs the oil from the pan.

It is not necessary to add any more oil to the pan after the first crêpe is made. The oil in the batter will prevent the crêpe from sticking. As each crêpe is baked, stack on a clean tea towel. The side of the crêpe that cooks first is the outside because it usually looks more attractive.

Preparation: 5 minutes
Standing: 1 hour
Cooking: 20-30 minutes
Protein g/s: 9 crêpes—6
              10 crêpes—5.5

Feta Spinach Crêpes

8 crêpes

1 recipe Whole Wheat Crêpes or Whole Wheat
   Sesame Crêpes (see index)
1 medium onion
2 tablespoons oil
8 ounces ricotta cheese or
   cottage cheese, well-drained
4 ounces Danish Feta cheese, well-rinsed
2 eggs
1 10-ounce package frozen leaf spinach, cooked,
   cooled, squeezed dry
½ teaspoon dry dill weed
⅛ teaspoon ground nutmeg
¼ teaspoon salt, as needed
yogurt and paprika for garnish, optional

METAL BLADE: Add onion, cut into 1-inch pieces, to work bowl. Pulse on/off until coarsely chopped. In a skillet, heat oil over medium-high heat. Add onions and sauté until soft and transparent, 3-5 minutes. Remove from heat and set aside. Add Feta cheese, cut into small chunks, ricotta cheese (or cottage cheese) and eggs to work bowl. Process until smooth. Stop machine, add spinach, onions, dill, nutmeg and salt. Pulse on/off until spinach is finely chopped.

Place about ¼ cup of filling in each crêpe. Roll the crêpes and place in a well-greased or buttered 8½ x 13½-inch or similar size baking dish. Cover with aluminum foil. With a knife, gently make about a dozen small slits in the foil to allow some of the steam to escape. Bake at 350° for 15-20 minutes. Garnish with yogurt and paprika.

Preparation: 10-15 minutes
Cooking/Baking: 35 minutes
Protein g/s: 12.5

Feta Cheese Broccoli Crêpes

8 crêpes

1 recipe Whole Wheat Crêpes (see index)
flowerets from 1 bunch broccoli, about 3-3½ cups
1 medium onion
2-3 tablespoons oil
8 ounces Danish Feta cheese
8 ounces ricotta cheese
2 eggs
yogurt and paprika for garnish

Trim broccoli, peel off tough outer portion. Blanch in salted water and allow to drain.

METAL BLADE: Add onion, cut into 1-inch pieces, to work bowl. Pulse on/off until finely chopped. In a skillet, heat oil over medium-high heat. Add onions and sauté until soft and transparent, 3-5 minutes.

Remove from heat and set aside. Add Feta cheese, broken into small chunks, and ricotta cheese to work bowl. Process until smooth. Add eggs and onions; combine with 2-3 on/off pulses.

Place about ⅓ cup of filling in each crêpe. Roll the crêpes and place in a greased 8½ x 13½-inch or similar size baking dish. Tuck broccoli flowerets, stem portion first, in both end of the crêpes. Set aside remaining flowerets. Cover with aluminum foil. With a knife, gently make about a dozen small slits in the foil to allow some of the steam to escape.

Bake at 350° for 15-20 minutes. Top each crêpe with a dab of yogurt and a sprinkle of paprika. Garnish with extra broccoli flowerets.

Preparation: 10-15 minutes
Cooking/Baking: 20-25 minutes
Protein g/s: 15.5

Fragrant Herbed Manicotti

10 crêpes

Contrary to popular belief, manicotti isn't authentically Italian but an Italian-American invention. In our version, crêpes encase a filling that is aromatically seasoned with herbs. Serve with whole wheat French bread and a tossed green salad.

1 recipe Whole Wheat Sesame Crêpes (see index)
4 ounces Parmesan cheese, room temperature
2 ounces provolone cheese, well-chilled
2 cups ricotta cheese or
    well-drained cottage cheese
1 egg
½ bunch chives, about 1 ounce
½ cup fresh basil leaves, packed, omit if fresh
    leaves are not available
¼ cup fresh parsley leaves
1-1¼ cups Basic Marinara Sauce (see index) or
    similar tomato-based sauce

Prepare crêpes according to directions, set aside. Crêpes may be made earlier in the day or the night before.

METAL BLADE: Add Parmesan cheese, cut into 1-inch pieces, to work bowl. Process until finely grated.

SHREDDING DISC: Cut provolone cheese to fit feed tube; shred.

METAL BLADE: Add ricotta or cottage cheese to work bowl with cheeses and combine with 2-3 on/off pulses. Add chives, cut into 2-inch pieces, along with basil and parsley. Pulse on/off until finely chopped.

Preheat oven to 350°. Place about ¼ cup filling in each crêpe. Roll the crêpes and arrange, in a single layer, in a well-buttered baking dish. Cover with aluminum foil. With a knife, gently make about a dozen small slits in the foil to allow some of the steam to escape. Bake 15-20 minutes. Heat marinara sauce, pour over crêpes and serve.

Preparation: 25 minutes
Cooking/Baking: 25 minutes
Protein g/s: 15

Fresh Corn Enchiladas

Serves 6

High in protein and tasty—a winning combination. Exprience with chiles will allow you to determine how many you wish to use.

1½ cups fresh or frozen corn, cooked and drained
1½-2 medium onions
2-4 canned whole green chiles, rinsed and seeded
¼-½ teaspoon salt
¼ teaspoon ground pepper
½ teaspoon ground cumin
½ teaspoon chili powder
pinch cayenne pepper
12 ounces Monterey Jack cheese, well-chilled or
     mild Cheddar cheese, well-chilled
1 cup low-fat cottage cheese
1¼ cups Enchilada Sauce (see index) or
     1 10-ounce can purchased enchilada sauce
12 Corn Tortillas (see index) or
     purchased tortillas
oil for frying tortillas
3 sprigs fresh coriander, optional

METAL BLADE: Add onions, cut into 1-inch pieces, to work bowl. Pulse on/off until chopped medium-fine. In a skillet, heat oil over medium-high heat. Add onions and sauté until soft and transparent, 3-5 minutes. Dry chiles with paper towels, cut into thirds and add to work bowl. Pulse on/off until coarsely chopped. Add chiles and corn to skillet; sauté 1-2 minutes. Stir in salt, pepper, cumin, chili powder and cayenne. Remove from heat.

SHREDDING DISC: Cut Monterey Jack or Cheddar cheese to fit feed tube; shred. Remove about 1½ cups of cheese and set aside for topping.

METAL BLADE: Add cottage cheese to work bowl and process with remaining cheese until smooth. In a large bowl, combine cheese and corn mixtures. Pour enchilada sauce into a shallow dish. Preheat oven to 350°.

Heat ⅛-inch oil in a frying pan over medium heat. Fry tortillas only long enough to soften. Do not allow them to get too crisp or they will be hard to roll. Rest the fried tortilla briefly on a paper towel to absorb excess oil; then dip into enchilada sauce. Fill with ⅓ cup of filling, roll up and arrange in a single layer in a long, well-greased baking dish. Spoon on remaining sauce, taking care to cover the edges of the tortillas. Top with reserved cheese. Bake, un-

covered, 15-20 minutes, or until hot. Garnish with fresh coriander.

Preparation: 20-minutes
Cooking/Baking: 25-30 minutes
Protein g/s: 23

Sonora-Style Enchiladas

Serves 4-6

These mouth-watering stacked enchiladas originated in the Mexican province of Sonora. Serve with Spanish Rice or Refried Beans (see index) and a salad.

6 ounces Monterey Jack cheese, well-chilled
6 ounces Cheddar cheese, well-chilled
1 can whole pitted black olives, drained weight 6
     ounces
8-10 green onions, 6 ounces
1¼ cups Enchilada Sauce (see index) or
     1 10-ounce can purchased enchilada sauce
¾ cup tomato sauce
12 Corn Tortillas (see index) or
     purchased corn tortillas
oil for frying tortillas

SHREDDING DISC: Cut Monterey Jack and Cheddar cheeses to fit feed tube; shred. Remove from bowl, toss to mix and set aside.

SLICING DISC: Drain olives, stack in feed tube; slice. Remove from work bowl and set aside.

METAL BLADE: Add green onions, cut into 1-inch pieces, to work bowl; pulse on/off until finely minced. Or cut into ¼-inch pieces with a sharp knife. Grease a large baking dish and set aside. Assemble stacks using 6 tortillas for 2 stacks; or 4 tortillas for 3 stacks. Divide filling ingredients into portions so that each layer will have roughly the same amount of filling. Stack and fill the tortillas on the baking dish as they are fried and sauced. In a shallow dish, stir together enchilada sauce and tomato sauce. Preheat oven to 350°.

Heat ⅛-inch oil in a frying pan over medium heat. Fry tortilla only long enough to soften. Do not allow tortilla to crisp. Rest the fried tortilla briefly on a paper towel to absorb excess oil; then dip into enchilada sauce. Place in the prepared baking dish and fill with portions of the cheese, olives and green onions. Continue frying, saucing and layering until all tortillas are stacked, ending with a tortilla topped with about 1 ounce cheese, ½ ounce green onions and a sprinkling of olives. Bake, uncovered, 10 minutes or until heated through. To serve, cut 4-tortilla stacks in half; 6-tortilla stacks in quarters.

Preparation: 15 minutes
Cooking/Baking: 20 minutes
Protein g/s: 4 servings—26
           6 servings—17.5

Bean and Raisin Enchiladas

Serves 6

Serve these slightly sweet and sour enchiladas with Spanish Rice (see index) and a tossed green salad with avocados.

⅔ cup raisins
2 medium onions
½ large bell pepper, seeded
2 canned whole green chiles, rinsed and seeded
2-3 tablespoons oil
2½ cups cooked pinto beans (1¼ cups dry)
½ teaspoon salt
1 8-ounce can tomato sauce
1½ teaspoons chili powder, increase for a spicier
    dish
¼ teaspoon ground cumin
3-4 tablespons Japanese rice vinegar or
    other mild vinegar
1¼ cups Enchilada Sauce (see index) or
    1 10-ounce can purchased enchilada sauce
12 Corn Tortillas (see index) or purchased tortillas
oil for frying tortillas
4-6 ounces Monterey Jack cheese, well-chilled

Plump raisins by boiling 1-2 minutes in water to cover over high heat. Drain and set aside.

METAL BLADE: Add onions, cut into 1-inch pieces, to work bowl. Pulse on/off until coarsely chopped. Add bell pepper, cut into 1-inch pieces; pulse on/off

until coarsely chopped. Dry chiles with paper towels, cut into thirds; add to work bowl. Pulse on/off until coarsely chopped.

In a 3 or 4-quart saucepan or dutch oven, heat oil over medium-high heat. Add onion mixture and sauté until onions are soft and transparent, 4-5 minutes. Stir in pinto beans, salt, tomato sauce, chili powder, cumin, vinegar and raisins. Cover and simmer 3-4 minutes, stirring occasionally. Pour enchilada sauce into a shallow dish. Preheat oven to 350°.

Heat ⅛-inch oil in a frying pan over medium heat. Fry tortillas only long enough to soften. Do not allow them to get too crisp or they will be hard to roll. Rest the fried tortilla briefly on a paper towel to absorb excess oil; then dip into enchilada sauce. Fill with ¼ cup of filling, roll up and arrange in a single layer in a long, well-greased baking dish. Spoon on remaining sauce, taking care to cover the edges of the tortillas.

SHREDDING DISC: Cut Monterey Jack cheese to fit feed tube; shred. Sprinkle evenly over the top of the enchiladas. Bake, uncovered, 15-20 minutes or until hot.

Preparation: 15 minutes
Cooking/Baking: 30 minutes
Protein g/s: 17

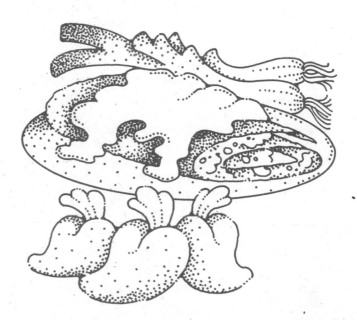

Enchiladas Coloradas

Serves 6

Homemade corn tortillas surround a low-fat filling of cottage cheese and Cheddar cheese, flavored with black olives and green onions.

8-10 green onions, about 6 ounces
2 tablespoons oil
1 cup low-fat cottage cheese
8 ounces Cheddar cheese, well-chilled
1 can pitted black olives, drained weight 6 ounces
1¼ cups Enchilada Sauce (see index) or
    1 10-ounce can purchased enchilada sauce
1 8-ounce can tomato sauce
12 Corn Tortillas (see index) or
    purchased tortillas
oil for frying tortillas

METAL BLADE: Add green onions, cut into 1-inch lengths, to work bowl. Pulse on/off until finely minced. Stop machine and scrape down sides of bowl as needed. Or, with a sharp knife, cut green onions into ¼-inch pieces. In a 2 or 3-quart saucepan, heat oil over medium-high heat. Add green onions and sauté until just beginning to soften, 30-60 seconds. Remove from heat. Add cottage cheese to work bowl. Process until smooth. Carefully remove metal blade and insert shredding disc.

SHREDDING DISC: Cut Cheddar cheese to fit feed tube; shred into cottage cheese.

SLICING DISC: Drain olives; wedge into feed tube; slice. Reserve a few sliced olives for garnish. Combine cheese-olive mixture with onions in the saucepan. Stir gently to mix well. In a shallow dish, stir together enchilada and tomato sauces. Preheat oven to 350°.

Heat ⅛-inch oil in a frying pan over medium heat. Fry tortillas only long enough to soften. Do not allow them to get too crisp or they will be hard to roll. Rest the fried tortilla briefly on a paper towel to absorb excess oil; then dip into enchilada sauce. Fill with ¼ cup of filling, roll up and arrange in a single layer in a long well-greased baking dish. Spoon on remaining sauce, taking care to cover the edges of the tortillas. Bake, uncovered, 15-20 minutes or until hot. Garnish with reserved olives.

Preparation: 15 minutes
Cooking/Baking: 25-30 minutes
Protein g/s: 17

Enchilada Sauce

6½ cups

In Mexico, this red chile sauce is made without tomato sauce. In our vegetarian version, tomato sauce provides added flavor. We suggest that you taste the chiles before proceeding with the recipe to be sure they're mild enough. Unless you like your sauce really hot, remove all the seeds from the chiles. The capsaicin that makes peppers hot is concentrated in and near the seeds.

4 ounces dried mild red chiles*, no substitute for
    dry chiles
4 cups hot water
2 8-ounce cans tomato sauce
2 tablespoons tomato paste
2-3 large cloves garlic, pressed
¼ teaspoon ground cumin
1 teaspoon salt
1 teaspoon dry leaf oregano, crumbled
cayenne pepper to taste, optional

Preheat oven to 375°. Place chiles on a cookie sheet and toast 3-5 minutes. Watch carefully so chiles do not burn—you won't like the flavor! Remove from oven and allow to cool. Remove and discard stems, seeds and pulp.

METAL BLADE: Add chiles, torn into small pieces, to work bowl. Process until ground to a coarse powder. With machine running, pour in part of the water: 1 cup for small machines, 1½-2 cups for larger capacity machines. Process until mixture is thick. Pour in tomato sauce, tomato paste, garlic, cumin, salt and oregano. Process until mixed.

Carefully remove work bowl and pour mixture into a large mixing bowl; stir in remaining water. Taste sauce and add cayenne a pinch or two at a time until desired degree of hotness is reached. Freeze in containers holding 1¼-1½ cups sauce. Makes enough sauce for 4-5 recipes of enchiladas.

*A mixture of ancho, Anaheim or California chiles, New Mexico mild, pasilla, with equal parts medium red and very dark red—almost black chiles. In some parts of the country, California or New Mexico chiles are packaged in plastic as loose string chiles.

Preparation: 15 minutes

Tofu

Scrambled Tofu

Serves 4

Our friend, Donna Howard, a public health nutritionist, contributes this versatile dish. It's ideal for breakfast or brunch. When served with rice and a tossed salad, it's a quick supper dish.

1 ounce Parmesan cheese, room temperature
3 tablespoons oil
1 medium onion
½ pound fresh mushrooms
¼ teaspoon ground turmeric
¼ teaspoon ground cumin
1 tablespoon Madras curry powder
1 block tofu, 20-22 ounces, drained
1 tablespoon tamari sauce
¼-½ teaspoon salt
1 tomato, diced

METAL BLADE: Add Parmesan cheese, cut into small pieces, to work bowl; process until finely grated. Remove and set aside.

SLICING DISC: Quarter onion and insert vertically into feed tube; slice, using light pressure. In a large skillet, heat oil over medium heat. Add onions and sauté 2-3 minutes. Stir in turmeric, cumin and curry powder. Continue cooking 1 minute to bring out the flavors of the spices.

Stack mushrooms in feed tube; slice. Add to skillet and sauté until soft. Break tofu into large chunks and add to skillet. Stir in tamari and salt. Cook for 1-2 minutes, stirring and breaking tofu into smaller chunks. Add diced tomatoes and cook until soft and ingredients are hot. Sprinkle in Parmesan and toss to mix.

Preparation: 5-8 minutes
Cooking: 10 minutes
Protein g/s: 12

Tofu with Asparagus and Mushrooms

Serves 4

Serve this quickly prepared dish often when asparagus is in season.

1½ pounds asparagus
4 green onions
8 ounces fresh mushrooms
3 tablespoons oriental sesame oil
1 piece fresh ginger root, 1 x ¼-inch
2 large cloves garlic, pressed
1 block tofu, 20-22 ounces, drained, cut into 1-inch squares
2 tablespoons low-sodium soy sauce or 1-2 tablespoons regular soy sauce

Snap off the lower tough part of the asparagus stalk, discard. Blanch spears in lightly salted water, drain. Cut into 1½-inch pieces and set aside. Cut green onions into 1-inch lengths and set aside.

SLICING DISC: Stack mushrooms sideways into feed tube; slice using medium pressure. Remove from work bowl and set aside. Wipe work bowl dry.

METAL BLADE: Cut ginger root into small pieces. Turn machine on and drop in ginger pieces; process until finely minced. In a frying pan, heat oil over medium heat. Add ginger and garlic; sauté 45-60 seconds or until the aroma starts to permeate the kitchen. Add mushrooms and continue cooking until just done. Stir in onions; sauté 1 minute. Add asparagus, tofu and soy sauce. Continue cooking, stirring gently until tofu is hot and has absorbed the flavor of the seasonings, 3-4 minutes.

Preparation: 10 minutes
Cooking: 10 minutes
Protein g/s: 10

Stir-Fry Teriyaki Tofu

Serves 4-6

Serve this tasty dish with simple steamed greens—cabbage, spinach or won bok (Chinese cabbage), and brown rice. Long rice, also known as cellophane noodles or bean threads, and dried bean curd are available in oriental markets.

1 package long rice, about 2 ounces
4 ounces dried bean curd, round-type, broken into
   3-inch lengths
2 tablespoons cornstarch
2 tablespoons water
1 piece fresh ginger root, about 1-inch square
1 clove garlic
3 tablespoons sherry
2 tablespoons brown sugar
¼ cup soy sauce
1 tablespoon oriental sesame oil
¼ teaspoon dry mustard
1 block firm tofu, 20-22 ounces, drained, cut into
   1-inch squares
8 ounces fresh mushrooms
1 15-ounce can bamboo shoots, drained
1 tablespoon oil
½ cup water
4 ounces snow peas

Early in the day or at least 60 minutes before cooking time, place long rice and bean curd in separate bowls. Pour in warm water to cover and let stand to soften. Drain. Combine cornstarch and 2 table-spoons water; set aside.

METAL BLADE: Cut ginger into small pieces. With machine running, drop in ginger and garlic and process until finely minced. In a measuring cup, combine ginger, garlic, sherry, brown sugar, soy sauce, sesame oil and dry mustard. Place tofu squares in a shallow dish, pour in marinade and let stand at least 30 minutes. Gently tilt pan occasion-ally to allow marinade to cover tofu squares.

SLICING DISC: Wedge mushrooms in feed tube; slice. Remove from bowl and set aside. Insert bamboo shoots vertically; slice. Heat a 4 or 5-quart dutch oven over medium heat for 30 seconds. Add 1 table-spoon oil and heat 15-30 seconds longer. Add mushrooms; stir-fry about 1 minute. Add bamboo shoots, long rice, bean curd and ½ cup water. Cover pot and bring mixture to a boil; lower heat and simmer 5 minutes. Place snow peas in a bowl, pour in boiling water to cover and let stand 30 seconds. Drain and cover to keep warm.

Add tofu cubes and marinade to the pot and stir gently to mix. Cover and cook 2 minutes. Give the cornstarch mixture a quick stir and add to the pot. Toss to mix. Add snow peas. Serve with brown rice.

Preparation: 15-20 minutes
Standing: 1-1½ hours
Cooking: 8-10 minutes
Protein g/s: 4 servings—24.5
             6 servings—16

Tofu with Fresh Mushrooms

Serves 4

Serve with a grain or milk product to complement the protein in the tofu. This is especially nice with Chinese Style Fried Rice (see index).

2 tablespoons oil
2 medium carrots, peeled
8 ounces fresh mushrooms
1 piece fresh ginger root, 1 x ¼-inch
1 large clove garlic, pressed
1 block tofu, drained, 20-22 ounces, cut into 1-inch
   cubes
2-3 tablespoons low sodium soy sauce or
     1-2 tablespoons regular soy sauce
4 green onions, cut into 1-inch lengths
salt to taste

SLICING DISC: Cut carrots to fit feed tube vertically; slice. In a large frying pan, heat oil over medium heat. Add carrots and sauté 4-5 minutes. Stack mushrooms sideways into feed tube; slice with firm pressure. Add to carrots and mix. Sauté 3-4 minutes or until mushrooms are tender.

METAL BLADE: Cut ginger into small pieces. With machine running, drop in ginger pieces and process until finely grated. Stir ginger and garlic into vegetable mixture. Gently stir in tofu cubes and soy sauce. Cook 2-3 minutes to heat tofu. Add green onions, toss gently to mix.

Preparation: 10 minutes
Cooking: 10 minutes
Protein g/s: 10

Tofu with Sprouts and Black Mushrooms

Serves 4

A steamed green vegetable and brown rice completes this quick meal.

1 package dry black mushrooms, ¾ ounce, about 15 mushrooms
1 block firm tofu, drained, 20-22 ounces
2 green onions
1 small onion
2 tablespoons oil
1 can bamboo shoots, drained weight 8.5 ounces
12 ounces mung bean sprouts
3 tablespoons soy sauce
1 tablespoon cornstarch
1 teaspoon oriental sesame oil
1 tablespoon sherry
1 teaspoon brown sugar
fresh coriander for garnish, optional

Soak mushrooms in warm water 15-20 minutes to soften. Rinse under running water to remove dirt. Squeeze out excess water and cut each mushroom into quarters. Set aside. Cut tofu crosswise into thirds. Place in a shallow pan and add water to cover. Bring water to a boil and cook, covered, 5 minutes. Carefully remove to a colander and allow to drain. When tofu is cool enough to handle, cut into 1-inch cubes. Parboiling produces a firmer tofu.

METAL BLADE: Add green onions, cut into 1-inch lengths, to work bowl. Pulse on/off until finely minced. Remove metal blade, leaving green onions in the bowl.

SLICING DISC: Cut onion to fit feed tube; slice with light pressure. In a large saucepan or 4-quart dutch oven, heat 2 tablespoons oil over medium-high heat. Add onions and sauté 1 minute. Cut bamboo shoots to fit feed tube; slice. Add bamboo shoots and mushrooms to pan with onions and sauté 1 minute. Stir in sprouts and ½ cup water. Cover pan and cook over medium heat 4 minutes or until sprouts are tender. Gently stir in tofu and cook 2 minutes. Stir together soy sauce, cornstarch, sesame oil, sherry and brown sugar. Pour over tofu/sprout mixture, stirring to mix well. Cook 15 seconds. Garnish with fresh coriander and serve.

Preparation: 10 minutes
Cooking: 15 minutes
Protein g/s: 13

Tofu with Carrots and Zucchini

Serves 4

Serve with brown rice or whole grain bread.

2-3 tablespoons oil
2 large carrots, peeled
1 medium zucchini, scrubbed
4 green onions
1 piece fresh ginger root, 1 x ¼-inch
1 large clove garlic, pressed
1½ cups mung bean sprouts
1 block tofu, drained, 20-22 ounces, cut into 1-inch cubes
2-3 tablespoons low-sodium soy sauce or 1-2 tablespoons regular soy sauce
½ teaspoon Vegit seasoning
salt to taste

JULIENNE DISC or SHREDDING DISC: Cut carrots to fit feed tube horizontally; shred. In a large frying pan, heat oil over medium heat. Add carrots and sauté 30 seconds. Cut zucchini to fit feed tube horizontally and shred. Add to pan with carrots and continue sautéing while you process remaining ingredients.

METAL BLADE: Add green onions, cut into 1-inch lengths, to work bowl. Pulse on/off until chopped medium-fine and stir into vegetables. Wipe work bowl dry. Cut ginger into small pieces and with machine running, drop in ginger pieces and process until finely grated. Add to pan along with garlic and bean sprouts and sauté 1 minute. Gently stir in tofu, soy sauce, Vegit seasoning and salt. Continue cooking 2-3 minutes or until tofu is heated through. Serve immediately.

Preparation: 10 minutes
Cooking: 10 minutes
Protein g/s: 11

Tofu Squares with Mushroom Tomato Sauce

Serves 6

Serve with brown rice and a steamed green vegetable.

2 blocks firm tofu, 20-22 ounces each, drained
1 slice whole wheat bread
3 green onions
2 stalks celery
1 teaspoon Spike seasoning or
    similar vegetable broth seasoning
dash pepper
5 eggs
½ cup skim milk
1 tablespoon oil
3 ounces Swiss cheese, well-chilled
8 ounces fresh mushrooms
5 large ripe tomatoes
1 tablespoon oil
1 teaspoon dry leaf oregano, crumbled
¼ teaspoon salt

Break tofu into small pieces and place in a saucepan. Pour in 2 cups water. Cover and bring water to a boil; reduce heat and simmer 2 minutes. Line a colander with several thicknesses of cheesecloth. Pour the tofu into the colander. Rinse with cold water. Using a potato masher or large spoon, press tofu firmly against the bottom and sides of the colander to remove excess water. Empty the crumbled tofu into a mixing bowl and allow to cool slightly. Preheat oven to 350°.

METAL BLADE: Add bread, torn into pieces, to work bowl. Process until coarsely chopped. Add green onions and celery, cut into 1-inch pieces; pulse on/off until coarsely chopped. Turn machine off and add seasoning, pepper, eggs, milk and 1 tablespoon oil. Combine with 3-4 on/off pulses. Pour into bowl with tofu, stir to mix well. Spread tofu mixture over the bottom of a well-oiled 8 x 8-inch baking pan. Gently press into an even layer. Cover with foil and bake for 35-40 minutes, until firm but not dry. While tofu is baking, prepare sauce. Wash and dry work bowl.

SHREDDING DISC: Cut Swiss cheese to fit feed tube; shred using light pressure. Remove from bowl and set aside.

SLICING DISC: Stack mushrooms sideways into feed tube; slice with firm pressure; remove from bowl and set aside.

METAL BLADE: Add tomatoes, cut into quarters, to work bowl; pulse on/off until coarsely chopped. Heat 1 tablespoon oil over high heat in a medium saucepan. Add mushrooms and sauté for 1 minute. Add tomatoes with liquid, oregano and salt. Cover and cook 2 minutes. Remove cover, turn heat to medium and cook 15-20 minutes until slightly thickened. Remove from heat, add cheese and stir until melted. Cut tofu into squares and top with mushroom tomato sauce.

Preparation: 15 minutes
Cooking/Baking: 35-40 minutes
Protein g/s: 23.5

Vegetable Tofu Curry

Serves 4

This spicy dish is delicious served over brown rice. When using Madras or Indian curry powder, decrease the amount slightly as this mixture tends to be a bit more spicy. DO NOT use the food processor to grind your own curry powder. The turmeric stains the lexan bowl a bright yellow and the hard spices produce deep scratches.

2 cloves garlic
1 small onion
2 tablespoons each butter and oil
2 tablespoons curry powder* or
    purchased curry powder
8 ounces string beans
1 small cauliflower, broken into flowerets
1 bunch broccoli, about 1 pound, trimmed and broken into flowerets
3 carrots, peeled
2 zucchini, scrubbed
1 block tofu, drained, 20-22 ounces, cut into 1-inch squares
½ teaspoon salt
1 teaspoon brown sugar
1 cup yogurt

METAL BLADE: Add garlic and onion, cut into 1-inch pieces, to work bowl. Pulse on/off until finely minced. In a 5- or 6-quart dutch oven, heat butter and oil over medium to medium-high heat. Add garlic and onions and sauté until clear but not brown, 3-4 minutes. Stir in curry powder, reduce heat to low and cook 15 minutes, stirring frequently to avoid burning and sticking. Pour in ½ cup water, cover and continue cooking 15 minutes. Meanwhile prepare and steam each vegetable separately to maintain individual textures. Do not overcook, vegetables should be tender-crisp.

SLICING BLADE: Cut carrots to fit feed tube vertically; slice. Remove from bowl. Cut zucchini to fit feed tube vertically and slice; remove from bowl. Place broccoli stalks into feed tube vertically; slice. Snap string beans into 1-2-inch lengths. Add cooked vegetables, tofu, salt, brown sugar and yogurt to spice mixture. Mix gently, cover and simmer about 10 minutes.

*To make your own curry powder, in a heavy-duty blender or electric spice grinder grind:
2 teaspoons ground turmeric
½ teaspoon ground ginger
3 whole cloves
2 cardamon seeds
½ stick cinnamon, broken into pieces
¼-½ teaspoon crushed red pepper
½ teaspoon white peppercorns
½ teaspoon whole mustard seed
½ teaspon cumin seed
2 teaspoons whole coriander seed

Preparation: 5-10 minutes
Cooking: 40 minutes
Protein g/s: 12

Sweet and Sour Tofu

Serves 4

The surprise ingredients in the sauce are tomato, honey and lemon. Serve with brown rice topped with toasted sesame seeds.

4 tablespoons oil
2 large onions
2 large carrots, peeled
2 stalks celery, trimmed
1 large green pepper, quartered and seeded
2 8-ounce cans tomato sauce
½ cup water
4-5 tablespoons honey, or to taste
2½ tablespoons lemon juice, or to taste
1 block tofu, 20-22 ounces, drained

In a dutch oven heat oil over medium heat. As the vegetables are chopped and sliced, add to dutch oven and sauté.

METAL BLADE: Add onions, cut into 1-inch pieces, to work bowl; pulse on/off until chopped medium-fine. Add to dutch oven and begin sautéing.

SLICING DISC or THIN SLICING DISC: Cut carrots to fit feed tube vertically; slice using light pressure. Add to onions. Cut celery to fit feed tube vertically; slice; add to dutch oven. Wedge pepper quarters into feed tube vertically; slice; add to vegetables. Continue cooking until vegetables are tender-crisp. Stir in tomato sauce, water, honey and lemon juice. Simmer until sauce is thick, about 10 minutes. Cut tofu into 1-inch cubes and add to sauce. Cover and cook 1-2 minutes or until tofu is heated. Do not allow tofu to boil vigorously or the cubes will break apart. Stir gently to mix.

Preparation: 10 minutes
Cooking: 15-20 minutes
Protein g/s: 10

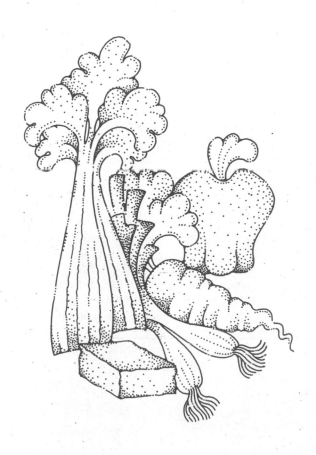

Side Dishes

Vegetables

Braised Eggplant with Garlic

Serves 4

You can remove the garlic before serving or leave it in. The choice is yours.

1 *pound long, thin eggplant, if not available substitute round eggplant*
4 *medium cloves garlic*
4 *tablespoons oil*
1 *tablespoon soy sauce*
1 *tablespoon dry sherry*
1 *teaspoon brown sugar*

Wash and trim eggplant, do not peel.

SLICING DISC: Cut eggplant into lengths to fit feed tube horizontally, slice. If using round eggplant, quarter or cut into pieces to fit feed tube, slice. In a small dish, combine soy sauce, sherry and sugar. Crush each garlic clove and discard peel.

Heat a 10-inch skillet or 12-inch wok over medium heat for 30 seconds. Add oil and heat for 30 seconds. Add garlic and eggplant, reduce heat to low. Cook, stirring frequently, for about 15 minutes or until lightly browned. Pour in soy sauce mixture, stir to mix. Cover pan and cook for 10 minutes until liquid has evaporated and eggplant is just tender. Serve hot.

Preparation: 5 minutes
Cooking: 30 minutes

Snow Peas with Bamboo Shoots

Serves 2-3

Delicate snow peas are flavored with brown bean sauce or "mein see." The sauce can be purchased from stores specializing in oriental foods. The unused portion will keep for months in a jar in the refrigerator.

1 *tablespoon oil*
1 *small onion*
1 *can bamboo shoots, 8.5 ounces, drained weight*
8 *ounces snow peas, also called edible pea pods*
½ *cup water*
2 *teaspoons sherry*
1 *tablespoon brown bean sauce*
1 *teaspoon cornstarch*
oriental sesame oil

SLICING DISC: Cut onion in half, stack in feed tube, slice. In a skillet, heat 1 tablespoon oil over medium-high heat. Add onions, stir-fry 3-4 minutes until onions are soft. Cut drained bamboo shoots to fit feed tube, slice. Add to onions and continue to cook 1-2 minutes. Add snow peas, toss to mix in. In a measuring cup, stir together water, sherry, brown bean sauce and cornstarch. Pour into a vegetable mixture, stir gently to mix. Reduce heat to low, cover skillet and cook 2-3 minutes until snow peas are crispy-tender. Do not overcook. Add a few drops sesame oil. Serve immediately.

Preparation: 5 minutes
Cooking: 6-8 minutes

Ratatouille

Serves 6-8

A version of a popular vegetable dish. Serve hot or at room temperature. For a picnic treat, stuff halved pita bread with ratatouille and top with shredded lettuce or sprouts.

2 large cloves garlic
2 green peppers, halved, seeded
2 green onions
1 pound long eggplant, or round eggplant, un-
    peeled
2 zucchini, scrubbed
2 firm tomatoes
½ teaspoon dry leaf basil
½ teaspoon dry leaf thyme
½ teaspoon dry leaf oregano
pinch marjoram
pinch rosemary
¾ teaspoon salt
¼ teaspoon pepper
1 6-ounce can tomato paste
¼ cup olive oil

METAL BLADE: Add garlic cloves to work bowl. Pulse on/off until finely minced. Remove from bowl and set aside. Add green onions, cut into 2-inch lengths, pulse on/off until finely minced. Remove from bowl and set aside.

SLICING DISC: Stack green peppers in feed tube, slice. In a 5-quart dutch oven, heat ¼ cup olive oil over medium-high heat. Add garlic and cook, stirring constantly until soft but not browned. Add green onions and green peppers and continue to cook, 3 minutes. Cut long eggplant and zucchini to fit feed tube vertically, slice. (Use thick slicing disc if available). If using round eggplant, cut into wedges to fit feed tube, slice. Cut tomatoes in half, stack in feed tube, slice.

Add vegetables to dutch oven and stir gently to mix. Reduce heat to medium and cook about 5 minutes, stirring occasionally. Add basil, thyme, oregano, marjoram, rosemary, salt, pepper and tomato paste. Stir to mix. Cover and simmer until vegetables are done to your liking. Stir occasionally. Vegetables should have some texture and not be mushy. To evaporate excess liquid, remove cover, increase heat and cook. Watch carefully so bottom does not burn.

Preparation: 10 minutes
Cooking: 20 minutes

Soy Sprout Sauté

Serves 4-6

A tasty filling for Mandarin Pancakes (see index).

¼ cup water
1 tablespoon soy sauce
1 tablespoon cornstarch
1 small onion
4 ounces fresh mushrooms
1 medium green pepper, halved, seeded
1 5-6 ounce can water chestnuts, drained
1 zucchini, scrubbed
1 large carrot, pared
8 ounces soy bean sprouts
fresh coriander or minced green onions for garnish,
    optional

In a measuring cup, stir together water, soy sauce and cornstarch. Set aside.

SLICING DISC: Cut onion in half, stack in feed tube and slice. Remove from bowl and set aside. Stack mushrooms in feed tube and slice. Remove from bowl and set aside. Place green pepper and water chestnuts in feed tube; slice. Remove slicing disc; insert shredding disc or ¼-inch square julienne disc.

SHREDDING DISC: Cut carrot and zucchini into lengths to fit feed tube horizontally. Shred into bowl with green pepper and water chestnuts.

In a 12-inch skillet or wok, heat 1 tablespoon oil over high heat. Add onions; stir-fry 1 minute. Add mushrooms; stir-fry 1 minute. Add sprouts, cover and cook over medium-low heat for 5 minutes. Add remaining vegetables and toss gently to mix. Cover and cook additional 1-2 minutes until vegetables are just heated. Do not overcook. Give the water, soy sauce, cornstarch mix a quick stir and pour into vegetables. Mix well. Garnish with fresh coriander or minced green onions if desired. Serve immediately.

Preparation: 10 minutes
Cooking: 10 minutes
Protein g/s: 4 servings—3.5
                    6 servings—2

Red Cabbage with Apples

Serves 8

We like to serve this with German Potato Pancakes or noodles with Hungarian Paprika Noodles (see index).

1 *large head red cabbage, 3 pounds*
2 *tablespoons oil*
2 *large cooking apples, Pippin, Granny Smith or Newtons*
½-1 *teaspoon salt*
½ *cup water*
4 *tablespoons white vinegar*
3 *tablespoons dark brown sugar, firmly packed*

SLICING DISC: Trim cabbage; core and cut into wedges to fit feed tube. Slice. In a large dutch oven, heat oil and butter over medium heat. Add cabbage and sauté 5 minutes. Add salt. Peel, core and quarter apples. Stack into feed tube vertically and slice. Add to cabbage. Stir to mix well and continue cooking 5 minutes. Add water, cover and cook until tender-crisp, about 20 minutes, stirring occasionally. Add vinegar and brown sugar. Taste and adjust seasoning.

Preparation: 5 minutes
Cooking: 20-25 minutes

Vegetable Parmesan

Serves 4-5

The heat from the cooked crisp vegetables melts the Parmesan to create a delightful sauce.

2 *ounces Parmesan cheese, at room temperature*
8 *ounces carrots, pared*
1 *small onion*
1 *large green pepper, halved, seeded*
2 *zucchini, about 12 ounces, scrubbed*
¼ *teaspoon salt*
½ *teaspoon dry leaf oregano*
2 *tablespoons oil*

METAL BLADE: Add Parmesan cheese, cut into 1-inch pieces, to work bowl. Process until finely grated. Remove from bowl and set aside.

SLICING DISC: Cut carrots into lengths to fit feed tube horizontally. Slice. Remove the slices. Insert the pusher in the feed tube, leaving a space at the bottom. Hold the cover sideways and wedge a stack of carrots in horizontally with cut sides of stack at right angle to cover. Slice again to produce julienne carrots (or use french fry/vegetable disc).

Steam carrots until tender but crisp. Remove from heat and keep warm.

SLICING DISC: Cut onion and green pepper to fit feed tube. Slice with light pressure. In a 10-inch skillet, heat 2 tablespoons oil over medium-high heat. Add onions and green pepper, sauté 1 minute. Cut zucchini to fit feed tube vertically, slice. Add zucchini to skillet. Sauté 2 minutes. Cover and cook 3-5 minutes over medium heat until zucchini is just tender. Do not overcook. Zucchini should remain somewhat crisp. Stir in cooked carrots, salt and oregano. Remove skillet from heat, top with Parmesan and toss gently to mix. Serve immediately.

Preparation: 10-15 minutes
Cooking: 10 minutes
Protein g/s: 4 servings— 4.5
　　　　　　6 servings—3

Stir-Fried Chinese Cabbage with Water Chestnuts

Serves 4-6

Brown bean sauce or "mein see" is available in stores specializing in oriental foods. It will keep in a jar in the refrigerator for many months. The sauce is used to flavor bland vegetables.

1 *tablespoon brown bean sauce*
2 *tablespoons soy sauce*
1 *tablespoon cornstarch*
1 *tablespoon water*
1 *small onion*
2 *tablespoons oil*
8 *ounces fresh mushrooms*
1 *pound chinese cabbage, also called won bok, celery cabbage, Napa cabbage*
1 *5-ounce can water chestnuts, drained*
6 *ounces mung bean sprouts*
fresh coriander leaves for garnish

In a measuring cup, combine brown bean sauce, soy sauce, cornstarch and water. Set aside.

SLICING DISC: Cut onion to fit feed tube; slice. In a large skillet, heat 2 tablespoons oil over medium-high heat. Add sliced onions, cook 1 minute. Stack mushrooms sideways to fit feed tube. Slice with firm pressure. Add to skillet with onions; continue to cook until soft, 2-3 minutes. Cut cabbage into lengths to fit feed tube vertically, slice. Add water chestnuts to feed tube, slice.

Add cabbage, water chestnuts and sprouts to skillet. Toss to mix. Cover and cook over medium-low heat 3-4 minutes. Cabbage should be crisp. Give the brown bean sauce mixture a quick stir and pour into skillet. Stir and cook until sauce thickens. Serve immediately. Garnish with fresh coriander.

Preparation: 10 minutes
Cooking: 8-10 minutes
Protein g/s: 4 servings—1.5
          6 servings—1

Chinese Stir-Fried Vegetables with Cashews

Serves 4

A nice accompaniment to Fried Rice (see index). Reduce the amount of nuts when serving as a side dish. As part of a main course, serve with a grain product and a milk or soy product such as Chinese Style Stir-Fry Noodles. The texture of the individual vegetables is maintained by slicing and cooking each separately.

1 teaspoon cornstarch
1 tablespoon dry sherry
2-3 tablespoons low sodium soy sauce, reduce
     when using regular soy sauce
6 ounces raw cashews
1 medium or large onion
2 large carrots, pared
1 medium zucchini, scrubbed
1 medium green pepper, halved, seeded
1 piece fresh ginger root, 1-inch diameter, ¼-inch
     thick
1 clove garlic
oil
fresh coriander, garnish

In a measuring cup, stir together cornstarch, sherry and soy sauce. Set aside. Spread cashews in a bak-

ing pan. Bake in a 350° oven 10-15 minutes or until lightly browned. Set aside.

SLICING DISC: Cut onion in half, stack into feed tube, slice. Remove and set aside. Cut carrots to fit feed tube vertically, slice. Remove and set aside. Cut zucchini to fit feed tube vertically, slice. Remove and set aside. Stack green pepper into feed tube, slice. Remove and set aside. In a large wok or skillet, heat a teaspoon or so of oil over medium-high heat. Stir-fry each vegetable until tender but crisp. As each vegetable is cooked, remove to large mixing bowl.

METAL BLADE: Cut ginger into small pieces. With machine running, drop in pieces and process until finely minced. Add garlic, pulse on/off until finely minced. Heat about 1 teaspoon oil in the large wok over medium-high heat for 20 seconds. Add ginger and garlic, stir-fry 15-20 seconds. Add vegetables and toss gently to mix. Give the soy sauce mixture a quick stir and add to wok. Stir to mix and cook until liquid has thickened. Remove to serving platter and top with cashews and coriander.

Preparation: 10 minutes
Cooking: 20 minutes
Protein g/s: 7.5

Zucchini Onion Sauté

Serves 4

1 medium onion
2 tablespoons oil
1 pound zucchini
¼ teaspoon salt
½ teaspoon Vegit seasoning
2 medium cloves garlic, pressed

SLICING DISC: Cut onion in half, stack into feed tube, slice. In a 10-inch skillet, heat 2 tablespoons oil over medium-high heat. Add onions and sauté 1-2 minutes. Cut zucchini to fit feed tube vertically, slice. Add to skillet. Add salt, Vegit seasoning and garlic. Stir to mix. Sauté until zucchini is tender-crisp. Do not overcook.

Preparation: 5 minutes
Cooking: 5 minutes

Marinated Carrot Strings

Serves 8-10

Your food processor takes the chore out of shredding 2 pounds of carrots for this dish. The recipe makes a large amount, perfect for entertaining. Wine in the marinade keeps the carrots crisp. Allow the carrots to marinate at least 24 hours but no longer than 5-6 days.

2 cups water
3 tablespoons chicken-flavored vegetable broth
  granules
2 cups dry white wine, no substitute
4-6 tablespoons white or wine vinegar
6 green onions
3 large cloves garlic, pressed
½ cup olive oil
2 teaspoons brown sugar
¾-1 teaspoon salt
½-¾ teaspoon pepper
1 bay leaf
1 teaspoon dry leaf thyme
2 pounds carrots, pared
1 lemon
2 sprigs parsley for garnish

METAL BLADE: Add green onions, cut into 2-inch lengths, to work bowl. Pulse on/off until just minced. In a 4-5 quart pot, bring 2 cups of water to a boil. Add vegetable broth and stir to dissolve. Add wine, green onions, garlic, olive oil, brown sugar, salt, pepper, bay leaf and thyme. Boil for 6 minutes.

SHREDDING DISC: Cut carrots to fit feed tube horizontally, shred. Add to boiling marinade and cook, uncovered, 5-7 minutes or until carrots are done but crisp. Allow to cool slightly, transfer to a glass or ceramic jar or bowl, cover and refrigerate at least 24 hours. Remove bay leaf before serving. Squeeze in the juice of half a lemon. Cut remaining lemon into thin slices, arrange attractively on carrots and top with parsley sprigs.

Preparation: 5 minutes
Cooking: 15 minutes
Chilling: 24 hours

Cheesy Zucchini Slices

Serves 4-6

Serve with fresh baked whole wheat rolls and a tossed salad.

4 zucchini, each about 6-inches long, 1½-2 pounds
  total
3 ounces Parmesan cheese, at room temperature
2 cloves garlic
2 eggs
3 tablespoons whole wheat flour
½ teaspoon salt
¼ teaspoon pepper
2 tablespoons parsley flakes
¼ cup skim milk
½ cup whole wheat flour measured, scoop and level
¼ cup oil

SLICING DISC: Trim zucchini, do not pare. Cut into lengths to fit feed tube horizontally. Slice. Remove from bowl and set aside. Wipe work bowl dry with a paper towel.

METAL BLADE: Add Parmesan cheese, cut into 1-inch pieces, to work bowl. Process until finely grated. Add garlic, pulse on/off until garlic is finely minced. Add eggs, 3 tablespoons whole wheat flour, salt, pepper, parsley flakes, and milk. Process to mix well. Remove to a shallow dish, cover and refrigerate at least 15 minutes. Place ½ cup whole wheat flour in a bag. Add zucchini slices. Shake to dust zucchini lightly.

In a large frying pan, heat ¼ cup oil over medium-high heat. Using a fork, dip each zucchini slice in the cheese mixture to coat both sides. Cook until golden brown on both sides, 5-7 minutes. Drain on paper towels and transfer to serving plate. Keep warm until all slices are cooked. These may be cooked ahead of time and reheated. Place slices on an ungreased pan and heat at 325° for 10-15 minutes.

Preparation: 10 minutes
Cooking/Baking: 20-25 minutes
Chilling: 15 minutes
Protein g/s: 4 servings—10.5
            6 servings—7

Zucchini Pancakes

10 pancakes

Add brown rice and a tossed green salad for a quick meal.

2 *medium zucchini, 12 ounces, scrubbed*
1 *small onion*
4 *eggs*
2 *teaspoons soy sauce*
dash pepper

SHREDDING DISC: Cut zucchini into lengths to fit feed tube horizontally. Shred. Cut onion to fit feed tube, shred. Remove to mixing bowl.

METAL BLADE: Add eggs, soy sauce and pepper. Process until well-mixed. Pour into zucchini mixture. Stir to mix. In a skillet, heat 1 teaspoon oil over medium heat. Drop the vegetable mixture from a ¼-cup measure onto hot skillet. Flatten to form 3-4 inch pancakes. Cook until lightly browned, about 2 minutes. Turn and cook other side. Keep warm until all the pancakes are cooked.

Preparation: 5 minutes
Cooking: 10-15 minutes
Protein g/s: 8.5 per 3 pancakes

Grains and Legumes

Chinese Style Fried Rice

Serves 6

Traditionally, fried rice is prepared with cold left-over rice. Cook the rice the night before or earlier in the day. Add variety to this dish by adding your choice of "extras"—fresh minced chives, chopped water chestnuts, shredded carrots or sliced bamboo shoots.

3-4 *tablespoons oil*
3 *eggs beaten, to make an egg pancake*
3-4 *green onions*
1 *large onion*
5-6 *ounces fresh mushrooms*
½ *cup frozen peas, thawed, uncooked*
3 *cups cold cooked brown rice (1 cup raw)*
2-3 *tablespoons low sodium soy sauce or*
     1-2 tablespoons regular soy sauce
1-2 *tablespoons oriental sesame oil, optional*

To make egg pancake, heat a 10 or 12-inch frying pan over moderate heat for about 30 seconds. With a paper towel or pastry brush, brush the bottom of the pan with 1 teaspoon oil. Pour in the beaten eggs. Reduce heat to low and working quickly, tip the pan from side to side until a thin round pancake forms. Cook over low heat until firm. Flip over and cook briefly, 15-20 seconds. Fold into thirds and remove from pan. When cool enough to handle, cut crosswise into ¼-inch shreds. Set aside

METAL BLADE: Add green onions, cut into 1-inch lengths, to work bowl. Pulse on/off until finely minced, or with a sharp knife, cut into ¼-inch pieces. Remove from bowl and set aside. Add onion, cut into 1-inch pieces, to work bowl; pulse on/off until chopped medium-fine. Heat 1 tablespoon oil in a 4 or 5-quart dutch oven over medium-high heat. Add chopped onions and sauté until soft and transparent, 3-5 minutes. Remove to a medium mixing bowl and set aside.

SLICING DISC: Stack mushrooms in feed tube, sideways; slice with firm pressure. In the same dutch oven, heat 1 tablespoon oil over medium-high heat. Add mushrooms and cook until soft. Add to sautéed onions. Sauté peas until hot and add to mushrooms. Heat about 1 tablespoon oil in the

dutch oven. Add rice and stir-fry until rice begins to warm. Add green onions, cooked vegetables, egg shreds, sesame oil and soy sauce. Toss gently to mix and stir-fry 2-3 minutes until ingredients are mixed and rice is hot. Taste and adjust seasoning.

Preparation: 10 minutes
Cooking: 10 minutes
        allow time to cook rice in advance
Protein g/s: 6

Spanish Rice (Sopa Seca de Arroz)

Serves 6

Serve with beans or a milk product. Especially good with our enchilada recipes, Chiles Rellenos, Mexican Quiche or Tamale Pie (see index).

1 *medium onion*
½ *green pepper, seeded*
½ *red bell pepper, seeded*
2 *canned whole green chiles, rinsed and seeded*
2-3 *tablespoons oil*
2 *cups boiling water*
2 *vegetable bouillon cubes*
1 *cup long grain brown rice*
1 *clove garlic, pressed*
1 *cup stewed tomatoes with liquid*
salt to taste

METAL BLADE: Add onion, cut into 1-inch pieces, to work bowl; pulse on/off until coarsely chopped. Add green and red peppers, cut into 1-inch pieces, to work bowl; pulse on/off until coarsely chopped. Dry green chiles with paper towels and cut into thirds. Add to work bowl; pulse on/off until coarsely chopped.

In a large skillet or 3-quart dutch oven with a tight-fitting lid, heat oil over medium-high heat. Add onion mixture and sauté until soft, 3-5 minutes. Rinse rice, add to vegetable mixture; stir to mix well. Sauté 1-2 minutes but do not allow to brown. Dissolve bouillon cubes in boiling water and stir into rice along with garlic. Bring to a boil. Lower heat, cover and simmer 35-40 minutes or until rice is tender. Do not lift lid during cooking. Add tomatoes and liquid to work bowl; pulse on/off until coarsely chopped. Stir into cooked rice, cover and simmer 3-5 minutes. Add salt to taste.

Preparation: 10 minutes
Cooking: 40-45 minutes
Protein g/s: 2.5

Yellow Rice Pilaf

Serves 4-6

With the price of saffron on the rise, we developed this variation substituting turmeric. A nice accompaniment to our curried dishes and dals.

1 medium onion
3 tablespoons oil
1 large clove garlic, pressed
¼ teaspoon ground black pepper
6 whole cloves
6 whole cardamom seeds
1 cinnamon stick
¼ teaspoon ground allspice
¼ teaspoon ground turmeric
1 cup long grain brown rice
2¾ cups boiling water
½ teaspoon salt
½ cup raisins
1 teaspoon brown sugar
⅓ cup unroasted pistachio nuts or
    roasted cashew nuts

METAL BLADE: Add onion, cut into 1-inch pieces, to work bowl; pulse on/off until chopped medium-fine. In a frying pan or dutch oven with a tight-fitting lid, heat oil over medium heat. Add onions and sauté until transparent, 3-5 minutes. Stir in garlic, pepper, cloves, cardamom, cinnamon, allspice and turmeric. Continue cooking, stirring constantly, 1-2 minutes. Add rice and stir until coated with spices. Pour in water and bring to a boil; reduce heat, cover and simmer 30 minutes. Remove lid, stir in salt, raisins, sugar and nuts. Cover and continue cooking 10-15 minutes or until rice is

tender and liquid is absorbed. Pick out whole spices; serve.

Preparation: 5 minutes
Cooking: 45-50 minutes
Protein g/s: 4 servings—5.5
              6 servings—3.5

Millet Vegetable Pilaf

Serves 6

An ideal accompaniment for dishes containing beans, peas, or tofu.

2-3 tablespoons oil
1 large onion
2 large carrots, 8 ounces, peeled
2-3 medium stalks celery, 4 ounces, trimmed
1 medium green pepper, halved and seeded
3 vegetable bouillon cubes
2½ cups boiling water
1 cup millet
1-2 cloves garlic, pressed

METAL BLADE: Add onion, cut into 1-inch pieces, to work bowl; pulse on/off until chopped medium-fine. In a frying pan or skillet with a tight-fitting lid, heat oil over medium heat. Add onions and sauté while preparing other vegetables.

SLICING DISC: Cut carrots in half vertically. Cut each half in quarters to make 8 long strips. Cut strips to fit feed tube vertically; slice. Cut celery to fit feed tube vertically, slice. Quarter each green pepper half, wedge into feed tube vertically, slice.

Add vegetables to onions and sauté until tender-crisp. For more rapid cooking, place lid on pan to steam vegetables. Add millet; stir until just coated with oil. Do not brown. Dissolve bouillon cubes in water and stir in along with garlic. Bring to a boil, reduce heat, cover and simmer 40-45 minutes or until millet grains are soft, puffed and liquid is absorbed.

Preparation: 5 minutes
Cooking: 45-50 minutes
Protein g/s: 3.5

Herbed Millet

Serves 4-6

This neglected grain is delicately seasoned so it doesn't overwhelm the dishes you serve it with. Millet complements beans or lentils and dishes containing milk or cheese.

1 bunch chives
½ bunch parsley
1 large onion
2-3 tablespoons oil
1 cup millet
3 vegetable bouillon cubes
2½ cups boiling water
½-¾ teaspoon dry leaf marjoram
½-¾ teaspoon dry leaf thyme
pinch salt
pinch or two reserved minced chives and parsley

METAL BLADE: Add parsley and chives, cut into 2-inch lengths, to work bowl; pulse on/off until finely minced. Remove from bowl and set aside. Add onion, cut into 1-inch pieces, to work bowl; pulse on/off until chopped medium-fine.

In a frying pan or skillet with a tight-fitting lid, heat oil over medium-high heat. Add onions and sauté until soft and transparent, 3-5 minutes. Add millet; stir until coated with oil. Do not brown. Dissolve bouillon cubes in water; stir in with chives, parsley, marjoram, thyme, and salt. Bring to a boil, reduce heat, cover, and simmer 45 minutes or until millet grains are soft and puffed and liquid is absorbed. Garnish with reserved chives and parsley and serve.

Preparation: 6 minutes
Cooking: 45-50 minutes
Protein g/s: 4 servings—5
            6 servings—3.5

Refried Beans

4 cups, serves 8

A nice accompaniment to many of our enchiladas, Chiles Rellenos, and Spanish Rice (see index).

1 medium onion
3½ cups well-cooked pinto beans (1½ cups dry)
3-4 tablespoons oil
salt to taste

Drain pinto beans, reserving cooking liquid.

METAL BLADE: Add onion, cut into 1-inch pieces, to work bowl; pulse on/off until finely minced. In a large skillet, heat oil over medium heat. Add onions and sauté until soft, 3-5 minutes. Add half the cooked beans to work bowl; process until smooth. Add puréed beans and whole beans to skillet with onions. Cook, mashing whole beans and adding reserved liquid until they are the desired consistency. Taste and adjust seasoning.

Preparation: 5 minutes
Cooking: 10 minutes
            allow time to cook beans
Protein g/s: 8

Mushroom Rice Pilaf

Serves 6

1 small onion
3 stalks celery, trimmed
4 ounces fresh mushrooms
3 tablespoons oil
1½ cups brown rice
3 cups boiling vegetable stock or water
½ teaspoon salt
½ teaspoon dry leaf thyme
pinch ground pepper

METAL BLADE: Add onion, cut into 1-inch pieces, to work bowl, pulse on/off until finely chopped. Remove from bowl and set aside. Add celery, cut into 1-inch lengths, to work bowl. Pulse on/off until finely chopped.

SLICING DISC: Stack mushrooms in feed tube sideways; slice with firm pressure. In a 3-quart dutch oven, heat 3 tablespoons oil over medium-high heat. Add onion, celery and mushrooms; sauté until onion is tender, about 5 minutes. Stir in rice and continue cooking 2-3 minutes. Carefully pour in boiling stock; do not stir. Add seasoning. Cover and simmer until liquid is absorbed and rice is tender, about 1 hour. Fluff with a fork and serve.

Preparation: 10 minutes
Cooking: 70 minutes
Protein g/s: 3.5

Buckwheat Mushroom Pilaf

Serves 4-6

Somewhat reminiscent of wild rice stuffing, this dish is best served with beans, peas, or lentils. Buckwheat cooks in 7-12 minutes.

2 tablespoons oil
3 sprigs parsley
1 large onion
1 large stalk celery, trimmed
1 medium green pepper, halved and seeded
8 ounces fresh mushrooms
¼-½ bunch fresh chives, about 1 ounce
1 cup buckwheat kernels
3 vegetable bouillon cubes
1¾ cups boiling water
½-¾ teaspoon dry leaf thyme
½ teaspoon dry leaf summer savory
1-2 large cloves garlic, pressed
salt to taste

Select a frying pan with a tight fitting lid. Heat oil over medium-high heat and sauté vegetables as they are prepared.

METAL BLADE: Add parsley to work bowl; pulse on/off until finely minced. Add to frying pan and sauté. Add onions, cut into 1-inch pieces, to work bowl; pulse on/off until finely chopped. Stir into parsley.

SLICING DISC: Cut celery to fit feed tube vertically; slice using medium pressure. Quarter each green pepper half; stack into feed tube vertically and slice. Add to frying pan. Wedge mushrooms in feed tube sideways; slice with firm pressure. Stir into frying pan. Wipe work bowl dry.

METAL BLADE: Add chives, cut into 1-inch lengths, to work bowl; pulse on/off until finely minced or cut into ¼-inch pieces using a sharp knife. Add to vegetables and sauté until vegetables

are tender and all the liquid has evaporated, 5-8 minutes. Add buckwheat kernels and stir until well-mixed. Dissolve bouillon cubes in water and add to pan. Stir in thyme, summer savory, and garlic. Bring liquid to a boil; reduce heat to low, cover and simmer 10 minutes. Remove lid; water should be absorbed and kernels tender. If not, continue cooking 2-3 minutes. Taste and adjust seasonings. Fluff with a fork and serve.

Preparation: 5 minutes
Cooking: 15-20 minutes
Protein g/s: 4 servings—5
          6 servings—3

Hummus Bi Tahini

Serves 4-6

This tasty purée is a nutritious main dish when served as a filling for Whole Wheat Pita Bread (see index) or an excellent appetizer when served with raw vegetables.

1 clove garlic
2 cups well-cooked garbanzo beans
juice of 1 lemon
3-4 tablespoons cold water
¼ cup Sesame Tahini (see index) or
     purchased sesame tahini
½ teaspoon salt
1 tablespoon olive oil
dash cayenne pepper, optional
fresh coriander for garnish
crushed red pepper, optional

METAL BLADE: Add garlic to work bowl and process until finely minced. Add garbanzo beans, lemon juice, water, tahini and salt. Process until smooth, scraping down the sides of the bowl with a spatula as needed. Taste and adjust seasoning. Spread hummus in a shallow dish. Dribble on olive oil, place a pinch of crushed red pepper in the center and garnish with coriander.

Preparation: 5 minutes
Protein g/s: 4 servings—13
          6 servings—9

Breads

Supplying several of the B vitamins, iron, protein, fiber, and food energy—whole grain breads are the staff of life in a vegetarian diet. We've enhanced the protein power of many of our breads with the addition of dry milk solids, wheat germ, nuts, seeds, cheeses, and non-wheat whole grains or flours—buckwheat, corn, oat, dark rye, triticale, and soy.

Nothing could replace the satisfaction of manually kneading dough for a loaf of yeast bread, a friend recently remarked. A machine to make a wholesome, old-fashioned loaf of bread? Never! Later, we were quick to note that while we were enjoying a variety of homebaked breads with our lunches, she brought only bread from the supermarket . . . didn't have time to bake, she said.

Friends often ask how we find time to bake yeast bread regularly. We explain that bread baking, contrary to popular belief, is not a time-consuming chore. The entire process from mixing the dough to eating the first slice does take about 2½-3 hours, but the actual time spent tending to the dough is about 20 minutes—10 minutes to mix and knead and another 10 minutes to shape. The remainder of the time, the bread is left to take care of itself—rising and baking. Meanwhile, relax with the book you've been wanting to read, prune and fertilize your plants, do some shopping, or put on your running shoes and go for a run around the neighborhood.

We started as only occasional weekend bakers. With thoughts of mixing and kneading that sticky glob of dough until our arms ached and of scraping the counter clean afterwards, we usually found something else to do.

But now, the food processor has so simplified bread making that tasty and nutritious, whole grain breads are an essential part of our diets and baking schedules. Flour and liquid are quickly mixed and transformed into an elastic ball of dough in the work bowl, eliminating lengthy manual mixing and kneading and greatly reducing the clean-up time.

Most machines on the market will process yeast dough from recipes calling for 2¾ to 3 cups of flour. The Cuisinart CFP5A and 9 can now process bread dough calling for up to 4 cups of flour with the new plastic dough-kneading blade. Be sure to follow the instructions that accompany the new blade. The basic procedure is the same as that presented in the recipes, but, ice water is used to prevent overheating of the machine. A small amount of warm water is still used to dissolve the yeast.

The Cuisinart DLC7 can handle yeast doughs using up to 6 cups of flour. Our recipes were developed and tested using the Cuisinart CFP5A (metal and plastic dough blade) and the DLC7. Check your instruction manual for flour capacity before you try the recipes. Experience will allow you to adjust the recipes to your machine's capabilities.

Baking Ingredients

Grains, Flours, and Cereals

Whole wheat, graham, or *wholemeal flour* is milled from the whole kernel and contains the bran and wheat germ which provides protein, all the B vitamins, iron, and other nutrients naturally present in wheat. When whole wheat flour is called for in this book it is *Gold Medal Whole Wheat Flour.* We use this flour as our all-purpose flour for breads, pastries, and other baked goods. The volume of breads made with whole wheat flour is slightly lower and the texture coarser than those of bread made with unbleached white flour.

Wheat flour contains a substance called *gluten*, an elastic protein. When wheat flour is mixed and kneaded with liquid, gluten forms an elastic framework that traps the bubbles of gas produced by leavening. The bread rises and achieves a light texture. Without gluten, a leavened bread cannot be produced.

Wheat flakes are made from whole wheat, steamed and rolled to form flakes. The flakes may be substituted for rolled oats in yeast breads and muffins.

Cracked wheat or *bulgur wheat* is wheat that is cracked or cut rather than ground. It is usually softened in hot water before use and adds a nice chewy texture.

Bran, miller's bran, or *unprocessed bran flakes* is the skin of wheat. A number of our recipes include bran for extra fiber. When bran is called for in this book, it is the *unprocessed bran flakes*. You may increase the amount of bran, but do so slowly as the resulting product will be more compact. Try adding about ¼ cup bran to your favorite recipes. You can increase the amount as long as the product is acceptable.

Wheat germ is the part of the wheat that germinates when the kernel is planted. It is rich in B and E vitamins and contains protein, iron, and fat. Store wheat germ in an airtight container in the refrigerator.

Buckwheat flour is milled much the same way as wheat flour but is an herb rather than a true grain. It has a rather strong flavor, has no gluten power, and is generally combined with a large proportion of wheat flour.

Cornmeal is ground corn. When water-ground or stone-ground, it retains the germ. Cornmeal does not contain gluten, so is not used alone for making most breads, but small amounts added to recipes give a nice crunch. When sprinkled on the baking sheet or in the bottom of a loaf pan, it keeps the bread from sticking.

Rolled oats, old-fashioned oats, or *oatmeal* are made from whole oat groats softened by steam and crushed between rollers. Unless otherwise noted, we do not use instant or quick-cooking oatmeal. Oats have the highest protein content of any cereal grain, and breads containing oats are tender, moist, and chewy.

Oat flour is easily made in your processor. For 1 cup of flour, process 1-1½ cups uncooked rolled oats with the metal blade for about 60 seconds. Store in a tightly covered container in a cool dry place. Oat flour has no gluten strength.

Dark rye flour is milled from whole rye and contains all of the grain. Rye flour is usually mixed with wheat flour because the rye flour gluten provides stickiness but lacks elasticity. Breads made with a large proportion of rye flour are moist and compact.

Rye flakes are made by rolling the grain and are similar to rolled oats.

Soy flour is made by grinding whole raw soy beans. This flour has a slightly sweet flavor and is high in protein. Breads and cakes containing soy flour tend to brown more quickly, so watch carefully.

Triticale flour is milled from a hybrid plant, a cross of rye and wheat. It is reported to have a slightly better amino acid balance than wheat alone.

Leavening Agents

Light breads, muffins, and cakes are the result of the action of leavening. Leavening agents include yeast, baking powder, baking soda, buttermilk, air, and steam.

Yeast feeds on sugars in the flour and forms carbon dioxide gas. These gas bubbles raise the dough. Yeast needs a warm temperature for growth; too low a temperature inhibits growth; too high a temperature kills yeast.

When yeast is called for in this book it is *El Molino Active Dry Yeast*. We dissolve it by sprinkling the granules into warm water (105°-115°F) and allowing it to stand for about 5 minutes until bubbly. If you don't have a thermometer, combine equal parts boiling water and ice water. Although improvements in yeast have ensured its reliability (when used within the time period stamped on the package), we always test it to make sure that the yeast is alive and ready to work. Nothing can be more disappointing than to discover two hours later that the yeast is not active. Purchase yeast in bulk and refrigerate in an airtight container.

Baking powder is a combination of baking soda and an acid ingredient that reacts in the batter to form gas bubbles. Two types of baking powder are available: double-acting and quick acting. Double-acting baking powder reacts and produces gas bubbles twice—first during mixing and again during baking. Quick-acting baking powder reacts to form gas bubbles only once—as soon as the batter is mixed. Batters containing quick-acting baking powder need to be baked as soon as mixed. When baking powder is called for in this book it is *double-acting baking powder*.

Baking soda is used when the batter contains acid ingredients such as buttermilk, honey, molasses, or fruit juice. Gas bubbles form in the same way as when baking powder is used, but the action is immediate. The product must be baked as soon as it is mixed.

Air in beaten egg whites is a leavening agent. Be sure that the bowl and beater are free of oil. Allow the whites to come to room temperature for maximum volume.

Steam leavens the mixture in some quick breads such as popovers.

Fat

Margarine, vegetable oil or butter makes bread more tender, adds flavor, and prevents rapid spoiling. Small amounts are used to prevent interference with the formation of gluten in the dough. Some breads, such as French bread, contain no fat.

Eggs

Eggs add flavor and nutritive value to baked products. The proteins in eggs coagulate when heated, strengthening the framework of batters and doughs.

Sweeteners

Honey, maple syrup, molasses, and brown sugar flavor baked goods and increase tenderness, volume, and keeping qualities. These sweeteners also help to brown crusts. In yeast-raised breads, the sweetener is food for the yeast.

Liquids

Water, fruit juice, liquid buttermilk, and liquid skim milk are among the liquids used to blend dry ingredients in making doughs and batters. It is the amount of liquid in a mixture that determines its bulk—whether it is a dough or batter. A dough is any mixture thick enough to be rolled or kneaded. A batter is thin enough to pour or drop from a spoon.

Water makes crusty breads. Bread made with milk has higher protein value. The crust is softer and browner, and the crumb is tender. Most of the recipes in this book call for *non-instant, non-fat milk powder.* The milk powder is added to the flour along with other dry ingredients, eliminating the step of heating fresh milk. Unheated fresh milk often contains an ingredient that produces a soft dough. This dough lacks the strength to hold the gas bubbles during rising and causes the loaf to collapse during baking.

Salt

A small amount of salt flavors the bread but, more importantly, inhibits and regulates the growth of yeast. Yeast dough without salt rises dramatically. A word of caution—if you eliminate the salt from the recipes, do not allow the dough to rise above the level of the pan as it may collapse.

Processor Bread Baking Basics

Measuring Ingredients

Though precise measurements of flours and liquids for yeast doughs are not critical, accuracy is important for other baked products. Using the right utensil and method will ensure a perfect product each time. We use standard measuring cups and spoons.

Flours: When flours, grains, and cereals are called for in bread recipes, except when noted, we measure by the *scoop and level method*. Stir the flour with a spoon to loosen, then *scoop* the flour directly from the container with a dry measuring cup and *level* it off with the straight edge of a knife or spatula. Do not tap or shake the cup.

Liquids: A measuring cup with space above the 1 cup line helps to avoid spills and makes measurements more accurate. Place the cup on a flat surface to check the measure at eye level.

Brown sugar: When brown sugar is called for, we pack it lightly into the cup or spoon and level off the top with the straight edge of a knife or spatula.

Baking powder, spices, baking soda, etc.: Dip the spoon into the container and bring it up heaping full. Level off the top with a straight edge.

Honey, molasses, maple syrup: In recipes calling for both oil and a liquid sweetener, measure the oil first. Using the same cup or spoon, measure the honey. The small bit of oil coating the cup or spoon will allow the honey to slip right off. In recipes not calling for oil, place a drop of oil in the cup or spoon, spread it around with a finger, and then measure the honey.

Mixing

Methods of mixing vary for different types of baked products. In the preparation of yeast bread dough, liquid and yeast are added to the flour. This mixture is vigorously mixed and kneaded to develop the gluten in wheat flour. The elasticity of the gluten allows the dough to rise as carbon dioxide is produced by the yeast. In yeast-raised breads, gluten must be developed to give volume to the loaf.

Muffins are processed with a few on/off pulses until the dry ingredients are just moistened. Overmixing results in poor texture with large holes and tunnels.

Mixing batter for breads leavened by baking soda, baking powder, or other means requires a light touch. You do not want the gluten to develop, or the product will be tough. The flour is added last and combined with a few quick on/off pulses until barely moist.

Step-By-Step Method

Experienced and first-time bread bakers will benefit from reading through this simplified lesson in the preparation of yeast dough using the food processor. Ingredients are listed in the order of use. The first loaf you make may take more time than subsequent loaves, as is the case when learning any new technique. Be sure to check the instructions that are included with your processor.

Basic Bread Recipe
Have all ingredients at room temperature.

active dry yeast
warm water (105°-115°F)
oil
honey
whole wheat flour, measured scoop and level
non-instant, non-fat milk powder
salt
warm water as needed to form ball of dough
   (ice water when using plastic dough blade with
   Cuisinart CFP5A or 9)

Dissolving the Yeast
Measure warm water (105°-115°F) into a glass measuring cup. If you don't have a thermometer, mix equal parts of boiling water and ice water. Too much heat will kill the yeast, while too little will delay its growth. Sprinkle the yeast over the liquid and let it sit for about 5 minutes until it dissolves or puffs. Meanwhile, you can be assembling and measuring the remaining ingredients. When the yeast has dissolved, add oil and honey to the measuring cup; stir to mix slightly.

Adding the Liquid to the Flour Mixture
With the proper blade in a dry work bowl, add flour, *measured scoop and level*, milk powder and salt. Pulse on/off to mix.

With the processor on, add the yeast mixture. Pour in the remaining liquid in a steady stream, only as fast as the flour absorbs it. All the liquid may not be needed. When the flour and liquid proportion is correct, the dough will form into a ball. With experience, you will know just when to stop adding the liquid.

If too much liquid is added, the motor slows. You will hear this; don't worry, just throw in 1-2 tablespoons of flour and the speed should pick up. Sometimes the dough will be very sticky—did you pour in too much liquid too fast? Stop the machine, scrape the dough from the sides of the bowl with the spatula, sprinkle with 1-2 tablespoons flour, and continue processing.

Due to the varying moisture content of flours, you may need more liquid. Dribble the additional amount in slowly, stopping as soon as the dough forms into a ball.

Kneading
Process the ball of dough for 20 seconds. Stop the machine and feel the dough. It should be elastic, sticky, and wet. If not, process 10 seconds longer. Sprinkle dough with an additional 1-2 tablespoons flour, pulse machine on/off to coat dough for easy removal from work bowl.

The food processor method of preparing yeast doughs differs from the traditional method in that the consistency of the dough is controlled by the amount of liquid added rather than by the addition of flour.

Preparing the Bowl for Rising
Place about 1 teaspoon of oil in a ceramic bowl and swirl to coat bottom. Place the ball of dough in the bowl and turn the bottom to the top so entire surface is oiled. Cover with *plastic bag* or damp cloth to keep dough from drying out. Plastic bags, unlike plastic wrap, have their own film of oil that keeps dough from sticking.

First Rising, Creating a Warm Place
Let rise in a warm place (80°-85°F) free from drafts until doubled in bulk. There are several ways to create a "warm place":
• Fill a large bowl with steaming hot water and place it on the bottom shelf of an unheated oven. Then put the bowl of dough, covered with a damp towel to keep it moist, on the shelf above. *This method doesn't work if the pilot light is on.*
• Fill a bowl with steaming water, top it with a wire rack and the bowl of dough and leave it on the counter to rise.
• The dough can be placed in a turned-on convection oven. Follow manufacturer's instructions if using this method.
• Yeast doughs can rise in a microwave oven. Check your instruction manual for directions.

This first rising will take about an hour. Whole grain breads take longer to rise. When your eyes tell you that the dough has doubled in bulk, test it. Poke two fingers one-half inch into the dough midway between the center and edge of the bowl. Quickly pull your fingers out. The dough is ready if the imprint remains. If the holes start filling in, give the dough more time.

Punching Down Dough

When the dough has doubled in bulk, you are ready to punch it down. Sink your fist down to the bottom of the center of the bowl. Pull the dough from the edge of the bowl into the center imprint left by your fist. Remove from the bowl.

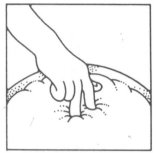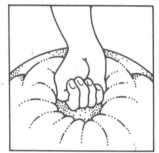

Lightly flour a pastry cloth or your counter. Knead the dough for 30 seconds as follows: Pat dough out one-inch thick; lift rear half up and fold over front. Press the dough down with the heels of your hands and push the dough away. Turn the dough one-quarter turn around and repeat the fold-over-push-turn process. This will break up the large air bubbles that form while the dough is rising and turn them into smaller ones, giving the bread an even grain. When making two loaves, divide the dough into two pieces.

Cover the dough and allow it to rest on the counter for about 5 minutes. During this time, the gluten relaxes, making the dough easier to roll and shape.

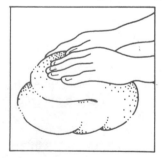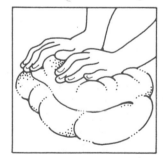

Shaping Loaf

Roll or pat the dough into a rectangle with the short side as long as the bread pan you are using. When using a 8½ x 4½-inch loaf pan, roll out a rectangle approximately 8 x 12 inches. Starting at the 8-inch end, tightly roll dough jelly-roll style.

Stop after each full turn to press the edge of the roll firmly into the flat sheet of dough to seal. Press with fingertips. Pinch seam to seal. With roll seam-side down, press the ends of the loaf down with the edges of your hands. Tuck flattened ends under and pinch gently to seal.

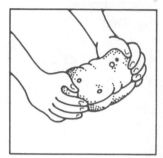

Or you can press the ball of dough into a flat oval, about the length of the baking pan. Fold the oval in half, pinch the seam tightly to seal. Place roll seam-side down, press the ends of the loaf down with the edges of your hands. Tuck flattened ends under and pinch gently to seal.

Panning

Place shaped loaf into a greased 8½ x 4½-inch loaf pan, seam-side down. Gently press the loaf into the pan so that both ends touch the edge of the pan. Use a vegetable shortening to grease the baking pans. Oils tend to be absorbed by the dough, causing the loaf to stick.

Second Rising

Cover and let rise again in warm place, free from drafts until doubled in bulk—about 45 minutes. The center of the dough will rise about 1 inch above the level of the pan. To test, press finger gently into a corner. It's ready to bake if an imprint remains.

Baking

Preheat oven 10 minutes. *Reminder! Remove the bowl of water and the bread from the oven during preheating.* Place pan(s) in center of middle shelf of oven. Do not let the pans touch each other or the sides of the oven.

Before baking you may brush the bread with a beaten egg for a shiny crust or milk or butter for a soft crust. Most of our breads go into the oven without a glaze. We keep the crusts soft by covering the loaf with a cloth while it cools.

Bake the loaves for the specified period of time. Resist peeking during the first 20 minutes of baking, or the loaf may collapse. Open the door gently and quickly. If the tops are browning too quickly, cover loosely with foil.

If using a convection oven, follow manufacturer's instructions. We've tested many of our recipes in the Farberware oven with excellent results. The loaves browned evenly and rose dramatically. Reduce the temperature by 75°; place loaf on lowest position in a cold oven; bake. You may need to adjust the baking times.

Testing the Loaf

Slip the loaf from its baking pan and tap the bottom crust with an index finger. It will sound hard and hollow when done. If it is soft, return the bread to the oven for an additional 5-10 minutes. Test again.

Cooling and Storing

Remove bread from pans immediately to avoid soggy crusts. Place on wire rack to cool.

It's important to allow bread to cool completely before storing as condensation can cause rapid molding. When cooled, place bread in a plastic bag and seal with a wire twist. Store at room temperature if it is to be eaten in a few days.

For longer storage, slice the loaf, wrap, and freeze. Remove individual slices as needed. Whole loaves of bread may also be frozen unsliced. Place in a plastic bag and freeze. Thaw wrapped loaf at room temperature. Remove from plastic, wrap in foil and reheat for 15 minutes in a 350°F oven.

Slicing

A serrated bread knife, kept razor-sharp, is an indispensable piece of equipment. Use your bread knife only for slicing bread and it will last for years. Even a hot loaf of bread can be sliced when using the right knife. For even slices, place the loaf on its side and slice with a gentle sawing motion.

Create Your Own Dough

Puréed vegetables (potatoes, pumpkin, carrots), fruits (applesauce), grated and shredded cheese, seeds, nuts, raisins, dates, and other chopped dried fruits are some of the "extras" we've put into our breads for flavor, texture, and increased food value.

It's easy to master bread baking using the food processor method. Soon you'll be creating your own breads or making variations of the recipes we offer. How about adding raisins to the honey whole wheat loaf or substituting rye flakes for oat flakes? Be creative! The combinations are endless.

Don't let loaf pans limit the shape of your loaves. Any decorative mold that can be placed in the oven can be used. Try 1-pound coffee cans for an interesting shape. You can usually fit more coffee cans in your oven than loaf pans—perfect for the times you want to make great quantities of bread.

Almost any yeast bread can be baked as rolls. This is a time-saver, as rolls take less time to rise and bake.

Here are a few tips to remember when creating your own dough:

- 3 cups of flour yields a 1½-pound loaf.

- 3 cups of flour will absorb about 1 cup liquid.

- 1 large egg equals ¼ cup liquid.

- Use 1 tablespoon active dry yeast, ½ tablespoon salt, 2 tablespoons oil and 2-4 tablespoons sweetener for a 3-cup flour loaf.

- Substitute no more than ⅓ of the total amount of whole wheat flour with a cereal or non-wheat flour. In a 3-cup flour recipe you might substitute 1 cup of whole wheat flour with some oat flour, rye flour, soy flour, or cornmeal. Remember, gluten found in whole wheat flour is essential for the bread to rise.

Pans

The kind of pan you use affects the final baking results. Shiny pans reflect heat; their use results in pale, tender crusts. Dull, dark-colored, very heavy-gauge pans absorb heat, which results in dark, thick crusts. Glass (Pyrex) and Corning Ware absorb and hold heat exceptionally well and produce a golden crust. Reduce the oven temperature by 25° when using glass or Corning Ware. A teflon-coated or other non-stick surface eliminates greasing and is easy to clean. The Brick Oven Bread Pan, marketed by Copco is a clay pan that produces a loaf that "bread eaters dream about—high-rising, fine-grained, with a crisp crust." Reduce the baking temperature by 25° and adjust the baking time. The pan needs to be well-greased to prevent sticking the first few times it is used.

Using the pan size specified in the recipes will give you the best result. If you must substitute, remember that a larger pan will cause the batter or dough to spread out and bake faster. Breads baked in smaller pans will take longer. Quick bread batter should fill no more than ½ the pan or it may overflow before it's set. A pan filled ⅔ with yeast-raised dough produces a nice high loaf.

Evenly baked goods result when air is allowed to circulate around the items as they bake. Try to allow at least two inches between each pan and the oven sides, back and door. Place the oven rack so that the food, not the rack is as close to the center of the oven as possible. When using two racks, position them so the pans are evenly spaced between the oven top and bottom. Stagger pans so one is not directly above the other.

Timing

A change in plans can sometimes interrupt the usual sequence of yeast bread baking, but you needn't be a slave to your bread. Should the loaf expand to more than double it's bulk because you didn't get home in time to check, simply punch it down, reshape, and set to rise again. The dough is ready to bake, but you aren't? Refrigerate the loaf, covered with a plastic bag of course. Let it come to room temperature while the oven is preheating and bake as usual.

No time to wait for the bread to rise? Bake bread after one rising, starting in a *cold oven*. The texture of this loaf will be coarser than if allowed to rise twice, but the flavor is not sacrificed.

Or try the "Coolrise Method" developed in the Consumer Kitchens, Robin Hood Flour. Almost any yeast bread recipe can be prepared with the "Coolrise Method" by doubling the amount of yeast. The loaves tend to be more compact but still delicious!

After kneading the ball of dough for 20 seconds, remove from work bowl and place on a pastry cloth or counter top. Cover with a plastic bag or inverted bowl and let rest 20 minutes. Punch down the dough, shape, and place seam-side down in a greased baking pan. Brush top of loaf with cooking oil. Cover loosely with plastic to allow for an expansion of 1-2 inches above the edge of the pan. Refrigerate 2-24 hours. Loaves may be removed and baked whenever it is convenient during that time span. Remove the loaves from the refrigerator. Peel back the plastic wrap. Let stand, uncovered, for 15 minutes while the oven heats to 400°F. Bake 35-40 minutes or until loaves are golden brown and sound hollow when tapped on the bottom crust. Remove to a wire rack to cool completely before storing.

What Went Wrong?

Heavy compact texture, dry crumb:	*too much flour, under-rising*
Coarse texture:	*under-kneading, too little flour, over-rising*
Uneven shape:	*too much dough for pan, improper shaping*
Porous bread:	*over-rising*
Small flat loaf:	*inactive yeast, ingredients too warm, old yeast, under-rising*
Pale crust:	*oven temperature too low, drying of dough during rising*
Yeasty flavor, fallen center:	*dough allowed to rise too long*
Cracks and bulging crust:	*dough too stiff, uneven heat in oven*
Holes in the center:	*air bubbles not pressed out before shaping, over-rising*

Yeast Breads

Complementary Bread

1 small loaf, 15 slices; 1 medium loaf, 16 slices

A moist high-protein all-purpose bread. Measure both wheat and soy flours, scoop and level. Double recipe for 2 small loaves if your machine can handle 5½ cups flour.

1 Loaf 7⅞ x 3⅞ inches

1 tablespoon active dry yeast
¼ cup warm water (105°-115°F)
1½ tablespoons oil
2 tablespoons honey
2¾ cups whole wheat flour
½ cup + 3 tablespoons soy flour
¾ teaspoon salt
¾ cup additional water

1 Loaf 8½ x 4½ inches

1 tablespoon active dry yeast
¼ cup warm water (105°-115°F)
2 tablespoons oil
3 tablespoons honey
3½ cups whole wheat flour
¾ cup + 2 tablespoons soy flour
1 teaspoon salt
1 cup additional water

In a measuring cup, sprinkle yeast over ¼ cup warm water. Let stand in warm place about 5 minutes until it dissolves or puffs. Add oil and honey.

METAL BLADE or PLASTIC DOUGH BLADE: Add whole wheat flour, soy flour and salt to work bowl. Pulse on/off to mix. With machine running, pour yeast mixture through feed tube. Pour in remaining water in a steady stream, only as fast as the flour absorbs it. All the water may not be needed to form a ball of dough. Process ball of dough for 20 seconds. Stop the machine and feel the dough. It should be elastic, sticky and wet. If not, process 10 seconds longer. Sprinkle dough with an additional 1-2 tablespoons flour. Pulse machine on/off to coat dough for easy removal from work bowl.

Transfer dough to an oiled bowl and turn so entire surface is oiled. Cover with plastic bag or damp cloth and let rise in a warm place, free from drafts, until doubled in bulk, about 1 hour. Punch down dough and knead for 30 seconds to press out the bubbles. Divide in half if making two loaves. Shape into a ball, let rest, covered, 5 minutes. Shape into a loaf and place in a greased loaf pan. Cover and let rise in warm place, free from drafts, until doubled, about 45 minutes.

Bake on middle rack in a preheated 375° oven 35-40 minutes or until golden brown and bottom crust of loaf has a hard hollow sound when tapped. Remove from loaf pan immediately and place on metal rack to cool.

Note: When doubling the recipe for 2 small loaves, with 5½ cups whole wheat flour, the machine may not be able to process the ball of dough easily. If this is the case, remove a portion of the dough and set aside. Continue processing the remaining portion of dough until it is elastic and sticky. Remove from bowl. Process second portion; knead the two portions together and proceed as directed.

Preparation: 10 minutes
Standing: allow 2-2½ hours for dough to rise
Baking: 35-40 minutes
Protein g/s: small loaf—4
              medium loaf—5

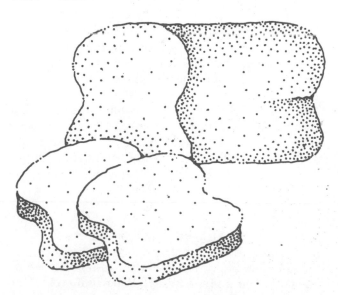

Braided Sesame Seed Bread

1 loaf, 20 slices

This large braid was developed for the larger capacity machine, such as the Cuisinart DLC7. For smaller machines, divide the recipe roughly in half and process to form two portions of dough. Knead the two portions together on a lightly floured board and proceed as directed.

1 *tablespoon plus 1 teaspoon active dry yeast*
½ *cup warm water (105°-115°F)*
2 *tablespoons oil*
3 *tablespoons honey*
4½ *cups whole wheat flour, measured scoop and*
      level
½ *cup gluten flour, measured scoop and level*
⅓ *cup non-instant, non-fat milk powder*
¾ *teaspoon salt*
1 *cup plus 1-3 tablespoons water, as needed*
1-3 *tablespoons sesame seeds for topping*

Glaze: 1 *egg beaten with*
       2 *tablespoons water*

In a measuring cup, sprinkle yeast over ½ cup warm water. Let stand in warm place about 5 minutes until it dissolves or puffs. Add oil and honey.

PLASTIC DOUGH BLADE: Add whole wheat flour, gluten flour, milk powder and salt to work bowl. Pulse on/off to mix. With machine running, pour yeast mixture through feed tube. Pour in remaining water in a steady stream, only as fast as the flour absorbs it. All the water may not be needed to form a ball of dough. Process ball of dough for 20 seconds. Stop the machine and feel the dough. It should be elastic, sticky and wet. If not, process 10 seconds longer. Sprinkle dough with an additional 1-2 tablespoons flour. Pulse machine on/off to coat dough for easy removal from work bowl.

Transfer dough to an oiled bowl and turn so entire surface is oiled. Cover with plastic bag or damp cloth and let rise in a warm place, free from drafts, until doubled in bulk, about 1-1¼ hours. Punch down dough and knead for 30 seconds to press out the bubbles. Divide dough into 3 parts. Shape into balls, let rest, covered, 10-15 minutes.

TO SHAPE BRAID: Roll each ball into strands 14 inches long. Line the strands together, pinch tops together and braid. Pinch ends together. Tuck both ends under and pinch to seal. Place braid on a well-greased cookie sheet. Cover with plastic bag and let rise in warm place, free from drafts, until doubled, about 45-60 minutes.

Brush with egg glaze and sprinkle on sesame seeds. Bake in a preheated 350° oven, 30-40 minutes or until golden brown and loaf sounds hollow when tapped. Using a wide spatula, carefully remove loaf to metal rack to cool. The bread is fragile.

Preparation: 10 minutes
Standing: allow 2-2½ hours for dough to rise
Baking: 30-40 minutes
Protein g/s: 5.5

Applesauce Cinnamon Whole Wheat Bread

2 loaves, 16 slices per loaf

Delicious breakfast toast or serve with Cheddar or Monterey Jack cheese. Recipe may be halved to make one loaf.

2 *tablespoons active dry yeast*
⅓ *cup warm water (105°-115°F)*
2 *tablespoons oil*
2 *tablespoons honey*
2 *cups applesauce, room temperature*
6 *cups whole wheat flour, measured scoop and level*
2 *teaspoons salt*
1 *tablespoon ground cinnamon*
1 *cup raisins*
about ⅓ *cup additional water*

In a measuring cup, sprinkle yeast over ⅓ cup warm water. Let stand in warm place about 5 minutes until it dissolves or puffs. Add oil and honey.

PLASTIC DOUGH BLADE: Add flour, salt and cinnamon to work bowl. With machine running, pour yeast mixture through feed tube. Pour in applesauce and enough additional water to form a ball of dough. It may be necessary to stop machine and scrape the dough down sides of bowl. Process ball of dough for 20 seconds. Stop the machine and feel the dough. It should be elastic, sticky and wet. If not, process 10 seconds longer. Sprinkle dough with an additional 1-2 tablespoons flour. Pulse machine on/off to coat dough for easy removal from work bowl.

Place dough on a lightly floured surface and knead in raisins. Transfer dough to an oiled bowl and turn so entire surface is oiled. Cover with plastic bag or damp cloth and let rise in a warm place, free from drafts, until doubled in bulk, about 1-1½ hours. Punch down dough and knead to press out the bubbles. Divide the dough into two pieces. Shape into balls, let rest, covered 5 minutes. Shape each ball into a loaf and place in a greased 8½ x 4½-inch loaf pan. Cover and let rise in warm place, free from drafts, until doubled, about 1 hour.

Bake on middle rack in a preheated 375° oven 30-35 minutes until golden brown and bottom crust of loaf has a hard hollow sound when tapped. Remove from loaf pan immediately and place on metal rack to cool.

Preparation: 10 minutes
Standing: allow 2 hours for dough to rise
Baking: 30-35 minutes
Protein g/s: 3

Challah

1 or 2 loaves, 16 slices per loaf

A light moist bread that slices with ease.

Amounts for 3 cup and 2¾ cup flour capacity machines given in parentheses.

2 (1,1) *tablespoons active dry yeast*
½ (¼,¼) *cup warm water (105°-115°F)*
3 (1½, 1½) *tablespoons melted butter*
3 (1½, 1½) *tablespoons oil*
¼ (⅛,⅛) *cup honey*
3 (2,1) *eggs, lightly beaten, reserve 2 (1, 1) tablespoons for glaze*
6 (3, 2¾) *cups whole wheat flour, measured scoop and level*
½ (¼,¼) *cup non-instant, non-fat milk powder*
2 (1, 1) *teaspoons salt*
¾ (⅜,⅛) *cup additional water*
poppy seeds for topping

In a measuring cup, sprinkle yeast over ½ (¼, ¼) cup warm water. Let stand in warm place about 5 minutes until it dissolves or puffs. Stir in melted butter, oil and honey.

METAL BLADE or PLASTIC DOUGH BLADE: Add whole wheat flour, salt and milk powder to work bowl. With machine running, pour in yeast mixture and eggs in a steady stream. Pour in enough additional water to form a stiff ball of dough. Process ball of dough for 20 seconds. Stop the machine and feel the dough. It should be elastic, sticky and wet. If not, process 10 seconds longer. Sprinkle dough with additional 1-2 tablespoons flour. Pulse machine on/off to coat dough for easy removal from work bowl.

Transfer dough to an oiled bowl and turn so entire surface is oiled. Cover with plastic bag or damp cloth and let rise in a warm place, free from drafts, until doubled in bulk, 1-1½ hours. Punch down dough and knead for 30 seconds to press out the bubbles. Divide dough in half when making 2 loaves. Divide each half portion into 3 parts. Shape into balls, let rest, covered, 15 minutes.

TO SHAPE STRAIGHT BRAID: Roll each part into strands 12 inches long. Line 3 strands together, pinch tops together and braid. Pinch ends together. Tuck both ends under and pinch to seal. Place each braid on a greased cookie sheet. Cover with plastic bag; let rise in warm place, free from drafts, until doubled, 1 hour.

TO SHAPE RING: Roll strands 18 inches long. Line 3 strands together, pinch top together and braid. Form braid into a ring, pinch ends together. Place ring in a greased 8-inch cake pan (or on a greased cookie sheet or 8-inch pie pan). Cover with plastic bag and let rise in warm place, free from drafts, until doubled, about 1 hour.

Just before baking, brush loaves with reserved egg. Sprinkle on poppy seeds. Bake in preheated 350° oven 25-30 minutes or until golden brown and bottom crust sounds hard and hollow when tapped. Remove to a metal rack to cool.

Preparation: 15 minutes
Standing: allow 2½-3 hours for dough to rise
Baking: 25-30 minutes
Protein g/s: 4.5

Bran Bread

1 loaf, 15 slices

A light, moist bread that provides extra fiber.

1 *tablespoon active dry yeast*
¼ *cup warm water (105°-115°F)*
2 *tablespoons oil*
2 *tablespoons honey*
2¾ *cups whole wheat flour, measured scoop and level*
½ *cup bran*
½ *teaspoon salt*
½-¾ *cup water, as needed*

In a measuring cup, sprinkle yeast over ¼ cup warm water. Let stand in warm place about 5 minutes until it dissolves or puffs. Add oil and honey.

METAL BLADE: Add flour, bran, and salt to the work bowl. With machine running, pour in yeast mixture through feed tube. Pour in remaining water in a steady stream, only as fast as the flour absorbs it. All the water may not be needed to form a ball of dough. Process ball of dough for 20 seconds. Stop the machine and feel the dough. It should be elastic, sticky and wet. If not, process 10 seconds longer. Sprinkle dough with an additional 1-2 tablespoons flour. Pulse on/off to coat dough for easy removal from work bowl.

Transfer dough to an oiled bowl and turn so entire surface is oiled. Cover with plastic bag or damp cloth and let rise in a warm place, free from drafts, until doubled in bulk, about 1 hour. Punch down dough and knead for 30 seconds to press out the bubbles. Shape into a ball, let rest, covered, 5 minutes. Shape into a loaf and place in a greased 7⅞ x 3⅞-inch loaf pan. Cover and let rise in warm place, free from drafts, until doubled, about 45 minutes.

Bake on middle rack in a preheated 375° oven 30-35 minutes or until golden brown and bottom crust of loaf has a hard hollow sound when tapped. Remove from loaf pan immediately and place on metal rack to cool.

Preparation: 10 minutes
Standing: allow 2 hours for dough to rise
Baking: 30-35 minutes
Protein g/s: 3.5

Carrot Whole Wheat Bread

2 loaves, 16 slices per loaf

For machines with smaller capacities, cut recipe in half to make one loaf. Speckled with shredded carrots, this loaf makes excellent sandwiches.

2 *tablespoons active dry yeast*
⅓ *cup warm water (105°-115°F)*
2 *tablespoons oil*
¼ *cup honey*
3 *medium carrots, pared*
6 *cups whole wheat flour, measured scoop and level*
¼ *cup non-instant, non-fat milk powder*
2 *teaspoons salt*
1¼-1½ *cups water*

In a measuring cup, sprinkle yeast over ⅓ cup warm water. Let stand in warm place about 5 minutes until it dissolves or puffs. Add oil and honey.

SHREDDING DISC: Cut carrots to fit feed tube vertically. Shred. Remove shredding disc. Insert plastic dough blade.

PLASTIC DOUGH BLADE: Add flour, milk powder and salt to work bowl. Pulse on/off to mix. With machine running, pour yeast mixture through feed tube. Pour in remaining water in a steady stream, only as fast as the flour absorbs it. All the water may not be needed; add only enough to form a soft ball of dough. Process ball of dough for 20 seconds. Stop the machine and feel the dough. It should be elastic, sticky and wet. If not, process 10 seconds longer. Sprinkle dough with additional 1-2 tablespoons flour. Pulse machine on/off to coat dough for easy removal from work bowl.

Transfer dough to an oiled bowl and turn so entire surface is oiled. Cover with plastic bag or damp cloth and let rise in a warm place, free from drafts, until doubled in bulk, about 1 hour. Punch down dough and knead for 30 seconds to press out the bubbles. Divide the dough into two pieces. Shape into balls; let rest, covered, 5 minutes. Shape each ball into a loaf and place in a greased 8½ x 4½-inch loaf pan. Cover and let rise in warm place, free from drafts, until doubled, about 45 minutes.

Bake on middle rack in a preheated 375° oven 35-40 minutes or until golden brown and bottom crust of loaf has a hard hollow sound when tapped. Remove from loaf pan immediately and place on metal rack to cool.

Preparation: 10 minutes
Standing: allow 2-2½ hours for dough to rise
Baking: 35-40 minutes
Protein g/s: 3.5

Cottage Wheat Loaf

1 loaf, 16 slices

Cottage cheese and milk powder give this tangy loaf "extra" protein.

1 tablespoon active dry yeast
¼ cup warm water (105°-115°F)
2 tablespoons oil
2 tablespoons honey
½ cup small curd cottage cheese
2¾ cups whole wheat flour, measured scoop and
*   level*
¼ cup rye flour, measured scoop and level
2 tablespoons bran
1 teaspoon salt
¼ cup non-instant, non-fat milk powder
about ½ cup additional water

In a measuring cup, sprinkle yeast over ¼ cup warm water. Let stand in warm place about 5 minutes until it dissolves or puffs. Add oil, honey and cottage cheese. Stir to mix.

METAL BLADE: Add wheat and rye flours, bran, milk powder and salt to work bowl. Pulse on/off to mix. With machine running, pour yeast mixture through feed tube. Pour in remaining water in a steady stream only as fast as the flour absorbs it. All the water may not be needed to form a ball of dough. Process ball of dough for 20 seconds. Stop the machine and feel the dough. It should be elastic, sticky and wet. If not, process 10 seconds longer. Sprinkle dough with additional 1-2 tablespoons flour. Pulse machine on/off to coat dough for easy removal from work bowl.

Transfer dough to an oiled bowl and turn so entire surface is oiled. Cover with plastic bag or damp cloth, and let rise in a warm place, free from drafts, until doubled in bulk, about 1 hour. Punch down dough and knead for 30 seconds to press out the bubbles. Shape into a ball, let rest, covered, 5 min-

utes. Shape into a loaf and place in a greased 7⅞ x 3⅞-inch loaf pan. Cover and let rise in warm place, free from drafts, until doubled, about 1 hour.

Bake on middle rack in a preheated 375° oven 30-35 minutes or until golden brown and bottom crust of loaf has a hard hollow sound when tapped. Remove from loaf pan immediately and place on metal rack to cool.

Preparation: 10 minutes
Standing: allow 2-2½ hours for dough to rise
Baking: 35 minutes
Protein g/s: 4.5

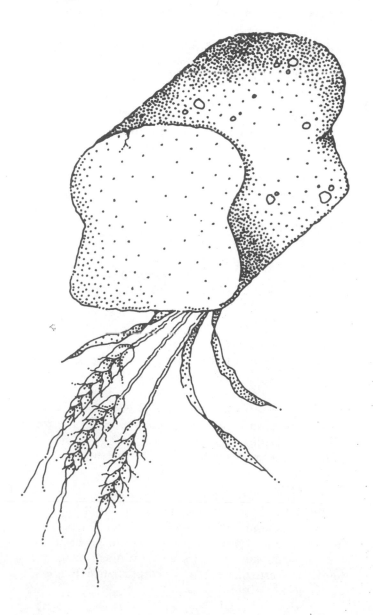

Herb Buttermilk Bread

1 loaf, 14 slices

A hint of herbs will make this the star at the dinner table. Double the recipe to process dough for 2 loaves in the larger capacity machine.

1 tablespoon active dry yeast
¼ cup warm water (105°-115°F)
2 tablespoons oil
1 tablespoon honey
2½ cups whole wheat flour, measured scoop and level
¼ cup buttermilk powder
½ tablespoon salt
1½ tablespoons mixed dried herbs
½ to ¾ cup additional water (or liquid buttermilk if used in place of buttermilk powder)

In a measuring cup, sprinkle yeast over ¼ cup warm water. Let stand in warm place about 5 minutes until it dissolves or puffs. Add oil and honey.

METAL BLADE: Add flour, salt, milk powder and herbs to work bowl. Pulse on/off to mix. With machine running, pour yeast mixture through feed tube. Pour in remaining water in a steady stream, only as fast as the flour absorbs it. All the water may not be needed to form a ball of dough. Process ball of dough for 20 seconds. Stop the machine and feel the dough. It should be elastic, sticky and wet. If not, process 10 seconds longer. Sprinkle dough with an additional 1-2 tablespoons flour. Pulse machine on/off to coat dough for easy removal from work bowl. Dough will be firm to hold the shape of the braid.

Transfer dough to an oiled bowl and turn so entire surface is oiled. Cover with plastic bag or damp cloth and let rise in a warm place, free from drafts, until doubled in bulk, about 1 hour. Punch down dough and knead for 30 seconds to press out the bubbles. Divide the dough into two pieces if making 2 loaves. Divide each half portion into 3 parts. Shape into balls, let rest, covered, 10-15 minutes.

TO SHAPE BRAID: Roll each part into strands 12 inches long. Line 3 strands together, pinch tops together and braid. Pinch ends together. Tuck both ends under and pinch to seal. Place each braid on a greased cookie sheet. Cover with plastic bag and let rise in warm place, free from drafts, until doubled, about 45-60 minutes.

Bake on middle rack in a preheated 350° oven 30-35 minutes until golden brown and bottom crust of loaf has a hard hollow sound when tapped. Transfer the loaf carefully to a metal rack to cool.

Preparation: 15 minutes
Standing: allow 2½-3 hours for dough to rise and to shape braid
Baking: 30-35 minutes
Protein g/s: 3.5

Cracked Wheat Buttermilk Bread

1 loaf, 15 slices

Softened cracked wheat adds an interesting texture to this bread.

½ cup cracked wheat
2 tablespoons butter or safflower margarine
½ cup boiling water
1 tablespoon active dry yeast
⅓ cup warm water (105°-115°F)
2 tablespoons honey
2½ cups plus 2 tablespoons whole wheat flour, measured scoop and level
½ teaspoon salt
⅓ cup buttermilk, at room temperature
1-3 tablespoons water, as needed

In a small bowl, combine cracked wheat, butter and ½ cup boiling water. Let stand until cracked wheat, is softened, about 20 minutes. In a measuring cup, sprinkle yeast over ⅓ cup warm water. Let stand in warm place about 5 minutes until it dissolves or puffs. Add honey.

METAL BLADE: Add flour and salt to work bowl. Pulse on/off to mix. Remove work bowl cover; add cracked wheat mixture. Pulse on/off to mix. With machine running, pour yeast mixture through feed tube. Pour in buttermilk in a steady stream, only as fast as the flour absorbs it. Add only enough additional water to form a ball of dough. Process ball of dough for 20 seconds. Stop the machine and feel the dough. It should be elastic, sticky and wet. If not, process 10 seconds longer. Sprinkle dough with an additional 1-2 tablespoons flour. Pulse machine on/off to coat dough for easy removal from work bowl.

Transfer dough to an oiled bowl and turn so entire surface is oiled. Cover with plastic bag or damp cloth and let rise in a warm place, free from drafts, until doubled in bulk, about 1 hour. Punch down dough and knead for 30 seconds to press out the bubbles. Shape into a ball, let rest, covered, 5 minutes. Shape into a loaf and place in a greased 8½ x 4½-inch loaf pan. Cover and let rise in warm place, free from drafts, until doubled, about 40-45 minutes.

Bake on middle rack in a preheated 350° oven 40-45 minutes or until golden brown and bottom crust of loaf has a hard hollow sound when tapped. Remove from loaf pan immediately and place on metal rack to cool.

Preparation: 10 minutes
Standing: allow 20 minutes for cracked wheat to soften; 1½-2 hours for dough to rise
Baking: 40-45 minutes
Protein g/s: 3.5

Double Cheese Bread

1 loaf, 16 slices

The combination of Cheddar and cottage cheeses makes this moist loaf a tasty treat.

1 tablespoon active dry yeast
¼ cup warm water (105°-115°F)
1 tablespoon oil
2 tablespoons honey
4 ounces Cheddar cheese
3 cups whole wheat flour, measured scoop and level
1 teaspoon salt
2 teaspoons dill seed
1 cup low-fat cottage cheese
additional ¼ cup water

In a measuring cup, sprinkle yeast over ¼ cup warm water. Let stand in warm place about 5 minutes until it dissolves or puffs. Add oil and honey.

SHREDDING DISC: Place Cheddar cheese in feed tube, shred using light pressure. Remove shredding disc.

METAL BLADE: Add to work bowl with cheese, the flour, salt, dill seed and cottage cheese. Pulse on/off to mix. With machine running, pour yeast mixture through feed tube. Pour in remaining water in a steady stream, only as fast as the flour absorbs it. All the water may not be needed to form a ball of dough. Process ball of dough for 20 seconds. Stop the machine and feel the dough. It should be elastic, sticky and wet. If not, process 10 seconds longer. Sprinkle dough with an additional 1-2 tablespoons flour. Pulse machine on/off to coat dough for easy removal from work bowl.

Transfer dough to an oiled bowl and turn so entire surface is oiled. Cover with plastic bag or damp cloth and let rise in a warm place, free from drafts, until doubled in bulk, about 1 hour. Punch down dough and knead for 30 seconds to press out the bubbles. Shape into a ball, let rest, covered, 5 minutes. Shape into a loaf and place in a greased 8½ x 4½-inch loaf pan. Cover and let rise in warm place until doubled, about 45 minutes.

Bake on middle rack in a preheated 375° oven 30 minutes or until golden brown and bottom crust of loaf has a hard hollow sound when tapped. Remove from loaf pan immediately and place on metal rack to cool.

Preparation: 10 minutes
Standing: allow 2-2½ hours for dough to rise
Baking: 30-35 minutes
Protein g/s: 6.5

Honey Wheat Bread

1 small loaf, 15 slices; 1 medium loaf, 16 slices

An all-around sandwich bread sweetened with honey. Double the recipe for 2 small loaves if your machine can handle 6 cups flour.

1 Loaf 7⅞ x 3⅞ inches

1 *tablespoon active dry yeast*
¼ *cup warm water (105°-115°F)*
2 *tablespoons oil*
2 *tablespoons honey*
3 *cups whole wheat flour, measured scoop and level*
¼ *cup non-instant, non-fat milk powder*
½ *tablespoon salt*
¾ *cups additional water*

1 Loaf 8½ x 4½ inches

1 *tablespoon active dry yeast*
⅓ *cup warm water (105°-115°F)*
2 *tablespoons oil*
3 *tablespoons honey*
3¾ *cups whole wheat flour, measured scoop and level*
¼ *cup non-instant, non-fat milk powder*
½ *tablespoon salt*
scant 1 *cup additional water*

In a measuring cup, sprinkle yeast over warm water. Let stand in a warm place about 5 minutes until it dissolves or puffs. Add oil and honey.

METAL BLADE or PLASTIC DOUGH BLADE: Add flour, milk powder and salt to work bowl. Pulse on/off to mix. With machine running, pour yeast mixture through feed tube. Pour in remaining water in a steady stream, only as fast as the flour absorbs it. All the water may not be needed to form a ball of dough. Process ball of dough for 20 seconds. Stop the machine and feel the dough. It should be elastic, sticky and wet. If not, process 10 seconds longer. Sprinkle dough with an additional 1-2 tablespoons flour. Pulse machine on/off to coat dough for easy removal from work bowl.

Transfer dough to an oiled bowl and turn so entire surface is oiled. Cover with plastic bag or damp cloth and let rise in a warm place, free from drafts, until doubled in bulk, about 1 hour. Punch down dough and knead for 30 seconds to press out the bubbles. Divide dough into halves (if making two loaves). Shape each portion into a ball; let rest, covered, 5 minutes. Shape into a loaf and place in a greased loaf pan. Cover and let rise in warm place, free from drafts, until doubled, about 45 minutes.

Bake on middle rack in a preheated 375° oven 30-35 minutes or until golden brown and bottom crust of loaf has a hard hollow sound when tapped. Remove from loaf pan immediately and place on metal rack to cool.

Preparation: 10 minutes
Standing: allow 2-2½ hours for dough to rise
Baking: 30-35 minutes
Protein g/s: small loaf—4
            medium loaf—4.5

Irish Oatmeal Bread

1 loaf, 15 slices

One of our all-time favorites. The rolled oats are added last to keep the texture.

1 *tablespoon active dry yeast*
½ *cup warm water (105°-115°F)*
1 *tablespoon oil*
2 *tablespoons honey*
1 *egg*
2¼ *cups whole wheat flour, measured scoop and level*
3 *tablespoons non-instant, non-fat milk powder*
½ *teaspoon salt*
⅔ *cup rolled oats*
1-4 *tablespoons water, as needed*
½ *cup raisins or currants*

Glaze: 1 *egg beaten with* ¼ *cup water*

In a measuring cup, sprinkle yeast over ½ cup warm water. Let stand in a warm place about 5 minutes until it dissolves or puffs. Stir in oil, honey and 1 egg.

METAL BLADE: Add flour, milk powder and salt to work bowl. Pulse on/off to mix. With machine running, pour in yeast mixture through feed tube. Stop the machine when all the liquid has been added. Add rolled oats and continue to process until a ball of dough is formed, adding additional water as needed. Process ball of dough for 20 seconds. Stop the machine and feel the dough. It should be elastic, sticky and wet. If not, process 10 seconds longer. Sprinkle dough with an additional 1-2 tablespoons flour. Pulse machine on/off to coat dough for easy removal from work bowl.

Transfer dough to an oiled bowl and turn so entire surface is oiled. Cover with plastic bag or damp cloth and let rise in a warm place, free from drafts, until doubled in bulk, about 1 hour. Punch down dough and knead for 30 seconds to evenly distribute the ½ cup raisins and to press out the bubbles. Shape into a ball; let rest, covered, 5 minutes. Shape into a high-rounded loaf, about 6½ inches across. Place on a well-greased cookie sheet. Cover and let rise in warm place, free from drafts, until doubled, about 45 minutes.

Brush top of loaf with egg glaze. Bake on middle rack in a preheated 350° oven 35-45 minutes or until golden brown and loaf sounds hollow when tapped. Remove to metal rack to cool.

Preparation: 10 minutes
Standing: allow 2-2½ hours for dough to rise
Baking: 35-45 minutes
Protein g/s: 4

Mixed Grain Bread

1 loaf, 16 slices

Oats, cornmeal, rye and wheat flavor this bread. The dough will be stiff but the finished product is light and moist.

1 tablespoon active dry yeast
¼ cup warm water (105°-115°F)
2½ tablespoons oil
2 tablespoons molasses
1 egg
3 cups whole wheat flour, measured scoop and level
⅓ cup non-instant, non-fat milk powder
¼ cup rolled oats, measured scoop and level
¼ cup cornmeal, measured scoop and level
¼ cup bran, measured scoop and level
½ cup rye flour, measured scoop and level
1½ teaspoons salt
¾-1 cup water

In a measuring cup, sprinkle yeast over ¼ cup warm water. Let stand in a warm place about 5 minutes until it dissolves or puffs. Add oil and molasses.

PLASTIC DOUGH BLADE: Add whole wheat flour, milk powder, rolled oats, cornmeal, bran, rye flour and salt to work bowl. Pulse on/off to mix. Remove work bowl cover and pour in yeast mixture. Pulse on/off to mix. Add egg. With machine running, pour in remaining water in a steady stream, only as fast as the flour absorbs it. All the water may not be needed to form a ball of dough. Process ball of dough for 20 seconds. Stop the machine and feel the dough. It should be elastic, sticky and wet. If not, process 10 seconds longer. Sprinkle dough with an additional 1-2 tablespoons flour. Pulse on/off to coat dough for easy removal from work bowl.

Transfer dough to an oiled bowl and turn so entire surface is oiled. Cover with plastic bag or damp cloth and let rise in a warm place, free from drafts, until doubled in bulk, about 1 hour. Punch down dough and knead for 30 seconds to press out the bubbles. Shape into a ball, let rest, covered, 5 minutes. Shape into a loaf and place in a greased 8½ x 4½-inch loaf pan. Cover and let rise in warm place, free from drafts, until doubled, about 45-60 minutes.

Bake on middle rack in a preheated 375° oven 25 minutes; reduce oven temperature to 350° and continue to bake 20 minutes or until loaf is golden brown and bottom crust of loaf has a hard hollow sound when tapped. Remove from pan immediately and place on metal rack to cool.

Preparation: 10 minutes
Standing: allow 2½ hours for dough to rise
Baking: 45 minutes
Protein g/s: 5

Limpa Swedish Rye Bread

1 loaf, 15 slices

This uncommonly delicious bread is flavored with caraway and anise seeds and sweetened with blackstrap molasses and honey. It's a perfect accompaniment to a bowl of Boston baked beans or any hearty bean soup. Use dark rye flour if available. It's higher in protein.

1 *tablespoon active dry yeast*
¼ *cup warm water (105°-115°F)*
1 *tablespoon blackstrap molasses*
3 *tablespoons honey*
2 *cups plus 2 tablespoons whole wheat flour,*
  measured scoop and level
⅔ *cup rye flour, measured scoop and level*
¼ *cup non-instant, non-fat milk powder*
½ *teaspoon salt*
2 *teaspoons grated orange rind*
2 *tablespoons butter or safflower margarine*
½-⅔ *cup water as needed*
2 *teaspoons each caraway and anise seeds*
additional caraway seeds for topping

Glaze: 1 *egg beaten with 2 tablespoons water*

In a measuring cup, sprinkle yeast over ¼ cup warm water. Let stand in a warm place about 5 minutes until it dissolves or puffs. Stir in molasses and honey.

METAL BLADE: Add wheat and rye flours, milk powder, salt and orange rind to work bowl. Pulse on/off to mix. Add butter, pulse on/off to cut in. With machine running, pour yeast mixture through feed tube. Pour in remaining water in a steady stream, only as fast as the flour absorbs it. All the water may not be needed to form a ball of dough. Process ball of dough for 20 seconds. Stop the machine and feel the dough. It should be elastic, sticky and wet. If not, process 10 seconds longer. With machine running, add caraway and anise seeds. Process only until just mixed. Sprinkle dough with an additional 1-2 tablespoons flour. Pulse machine on-off to coat dough for easy removal from work bowl.

Transfer dough to an oiled bowl and turn so entire surface is oiled. Cover with plastic bag or damp cloth and let rise in a warm place, free from drafts, until doubled in bulk, 1-1¼ hours. Punch down dough and knead for 30 seconds to press out the bubbles. Shape into a ball, let rest, covered 5 minutes. Shape into a rounded high loaf measuring about 5-6 inches across. Place loaf on a well-greased cookie sheet. Cover and let rise in warm place, free from drafts, until doubled, about 45 minutes.

Brush with egg glaze, sprinkle on caraway seeds. Bake on middle rack in a preheated 350° oven 40-45 minutes or until bottom crust of loaf has a hard hollow sound when tapped. Remove to metal rack to cool.

Preparation: 10 minutes
Standing: allow 2½ hours for dough to rise
Baking: 40-45 minutes
Protein g/s: 3.5

Malted Milk Bread

1 loaf, 15 slices

The gluten flour may be omitted, producing a more compact but delicious, moist loaf. Increase the whole wheat flour to 3 cups.

1 *tablespoon active dry yeast*
¼ *cup warm water (105°-115°F)*
1 *tablespoon oil*
2¾ *cups whole wheat flour, measured scoop and*
  level (increase to 3 cups if gluten flour is
  omitted)
¼ *cup gluten flour (optional)*
½ *cup malted milk (Carnation Brand)*
½ *teaspoon salt*
¾-1 *cup water, as needed*

In a measuring cup, sprinkle yeast over ¼ cup warm water. Let stand in a warm place about 5 minutes until it dissolves or puffs. Add oil.

METAL BLADE Add whole wheat flour, gluten flour, malted milk and salt to work bowl. Pulse on/off to mix. With machine running, pour yeast mixture through feed tube. Pour in remaining water in a steady stream, only as fast as the flour absorbs it. All the water may not be needed to form a ball of dough. Process ball of dough for 20 seconds. Stop the machine and feel the dough. It should be elastic, sticky and wet. If not, process 10 seconds longer. Sprinkle dough with an additional 1-2 tablespoons flour. Pulse machine on/off to coat dough for easy removal from work bowl.

Transfer dough to an oiled bowl and turn so entire surface is oiled. Cover with plastic bag or damp cloth and let rise in a warm place, free from drafts, until doubled in bulk, about 45-60 minutes. Punch down dough and knead for 30 seconds to press out the bubbles. Shape into a ball, let rest, covered, 5 minutes. Shape into a loaf and place in a greased 8½ x 4½-inch loaf pan. Cover and let rise in warm place, free from drafts, until doubled, about 45 minutes.

Bake on middle rack in a preheated 350° oven 45-55 minutes or until golden brown and bottom crust of loaf has a hard hollow sound when tapped. Remove from loaf pan immediately and place on metal rack to cool.

Preparation: 10 minutes
Standing: allow 2 hours for dough to rise
Baking: 45-55 minutes
Protein g/s: 4

Oat Bran Bread

1 loaf, 16 slices

Try this recipe after you are familiar with your machine and have made a few loaves following the procedure outlined in the beginning of the chapter. We suggest this because the steps to produce this bread are a variation of the standard. This loaf is light, moist and has a chewy texture due to the oats.

½ cup rolled oats
½ cup bran
1 tablespoon oil
2 tablespoons molasses
1 cup boiling water
1 tablespoon active dry yeast
¼ cup warm water (105°-115°F)
3¾ cups whole wheat flour, measured scoop and
      level
1 teaspoon salt
¼-½ cup water, as needed

In a medium bowl, combine oats, bran, oil and molasses. Pour in boiling water. Stir and allow to cool to lukewarm, about 30 minutes. To hasten cooling, place in a cold water bath. Test with a thermometer or finger to make sure that it is not over 115°F. In a measuring cup, sprinkle yeast over ¼ cup warm water. Let stand in a warm place about 5 minutes until it dissolves or puffs.

PLASTIC DOUGH BLADE: Add flour and salt to work bowl. Add yeast mixture through feed tube; pulse on/off to mix. Remove cover, pour in oat/bran mixture all at once. Use spatula to mix slightly. Turn on machine and process to make a ball of dough. Gradually add remaining water if needed. Have patience and do not add too much water too fast. It takes a moment for the flour to absorb the oat/bran mixture. It may be necessary to stop machine and push dough to loosen the ball to help distribute the liquid. Process the ball of dough for 20 seconds. Stop the machine and feel the dough. It should be elastic, sticky and wet. If not, process 10 seconds longer. Sprinkle dough with an additional 1-2 tablespoons flour. Pulse machine on/off to coat dough for easy removal from work bowl.

Transfer dough to an oiled bowl and turn so entire surface is oiled. Cover with plastic bag or damp cloth and let rise in a warm place, free from drafts, until doubled in bulk, about 1 hour. Punch down dough and knead for 30 seconds to press out bubbles. Shape into a ball, let rest, covered, 5 minutes. Shape into a loaf and place in a greased 8½ x 4½-inch loaf pan. Cover and let rise in warm place, free from drafts, until doubled, about 45 minutes.

Bake on middle rack in a preheated 350° oven 40-45 minutes or until golden brown and bottom crust of loaf has a hard hollow sound when tapped. Remove from loaf pan immediately and place on metal rack to cool.

Preparation: 10 minutes
Standing: 30 minutes for oat/bran mixture to cool
              2 hours for dough to rise
Baking: 40-45 minutes
Protein g/s: 4.5

Nut Butter Bread

1 loaf, 16 slices

This moist close-grained loaf slices easily. Try it with sliced apples topped with Cheddar cheese.

1 *tablespoon active dry yeast*
¼ *cup warm water (105°-115°F)*
2 *tablespoons honey*
½ *cup crunchy unsalted peanut butter (or nut butter of your choice)*
3½ *cups whole wheat flour, measured scoop and level*
¼ *cup non-instant, non-fat milk powder*
½ *tablespoon salt*
about 1 cup water

In a measuring cup, sprinkle yeast over ¼ cup warm water. Let stand in warm place about 5 minutes until it dissolves or puffs. Add honey.

METAL BLADE or PLASTIC DOUGH BLADE: Add whole wheat flour, milk powder and salt to work bowl. Pulse on/off to mix. With machine off, spoon in peanut butter. With machine running, pour yeast mixture through feed tube. Pour in remaining water in a steady stream, only as fast as the flour absorbs it. All the water may not be needed to form a ball of dough. Process ball of dough for 20 seconds. Stop the machine and feel the dough. It should be elastic, sticky and wet. If not, process 10 seconds longer. Sprinkle dough with an additional 1-2 tablespoons flour. Pulse machine on/off to coat dough for easy removal from work bowl.

Transfer dough to an oiled bowl and turn so entire surface is oiled. Cover with plastic bag or damp cloth and let rise in a warm place, free from drafts, until doubled in bulk, about 1 hour. Punch down dough and knead for 30 seconds to press out the bubbles. Shape into a ball; let rest, covered, 5 minutes. Shape into a loaf and place in a greased 8½ x 4½-inch loaf pan. Cover and let rise in warm place, free from drafts, until doubled, about 1 hour.

Bake on middle rack in a preheated 375° oven 30-35 minutes or until golden brown and bottom crust of loaf has a hard hollow sound when tapped. Remove from loaf pan immediately and place on metal rack to cool.

Preparation: 10 minutes
Standing: allow 2-2½ hours for dough to rise
Baking: 30-35 minutes
Protein g/s: 6.5

Oat Flour Whole Wheat Bread

1 small loaf, 15 slices; 1 medium loaf, 16 slices

Choose the size of the loaf you want to bake to match the capacity of your machine. This is a moist loaf that makes delicious toast or a nice sandwich bread. Double the recipe for 2 small loaves if your machine can handle 6 cups of flour.

1 Loaf 7⅞ x 3⅞ inches
1 *cup rolled oats*
1 *tablespoon active dry yeast*
¼ *cup warm water (105°-115°F)*
1½ *tablespoons oil*
1½ *tablespoons honey*
2½ *cups whole wheat flour, measured scoop and level*
3 *tablespoons non-instant, non-fat milk powder*
½ *tablespoon salt*
¾ *cup plus 1 tablespoon water*
additional flour as needed

1 Loaf 8½ x 4½ inches
1½ *cups rolled oats*
1 *tablespoon active dry yeast*
⅔ *cup warm water (105°-115°F)*
2 *tablespoons oil*
2 *tablespoons honey*
3-3¾ *cups whole wheat flour, measured scoop and level*
½ *cup non-instant, non-fat milk powder*
½ *tablespoon salt*
1 *cup water*
additional flour as needed

METAL BLADE: Add rolled oats to work bowl and process until a fine flour is made, about 60 seconds. Remove from bowl and set aside. In a measuring cup, sprinkle yeast over warm water. Let stand in a warm place about 5 minutes until it dissolves or puffs. Add oil and honey.

METAL BLADE or PLASTIC DOUGH BLADE: Add whole wheat flour, milk powder and salt to work bowl. Pulse on/off to mix. With machine running, pour yeast mixture through feed tube. Pour in *all* of the remaining water in a steady stream, only as fast as the flour absorbs it. Process 20 seconds. Dough will be sticky and wet.

Turn off machine, add oat flour. Pulse on/off to mix in, scraping down sides of bowl if necessary. Process to knead ball of dough 20 seconds. Add flour needed to produce a ball of dough—but do so sparingly. Turn off machine and feel dough. It should be elastic, sticky and wet. If not, process 10 seconds longer. Sprinkle dough with an additional 1-2 tablespoons flour. Pulse machine on/off to coat dough for easy removal from work bowl.

Transfer dough to an oiled bowl and turn so entire surface is oiled. Cover with plastic bag or damp cloth and let rise in a warm place, free from drafts, until doubled in bulk, about 1 hour. Punch down dough and knead for 30 seconds to press out the bubbles. Shape into a ball, let rest, covered, 5 minutes. Shape into loaf and place in a greased loaf pan. Cover and let rise in warm place, free from drafts, until doubled, about 45-60 minutes.

Bake on middle rack in a preheated 375° oven 35-40 minutes or until golden brown and bottom crust of loaf has a hard hollow sound when tapped. Remove from loaf pan immediately and place on metal rack to cool.

Preparation: 10-15 minutes
Standing: allow 2-2½ hours for dough to rise
Baking: 35-40 minutes.
Protein g/s: small loaf—3.5
              medium loaf—5.5

PLASTIC DOUGH BLADE: Add flour, salt and milk powder to work bowl. Pulse on/off to mix. With machine running, pour yeast mixture through feed tube. Pour in remaining water in a steady stream, only as fast as the flour absorbs it. All the water may not be needed to form a ball of dough. Process ball of dough for 20 seconds. Stop the machine and feel the dough. It should be elastic, sticky and wet. If not, process 10 seconds longer. Sprinkle dough with an additional 1-2 tablespoons flour. Pulse machine on/off to coat dough for easy removal from work bowl.

Transfer dough to an oiled bowl and turn so entire surface is oiled. Cover with plastic bag or damp cloth and let rise in a warm place, free from drafts, until doubled in bulk, 1-1½ hours. Punch down dough and knead for 30 seconds to press out the bubbles. Shape into a ball; let rest, covered, 5 minutes. Shape into a loaf and place in a greased 8½ x 4½-inch or 9 x 5-inch loaf pan. Cover and let rise in warm place, free from drafts, until doubled, about 1 hour.

Bake on middle rack in a preheated 375° oven 30-35 minutes or until golden brown and bottom crust of loaf has a hard hollow sound when tapped. Remove from loaf pan immediately and place on metal rack to cool.

Preparation: 10 minutes
Standing: allow 2-2½ hours for dough to rise
Baking: 30-35 minutes
Protein g/s: 4.5

Molasses Wheat Bread

1 loaf, 16 slices

This is a good all-around sandwich bread, not too sweet.

1 tablespoon active dry yeast
¼ cup warm water (105°-115°F)
2 tablespoons oil
¼ cup molasses
4 cups whole wheat flour, measured scoop and
   level
½ tablespoon salt
¼ cup non-instant, non-fat milk powder
about 1 cup additional water

In a measuring cup, sprinkle yeast over ¼ cup warm water. Let stand in a warm place about 5 minutes until it dissolves or puffs. Add oil and molasses.

Orange Sunflower Seed Bread

1 loaf, 16 slices

Fresh squeezed orange juice and sunflower seeds flavor this loaf. Makes excellent breakfast toast or a lunchtime treat with homemade peanut butter.

1　*tablespoon active dry yeast*
¼　*cup warm water (105°-115°F)*
2　*tablespoons oil*
2　*tablespoons honey*
1　*egg*
3¾　*cups whole wheat flour, measured scoop and level*
¼　*cup non-instant, non-fat milk powder*
grated peel of 1 orange
½　*tablespoon salt*
⅓　*cup sunflower seeds*
½　*cup fresh squeezed orange juice*
¼　*cup water, as needed*

In a measuring cup, sprinkle yeast over ¼ cup warm water. Let stand in a warm place about 5 minutes until it dissolves or puffs. Stir in oil, honey and egg.

PLASTIC DOUGH BLADE: Add flour, milk powder, salt, grated orange peel and sunflower seeds to work bowl. Pulse on/off to mix. With machine running, pour yeast mixture and orange juice through feed tube. Pour in remaining water in a steady stream only as fast as the flour absorbs it. All the water may not be needed to form a ball of dough. Process the ball of dough 20 seconds. Stop the machine and feel the dough. It should be elastic, sticky and wet. If not, process 10 seconds longer. Sprinkle dough with an additional 1-2 tablespoons flour. Pulse machine on/off to coat dough for easy removal from work bowl.

Transfer dough to an oiled bowl and turn so entire surface is oiled. Cover with plastic bag or damp cloth and let rise in a warm place, free from drafts, until doubled in bulk, about 1 hour. Punch down dough and knead for 30 seconds to press out the bubbles. Shape into a ball; let rest, covered, 5 minutes. Shape into a loaf and place in a greased 8½ x 4½-inch loaf pan. Cover and let rise in warm place, free from drafts, until doubled, about 45 minutes.

Bake on middle rack in a preheated 375° oven 30-35 minutes or until golden brown and bottom crust of loaf has a hard hollow sound when tapped. Remove from loaf pan immediately and place on metal rack to cool.

Preparation: 10 minutes
Standing: allow 2-2½ hours for dough to rise
Baking: 30-35 minutes
Protein g/s: 5.5

Oatmeal Sesame Bread

2 loaves, 15 slices per loaf

Sesame seeds make this hearty loaf a taste treat with an interesting texture.

2　*tablespoons active dry yeast*
½　*cup warm water (105°-115°F)*
2　*tablespoons oil*
3　*tablespoons honey*
4　*cups whole wheat flour, measured scoop and level*
1　*teaspoon salt*
2　*cups rolled oats*
½　*cup sesame seeds*
½　*cup non-instant, non-fat milk powder*
1-1¼　*cups water*

In a measuring cup, sprinkle yeast over ½ cup warm water. Let stand in warm place about 5 minutes until it dissolves or puffs. Add oil and honey.

PLASTIC DOUGH BLADE: Add flour, salt, oats, sesame seeds and milk powder to work bowl. Pulse on/off to mix. With machine running, pour yeast mixture through feed tube. Pour in remaining water in a steady stream, only as fast as flour absorbs it. All the water may not be needed to form a ball of dough. Process the stiff ball of dough for 20 seconds. Stop the machine and feel the dough. It should be elastic, sticky and wet. If not, process 10 seconds longer. Sprinkle dough with an additional 1-2 tablespoons flour. Pulse machine on/off to coat dough for easy removal from work bowl.

Transfer dough to an oiled bowl and turn so entire surface is oiled. Cover with plastic bag or damp cloth and let rise in a warm place, free from drafts, until doubled in bulk, about 1 hour. Punch down dough and knead for 30 seconds to press out the bubbles. Divide dough in half. Shape each piece into a smooth round ball and place in greased 8-inch round pans. Loaves may also be baked in greased 7⅞ x 3⅞-inch pans. Cover and let rise in warm place, free from drafts, until doubled, about 40 minutes.

Bake on middle rack in a preheated 350° oven 30-35 minutes or until golden brown and bottom crust of loaf has a hard hollow sound when tapped. Remove from pan immediately and place on metal rack to cool.

Preparation: 10 minutes
Standing: allow 2½ hours for dough to rise
Baking: 30-35 minutes
Protein g/s: 4

Potato Loaf

1 loaf, 16 slices

Fresh mashed potatoes make this loaf moist and chewy. Slices thin with ease. Double recipe to make two loaves.

5 ounces potatoes
2 tablespoons cold water
1½ tablespoons oil
1½ tablespoons honey
1 tablespoon active dry yeast
¼ cup warm water (105°-115°F)
2¾ cups whole wheat flour, measured scoop and
      level
¾ teaspoon salt
2 tablespoons non-instant, non-fat milk powder
1 egg, slightly beaten

Cook whole potatoes in water to cover until tender. While hot, peel and mash. You will have about ⅔ cup. Allow to cool slightly; stir in cold water, oil and honey. In a measuring cup, sprinkle yeast over ¼ cup warm water. Let stand in warm place about 5 minutes until it dissolves or puffs.

METAL BLADE: Add flour, salt, and milk powder to work bowl. Pulse on/off to mix. With processor running, pour dissolved yeast, potato mixture and egg through feed tube. After liquid is absorbed, let processor knead the ball of dough for 20 seconds. Add only enough additional water or flour to form a ball of dough. Stop the machine and feel the dough. It should be elastic, sticky and wet. If not, process 10 seconds longer. Sprinkle dough with an additional 1-2 tablespoons flour. Pulse machine on/off to coat dough for easy removal from work bowl.

Transfer dough to an oiled bowl and turn so entire surface is oiled. Cover with plastic bag or damp cloth and let rise in a warm place, free from drafts, until doubled in bulk, about 1 hour. Punch down dough and knead for 30 seconds to press out the bubbles. Shape into a ball, let rest, covered, 5 minutes. Shape into a loaf and place in a greased 8½ x 4½-inch loaf pan. Cover and let rise in warm place, free from drafts, until doubled, about 45-60 minutes.

Bake on middle rack in a preheated 375° oven 30-35 minutes or until golden brown and bottom crust of loaf has a hard hollow sound when tapped. Remove from loaf pan immediately and place on metal rack to cool.

Preparation: 10 minutes
Standing: allow 2-2½ hours for dough to rise
Cooking/Baking: 30-35 minutes to bake
                20-25 minutes to cook potatoes
Protein g/s: 3.5

Protein Plus

2 loaves, 15 slices per loaf

A variation of a well-known recipe for bread which contains soy flour, wheat germ and milk powder. This close-grained loaf slices with ease. Recipe may be divided in half for smaller machines.

2　*tablespoons active dry yeast*
½　*cup warm water (105°-115°F)*
3　*tablespoons oil*
¼　*cup honey*
4½　*cups whole wheat flour, measured scoop and*
　　level
½　*cup oat flour**
⅓　*cup soy flour*
¼　*cup wheat germ*
½　*cup non-instant, non-fat milk powder*
2　*teaspoons salt*
1　*cup water, as needed*

In a measuring cup, sprinkle yeast over ½ cup warm water. Let stand in a warm place about 5 minutes until it dissolves or puffs. Add oil and honey.

PLASTIC DOUGH BLADE: Add wheat flour, oat flour, milk powder, soy flour, wheat germ, and salt to work bowl. Pulse on/off to mix. With machine running, pour yeast mixture through feed tube. Pour in remaining water in a steady stream, only as fast as the flour absorbs it. All the water may not be needed to form a ball of dough. Process ball of dough for 20 seconds. Stop the machine and feel the dough. It should be elastic, sticky and wet. If not, process 10 seconds longer. Sprinkle dough with an additional 1-2 tablespoons flour. Pulse machine on/off to coat dough for easy removal from work bowl.

Transfer dough to an oiled bowl and turn so entire surface is oiled. Cover with plastic bag or damp cloth and let rise in a warm place, free from drafts, until doubled in bulk, about 1-1½ hours. Punch down dough and knead for 30 seconds to press out the bubbles. Divide the dough into two pieces. Shape each portion into ball; let rest, covered 5 minutes. Shape into a loaf and place in a greased 7⅞ x 3⅞-inch loaf pan. Cover and let rise in warm place, free from drafts, until doubled, about 45-60 minutes.

Bake on middle rack in a preheated 375° oven 35-40 minutes. Cover loaves with a tent of aluminum foil during the last 10 minutes if tops are browning too quickly. Loaves are done when the bottom crust has a hard hollow sound when tapped. Remove from loaf pan immediately and place on metal rack to cool.

Preparation: 10-15 minutes
Standing: allow 2½ hours for dough to rise
Baking: 35-40 minutes
Protein g/s: 4

*To make oat flour, process rolled oats, using the metal blade until a finely ground flour is produced. 1½ cups rolled oats makes about 1 cup ground oat flour. Store in an airtight container in a cool place.

Pumpkin Bread

1 loaf, 16 slices

A nice way to use left-over pumpkin.

1　*tablespoon active dry yeast*
½　*cup warm water (105°-115°F)*
2　*tablespoons oil*
3-4　*tablespoons honey*
1　*egg*
½　*cup cooked pumpkin, mashed*
3　*cups whole wheat flour, measured scoop and*
　　level
¼　*cup non-instant, non-fat milk powder*
1　*teaspoon salt*
½　*teaspoon ground cinnamon*
¼　*teaspoon ground nutmeg*
¼　*teaspoon ground cloves*
pinch ground ginger
¼　*cup water*
½　*cup raisins*

In a measuring cup, sprinkle yeast over ½ cup warm water. Let stand in warm place about 5 minutes until it dissolves or puffs. Stir in oil, honey, egg and pumpkin.

METAL BLADE: Add whole wheat flour, milk powder, salt, and spices to work bowl. Pulse on/off to mix. With machine running, pour in yeast mixture through feed tube. Pour in remaining water in a steady stream, only as fast as the flour absorbs it. All the water may not be needed to form a ball of dough. Process ball of dough for 20 seconds. Stop machine and feel the dough. It should be elastic, sticky and wet. If not, process 10 seconds longer. Sprinkle dough with an additional 1-2 tablespoons flour. Pulse machine on/off to coat dough for easy removal from work bowl.

Transfer dough to an oiled bowl and turn so entire surface is oiled. Cover with plastic bag or damp cloth and let rise in a warm place, free from drafts until doubled in bulk, about 1 hour. Punch down dough and knead in ½ cup raisins. Shape into a ball, let rest, covered, 5 minutes. Shape into a loaf and place in a greased 8½ x 4½-inch loaf pan. Cover and let rise in warm place, free from drafts, until doubled, about 45-60 minutes.

Bake on middle rack in a preheated 375° oven 35-40 minutes or until golden brown and bottom crust of loaf has a hard hollow sound when tapped. Remove from loaf pan immediately and place on metal rack to cool.

Preparation: 10 minutes
Standing: allow 2½-3 hours for dough to rise
Baking: 35-40 minutes
Protein g/s: 4

Rye Bran Bread

1 loaf, 16 slices

Hearty moist loaves packed with bran and wheat germ. Double this recipe if your processor can handle a larger amount of dough.

1 tablespoon active dry yeast
¼ cup warm water (105°-115°F)
2 tablespoons oil
2 tablespoons honey
1 egg
2 cups whole wheat flour, measured scoop and level
1 cup rye flour, measured scoop and level
½ cup bran
¼ cup wheat germ
1 teaspoon salt
¼ cup non-fat, non-instant milk powder
½ to ¾ cup additional water
cornmeal

In a measuring cup, sprinkle yeast over ¼ cup warm water. Let stand in warm place about 5 minutes until it dissolves or puffs. Add oil, honey and egg. Stir to mix.

METAL BLADE or PLASTIC DOUGH BLADE: Add whole wheat flour, rye flour, wheat germ, bran, salt and milk powder to work bowl. Pulse on/off to mix. With machine running, pour yeast mixture through feed tube. Pour in remaining water in a steady stream, only as fast as the flour absorbs it. All the water may not be needed to form a ball of dough. Process ball of dough for 20 seconds. Stop the machine and feel the dough. It should be elastic, sticky and wet. If not, process 10 seconds longer. Sprinkle dough with an additional 1-2 tablespoons flour. Pulse machine on/off to coat dough for easy removal from work bowl.

Transfer dough to an oiled bowl and turn so entire surface is oiled. Cover with plastic bag or damp cloth and let rise in a warm place, free from drafts, until doubled in bulk, about 1 hour. Punch down dough and knead for 30 seconds to press out the bubbles. Shape into a ball, let rest, covered, 15 minutes. Shape dough into an oval. Place on a lightly greased cookie sheet sprinkled with cornmeal. Cover and let rise in warm place, free from drafts, until doubled, about 1 hour. Loaf may also be baked in a 8½ x 4½-inch greased loaf pan.

Make three diagonal slashes on top of oval loaf on cookie sheet. Bake on middle rack in a preheated 350°F oven 30-35 minutes or until loaf is golden brown and bottom crust has a hard hollow sound when tapped. Remove carefully to metal rack to cool.

Preparation: 10 minutes
Standing: allow 2-2½ hours for dough to rise
Baking: 30-35 minutes
Protein g/s: 4

Rye Bread

1 loaf, 16 slices

A small amount of gluten flour enhances the rising power, producing a bread with a light texture. For a more compact but equally delicious and moist loaf, omit the gluten flour and increase the whole wheat flour to 1½ cups. We use dark rye flour for its higher protein value. If you prefer a less sweet bread, use the smaller amount of honey.

1 *tablespoon active dry yeast*
¼ *cup warm water (105°-115°F)*
1 *tablespoon oil*
1-2 *tablespoons honey*
1¼ *cups whole wheat flour, measured scoop and*
    level (increase to 1½ cups if gluten flour is
    omitted)
1¼ *cups rye flour, measured scoop and level*
⅓ *cup gluten flour (optional)*
½ *teaspoon salt*
½ *to ¾ cup water, as needed*
2 *teaspoons caraway seeds*
additional caraway seeds for topping

Glaze: 1 egg beaten with 2 tablespoons water

In a measuring cup, sprinkle yeast over ¼ cup warm water. Let stand in a warm place about 5 minutes until it dissolves or puffs. Add oil and honey.

METAL BLADE: Add whole wheat flour, rye flour, gluten flour (if used) and salt to work bowl. Pulse on/off to mix. With machine running, pour yeast mixture through feed tube. Pour in remaining water in a steady stream, only as fast as the flour absorbs it. All the water may not be needed to form a ball of dough. Process ball of dough for 20 seconds. Stop the machine and feel the dough. It should be elastic, sticky and wet. Rye doughs are characteristically stickier and less elastic than those made with only whole wheat flour. Process 10 seconds longer if needed. With machine running, slowly add caraway seeds, processing only until just mixed. Sprinkle dough with an additional tablespoon of flour. Pulse machine on/off to coat dough for easy removal from work bowl.

Transfer dough to an oiled bowl and turn so entire surface is oiled. Cover with plastic bag or damp cloth and let rise in a warm place, free from drafts, until doubled in bulk, about 1-1¼ hours. Punch down dough and knead for 30 seconds to press out the bubbles. Shape into a ball, let rest, covered, 5 minutes.

On a lightly floured surface, roll the dough to form a rectangle roughly measuring 8 x 12-inches. Starting at the 12-inch end, tightly roll dough jelly-roll style; pinch seam to seal. Turn roll seam-side down, press the ends of the loaf down with the edges of your hands. Tuck flattened ends under and pinch gently to seal. Place loaf on a well-greased cookie sheet, seam-side down. Cover and let rise in warm place, free from drafts until doubled, about 40 minutes.

With a razor blade or sharp knife, slash the loaf with 3-4 diagonal cuts. Brush top with egg glaze and sprinkle on additional caraway seeds. Bake on middle rack in a preheated 350° oven 35-40 minutes or until golden brown and bottom crust of loaf has a hard hollow sound when tapped. Remove from sheet and place on metal rack to cool.

Preparation: 10 minutes
Standing: allow 2 hours for dough to rise
Baking: 35-40 minutes
Protein g/s: 3.5

Tofu Wheat Bread

1 loaf, 15 slices

This is a heavy moist bread. The dough has a consistency much like rye bread.

1 *tablespoon active dry yeast*
¼ *cup warm water (105°-115°F)*
9 *ounces firm tofu, drained, broken into pieces*
2 *tablespoons oil*
2 *tablespoons honey*
3 *cups whole wheat flour, measured scoop and level*
¼ *cup non-instant, non-fat milk powder*
½ *teaspoon salt*
1-2 *tablespoons additional water*

In a measuring cup, sprinkle yeast over ¼ cup warm water. Let stand in a warm place about 5 minutes until it dissolves or puffs.

METAL BLADE: Add tofu pieces, oil and honey to work bowl. Process until smooth. Turn machine off, add flour, milk powder, salt and yeast mixture.

Process to form a ball of dough. Pour in remaining water only as fast as the flour absorbs it. Process ball of dough for 20 seconds. Stop the machine and feel the dough. It should be plastic, sticky and wet. If not, process 10 seconds longer. Sprinkle dough with an additional 1-2 tablespoons flour. Pulse machine on/off to coat dough for easy removal from work bowl.

Transfer dough to an oiled bowl and turn so entire surface is oiled. Cover with plastic bag or damp cloth and let rise in a warm place, free from drafts, until doubled in bulk, about 1½ hours. Punch down dough and knead for 30 seconds to press out the bubbles. Shape into a ball, let rest, covered, 5 minutes. Shape into a loaf and place in a greased 7⅞ x 3⅞-inch loaf pan. Cover and let rise in warm place, free from drafts, until doubled, 45-60 minutes.

Bake on middle rack in a preheated 375° oven 35-40 minutes or until golden brown and bottom crust of loaf has a hard hollow sound when tapped. Remove from loaf pan immediately and place on metal rack to cool.

Preparation: 10 minutes
Standing: allow 2½-3 hours for dough to rise
Baking: 35-40 minutes
Protein g/s: 5

Soy Sesame Wheat Bread

1 small loaf, 15 slices; 1 medium loaf, 16 slices

Double this recipe to make 2 small loaves if your machine has the capacity.

1 Loaf 7⅞ x 3⅞ inches

1 *tablespoon active dry yeast*
¼ *cup warm water (105°-115°F)*
1½ *tablespoons oil*
1½ *tablespoons honey*
2¾ *cups whole wheat flour, measured scoop and
      level*
6 *tablespoons + 2 teaspoons soy flour*
6 *tablespoons + 2 teaspoons sesame seeds*
¼ *cup non-instant, non-fat milk powder*
¾ *teaspoon salt*
¼ *cup + 1-2 tablespoons additional water*

1 Loaf 8½ x 4½ inches

1 *tablespoon active dry yeast*
¼ *cup warm water (105°-115°F)*
2 *tablespoons oil*
2 *tablespoons honey*
3¼ *cups whole wheat flour, measured scoop and
      level*
½ *cup soy flour*
½ *cup sesame seeds*
¼ *cup non-instant, non-fat milk powder*
1 *teaspoon salt*
¾ *cup + 1-2 tablespoons additional water*

In a measuring cup, sprinkle yeast over ¼ cup warm water. Let stand in a warm place about 5 minutes until it dissolves or puffs. Add oil and honey.

METAL BLADE (Plastic Dough Blade when making 2 loaves): Add wheat flour, soy flour, sesame seeds, milk powder and salt to work bowl. Pulse on/off to mix. With machine running, pour in yeast mixture through feed tube. Pour in remaining water in a steady stream, only as fast as the flour absorbs it. All the water may not be needed to form a ball of dough. Process ball of dough for 20 seconds. Stop machine and feel the dough. It should be elastic, sticky and wet. If not, process 10 seconds longer. Sprinkle dough with an additional 1-2 tablespoons flour. Pulse machine on/off to coat dough for easy removal from work bowl.

Transfer dough to an oiled bowl and turn so entire surface is oiled. Cover with plastic bag or damp cloth and let rise in a warm place, free from drafts, until doubled in bulk, 1-1½ hours. Punch down dough and knead for 30 seconds to press out the bubbles. Shape into a ball, let rest, covered, 5 minutes. Shape into a loaf and place in a greased loaf pan. Cover and let rise in warm place, free from drafts, until doubled, about 45-60 minutes.

Bake on middle rack in a preheated 375° oven 35-40 minutes or until golden brown and bottom crust of loaf has a hard hollow sound when tapped. Remove from loaf pan immediately and place on metal rack to cool.

Preparation: 10 minutes
Standing: allow at least 2½ hours for dough to rise
Baking: 35-40 minutes
Protein g/s: small loaf—5
       medium loaf—5.5

Ricotta Swirl Bread

1 loaf, 20 slices

Ricotta cheese, delicately flavored with almond, swirls through this moist loaf.

1   *tablespoon active dry yeast*
¼   *cup plus 2 tablespoons warm water (105°-115°F)*
3   *tablespoons honey*
2¾   *cups whole wheat flour, measured scoop and
       level*
⅛   *cup non-instant, non-fat milk powder*
¼   *teaspoon salt*
¼   *cup butter or margarine, cut into 1-inch pieces*
2   *eggs*

Filling:
16   *ounces ricotta cheese*
2   *egg yolks*
2   *tablespoons honey*
¼   *teaspoon almond extract*

Stir filling ingredients together until smooth and well-mixed; set aside. In a measuring cup, sprinkle yeast over ¼ cup plus 2 tablespoons warm water. Let stand in warm place about 5 minutes until it dissolves or puffs. Add honey and eggs. Stir to mix.

METAL BLADE: Add flour, milk powder, salt and butter to work bowl. Pulse on/off to cut in butter. With machine running, pour in yeast mixture. Process until dough forms a ball, adding additional water or flour as needed. Process the ball of dough for 20 seconds. Stop the machine and feel the dough. It should be elastic, sticky and wet. If not, process 10 seconds longer. Sprinkle dough with an additional 1-2 tablespoons flour. Pulse machine on/off to coat dough for easy removal from work bowl.

Transfer dough to an oiled bowl and turn so entire surface is oiled. Cover with plastic bag or damp cloth and let rise in a warm place, free from drafts, until doubled in bulk, about 1 hour. Punch down dough and knead for 30 seconds to press out the bubbles. Shape into a ball, let rest, covered 10 minutes. On a lightly floured surface, roll dough into a 16 x 14-inch rectangle. Spread filling over dough, leaving a 1-inch border on all edges. Roll up, beginning at long side; pinch seam and ends to seal. Place on foil lined baking sheet. Cover and let rise in warm place, free from drafts, until doubled, 45 minutes.

Bake on middle rack in a preheated 350° oven 30-35 minutes or until golden brown and loaf sounds hollow when tapped. Carefully remove to wire rack. Brush with butter (optional) and allow to cool. Serve warm or cool.

Preparation: 10-15 minutes
Standing: allow about 2 hours for dough to rise
Baking: 30-35 minutes
Protein g/s: 6

Swiss and Rye Bread

1 loaf, 15 slices

Double the recipe if your processor can handle a larger amount of flour. This is a close-grained bread, moist and solid.

4   *ounces Swiss cheese*
1   *tablespoon active dry yeast*
¼   *cup warm water (105°-115°F)*
1   *tablespoon honey*
2¼   *cups whole wheat flour, measured scoop and
       level*
¾   *cup rye flour, measured scoop and level*
½   *teaspoon salt*
¼   *cup non-instant, non-fat milk powder*
¾   *cup water*

In a measuring cup, sprinkle yeast over ¼ cup warm water. Let stand in a warm place about 5 minutes until it dissolves or puffs. Add honey.

SHREDDING DISC: Shred cheese. Remove shredding disc; insert metal blade.

METAL BLADE: Add to bowl with cheese: the whole wheat flour, rye flour, salt and milk powder. Pulse on/off to mix. With machine running, pour yeast mixture through feed tube. Pour in remaining water in a steady stream, only as fast as the flour absorbs it. All the water may not be needed to form a ball of dough. Process the stiff ball of dough for 20 seconds. Stop the machine and feel the dough. It should be elastic, sticky and wet. If not, process 10 seconds longer. Sprinkle dough with an additional

1-2 tablespoons flour. Pulse on/off to coat dough for easy removal from work bowl.

Transfer dough to an oiled bowl and turn so entire surface is oiled. Cover with plastic bag or damp cloth and let rise in a warm place, free from drafts, until doubled in bulk, about 1 hour. Punch down dough and knead for 30 seconds to press out the bubbles. Shape into a ball, let rest, covered, 5 minutes. Shape into a loaf and place in a greased 7⅞ x 3⅞-inch pan. Cover and let rise in warm place, free from drafts until nearly doubled, about 30-45 minutes.

Bake on middle rack in a preheated 375° oven 35-40 minutes or until golden brown and bottom crust of loaf has a hard hollow sound when tapped. Cover top of loaf with foil tent during last 10 minutes to prevent overbrowning. Remove from loaf pan immediately and place on metal rack to cool.

Preparation: 10 minutes
Standing: allow 2½ hours for dough to rise
Baking: 35-40 minutes
Protein g/s: 5.5

Sunflower Seed Bread

1 loaf, 15 slices

Sunflower seeds add the crunch to this delicious loaf. A good all around sandwich bread.

1 *tablespoon active dry yeast*
¼ *cup warm water (105°-115°F)*
1 *tablespoon oil*
2 *tablespoons honey*
2¾ *cups whole wheat flour, measured scoop and level*
½ *teaspoon salt*
⅓ *cup sunflower seeds*
¾ *cup water*

In a measuring cup, sprinkle yeast over ¼ cup warm water. Let stand in a warm place about 5 minutes until it dissolves or puffs. Add oil and honey.

METAL BLADE: Add flour and salt to work bowl. Pulse on/off to mix. With machine running, pour yeast mixture through feed tube. Pour in remaining water in a steady stream, only as fast as the flour absorbs it. All the water may not be needed to form a ball of dough. Process ball of dough for 20 seconds. Stop the machine and feel the dough. It should be elastic, sticky and wet. If not, process 10 seconds longer. With machine running, gradually pour in the sunflower seeds and process until just mixed in. Sprinkle dough with an additional 1-2 tablespoons flour. Pulse machine on/off to coat dough for easy removal from work bowl.

Transfer dough to an oiled bowl and turn so entire surface is oiled. Cover with plastic bag or damp cloth and let rise in a warm place, free from drafts, until doubled in bulk, 1 hour. Punch down dough and knead for 30 seconds to press out the bubbles. Shape into a ball, let rest, covered, 5 minutes. Shape into a loaf and place in a greased 8½ x 4½-inch loaf pan. Cover and let rise in warm place, free from drafts, until doubled, about 45 minutes.

Bake on middle rack in a preheated 350° oven 35-40 minutes or until golden brown and bottom crust of loaf has a hard hollow sound when tapped. Remove from loaf pan immediately and place on metal rack to cool.

Preparation: 10 minutes
Standing: allow about 2 hours for dough to rise
Baking: 35-40 minutes
Protein g/s: 3.5

Triticale Wheat

1 loaf, 16 slices

Double the recipe to make two loaves if your machine can handle the larger amount of flour.

1 *tablespoon active dry yeast*
¼ *cup warm water (105°-115°)*
2 *tablespoons oil*
2 *tablespoons honey*
2 *cups whole wheat flour, measured scoop and level*
¾ *cup triticale flour, measured scoop and level*
1 *teaspoon salt*
¼ *cup non-instant, non-fat milk powder*
½ *cup water*

In a measuring cup, sprinkle yeast over ¼ cup warm water. Let stand in a warm place about 5 minutes until it dissolves or puffs. Add oil and honey.

METAL BLADE or PLASTIC DOUGH BLADE: Add flours, salt and milk powder to work bowl. Pulse on/off to mix. With machine running, pour yeast mixture through feed tube. Pour in remaining water in a steady stream, only as fast as the flour absorbs it. All the water may not be needed to form a ball of dough. Process ball of dough for 20 seconds. Stop the machine and feel the dough. It should be elastic, sticky and wet. If not, process 10 seconds longer. Sprinkle dough with an additional 1-2 tablespoons flour. Pulse machine on/off to coat dough for easy removal from work bowl.

Transfer dough to an oiled bowl and turn so entire surface is oiled. Cover with plastic bag or damp cloth and let rise in a warm place, free from drafts, until doubled in bulk, about 1 hour. Punch down dough and knead for 30 seconds to press out the bubbles. Shape into a ball, let rest, covered, 5 minutes. Shape into a loaf and place in a greased 7⅞ x 3⅞-inch loaf pan. Cover and let rise in warm place, free from drafts, until doubled, about 1 hour.

Bake on middle rack in a preheated 375° oven 30-35 minutes or until golden brown and bottom crust of loaf has a hard hollow sound when tapped. Remove from loaf pan immediately and place on metal rack to cool.

Preparation: 10 minutes
Standing: allow 2-2½ hours for dough to rise
Baking: 30-35 minutes
Protein g/s: 4

Whole Wheat French Bread

1 loaf, 12 slices

A delightful bread with the characteristic crunch and chewiness of the original but with the added goodness of whole grain and buttermilk. This recipe makes one long loaf. If you have a double french bread pan, you can quickly process the recipe twice.

1 *tablespoon active dry yeast*
¼ *cup warm water (105°-115°F)*
3 *cups whole wheat flour, measured scoop and level*
1 *teaspoon salt*
½ *cup buttermilk at room temperature*
¼-½ *cup water, as needed*
cornmeal for dusting pan

In a measuring cup, sprinkle yeast over ¼ cup warm water. Let stand in a warm place about 5 minutes until it dissolves or puffs.

METAL BLADE: Add flour and salt to work bowl. With machine running, pour yeast mixture and buttermilk through feed tube. Pour in remaining water in a steady stream, only as fast as the flour absorbs it. All the water may not be needed to form a ball of dough. Process ball of dough for 20 seconds. Stop the machine and feel the dough. It should be elastic, sticky and wet. If not, process 10 seconds longer. Sprinkle dough with an additional 1-2 tablespoons flour. Pulse machine on/off to coat dough for easy removal from work bowl.

Transfer dough to an oiled bowl and turn so entire surface is oiled. Cover with plastic bag or damp cloth and let rise in a warm place, free from drafts, until doubled in bulk, about 1 hour. Punch down dough and knead for 30 seconds to press out the bubbles. Shape into a ball, let rest, covered, 5 minutes.

On a floured surface, roll dough into a rectangle roughly 15 x 10-inches. Starting with 15-inch side, tightly roll dough, jelly-roll style. Pinch seam to seal. Turn roll seam-side down, press the ends of the loaf down with the edges of your hands. Tuck flattened ends under and pinch gently to seal. Place loaf on a greased cookie sheet or greased french bread pan sprinkled with cornmeal. Cover and let rise in a warm place, free from drafts, until doubled, about 45 minutes.

Approximately 15 minutes before putting dough in the oven, preheat to 400°. Prepare oven by placing a roasting pan or similar shallow pan on the lowest shelf. Five minutes before baking, pour about 1½ cups of hot tap water in the pan. Brush or spray loaf with cold water. With a razor blade or sharp knife, slash the loaf with diagonal cuts. Bake on middle rack 35-45 minutes or until golden brown and bottom crust of loaf has a hard hollow sound when tapped. Remove from baking sheet or pan immediately and place on metal rack to cool.

Preparation: 10 minutes
Standing: allow 2 hours for dough to rise
Baking: 35-45 minutes
Protein g/s: 4.5

Whole Wheat Pita Bread

Serves 8

Once you have eaten whole wheat pitas fresh out of the oven, you probably won't buy any more. The tricks to getting them to puff are: a super hot oven, kneading each portion of dough before shaping and an absolutely grease-free baking pan. After you make the basic whole wheat pita, we're sure you'll want to try the buttermilk and bran versions too.

Whole Wheat Pita

1 tablespoon active dry yeast
¼ cup warm water (105°-115°F)
3 cups flour, measured scoop and level
½ teaspoon salt
¾-1 cup water, as needed

Buttermilk Pita

1 tablespoon active dry yeast
¼ cup warm water (105°-115°F)
3 cups flour, measured scoop and level
½ teaspoon salt
½ cup buttermilk, brought to room temperature
¼ cup water, as needed

Bran Pita

1 tablespoon active dry yeast
¼ cup warm water (105°-115°F)
2¾ cups flour, measured scoop and level
¼ cup bran
½ teaspoon salt
¾-1 cup water, as needed

In a measuring cup, sprinkle yeast over ¼ cup warm water. Let stand in a warm place about 5 minutes until it dissolves or puffs.

METAL BLADE: Add flour, salt and bran (if used) to work bowl. Pulse on/off to mix. With machine running, pour yeast mixture through feed tube. Pour in remaining water in a steady stream, only as fast as the flour absorbs it. When making buttermilk version, pour in all the buttermilk, then the remaining water as needed. All the water may not be needed to form a ball of dough. Process ball of dough for 20 seconds. Stop machine and feel dough. It should be elastic, sticky and wet. If not, process 10 seconds longer. Sprinkle dough with an additional 1-2 tablespoons flour. Pulse machine on/off to coat dough for easy removal from work bowl.

Transfer dough to an oiled bowl and turn so entire surface is oiled. Cover with plastic bag or damp cloth and let rise in a warm place, free from drafts, until doubled in bulk, about 1-1¼ hours. Punch down dough. Divide into 8 pieces. Shape each piece into a ball and knead for about 30 seconds. Cover balls with plastic and allow to rest for 30 minutes. After 20 minutes, preheat oven to 500° and place oven rack at the lowest position.

When oven is hot, use a rolling pin to roll each ball into a circle about ¼-inch thick. Flour well on the "down" side and place on an ungreased baking sheet. Place the filled sheet immediately into the oven. Bake on the lower rack for about 4 minutes, or until they puff. Turn over and continue baking an additional 4 minutes. Remove from oven and serve at once. Pitas may also be kept warm by wrapping in a kitchen towel until ready to serve. If not serving immediately, remove to metal rack and allow to cool.

DO NOT ALLOW THE CIRCLES TO RISE AGAIN. They may not puff. Shape only the circles to be baked at one time.

Preparation: 20 minutes
Standing: allow 1½-1¾ hours for rising
Baking: 16 minutes
Protein g/s: with buttermilk—6.5
　　　　　with water—6

   or

Whole Wheat Cornell Bread

1 loaf, 15 slices

The Cornell Triple-Rich flour formula was originally developed to supplement baked goods using unbleached white flour. This loaf follows the basic principle and is an excellent sandwich bread.

1 tablespoon active dry yeast
¼ cup warm water (105°-115°F)
2 tablespoons oil
2 tablespoons honey
2¾ cups whole wheat flour, measured scoop and level
3 tablespoons non-instant, non-fat milk powder
3 tablespoons wheat germ
3 tablespoons soy flour
½ teaspoon salt
¾ cup water, as needed

In a measuring cup, sprinkle yeast over ¼ cup warm water. Let stand in warm place about 5 minutes until it dissolves or puffs. Add oil and honey.

METAL BLADE: Add whole wheat flour, milk powder, wheat germ, soy flour and salt to work bowl. Pulse on/off to mix. With machine running pour in yeast mixture and enough additional water to form a ball of dough. Pour in liquid in a steady stream to allow flour to absorb liquid. Process ball of dough for 20 seconds. Stop the machine and feel the dough. It should be elastic, sticky and wet. If not, process 10 seconds longer. Sprinkle dough with an additional 1-2 tablespoons flour. Pulse machine on/off to coat dough for easy removal from work bowl.

Transfer dough to an oiled bowl and turn so entire surface is oiled. Cover with plastic bag or damp cloth and let rise in a warm place, free from drafts, until doubled in bulk, about 1 hour. Punch down dough and knead for 30 seconds to press out the bubbles. Shape into a ball, let rest, covered, 5 minutes. Shape into a loaf and place in a greased 7⅞ x 3⅞-inch loaf pan. Cover and let rise in warm place, free from drafts, until doubled, about 45 minutes.

Bake on middle rack in a preheated 375° oven 30-35 minutes or until golden brown and bottom crust of loaf has a hard hollow sound when tapped. Remove from loaf pan immediately and place on metal rack to cool.

Preparation: 10 minutes
Standing: allow 2-2½ hours for dough to rise
Baking: 30-35 minutes
Protein g/s: 4

Yogurt Bran Bread

1 loaf, 16 slices

Double the recipe for two loaves.

1 tablespoon active dry yeast
¼ cup warm water (105°-115°F)
1 tablespoon oil
2 tablespoons honey
1 egg
½ cup yogurt
3 cups whole wheat flour, measured scoop and level
2 tablespoons non-instant, non-fat milk powder
2 tablespoons sesame seeds
1 teaspoon salt
½ cup bran
½ cup water

In a measuring cup, sprinkle yeast over ¼ cup warm water. Let stand in a warm place about 5 minutes until it dissolves or puffs. Add oil, honey, egg and yogurt. Stir to mix.

METAL BLADE: Add flour, milk powder, sesame seeds, salt and bran to work bowl. Pulse on/off to mix. With machine running, pour yeast mixture through feed tube. Pour in remaining water in a steady stream, only as fast as the flour absorbs it. All the water may not be needed to form a ball of dough. Process ball of dough for 20 seconds. Stop the machine and feel the dough. It should be elastic, sticky and wet. If not, process 10 seconds longer. Sprinkle dough with an additional 1-2 tablespoons flour. Pulse machine on/off to coat dough for easy removal from work bowl.

Transfer dough to an oiled bowl and turn so entire surface is oiled. Cover with plastic bag or damp cloth and let rise in a warm place, free from drafts, until doubled in bulk, about 1 hour. Punch down dough and knead for 30 seconds to press out the bubbles. Divide in half if making 2 loaves. Shape each portion into a ball, let rest, covered, 5 minutes. Shape into a loaf and place in a greased 8½ x 4½-

inch loaf pan. Cover and let rise in warm place, free from drafts, until doubled, about 45 minutes.

Bake on middle rack in a preheated 375° oven 30-35 minutes or until golden brown and bottom crust of loaf has a hard hollow sound when tapped. Remove from loaf pan immediately and place on metal rack to cool.

Preparation: 10 minutes
Standing: allow about 2 hours for dough to rise
Baking: 30-35 minutes
Protein g/s: 4.5

Whole Wheat Christmas Stollen

1 stollen, 16 slices

You don't have to wait till Christmas to bake this tender festive loaf filled with fruits—not the usual sweet candied type—nuts and spices. Vary the amount of the flavorings to suit your taste.

1 tablespoon active dry yeast
¼ cup warm water (105°-115°F)
⅓ cup milk, scalded, cooled to lukewarm
1 egg
2¾ cups whole wheat flour, measured scoop and
    level
¼ teaspoon salt
¼ cup brown sugar
4 tablespoons butter (½ stick) cut into 1-inch pieces
¾-1 teaspoon lemon extract
¾-1 teaspoon almond extract
1 teaspoon grated lemon rind
1½-2 teaspoons vanilla extract
½ cup raisins
¼ cup blanched almonds
½ cup dried apricots
½ cup dried unsugared pineapple
powdered sugar for topping

In a measuring cup, sprinkle yeast over ¼ cup warm water. Let stand in warm place about 5 minutes until it dissolves or puffs.

METAL BLADE: Add flour, salt, brown sugar and butter to the work bowl. Process until mixture resembles coarse meal. Add lemon, almond, and vanilla extracts and grated lemon rind. Stir together the yeast mixture, cooled scalded milk and egg. With machine running, pour in yeast/milk/egg mixture in a steady stream to allow flour to absorb liquid. An additional tablespoon or so of water may be added to form a ball of dough. Process the ball of dough for 20 seconds. Turn off machine and feel dough. It should be elastic, sticky and wet. If not, process 10 seconds longer. This will be a soft dough. Sprinkle dough with additional tablespoon flour. Pulse on/off to coat dough for easy removal.

Place dough in a buttered bowl, turn to coat surface. Cover with plastic bag; let rise in a warm place, free from drafts, until doubled in bulk, about 1-1½ hours. While dough is rising, process fruits and nuts.

METAL BLADE: To retain the texture of each ingredient, coarsely chop the nuts, apricots and pineapple separately. Add a bit of flour while chopping the fruit to prevent them from sticking together. Punch down dough. Turn out to a lightly floured board and knead in raisins, almonds, apricots and pineapple until evenly distributed throughout the dough.

SHAPING: Roll the dough into a square about 11 x 11 inches. Fold over the one side, lapping ⅔ over the other side. Press the center of the loaf upward between your palms to form the characteristic stollen "hump," as illustrated.

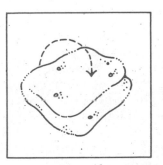 

Place stollen on a buttered cookie sheet. Cover with plastic bag and allow to rise in a warm place until doubled, about 1½ hours. Bake in preheated 325° oven 30 minutes or until golden. Carefully remove to metal rack to cool.

Preparation: 15-20 minutes
Standing: allow 3-3½ hours for dough to rise
Baking: 30 minutes
Protein g/s: 4

Wheat-Rye-Buckwheat Bread

1 loaf, 17 slices

This makes a large loaf. For small machines, cut the ingredients roughly in half and bake in a small loaf pan (7⅞ x 3⅞-inch).

1 tablespoon active dry yeast
½ cup warm water (105°-115°F)
2 tablespoons oil
2 tablespoons honey
4 cups whole wheat flour, measured scoop and level
½ cup rye flour, measured scoop and level
⅓ cup buckwheat flour, measured scoop and level
3 tablespoons cornmeal
½ tablespoon salt
1¼ cups water

In a measuring cup, sprinkle yeast over ½ cup warm water. Let stand in a warm place about 5 minutes until it dissolves or puffs. Add oil and honey.

PLASTIC DOUGH BLADE: Add wheat, rye, buckwheat flours, cornmeal and salt to work bowl. Pulse on/off to mix. With machine running, pour yeast mixture through feed tube. Pour in remaining water in a steady stream, only as fast as the flour absorbs it. All the water may not be needed to form a ball of dough. Process ball of dough for 20 seconds. Stop the machine and feel the dough. It should be elastic, sticky and wet. If not, process 10 seconds longer. Sprinkle dough with an additional 1-2 tablespoons flour. Pulse machine on/off to coat dough for easy removal from work bowl.

Transfer dough to an oiled bowl and turn so entire surface is oiled. Cover with plastic bag or damp cloth and let rise in a warm place, free from drafts, until doubled in bulk, 1 hour. Punch down dough and knead for 30 seconds to press out bubbles. Shape into a ball, let rest, covered, 5 minutes. Shape into a loaf and place in a greased 9 x 5-inch loaf pan. Cover and let rise in warm place, free from drafts, until doubled, about 45 minutes.

Bake on middle rack in a preheated 375° oven 45-50 minutes or until golden brown and bottom crust of loaf has a hard hollow sound when tapped. Remove from loaf pan immediately and place on metal rack to cool.

Preparation: 10 minutes
Standing: allow about 2 hours for dough to rise
Baking: 45-50 minutes
Protein g/s: 4

Hot Rolls with Lemon Butter

1 dozen rolls

A welcome addition to any meal!

1 tablespoon active dry yeast
½ cup warm water (105°-115°F)
¼ cup honey
1 egg
¼ cup butter
2 cups whole wheat flour, measured scoop and level
⅓ cup non-instant, non-fat milk powder
2 tablespoons wheat germ
1 teaspoon salt
1 teaspoon grated orange rind
1 teaspoon ground cinnamon
¼ teaspoon ground cloves
¼ teaspoon nutmeg
½ cup raisins

Glaze: 1 egg yolk beaten with 1 tablespoon water

Lemon Butter:
¼ cup softened butter
2-4 tablespoons honey
1½ teaspoons grated lemon rind

In a measuring cup, sprinkle yeast over ½ cup warm water. Let stand in a warm place about 5 minutes until it dissolves or puffs. Stir in honey and egg.

METAL BLADE: Add flour, milk powder, wheat germ, salt, cinnamon, cloves, nutmeg, and orange rind to the work bowl. Pulse on/off to mix. Add butter, cut into 1-inch pieces. Pulse on/off until mixture resembles coarse meal. With machine running, pour yeast mixture through feed tube. Process the ball of dough 20 seconds. Sprinkle in an additional 1-2 tablespoons of flour if needed. Stop the machine and feel the dough. It should be elastic, sticky and wet. If not, process 10 seconds longer. Sprinkle dough with an additional 1-2 tablespoons flour. Pulse machine on/off to coat dough for easy removal from work bowl.

Transfer dough to an oiled bowl and turn so entire surface is oiled. Cover with plastic bag or damp cloth and let rise in a warm place, free from drafts, until doubled in bulk, about 1-1½ hours. Punch down dough and knead for 30 seconds to press out bubbles and to evenly distribute ½ cup raisins. Divide the dough into 12 portions. Let rest, covered, 5 minutes. Shape each portion into a ball. Place balls about 1-inch apart on greased baking sheet.

Cover and let rise in warm place, free from drafts, until doubled, about 45-60 minutes.

Brush with glaze. Bake on middle rack in a preheated 375° oven 20-25 minutes. Remove from oven and serve hot with lemon butter.

LEMON BUTTER: Add butter, honey and lemon rind to a clean, dry work bowl. Process until smooth and blended.

Preparation: 15 minutes
Standing: allow 2-2½ hours for dough to rise
Baking: 20-25 minutes
Protein g/s: 4.5

Poppy Seed Milk Rolls

12 rolls

Milk powder enhances the protein quality of these delicious dinner rolls, which also make good sandwich buns.

1 tablespoon active dry yeast
¼ cup warm water (105°-115°F)
2 tablespoons oil
2 tablespoons honey
2¾ cups whole wheat flour, measured scoop and
    level
¼ cup non-instant, non-fat milk powder
¼ teaspoon salt
½-⅔ cup water, as needed
poppy seeds for topping

Glaze: 1 egg beaten with ¼ cup water

In a measuring cup, sprinkle yeast over ¼ cup warm water. Let stand in a warm place about 5 minutes until it dissolves or puffs. Add oil and honey.

METAL BLADE: Add flour, milk powder and salt to work bowl. Pulse on/off to mix. With machine running, pour yeast mixture through feed tube. Pour in remaining water in a steady stream, only as fast as the flour absorbs it. All the water may not be needed to form a soft ball of dough. Process ball of dough for 20 seconds. Stop the machine and feel the dough. It should be elastic, sticky and wet. If not,

process 10 seconds longer. Sprinkle dough with an additional 1-2 tablespoons flour. Pulse machine on/off to coat dough for easy removal from work bowl.

Transfer dough to an oiled bowl and turn so entire surface is oiled. Cover with plastic bag or damp cloth and let rise in a warm place, free from drafts, until doubled in bulk, about 1 hour. Punch down dough and knead for 30 seconds to press out the bubbles. Divide dough into 12 equal portions. Cover and let rest for 5 minutes. Shape each piece into a ball and place on a well-greased cookie sheet about 1½ inches apart. Let rise in a warm place, uncovered, until doubled, about 45 minutes.

Brush each roll with egg glaze; sprinkle on poppy seeds. Bake on middle rack in a preheated 350° oven for 15-20 minutes or until golden brown and rolls sound hollow when tapped. Remove to metal rack. Serve warm or allow to cool completely.

Preparation: 15-20 minutes
Standing: allow about 2 hours for dough to rise
Baking: 15-20 minutes
Protein g/s: 3.5

Mega Cinnamon Rolls

9 rolls

2 *tablespoons active dry yeast*
½ *cup warm water (105°-115°F)*
½ *cup butter*
½ *cup honey*
1 *egg*
1 *egg yolk*
4¾ *cups whole wheat flour, measured scoop and*
   level
¼ *cup non-instant, non-fat milk powder*
1 *teaspoon salt*
¼ *to ½ cup water*

Filling:
¼ *cup softened butter*
¼ *cup brown sugar, lightly packed*
1 *tablespoon ground cinnamon*
½ *cup raisins*
¼ *cup honey*

Glaze: *1 egg white beaten with 1 teaspoon water*

For processors with smaller capacities, roughly divide ingredients in half to make dough. Knead the two pieces of dough together by hand to mix and proceed as directed.

In a measuring cup, sprinkle yeast over ½ cup warm water. Let stand in a warm place about 5 minutes until it dissolves or puffs. Melt ½ cup butter, remove from heat, stir in ½ cup honey, set aside.

PLASTIC DOUGH BLADE: Add flour, milk powder, and salt to work bowl. Pulse on/off to mix. Pour in yeast mixture, pulse on/off to mix in. With machine running, pour in 1 whole egg, 1 egg yolk, butter/honey mixture and enough water to form a soft ball of dough. Process ball of dough for 20 seconds. Stop the machine and feel the dough. It should be elastic, sticky and wet. If not, process 10 seconds longer. Sprinkle dough with an additional 1-2 tablespoons flour. Pulse machine on/off to coat dough for easy removal from work bowl.

Transfer dough to an oiled bowl and turn so entire surface is oiled. Cover with plastic bag or damp cloth and let rise in a warm place, free from drafts, until doubled in bulk, about 1½-2 hours. Punch down dough and knead for 30 seconds to press out bubbles. Shape into a ball, let rest, covered, 10 minutes.

Roll dough into an 18 x 24-inch rectangle. Spread softened butter evenly over surface. Combine brown sugar and cinnamon; sprinkle evenly over butter. Top with raisins and dribble on honey. Roll dough up tightly, jelly-roll fashion, starting with 18-inch side. Moisten the end of the dough with water and pinch to seal well. With a sharp knife, cut the roll into 2-inch sections to make 9 rolls. Hold the roll cut side up. From the bottom, gently push the center up to form a slight peak. Repeat with remaining rolls.

Arrange rolls, peak side up in a well-greased 9 x 9-inch pan. Cover and let rise in a warm place until doubled, 1-1½ hours. Brush rolls with reserved egg white beaten with 1 teaspoon water. Bake on middle rack in a preheated 350° oven 30-35 minutes. Carefully transfer rolls to wire rack to cool slightly before serving.

Preparation: 15 minutes
              15 minutes to shape rolls
Standing: allow 2½-3 hours for dough to rise
Baking: 30-35 minutes
Protein g/s: 11

Quick Breads

Apple Bran Muffins

6-9 muffins

Your processor will quickly chop the apple for these moist muffins.

⅓ cup skim milk
1 egg
3 tablespoons oil
1 tablespoon honey
1 small Golden Delicious apple, unpeeled, cored, quartered
¾ cup whole wheat flour, measured scoop and level
½ cup bran
1¼ teaspoon baking powder
⅛ teaspoon baking soda
¼ teaspoon salt
½ teaspoon ground cinnamon

Preheat oven to 400°. In a measuring cup, stir together skim milk, egg, oil and honey. Set aside.

METAL BLADE: Add flour and apple quarters to the work bowl. Pulse on/off to coarsely chop apple. Add bran, baking powder, baking soda, salt and cinnamon. Pulse on/off to mix.

Stop machine, remove cover and pour in liquid mixture all at once. Pulse on/off 3-4 times until flour is just moistened. Spoon batter into greased muffin cups, filling each ⅔ full. Bake 18-22 minutes or until toothpick inserted in center comes out clean. Remove from muffin cups and serve hot or place on metal rack to cool.

Preparation: 5 minutes
Baking: 18-22 minutes
Protein g/s: 6 muffins—4.5
            9 muffins—3

Banana Walnut Bran Muffins

12 muffins

One tablespoon of baking powder is needed to produce a light muffin from the heavy bran batter. A delicious snack or accompaniment to any meal.

⅔ cup walnuts
1¼ cups whole wheat flour, measured scoop and level
2 tablespoons non-instant, non-fat milk powder
1 tablespoon baking powder
½ teaspoon baking soda
½ teaspoon salt
¾ cup bran
2 medium bananas, ripe
½ cup milk
1 egg
2 tablespoons oil
2 tablespoons honey
1 teaspoon vanilla extract

Preheat oven to 400°.

METAL BLADE: Add walnuts to work bowl. Pulse on/off to coarsely chop. Remove to medium mixing bowl. Set aside. Add flour, milk powder, baking powder, baking soda, salt and bran to work bowl. Pulse on/off to mix. Add to bowl with nuts, toss to mix. Add bananas, cut into pieces. Process until smooth. Add milk, egg, oil, honey and vanilla extract. Pulse on/off to combine. Remove cover of work bowl. Add flour mixture all at once. Pulse on/off 2-3 times until flour is just moistened. Do not overprocess. Spoon batter into 12 well-greased muffin cups, filling each ⅔ full. Bake 16-18 minutes or until toothpick inserted in center comes out clean. Remove from muffin cups and serve hot or place on metal rack to cool.

Preparation: 5 minutes
Baking: 16-18 minutes
Protein g/s: 4.5

Apricot Yogurt Bran Muffins

12 muffins

1 cup low-fat yogurt
1 egg
¼ cup oil
2 tablespoons honey
2 tablespoons molasses
1 cup whole wheat flour, measured scoop and level
3 ounces dried apricot halves
¾ cup bran
¾ teaspoon baking soda
¼ teaspoon salt

Preheat oven to 425°. In a measuring cup, stir together yogurt, egg, oil, honey and molasses. Set aside.

METAL BLADE: Add whole wheat flour and apricot halves to work bowl. Pulse on/off to coarsely chop apricots. Add bran, baking soda and salt. Pulse on/off to mix. Stop machine, remove cover and pour in liquid mixture all at once. Pulse on/off 3-4 times until flour is just moistened. Spoon batter into greased muffin cups, filling each ⅔ full. Bake 20-25 minutes or until toothpick inserted in center comes out clean. Remove from muffin cups and serve hot or place on metal rack to cool.

Preparation: 5 minutes
Baking: 20-25 minutes
Protein g/s: 3

High Protein Bran Popovers

12 popovers

Crisp on the outside and spongy on the inside, these popovers will make any weekend breakfast special. Serve these as soon as they are out of the oven with a little bit of margarine and honey.

12 teaspoons butter or safflower margarine
¾ cup whole wheat flour, measured scoop and level
¼ cup bran
¼ teaspoon salt
4 eggs
1 cup milk

Preheat oven to 375°. Place 1 teaspoon butter or margarine in each of 12 muffin cups. Place cups in hot oven for about 3 minutes to melt butter.

METAL BLADE: Add flour, bran, salt, eggs and milk to work bowl. Process 10 seconds until well mixed. Pour batter into muffin cups, filling each ¾ full. Bake 30 minutes. Do not peek or open the oven door or the popovers will collapse.

Preparation: 5 minutes
Baking: 30 minutes
Protein g/s: 4

Molasses Bran Muffins

12 muffins

1 cup buttermilk, room temperature
1 egg
¼ cup molasses
2 tablespoons oil
1 cup whole wheat flour, measured scoop and level
¾ cup bran
1 tablespoon brown sugar, optional
⅛ teaspoon salt
¾ teaspoon baking soda
½ cup raisins

Preheat oven to 350°. In a measuring cup, stir together buttermilk, egg, molasses and oil. Set aside.

METAL BLADE or PLASTIC MIXING BLADE: Add flour, bran, brown sugar, salt and baking soda to work bowl. Pulse on/off to mix. Remove work bowl cover and scatter raisins evenly over flour mixture. Pour in liquid mixture all at once. Replace cover; pulse on/off 3-4 times until flour is just moistened. Do not overprocess. Spoon batter into well-greased muffin cups, filling each ⅔ full. Bake 20-25 minutes or until toothpick inserted in center comes out clean. Remove from muffin cups and serve hot or place on metal rack to cool.

Preparation: 5 minutes
Baking: 20-25 minutes
Protein g/s: 2.5

Bran Prune Muffins

12 muffins

These are an especially nice accompaniment to a main-dish salad lunch or dinner. One tablespoon of baking powder is the minimum amount needed to raise the heavy bran batter.

1 cup milk
2 tablespoons oil
1 egg
9 ounces pitted prunes
1 tablespoon whole wheat flour
1 cup whole wheat flour, measured scoop and level
¾ cup bran
½ teaspoon salt
1 tablespoon baking powder

Preheat oven to 375°. In a measuring cup, stir together milk, oil and egg. Set aside.

METAL BLADE: Add prunes and 1 tablespoon whole wheat flour to work bowl. Pulse on/off to chop prunes.

METAL BLADE or PLASTIC MIXING BLADE: Add to the chopped prunes the whole wheat flour, bran, salt and baking powder. Pulse on/off to mix. Stop machine, remove cover and pour in liquid mixture all at once. Pulse on/off 3-4 times until flour is just moistened. Spoon batter into greased muffin cups, filling each ⅔ full. Bake 20-25 minutes or until toothpick inserted in center comes out clean. Remove from muffin cups and serve hot or place on metal rack to cool.

Preparation: 5 minutes
Baking: 20-25 minutes
Protein g/s: 3

Rye Wheat Biscuits

6-7 2-inch biscuits

Biscuits are quick to prepare. Larger biscuits can be shaped by doubling the recipe, rolling the dough to 1-inch thickness and cutting with a 3-inch cutter. Bake as directed, adding a few minutes to the baking time. Split and fill with sautéed vegetables.

½ cup rye flour, measured scoop and level
½ cup whole wheat flour, measured scoop and level
3 tablespoons non-instant, non-fat milk powder
1½ teaspoons baking powder
⅛ teaspoon salt
2 tablespoons butter, chilled, cut into small pieces
1 tablespoon honey
¼ cup cold water

VARIATION: Cheese Rye Wheat Biscuits. Shred one ounce cheese and add to bowl with dry ingredients. Proceed as directed.

Preheat oven to 450°.

METAL BLADE: Add rye flour, wheat flour, milk powder, baking powder and salt to work bowl. Pulse on/off to mix. Add butter, pulse on/off until mixture resembles coarse meal. With machine running, pour in honey and cold water. Stop machine as soon as a soft ball is formed. Do not overprocess.

Turn out dough onto a lightly floured board. Using a lightly floured rolling pin, roll the dough out to form a rectangle a little more than ¼-inch thick. Fold the dough over once. Cut straight down with a biscuit cutter, lightly dipped in flour. Be careful not to twist the cutter. Twisting may seal the cut edge and prevent rising. Place on an ungreased baking sheet. Bake on the middle shelf of the oven 10-12 minutes or until golden brown. Serve at once.

Preparation: 10 minutes
Baking: 10-12 minutes
Protein g/s: 3.5

Corn Muffins

6 muffins

These light, moist corn muffins make a nice addition to any meal. They are best when served fresh from the oven.

1 egg
2 tablespoons oil
2 tablespoons honey
½ cup water
¼ cup plus 2 tablespoons whole wheat flour,
    measured scoop and level
¾ cup cornmeal, measured scoop and level
½ tablespoon baking powder
¼ teaspoon salt
2 tablespoons non-instant, non-fat milk powder

Preheat oven to 425°. In a measuring cup, stir together egg, oil, honey and water. Set aside.

METAL BLADE or PLASTIC MIXING BLADE: Add flour, cornmeal, baking powder, salt and milk powder to work bowl. Pulse on/off to mix. Stop machine, remove cover and pour in liquid mixture all at once. Pulse on/off 3-4 times until flour is just moistened. Spoon batter into greased muffin cups, filling each ⅔ full. Bake 15-18 minutes or until lightly golden and toothpick inserted in center comes out clean. Remove from muffin cups and serve hot.

Preparation: 5 minutes
Baking: 15-18 minutes
Protein g/s: 4.5

Yogurt Sunflower Seed Muffins

12-14 muffins

1 cup low-fat yogurt
2 eggs
3 tablespoons oil
¼ cup honey
1¼ cups whole wheat flour, measured scoop and
    level
2 teaspoons baking powder
1 teaspoon baking soda
½ teaspoon salt
1 tablespoon soy flour
½ cup raisins
¼ cup and 2 tablespoons sunflower seeds

Preheat oven to 375°. In a large measuring cup, stir together yogurt, eggs, oil and honey. Set aside.

METAL BLADE or PLASTIC MIXING BLADE: Add flour, baking powder, baking soda, salt, and soy flour to work bowl. Pulse on/off to mix. Stop machine, remove cover and pour in liquid mixture all at once. Add raisins and sunflower seeds. Pulse on/off 3-4 times until flour is just moistened. Spoon batter into greased muffin cups, filling each ⅔ full. Bake 18-20 minutes or until toothpick inserted in center comes out clean. Remove from muffin cups and serve warm or let cool on metal rack.

Preparation: 5-8 minutes
Baking: 18-20 minutes
Protein g/s: 12 muffins—4.5
            14 muffins—4

Oat Raisin Muffins

12 muffins

This is sure to be one of your favorites. Substitute 4-grain cereal, rolled rye or wheat for variation.

1 cup rolled oats
1 cup warm water
¼ cup oil
¼ cup honey
1 egg
1 cup whole wheat flour, measured scoop and level
1 tablespoon baking powder
¾ teaspoon ground cinnamon
¼ teaspoon salt
¼ cup non-instant, non-fat milk powder
½ cup raisins

Preheat oven to 400°. In a large measuring cup stir together rolled oats and warm water. Allow to stand for 15 minutes. Stir in oil, honey and egg. Set aside.

METAL BLADE or PLASTIC MIXING BLADE: Add flour, baking powder, cinnamon, salt, milk powder and raisins to work bowl. Pulse on/off to mix. Stop machine, remove cover and pour in liquid mixture all at once. Pulse on/off 2-3 times until flour is just moistened. Batter will be lumpy. Spoon batter into greased muffin cups, filling each ⅔ full. Bake 20-22 minutes or until toothpick inserted in center comes out clean. Remove from muffin cups and serve hot or place on metal rack to cool.

Preparation: 5 minutes
Standing: allow 15 minutes to soften rolled oats
Baking: 20-22 minutes
Protein g/s: 3.5

Sunny Prune Muffins

8-10 muffins

Sunflower seeds and prunes add crunch and moistness to these tasty muffins.

½ cup water (or ½ cup milk, omit milk powder)
1 egg
3 tablespoons oil
3 tablespoons honey
12 pitted prunes
¾ cup whole wheat flour, measured scoop and level
1 teaspoon baking powder
⅛ teaspoon baking soda
¼ teaspoon salt
¼ teaspoon ground cinnamon
2 tablespoons non-instant, non-fat milk powder
¼ cup sunflower seeds

Preheat oven to 400°. In a measuring cup, stir together water (or liquid milk if used), egg, oil, and honey. Set aside.

METAL BLADE: Add whole wheat flour and prunes to work bowl. Pulse on/off to coarsely chop prunes. Add baking powder, baking soda, salt, cinnamon, milk powder and sunflower seeds. Pulse on/off to mix. Stop machine, remove cover and pour in liquid mixture all at once. Pulse on/off 3-4 times until flour is just moistened. Spoon batter into greased muffin cups, filling each ⅔ full. Bake 16-18 minutes or until toothpick inserted in center comes out clean. Remove from muffin cups and serve hot or place on metal rack to cool.

Preparation: 6 minutes
Baking: 16-18 minutes
Protein g/s: 8 muffins—4
              10 muffins—3.5

Whole Wheat Scones

12 scones

In Great Britain, scones are eaten with afternoon tea. Once you make a batch of these, you'll be serving them at breakfast, with a salad . . . whenever!

2 eggs
¼ cup water
1 tablespoon honey (optional)
2 cups whole wheat flour, measured scoop and level
1 tablespoon baking powder
½ teaspoon salt
¼ cup non-instant, non-fat milk powder
¼ cup butter or margarine, chilled, cut into 1-inch pieces
¼ cup raisins

Preheat oven to 425°. In a measuring cup, stir together eggs, water, and honey. Set aside.

METAL BLADE: Add flour, baking powder, salt, and milk powder to work bowl. Pulse on/off to mix. Add butter; pulse on/off until mixture has the consistency of coarse meal. Add raisins. With machine running, pour in liquid mixture through feed tube. Stop processing as soon as the dough begins to form a ball. Remove ball of dough to lightly floured board. Gently knead to form a smooth ball. Place dough on a lightly floured baking sheet; pat it until it forms an 8-inch circle, about ½-inch thick.

Using a large, floured knife, cut 12 pie-shaped wedges into the circle. Cut completely through dough but do not separate wedges. Bake 12-14 minutes or until lightly browned and a toothpick inserted into a scone comes out clean. Slide circle of scones onto a wire rack to cool. Serve warm with a little honey. These may be cooled completely, split and reheated in your toaster.

Preparation: 5-8 minutes
Baking: 12-14 minutes
Protein g/s: 4.5

Carrot Sesame Bread

1 loaf, 8-10 slices

A tender extra moist quick bread. Sesame seeds give this loaf an interesting texture. Serve warm or cold.

3 medium carrots, peeled
¾ cup *whole wheat flour, measured scoop and level*
½ cup *soy flour, measured scoop and level*
1 teaspoon baking powder
1 teaspoon baking soda
1 teaspoon ground cinnamon
¼ teaspoon salt
½ cup raisins
¼ cup sesame seeds
2 eggs
½ cup oil
½ cup honey

Preheat oven to 350°.

SHREDDING DISC: Cut carrots to fit feed tube vertically, shred to make about 1 cup packed. Remove shredding disc; replace with metal blade.

METAL BLADE: Add to the work bowl with shredded carrots: the whole wheat flour, soy flour, baking soda, cinnamon and salt. Pulse on/off to mix. Remove to medium mixing bowl, add raisins and sesame seeds. Toss to mix and set aside. Add eggs to work bowl. Process 30 seconds. Scrape down sides of work bowl. Add oil and honey. Process until well-mixed. Remove work bowl cover, scrape down sides and add all dry ingredients at once. Combine with 5 on/off pulses only until batter is mixed. Before last on/off, scrape down sides of work bowl. Do not overprocess.

Grease bottom and sides of a small foil pan, 7⅞ x 3⅞-inch. Line bottom with wax paper. Pour in batter. Bake at 350° 30 minutes. Reduce oven temperature to 325° and bake an additional 20-30 minutes until a toothpick inserted in the middle of the loaf comes out clean. Let cool in pan on a wire rack.

Preparation: 10 minutes
Baking: 50-60 minutes
Protein g/s: 8 slices—5.5
              10 slices—4.5

Banana Yogurt Nut Bread

1 loaf, 15 slices

Yogurt gives this spicy moist bread a tang!

1½ cups *whole wheat flour, measured scoop and level*
½ teaspoon baking soda
¼ teaspoon baking powder
¼ teaspoon salt
¼ teaspoon ground cinnamon
½ cup walnuts
1 egg
¼ cup low-fat yogurt
¼ cup oil
⅓ cup honey
1 large ripe banana

Preheat oven to 350°.

METAL BLADE: Add flour, baking soda, baking powder, salt, cinnamon and walnuts to work bowl. Pulse on/off to coarsely chop nuts. Remove and set aside. Add egg, process 30 seconds. Scrape down sides of work bowl. Add yogurt, oil, honey and banana (cut into small pieces). Pulse on/off until well-mixed and banana is puréed. Remove work bowl cover, scrape down sides and add all dry ingredients at once. Combine with 5 on/off pulses only until batter is mixed. Before last on/off, scrape down sides of work bowl. Do not overprocess.

Grease bottom and sides of a small foil pan, 7⅞ x 3⅞-inch. Line bottom with wax paper. Spoon batter into the pan. Bake 45-50 minutes or until a toothpick inserted into the center comes out clean. Cool for 15 minutes; remove bread from pan and allow to cool completely on a wire rack.

Preparation: 10 minutes
Baking: 40-45 minutes
Protein g/s: 3

Banana Nut Bread

1 loaf, 15 slices

Slice for slice, most banana nut breads contain too much sugar and oil. We've cut down on these two ingredients and have come up with a bread that's sure to be one of your favorites.

1½ cups whole wheat flour, measured scoop and
    level
½ teaspoon salt
½ teaspoon baking soda
1 teaspoon baking powder
½ cup walnuts
2 medium bananas, ripe
⅓-½ cup brown sugar
⅓ cup oil
2 eggs
1 teaspoon vanilla extract

Preheat oven to 350°.

METAL BLADE: Add flour, salt, baking soda, baking powder and walnuts to work bowl. Pulse on/off to coarsely chop nuts. Remove and set aside. Add bananas, cut into pieces; brown sugar; oil; eggs and vanilla extract to work bowl. Process until well-blended and bananas are smooth. Remove work bowl cover, scrape down sides and add all dry ingredients at once. Combine with 4-5 on/off pulses only until batter is mixed. Before last on/off, scrape down sides of work bowl. Do not overprocess.

Grease bottom and sides of a 8½ x 4½-inch loaf pan. Line bottom with wax paper. Pour batter into the pan. Bake 40-50 minutes or until a toothpick inserted into the center comes out clean. Cool for 10 minutes; remove bread from pan and allow to cool completely on a wire rack.

Preparation: 10 minutes
Baking: 40-50 minutes
Protein g/s: 3

Banana Carrot Bread

1 loaf, 16 slices

1¾ cups whole wheat flour, measured scoop and
    level
½ teaspoon baking soda
1 teaspoon baking powder
½ teaspoon ground cinnamon
2 medium carrots, pared
2 small bananas, ripe
2 eggs
½ cup low-fat yogurt
2 tablespoons oil
½ cup honey
2 teaspoons vanilla extract

Preheat oven to 350°.

METAL BLADE: Add flour, baking soda, baking powder and cinnamon to work bowl. Pulse on/off to mix. Remove to medium mixing bowl and set aside.

SHREDDING DISC: Cut carrots to fit feed tube vertically shred. Cut bananas to fit feed tube vertically, shred. Combine carrots and bananas in mixing bowl with flour. Toss gently to mix.

METAL BLADE: Add eggs to work bowl. Process 30 seconds. Scrape down sides of work bowl. Add yogurt, oil, honey and vanilla extract and mix with on/off pulses until well-blended. Remove work bowl cover, scrape down sides and add all dry ingredients at once. Combine with 5 on/off pulses only until batter is mixed. Before last on/off, scrape down sides of work bowl. Do not overprocess.

Grease bottom and sides of an 8½ x 4½-inch loaf pan. Line bottom with wax paper. Pour batter into pan. Bake 55-60 minutes or until a toothpick inserted in the center comes out almost clean. Cool in pan 10 minutes; turn out to wire rack to cool completely. Serve warm or cold.

Preparation: 8 minutes
Baking: 55-60 minutes
Protein g/s: 3

Fresh Mango or Peach Bread

1 loaf, 16 slices

Dozens of loaves of this bread are baked in homes throughout the Hawaiian Islands when the fruit is in season. Our version uses whole wheat flour and brown sugar. Substitute fresh firm peaches if mangoes are not available—the results are similar. Try to resist temptation and allow the loaf to "age," well-wrapped, overnight so the flavors can blend.

1 Loaf 9 x 5 inches

2 *cups whole wheat flour, measured scoop and level*
¾ *cup brown sugar, lightly packed*
2 *teaspoons baking soda*
¼ *teaspoon salt*
1 *teaspoon ground cinnamon*
3 *ounces walnuts*
2 *medium fresh mangoes or fresh peaches to yield 2 cups chopped*
3 *eggs*
½ *cup oil*
2 *teaspoons vanilla extract*

1 Loaf 8½ x 4½ inches

1⅓ *cups whole wheat flour, measured scoop and level*
½ *cup brown sugar, lightly packed*
1¼ *teaspoons baking soda*
⅛ *teaspoon salt*
¾ *teaspoon ground cinnamon*
2 *ounces walnuts*
2 *small mangoes or fresh peaches to yield 1⅓ cups chopped*
2 *eggs*
⅓ *cup oil*
1½ *teaspoons vanilla extract*

Preheat oven to 350°.

METAL BLADE: Add flour, brown sugar, baking soda, salt and cinnamon to work bowl. Pulse on/off to mix. Add walnuts, pulse on/off until coarsely chopped. Remove from bowl and set aside. Add mangoes, cut roughly into 1½-inch pieces, to work bowl. Pulse on/off to coarsely chop. Remove from bowl and set aside. Add eggs to work bowl; process 30 seconds. With machine running, pour in oil and vanilla extract. Process until well-mixed, 15-20 seconds. Turn machine off and add flour mixture all at once. Combine with 3-4 on/off pulses. Add mangoes; pulse on/off until mangoes are just mixed in. Do not overprocess or you will have puréed

mangoes. Scrape down sides of bowl and mix gently with the spatula, if necessary.

Grease the bottom and sides of a loaf pan; line bottom with wax paper. Pour batter into pan. Bake large loaf 55-60 minutes; small loaf 45-55 minutes or until a toothpick inserted in the center comes out clean. Cool in pan 15 minutes. Carefully turn out to wire rack to cool completely.

Preparation: 15 minutes
Baking: 55-60 minutes
Protein g/s: 3

Mango Bread II

1 loaf, 16 slices

This variation of an island favorite combines fresh mangoes and dates for a moist loaf. Make several loaves and freeze, well-wrapped.

1⅓ *cups whole wheat flour, measured scoop and level*
⅓ *cup brown sugar, lightly packed*
1¼ *teaspoons baking soda*
⅛ *teaspoon salt*
1 *teaspoon ground cinnamon*
⅓ *cup whole pitted dates, packed*
2 *ounces walnuts*
2 *small mangoes, to yield 1⅓ cups chopped or fresh peaches*
2 *eggs*
⅓ *cup oil*
1 *teaspoon vanilla extract*

METAL BLADE: Add flour, brown sugar, baking soda, salt and cinnamon to work bowl. Pulse on/off to mix. Add dates; pulse on/off until coarsely chopped. Add walnuts; pulse on/off until coarsely chopped. Remove from bowl and set aside. Add mangoes, cut roughly into 1½-inch pieces, to work bowl. Pulse on/off until coarsely chopped. Remove from bowl and set aside. Add eggs to work bowl. Process 30 seconds. With machine running, pour in oil and vanilla extract. Process until well-mixed, 15-20 seconds. Turn machine off and add flour mixture all at once. Combine with 3-4 on/off pulses. Add mangoes; pulse on/off until mangoes are just mixed in. Do not overprocess or you will have puréed mangoes. Scrape down sides of bowl and mix gently with the spatula, if necessary.

Grease the bottom and sides of an 8½- x 4½-inch loaf pan; line bottom with wax paper. Pour batter into pan. Let stand 10 minutes while oven preheats to 350°. Bake at 350° 15 minutes; reduce temperature to 300° and bake an additional 45 minutes or until a toothpick inserted in the center comes out clean. Place on a wire rack to cool completely, in the pan, before slicing.

Preparation: 10-15 minutes
Standing: 10 minutes
Baking: 55-60 minutes
Protein g/s: 3

Raisin Spice Bread

1 loaf, 15 slices

A slice of this moist bread will spice up any lunch.

1 cup whole wheat flour, measured scoop and level
½ teaspoon baking soda
1 teaspoon ground cinnamon
¼ teaspoon salt
⅛ teaspoon ground cloves
⅛ teaspoon ground nutmeg
1 egg
⅓ cup low-fat yogurt
¼ cup oil
⅓ cup honey
½ cup raisins

Preheat oven to 350°.

METAL BLADE or PLASTIC MIXING BLADE: Add flour, baking soda, cinnamon, salt, cloves, and nutmeg to work bowl. Pulse on/off to mix. Remove and set aside. Add egg to work bowl and process 30 seconds. Scrape down sides of work bowl. Add yogurt, oil and honey. Mix with on/off pulses until well-blended. Remove work bowl cover, scrape down sides and add all dry ingredients at once. Add raisins. Combine with 5 on/off pulses only until batter is mixed. Before last on/off, scrape down sides of work bowl. Do not overprocess.

Grease bottom and sides of a small loaf pan, 7⅞ x 3⅞-inch. Line bottom with wax paper. Pour in batter. Bake 30-35 minutes or until a wooden toothpick inserted in the center comes out almost clean. Cool in pan 10 minutes. Carefully turn out to wire rack. Serve warm or cold.

Preparation: 8 minutes
Baking: 30-35 minutes
Protein g/s: 1.5

Irish Soda Bread

1 loaf, 15 slices

No time for a yeast bread? This is a quick and easy loaf you can make for any meal.

2¾-3 cups whole wheat flour, measured scoop and level
1½ teaspoons baking powder
1½ teaspoons baking soda
¾ teaspoon salt
2 tablespoons honey
about 1 cup buttermilk, at room temperature
1 tablespoon melted margarine
½ cup raisins (optional)

Preheat oven to 375°.

METAL BLADE: Add whole wheat flour, baking powder, baking soda, and salt to work bowl. Pulse on/off to mix. Add honey. With machine running, pour in enough buttermilk to form a soft ball of dough. Remove dough to lightly floured surface; knead in raisins. Shape dough into a ball. Place on a greased cookie sheet; flatten into a 6½-7 inch circle (about 1½ inches thick). Press a large floured knife into center of loaf halfway through to bottom. Repeat, at right angle, to divide the loaf into quarters. Bake 30 minutes or until top is golden and loaf sounds hollow when tapped. Remove to wire rack. Brush top with melted butter and allow to cool.

Preparation: 10 minutes
Baking: 30 minutes
Protein g/s: 3.5

Pineapple Bran Bread

1 loaf, 15 slices

Pineapple and honey flavor this moist high fiber bread. Allow the loaf to age at least a day.

1 cup walnuts
1¾ cups whole wheat flour, measured scoop and level
1 teaspoon salt
¾ teaspoon ground cinnamon
2 teaspoons baking powder
1 cup bran
3 tablespoons oil
½ cup honey
1 egg
1 cup pineapple juice

Preheat oven to 350°. In a mixing bowl, combine flour, salt, cinnamon, baking powder and bran. Set aside.

METAL BLADE: Add walnuts to work bowl. Pulse on/off until coarsely chopped. Remove to bowl with flour. Add oil, honey and egg to work bowl. Process for 15 seconds. With machine running, pour in pineapple juice. Stop machine as soon as all the juice is added. Remove work bowl cover and add flour mixture all at once. Combine with 3-4 on/off pulses until flour is just moistened.

Grease a 9 x 5-inch pan; line bottom with wax paper. Pour batter into the pan. Bake 1-1¼ hours or until browned and a toothpick inserted in the center comes out clean and dry. Cover the loaf with a tent of foil during the last 10-15 minutes of baking to prevent top from overbrowning. Let cool in the pan for 10 minutes before removing to a wire rack. Cool completely.

Preparation: 10 minutes
Baking: 60-75 minutes
Protein g/s: 3

Cheese and Chile Corn Bread

Serves 6-9

This moist, mildly spicy bread is almost a meal in itself. Serve with a steamed vegetable and fresh fruit salad.

1 4-ounce can whole green chiles, rinsed and seeded
4 ounces sharp Cheddar cheese, well-chilled
½ small onion
1 cup corn
1¼ cup cornmeal, measured scoop and level
⅓ cup whole wheat flour, measured scoop and level
1 tablespoon brown sugar
1 teaspoon salt
2 teaspoons baking soda
¼ cup non-instant, non-fat milk powder
2 eggs
¾ cup warm water
¼ cup oil

Preheat oven to 425°.

METAL BLADE: Dry chiles on a paper towel and add to work bowl. Pulse on/off until coarsely chopped. Remove metal blade and insert shredding disc.

SHREDDING DISC: Cut cheese to fit feed tube, shred. Cut onion into small wedges, stack into feed tube, shred. Remove chiles, cheese and onions to a mixing bowl. Add corn and toss to mix. Set aside.

METAL BLADE: Add cornmeal, whole wheat flour, sugar, salt, baking soda and milk powder to work bowl. Pulse on/off to mix. In a measuring cup, stir together eggs, warm water and oil. With machine running, pour liquid through feed tube in a steady stream. Stop machine as soon as the liquid has been added. Remove work bowl cover and scrape down sides of bowl. Add the cheese corn mixture all at once. Combine with 2-3 on/off pulses. Do not over-process. Corn should remain whole.

Pour into a well-greased 9 x 9-inch baking pan and bake 25-30 minutes or until a toothpick inserted in the center comes out clean. Place on wire rack and allow to cool 5 minutes before cutting. Serve warm.

Preparation: 10 minutes
Baking: 25-30 minutes
Standing: 5 minutes
Protein g/s: 6 servings—13
              9 servings—8.5

Sesame Honey Poundcake

1 loaf, 16 slices

This not-too-sweet poundcake is moist and slices well.

1½ cups *whole wheat flour, measured scoop and*
level
¼ cup *non-instant, non-fat milk powder*
1 teaspoon *baking powder*
1 teaspoon *baking soda*
¼ teaspoon *salt*
1 teaspoon *grated lemon peel*
⅓ cup *toasted sesame seeds*
3 *eggs*
½ cup *butter or margarine*
½ cup *honey*
⅓ cup *water*
1 teaspoon *vanilla extract*
1 teaspoon *oriental sesame oil*
1 tablespoon *toasted sesame seeds for topping*

Preheat oven to 325°.

METAL BLADE: Add flour, milk powder, baking powder, baking soda, salt, lemon peel and ⅓ cup sesame seeds to work bowl. Pulse on/off to mix. Remove and set aside. Add eggs to work bowl. Process 30 seconds. Scrape down sides of work bowl. Add butter, cut into small pieces. Process 10-20 seconds until well-blended. Pour in honey, water, vanilla extract and sesame oil. Pulse on/off until blended. Remove work bowl cover, scrape down sides and add all dry ingredients at once. Combine with 5 on/off pulses only until batter is mixed. Before last on/off, scrape down sides of work bowl. Do not overprocess.

Grease sides and bottom of an 8½ x 4½-inch loaf pan. Line bottom with wax paper. Pour batter into pan. Sprinkle top with 1 tablespoon sesame seeds. Bake 40-45 minutes or until a wooden toothpick inserted in center comes out clean. Allow to cool in the pan on a wire rack.

Preparation: 10-15 minutes
Baking: 40-45 minutes
Protein g/s: 4

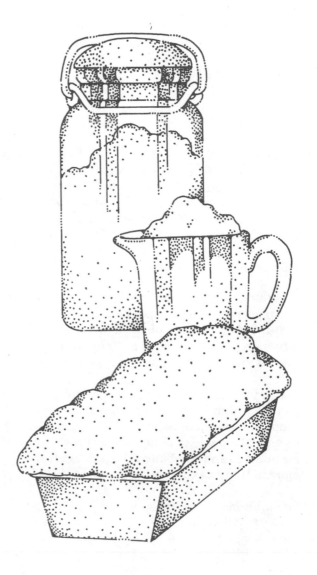

Unleavened Breads

Chapatis

Serves 8

This unleavened whole wheat bread is quite similar to our whole wheat flour tortillas. The food processor is perfect for kneading this heavy dough. An excellent accompaniment to dal, a standard in Indian cuisine.

1½ cups whole wheat flour, measured scoop and
      level
½ teaspoon salt
1 tablespoon oil
½ cup plus 1-2 tablespoons lukewarm water, as
      needed

METAL BLADE: Add flour and salt to work bowl. Pulse on/off to mix. Add oil and process until mixture resembles coarse meal. With machine running, pour in water in a slow steady stream. Add only enough water to form a stiff ball of dough and process 20 seconds. Stop machine and feel the dough. It should be smooth and elastic. It not, process 10 seconds more.

Divide dough into 8 portions. Knead each portion for about 10 seconds. Place ball on a lightly floured board. Using a rolling pin, roll out to a 7-inch circle 1/16-inch thin. If dough is difficult to shape, let rest several minutes to "relax."

Heat an ungreased SilverStone or similar non-stick pan over high heat. To test pan, sprinkle with few drops of water. If bubbles skitter around, heat is just right. Bake circle of dough until surface puffs with air bubbles and the bottom begins to brown. Turn and continue baking until done.

Preparation: 25 minutes
Cooking: 15-20 minutes
Protein g/s: 3

Whole Wheat Flour Tortillas

12 tortillas

Essentially an unleavened bread, these tasty tortillas contain a small amount of baking powder to produce a light texture. A good accompaniment to most of our Mexican main dishes.

2¼ cups whole wheat flour, measured scoop and
      level
½ teaspoon salt
¾ teaspoon double acting baking powder
2 tablespoons soy or safflower margarine
¾ cup warm water
1-2 tablespoons water, as needed

METAL BLADE: Add flour, salt and baking powder to work bowl. Pulse on/off. Add margarine, cut into small pieces. Process until mixture has the consistency of coarse meal. With machine running, pour in water through feed tube in a steady stream. When the proportion of flour and liquid is correct, the dough will begin to form into a ball. Stop processing as soon as a ball is formed. Remove dough from work bowl and divide into 12 portions. Place in plastic bag. Keep pieces well covered at all times as dough can dry out.

Form 1 piece of dough into a ball, coat with additional flour and roll out to a circle 6-7 inches in diameter. If dough is difficult to work with, cover, let "relax" for a few minutes. Make only 1 or 2 tortillas at a time, then bake. Repeat to make each tortilla.

Heat an ungreased SilverStone or similar non-stick pan over medium-high heat. Bake the tortillas until brown flecks appear, about 1½ minutes. Turn and cook the other side. Tortillas should puff up a bit during baking. Stack and cover tortillas, keeping warm until all tortillas are cooked and ready to be served.

Preparation: 5 minutes
Cooking: 25 minutes
Protein g/s: 3

Lavosh

Serves 16

2 cups whole wheat flour, measured scoop and
   level
1¼ teaspoons salt
2 tablespoons non-instant, non-fat milk powder
2 tablespoons butter
1 teaspoon honey
1 egg
½ cup water
toasted sesame seeds
poppy seeds

METAL BLADE: Add flour, salt, milk powder and
butter to work bowl. Process for 5 seconds or until
mixture has consistency of coarse meal. Add honey
and egg. With processor running, pour water
through feed tube in a steady stream. Stop processing as soon as dough begins to form a ball. Wrap in
plastic wrap and let rest 30 minutes. Prepare oven.
Place a pan of hot water on lower shelf. Preheat to
400°. Lightly grease a cookie sheet and place in hot
oven briefly to heat.

Divide dough into 8 portions. Roll out 2 portions at
a time. Keep remaining dough covered to prevent
drying. Dust the balls of dough with flour. Place on
floured pastry cloth and using a covered rolling pin,
roll dough to 1/16th-inch thickness. Sprinkle on
seeds during rolling to press seeds in. Set aside on a
sheet of waxed paper.

Carefully transfer dough to the hot, lightly greased
cookie sheet and bake 8-10 minutes or until lightly
browned. Watch carefully as these brown quickly.
Remove lavosh to metal racks to cool. Break into
pieces and store in airtight container. Repeat with
remaining dough. Cookie sheet does not need to be
greased after first baking. Makes eight 12 x 8-inch
rectangles.

Preparation: 20 minutes
Standing: 30 minutes
Baking: 30-40 minutes
Protein g/s: 3

Tofu Wheat Flour Tortillas

12 tortillas

6 ounces firm tofu, drained, broken into pieces
2 cups whole wheat flour, measured scoop and level
⅛ teaspoon salt (optional)
1-3 tablespoons water

METAL BLADE: Add tofu pieces, process until
smooth. Add flour and salt. With machine running,
slowly add enough water to form a ball of dough.
Process the ball of dough for 20 seconds. Divide the
dough into 12 pieces. Cover with plastic wrap and
allow to rest 30 minutes.

On a lightly floured board, using a rolling pin, roll
the pieces of dough into thin circles, 7-8 inches
across. Heat a non-stick skillet over medium heat.
Place the tortilla on the hot skillet and cook until
speckled brown. Turn and cook the other side. Place
the hot tortillas in a tea towel to keep warm while
baking the remaining circles.

Preparation: 5 minutes
Standing: 30 minutes
Cooking: allow 30 minutes to shape and cook
Protein g/s: 3.5

Mandarin Pancakes

12 pancakes

A tortilla press helps shorten the preparation time. When the correct amount of liquid is in the dough, the wax paper will peel easily off the pancake. If it cracks, add a little more water and knead well. If it sticks, add a little more flour to dough. Fill with Soy Sprout Sauté (see index).

1 cup whole wheat flour, measured scoop and level
⅓ cup boiling water
1-2 tablespoons boiling water
oriental sesame oil

METAL BLADE: Add flour to work bowl. With machine running, pour in ⅓ cup boiling water. Process to form a stiff ball of dough, adding boiling water if necessary. Process ball of dough 20 seconds. Remove dough from bowl, wrap well and let rest 30 minutes. Shape dough into a 6-inch long roll; cut into 12 pieces. Keep dough pieces covered to prevent them from drying.

Work with two pieces of dough at a time. Pat each of the pieces into 2-inch circles. Brush one circle with sesame oil, especially on the edges. Top with remaining circle. Place the circles on the tortilla press, inside a folded sheet of wax paper, slightly back of center. Close the lid and press. Lift lid and rotate circle a quarter turn, press. Continue rotating and pressing to form a 4½-5-inch circle. Make 1 or 2 pancakes and cook; repeat with remaining pieces of dough. When using rolling pin, to avoid wrinkling, roll in 1 stroke from center to outside, not in a back and forth motion.

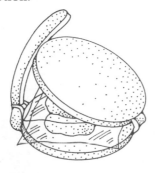

Heat a non-stick, ungreased skillet over medium-high heat. Cook pancakes until they are puffed and parchment colored, about 1 minute on each side. Remove from skillet; cool slightly and while hot, separate with a small pointed knife into two pancakes. Stack, cover and keep warm until all pancakes are cooked.

These can be made up to 2 weeks in advance. Stack, cover and cool completely. Wrap well and freeze. To reheat, steam frozen wrapped pancakes for about 12 minutes; thawed pancakes 6 minutes. Or heat frozen wrapped pancakes in a 325° oven for 20-30 minutes.

Preparation: 30 minutes
Standing: 30 minutes
Cooking: 24 minutes
Protein g/s: 1.5

Corn Tortillas

12 tortillas

After numerous attempts, we finally came up with a good tasting corn tortilla made with commercial masa harina. The secret—corn germ. This new product puts back flavor and nutrients that never should have been removed from the corn. A tortilla press is an essential piece of equipment if you make these often.

1½ cups Quaker Oats masa harina
½ cup corn germ
1⅛ cups water

METAL BLADE: Add masa harina and corn germ to work bowl. Process until the corn germ is cut into very small pieces. With machine running, add water in a steady stream until masa forms a ball. Stop processing as soon as a ball is formed. Remove dough from work bowl and divide into 12 portions. Place in a plastic bag. Keep pieces well covered at all times as dough can dry out.

SHAPING Tortilla Press Method: Line both sides of the tortilla press with heavy polyethylene plastic. (Cut open a sandwich bag or use a bag such as the kind you get in the produce section of the supermarket.) DO NOT use Saran or similar type of plastic wrap or wax paper. The dough will invariably stick to them.

Roll a piece of dough into a ball. Pat a few times to flatten slightly. Place flattened dough slightly off center, toward the back, on the tortilla press. Close the lid and press down hard on the handle. Be sure that dough is completely encased in the plastic sheet. Remove the tortilla from the press and peel off the plastic. With experience you will learn how the dough should feel. If the tortilla cracks around the edges, add a little more water to the dough and knead well. If it sticks to the plastic, add a little more masa harina to the dough.

Rolling Pin Method: Roll a piece of dough into a ball. Place between two sheets of polyethylene plastic, larger than the diameter of the finished tortilla. Roll out to form a circle 6-6½ inches in diameter. If you find that the tortilla sticks to the plastic, dust with a little masa harina before rolling out.

Heat an ungreased SilverStone or similar non-stick pan over medium-high heat. Bake tortilla until edges start to dry out, about 30 seconds. Flip and bake until lightly flecked on the underside, about 1 minute. Flip a second time and bake about 30 seconds. Wrap in a towel to keep soft and warm.

DO NOT substitute cornmeal in this recipe. It is about as far removed from the flavor of a Mexican tortilla as you can get.

Preparation: 15-20 minutes
Cooking: 25 minutes
Protein g/s: 2.5

Sandwiches and Spreads

Aioli Cheese-Avocado Open-Face

1 slice sandwich bread
2 teaspoons Aioli Mayonnaise (see index)
2 ounces Monterey Jack cheese, sliced
avocado slices
alfalfa sprouts

Spread bread with mayonnaise; top with cheese slices, avocado slices and sprouts.

Protein g/s: 14-17

Cheddar and Dijon Mustard Open-Face

1 slice sandwich bread
1 teaspoon Dijon mustard
2 ounces mild Cheddar cheese, sliced
2 slices tomato
alfalfa sprouts

Spread bread with Dijon mustard; top with cheese, tomato slices and sprouts.

Protein g/s: 14-17

Apple and Swiss Cheese Sandwich

2 slices sandwich bread (try one with raisins)
mayonnaise
1 small apple, thinly sliced
1 ounce Swiss cheese, sliced

Spread one or both slices of bread with mayonnaise. Arrange apple slices on the mayonnaise; top with Swiss cheese and cover with remaining slice of bread.

Protein g/s: 16

Chile Cheese Melt

2 slices sandwich bread
2 ounces sharp Cheddar cheese or Monterey Jack cheese
1 canned whole green chile, rinsed and seeded

Split chile and pat dry with paper towel. Arrange over one slice of bread; top with one ounce cheese. Top second slice of bread with remaining cheese. Broil until cheese is melted and bubbly. Carefully press slices together.

Protein g/s: 22

Banana Peanut Butter Sandwich

2 slices sandwich bread
2 tablespoons peanut butter
1 small ripe banana, sliced
honey
lettuce

Spread one slice of bread with peanut butter; top with banana slices (mashing slightly to keep them from sliding off). Dribble a small amount of honey over bananas; top with lettuce and remaining slice of bread.

Protein g/s: 17

Peanut Butter Surprise

2 slices sandwich bread
2 tablespoons peanut butter
mayonnaise
raisins
cucumber slices

Spread one slice of bread with peanut butter and the other with mayonnaise. Arrange raisins and cucumber slices on the mayonnaise topped slice of bread.

Protein g/s: 17

Plain Peanut Butter

Nothing plain about this combination!

2 slices orange sunflower seed bread
2 tablespoons peanut butter or sesame peanut butter

Protein g/s: 20

Swiss and Spinach Sandwich

2 slices rye bread
butter or margarine, optional
2 ounces Swiss cheese, sliced
fresh spinach leaves
2 tomato slices
alfalfa sprouts

Butter one slice of bread. Layer on cheese, spinach leaves, tomato slices and sprouts. Top with remaining slice of bread.

Protein g/s: 21

Sesame Peanut Spread

¾ cup, 4 servings

Try this spread on a warm Tofu Wheat Flour Tortilla (see index).

½ cup toasted sesame seeds
1 tablespoon sunflower seeds
1 tablespoon oil
1 tablespoon honey
½ cup peanut butter

METAL BLADE: Add sesame seeds and sunflower seeds to work bowl. Process until finely ground. With machine running, pour in oil and honey. Stop machine, scrape mixture down from the side of the bowl. Add peanut butter and process until well-mixed. Store in a covered container in the refrigerator.

Preparation: 5 minutes
Protein g/s: 14

Guacamole Cheese Sandwich

1 pita bread, halved
2 tomato slices
2 ounces Monterey Jack cheese
alfalfa sprouts

Guacamole:
½ small avocado, mashed
1 green onion, minced
1 tablespoon yogurt
pinch garlic salt
dash chili powder

Combine guacamole ingredients. Heat pita. Fill each half with tomato, cheese and guacamole. Top with alfalfa sprouts.

Protein g/s: 20.5

Sesame Tahini

1¾ cups

No need to purchase this sesame seed butter since it's so easy to make in the food processor. It's an essential ingredient in hummus and other Middle Eastern dishes.

3½ cups hulled (white) sesame seeds, about 1 pound

Spread sesame seeds evenly over the bottom of an ungreased baking pan. Toast in a 325° oven 8-10 minutes. Stir occasionally. The seeds will be lightly toasted to a pale straw color. DO NOT let seeds brown as this causes an undesirable bitter flavor to develop. Allow to cool slightly.

METAL BLADE: Add seeds to work bowl. Process until mixture becomes a smooth paste. It will first have the appearance of coarse meal, form a ball and finally become a smooth paste. It will take 4-5 minutes to form the paste. Stop the machine and scrape down sides as necessary.

Preparation: 20 minutes
Protein g/s: 3 per tablespoon

Swiss and Mushroom Sandwich

3　*fresh mushrooms, sliced*
1　*green onion, minced*
1　*tablespoon butter*
2　*slices sandwich bread*
2　*tomato slices*
1　*ounce Swiss cheese, shredded*

In a small skillet, heat butter over medium heat; add mushrooms and onion. Sauté until soft and liquid has evaporated, 3-5 minutes. Toast bread. Top each slice with tomato, mushroom mixture and cheese. Broil until cheese is melted and bubbly. Serve open-face.

Protein g/s: 15

Peanut Butter

1½-1¾　cups

This is peanut butter at its best—no salt, sugar or additives—just peanuts and a bit of oil as needed. Serve with a grain and a milk product!

1　*pound shelled unsalted peanuts, about 3 cups*
1-2　*tablespoons oil as needed*

Purchasing nuts: Purchase either shelled raw peanuts in the skins or skinned peanuts which have been pre-roasted specifically for making peanut butter. We don't recommend that you remove the skins. It's tedious and time-consuming. Besides, the extra fiber is a real advantage.

Roasting: If you buy peanuts which are lightly roasted, you may want to roast them in a slow oven 5-10 minutes to bring out the flavor. When using raw nuts, we roast them slowly at a low temperature; 35-45 minutes in a 325° oven is about right. The amount of roasting is a matter of individual preference. Over-roasting results in a bitter flavor and loss of nutrients.

METAL BLADE: Add peanuts to work bowl. Process until completely smooth. This may take 4-5 minutes. Scrape down sides of bowl as necessary. The mixture will first resemble coarse meal, form a ball and finally become a smooth paste. Add oil only as necessary to form the paste.

To make crunchy peanut butter, coarsely chop 1 cup peanuts, using several on/off pulses. Remove from the bowl and set aside. Process remaining 2 cups peanuts to make a smooth butter. Add chopped nuts and pulse on/off to mix in. Heat created by the rapid revolution of the blade causes homemade peanut butter to be runny until it is refrigerated.

Preparation: 5-6 minutes, excluding roasting time
Protein g/s: 3 tablespoons regular—15
　　　　　　3 tablespoons crunchy—12

Pancakes and Waffles

Spiced Fruit Pancakes

12 5-inch pancakes

These light, mildly flavored pancakes need no syrup. Try a different fruit each time you make them.

Any of these fresh or dry fruits:
- *½-1 cup whole berries*
- *1 unpeeled apple, halved cored, shredded*
- *1 large banana, shredded*
- *½ cup raisins*
- *½ cup dates, coarsely chopped*
- *1-2 peaches, coarsely chopped*
- 2 eggs
- 2 tablespoons oil
- 2 tablespoons honey
- 1 cup water
- 1¼ cups whole wheat flour, measured scoop and level
- 2½ teaspoons baking powder
- ½ teaspoon ground coriander
- ½ teaspoon ground cinnamon
- ½ teaspoon ground nutmeg
- ¼ teaspoon salt
- ¼ cup non-instant, non-fat milk powder

SHREDDING DISC or METAL BLADE: Shred or chop the fruit of your choice. Remove from work bowl and set aside. Wipe work bowl dry. In a measuring cup, combine eggs, oil, honey and water. Set aside.

METAL BLADE or PLASTIC MIXING BLADE: Add flour, baking powder, coriander, cinnamon, nutmeg, salt and milk powder to work bowl; pulse on/off to mix. With machine running, pour in liquid mixture. Stop machine as soon as all the liquid has been added. Scrape down sides of bowl and add fruit and combine with 2-3 on/off pulses. Do not overprocess.

Heat a lightly oiled non-stick frying pan over medium heat. Before baking, test the pan by sprinkling a few drops of cold water on it. If the water bounces and sputters, the pan is ready. Using a ¼-cup measure, pour batter onto pan. Pancakes are ready to turn when bubbles appear on top and the underside is light brown, 2-3 minutes. Turn pancakes only once and continue baking until the second side is done. Cooking the second side takes about half as long as cooking the first side.

Preparation: 5-7 minutes
Cooking: 23-25 minutes
Protein g/s: 4 per pancake

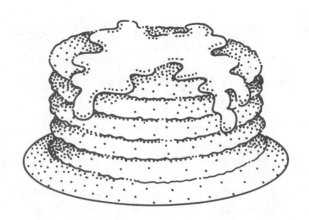

Oatmeal Pancakes

12 5-inch pancakes

Delicious with applesauce or maple syrup and just a bit of butter.

2 eggs
2 tablespoons oil
1 tablespoon honey
1¼ cups milk
1 cup rolled oats
1½ cups whole wheat flour, measured scoop and level
1 teaspoon baking powder
¼ teaspoon salt

In a measuring cup, stir together eggs, oil, honey and milk. Set aside.

METAL BLADE: Add rolled oats to work bowl. Process until oats resemble coarse meal. Add flour, baking powder and salt; pulse on/off to mix. With machine running, pour in liquid mixture. Stop machine as soon as all the liquid has been added. Do not overprocess. Scrape down sides of bowl.

Heat a lightly oiled non-stick frying pan over medium heat. Before baking, test the pan by sprinkling a few drops of cold water on it. If the water bounces and sputters, the pan is ready. Using a ¼-cup measure, pour batter onto pan. Pancakes are ready to turn when bubbles appear on top and the underside is light brown, 2-3 minutes. Turn pancakes only once and continue baking until the second side is done. Cooking the second side takes about half as long as cooking the first side.

Preparation: 5 minutes
Cooking: 15-25 minutes
Protein g/s: 5 per pancake

Oven Pancakes

2 large pancakes

Fresh lemon juice and a light dusting of powdered sugar top these puffy baked pancakes. Without a doubt, these are one of our all-time favorites. Sprinkle tops with cinnamon or serve with our Sautéed Apples (see index) for a variation.

4 tablespoons butter or margarine
½ cup whole wheat flour, measured scoop and level
2 eggs
½ cup milk
½ teaspoon ground nutmeg
juice of ½ lemon
powdered sugar
cinnamon, optional

Preheat oven to 425°. Place 2 tablespoons butter in each of two 9-inch round cake pans and heat briefly in the oven. Spread melted butter evenly over the bottom of the pans and set aside. When oven has reached 425°, prepare batter.

PLASTIC MIXING BLADE or METAL BLADE: Add flour, eggs, milk and nutmeg to work bowl. Combine with 3-4 on/off pulses. Do not overprocess. Immediately pour batter into the center of the prepared pans and bake 10-15 minutes. The tender pancakes will puff and become a golden brown. Carefully remove pancakes with a pancake turner to a serving dish. Sprinkle with lemon juice; dust lightly with powdered sugar and cut into wedges to serve.

Preparation: 3-5 minutes
Baking: 10-15 minutes
Protein g/s: 13 per pancake

Banana Nut Pancakes

10 5-inch pancakes

1 cup whole wheat flour, measured scoop and level
2 tablespoons non-instant, non-fat milk powder
1 tablespoon brown sugar
½ teaspoon baking powder
½ teaspoon baking soda
½ cup walnut pieces
⅞ cup skim milk
1 tablespoon oil
2 eggs
½ teaspoon vanilla extract
1 medium ripe banana

In a small bowl, stir together flour, milk powder, brown sugar, baking powder, walnut pieces, and baking soda. Set aside. In a measuring cup, combine milk, oil, eggs and vanilla extract. Set aside.

METAL BLADE: Add banana, broken into small chunks, to work bowl. Process until liquified. Stop machine and add flour mixture; combine with 2-3 on/off pulses. With machine running, pour in liquid mixture. Stop machine as soon as all the liquid has been added. Do not overprocess. Scrape down sides of bowl.

Heat a lightly oiled non-stick frying pan over medium heat. Before baking, test the pan by sprinkling a few drops of cold water on it. If the water bounces and sputters, the pan is ready. Using a ¼-cup measure, pour batter onto pan. Pancakes are ready to turn when bubbles appear on top and the underside is light brown, 2-3 minutes. Turn pancakes only once and continue baking until the second side is done. Cooking the second side takes about half as long as cooking the first side.

Preparation: 5 minutes
Cooking: 15 minutes
Protein g/s: 5 per pancake

Selma's Cottage Cheese Pancakes

8 5-inch pancakes

A favorite family recipe and a delicious high protein breakfast. Serve with a small amount of butter or margarine and honey or maple syrup.

4 eggs
¾ cup cottage cheese, drained
3 tablespoons oil
½ teaspoon vanilla extract
⅓ cup whole wheat flour, measured scoop and level
¼ teaspoon salt
1 tablespoon bran
1 tablespoon wheat germ

METAL BLADE: Add eggs to work bowl and process until foamy, 5-6 seconds. Add the cottage cheese and process until smooth, 4-5 seconds. Stop machine and add oil, vanilla extract, flour, salt, bran and wheat germ. Combine with 3-4 on/off pulses. Do not overprocess.

Heat a non-stick frying pan over medium-low to medium heat. Before baking, test the pan by sprinkling a few drops of cold water on it. If the water bounces and sputters, the pan is ready. Using a ¼-

cup measure, pour batter onto pan. Pancakes are ready to turn when bubbles appear on top and the underside is light brown, 2-3 minutes. Turn pancakes only once and continue baking until the second side is done. Cooking the second side takes about half as long as cooking the first side.

Preparation: 5 minutes
Cooking: 15 minutes
Protein g/s: 7 per pancake

Whole Wheat Pancakes

9 5-inch pancakes

This basic recipe calls for ingredients you'll usually have on hand.

2 eggs
1 tablespoon oil
⅞ cup skim milk
1 cup whole wheat flour, measured scoop and level
1 tablespoon brown sugar
1 teaspoon baking powder
¼ teaspoon salt

In a measuring cup, stir together eggs, oil and milk and set aside.

METAL BLADE or PLASTIC MIXING BLADE: Add flour, brown sugar, baking powder and salt to work bowl. Pulse on/off to mix, and with machine running, pour in liquid mixture. Stop machine as soon as all the liquid has been added. Do not overprocess. Scrape down sides of bowl.

Heat a lightly oiled non-stick frying pan over medium heat. Before baking, test the pan by sprinkling a few drops of cold water on it. If the water bounces and sputters, the pan is ready. Using a ¼-cup measure, pour batter onto pan. Pancakes are ready to turn when bubbles appear on top and the underside is light brown, 2-3 minutes. Turn pancakes only once and continue baking until the second side is done. Cooking the second side takes about half as long as cooking the first side.

Preparation: 5 minutes
Cooking: 15 minutes
Protein g/s: 4 per pancake

Whole Wheat Soy Pancakes

9 5-inch pancakes

2   *eggs*
1   *tablespoon oil*
1   *teaspoon vanilla extract*
⅞   *cup skim milk*
¾   *cup whole wheat flour, measured scoop and level*
¼   *cup soy flour, measured scoop and level*
1   *tablespoon brown sugar*
1   *teaspoon baking powder*
¼   *teaspoon salt*

In a measuring cup, stir together eggs, oil, vanilla extract and milk and set aside.

METAL BLADE or PLASTIC MIXING BLADE: Add wheat flour, soy flour, brown sugar, baking powder and salt to work bowl; pulse on/off to mix. With machine running, pour in liquid mixture. Stop machine as soon as all the liquid has been added. Do not overprocess. Scrape down sides of bowl.

Heat a lightly oiled non-stick frying pan over medium heat. Before baking, test the pan by sprinkling a few drops of cold water on it. If the water bounces and sputters, the pan is ready. Using a ¼ cup measure, pour batter onto pan. Pancakes are ready to turn when bubbles appear on top and the underside is light brown, 2-3 minutes. Turn pancakes only once and continue baking until the second side is done. Cooking the second side takes about half as long as cooking the first side.

Preparation: 5 minutes
Cooking: 15-25 minutes
Protein g/s: 4.5 per pancake

Whole Wheat or Buckwheat Buttermilk Pancakes

9 5-inch pancakes

This batter makes a pancake which is thick and light. If the batter thickens, thin with water. We like to serve these with a simple syrup made of honey and water. Stir together ½ cup honey and ⅓ cup water, bring to a boil and serve.

1 *egg*
2 *tablespoons oil*
1 *cup buttermilk*
1 *cup whole wheat flour, measured scoop and level**
1 *tablespoon brown sugar*
1 *teaspoon baking powder*
½ *teaspoon baking soda*
½ *teaspoon salt*

In a measuring cup, stir together egg, oil and buttermilk and set aside.

METAL BLADE or PLASTIC MIXING BLADE: Add flour, brown sugar, baking powder, baking soda and salt to work bowl. Pulse on/off to mix, and with machine running, pour in liquid mixture. Stop machine as soon as all the liquid has been added. Do not overprocess. Scrape down sides of bowl.

Heat a lightly oiled non-stick frying pan over medium heat. Before baking, test the pan by sprinkling a few drops of cold water on it. If the water bounces and sputters, the pan is ready. Using a ¼-cup measure, pour batter onto pan. Pancakes are ready to turn when bubbles appear on top and the underside is light brown, 2-3 minutes. Turn pancakes only once and continue baking until the second side is done. Cooking the second side takes about half as long as cooking the first side.

*½ cup dark buckwheat flour may be substituted for ½ cup of the whole wheat flour.

Preparation: 5 minutes
Cooking: 15 minutes
Protein g/s: 3.5 per pancake

Whole Wheat Hazelnut Pancakes

9 5-inch pancakes

The food processor is ideal for grinding the hazelnuts into a flour for this recipe. We enjoy these on special occasions topped with a dab of butter and a bit of maple syrup.

2 eggs
1 teaspoon vanilla extract
¾ cup skim milk
½ cup hazelnuts, shelled but not skinned
1 cup whole wheat flour, measured scoop and level
1 teaspoon baking powder
¼ teaspoon salt
1 tablespoon brown sugar
1 tablespoon margarine

In a measuring cup, stir together eggs, vanilla extract and milk. Set aside.

METAL BLADE: Add hazelnuts and ½ cup flour to the work bowl. Process until nuts are ground to a consistency of coarse flour. Add remaining ½ cup flour, baking powder, salt and brown sugar; pulse on/off to mix. Add margarine, cut into 4 pieces; pulse on/off to cut in. With machine running, pour in liquid mixture. Stop machine as soon as all the liquid has been added. Do not overprocess. Scrape down sides of bowl.

Heat a lightly oiled non-stick frying pan over medium heat. Before baking, test the pan by sprinkling a few drops of cold water on it. If the water bounces and sputters, the pan is ready. Using a ¼-cup measure, pour batter onto pan. Pancakes are ready to turn when bubbles appear on top and the underside is light brown, 2-3 minutes. Turn pancakes only once and continue baking until the second side is done. Cooking the second side takes about half as long as cooking the first side.

Preparation: 5-7 minutes
Cooking: 15 minutes
Protein g/s: 4.5 per pancake

Cinnamon Apple Pancakes

9 5-inch pancakes

Bits of shredded apple are the surprise in these light and fluffy pancakes.

⅞ cup skim milk
2 eggs
1 tablespoon oil
1 cup whole wheat flour, measured scoop and level
1 teaspoon baking powder
¼ teaspoon baking soda
½ teaspoon cinnamon
¼ teaspoon salt
1 large apple, peeled and cored

In a measuring cup, stir together milk, eggs and oil. Set aside.

METAL BLADE or PLASTIC MIXING BLADE: Add flour, baking powder, baking soda, cinnamon and salt to work bowl; pulse on/off to mix. With machine running, pour in liquid mixture. Stop machine as soon as all the liquid has been added. Do not overprocess. Carefully remove blade and insert shredding disc.

SHREDDING DISC: Quarter apple and insert vertically into feed tube; shred onto batter. Remove shredding disc and with a spatula or end of a wooden spoon, gently mix apple into batter.

Heat a lightly oiled non-stick frying pan over medium heat. Before baking, test the pan by sprinkling a few drops of cold water on it. If the water bounces and sputters, the pan is ready. Using a ¼-cup measure, pour batter onto pan. Pancakes are ready to turn when bubbles appear on top and the underside is light brown, 2-3 minutes. Turn pancakes only once and continue baking until the second side is done. Cooking the second side takes about half as long as cooking the first side.

Preparation: 5 minutes
Cooking: 15 minutes
Protein g/s: 4 per pancake

Ricotta Pancakes

14-16 5-inch pancakes

Top these pancakes with puréed fresh fruit of the season.

8 ounces ricotta cheese
3 eggs
1 teaspoon vanilla extract
5 drops lemon extract
grated rind from ½ lemon
⅔ cup skim milk
½ cup whole wheat flour, measured scoop and level
¼ teaspoon salt
1 teaspoon baking powder
3 tablespoons bran

METAL BLADE: Add ricotta cheese, eggs, vanilla extract, lemon extract and lemon rind to work bowl; process until well-mixed. With machine running, pour in skim milk. Stop machine and scrape down sides of bowl. Stir together flour, salt, baking powder and bran. Add to work bowl and combine with 3-4 on/off pulses; do not overprocess.

Heat a lightly oiled non-stick frying pan over medium heat. Before baking, test the pan by sprinkling a few drops of cold water on it. If the water bounces and sputters, the pan is ready. Using a ¼-cup measure, pour batter onto pan. Pancakes are ready to turn when bubbles appear on top and the underside is light brown, 2-3 minutes. Turn pancakes only once and continue baking until the second side is done. Cooking the second side takes about half as long as cooking the first side.

Preparation: 5-7 minutes
Cooking: 22-25 minutes
Protein g/s: 14—4 per pancake
              16—3.5 per pancake

Oatmeal Molasses Ginger Cakes

10 5-inch pancakes

A different taste to break the breakfast monotony. For a stronger ginger flavor, increase the amount of ground ginger by ⅛ teaspoon. Top these cakes with a dab of butter and maple syrup or fresh puréed fruit.

2 eggs
1 tablespoon oil
2 tablespoons molasses
1 tablespoon honey
1 teaspoon vanilla extract
1 cup milk
1 cup whole wheat flour, measured scoop and level
½ cup rolled oats
1 teaspoon baking powder
½ teaspoon ground ginger
¼ teaspoon salt

In a measuring cup, stir together eggs, oil, molasses, honey, vanilla extract and milk. Set aside.

METAL BLADE or PLASTIC MIXING BLADE: Add flour, oats, baking powder, ginger and salt to work bowl. Pulse on/off to mix. With machine running, pour in liquid mixture. Stop machine as soon as all the liquid has been added. Do not overprocess. Scrape down sides of bowl.

Heat a lightly oiled non-stick frying pan over medium heat. Before baking, test the pan by sprinkling a few drops of cold water on it. If the water bounces and sputters, the pan is ready. Using a ¼-cup measure, pour batter onto pan. Pancakes are ready to turn when bubbles appear on top and the underside is light brown, 2-3 minutes. Turn pancakes only once and continue baking until the second side is done. Cooking the second side takes about half as long as cooking the first side.

Preparation: 5 minutes
Cooking: 15-25 minutes
Protein g/s: 4.5 per pancake

Sunflower Seed Pancakes

10 5-inch pancakes

A delicious high protein breakfast with a crunch. Top with a bit of butter and maple syrup or honey.

2 eggs
2 tablespoons oil
1 tablespoon honey
1 teaspoon vanilla extract
1 cup skim milk
1 cup whole wheat flour, measured scoop and level
1 teaspoon baking powder
½ teaspoon salt
⅓ cup sunflower seeds

In a measuring cup, stir together eggs, oil, honey, vanilla extract and milk. Set aside.

METAL BLADE or PLASTIC MIXING BLADE: Add flour, baking powder, salt and sunflower seeds to work bowl. Pulse on/off to mix, and with machine running, pour in liquid mixture. Stop machine as soon as all the liquid has been added. Do not overprocess. Scrape down sides of bowl.

Heat a lightly oiled non-stick pan over medium heat. Before baking, test the pan by sprinkling a few drops of cold water on it. If the water bounces and sputters, the pan is ready. Using a ¼-cup measure, pour batter onto pan. Pancakes are ready to turn when bubbles appear on top and the underside is light brown, 2-3 minutes. Turn pancakes only once and continue baking until the second side is done. Cooking the second side takes about half as long as cooking the first side.

Preparation: 5 minutes
Cooking: 15 minutes
Protein g/s: 6 per pancake

Bran Cheese Waffles

4-6 large waffles

Top with warm applesauce, spiced with cinnamon. These freeze well; reheat in a 350° oven about 10 minutes or until crisp and hot.

2 eggs, separated
¼ cup oil
1½ cups water
3 ounces sharp Cheddar cheese, well-chilled
*1¾ cups whole wheat flour, measured scoop and
    level*
1 tablespoon baking powder
¾ cup bran
½ cup non-instant, non-fat milk powder
1 teaspoon salt

In a measuring cup stir together egg yolks, oil and water and set aside.

SHREDDING DISC: Cut Cheddar cheese to fit feed tube; shred. Leave cheese in work bowl.

METAL BLADE: Add flour, baking powder, bran, milk powder and salt to cheese in work bowl and pulse on/off to mix. With machine running, pour in liquid mixture. Stop machine as soon as all the liquid has been added. Do not overprocess. Pour the batter into a medium mixing bowl. Wash and dry bowl and metal blade.

METAL BLADE: Add egg whites to work bowl. Process until stiff but not dry. Fold into batter. Bake in a hot waffle iron according to manufacturer's directions. Thin batter with milk if it gets too thick.

Preparation: 10-15 minutes
Baking: 20-30 minutes
Protein g/s: 4—23 per waffle
              6—15 per waffle

Enriched French Toast

4 slices

Top these with a dab of butter or margarine and a bit of honey.

¼ cup non-instant, non-fat milk powder
½ cup milk
2 eggs
1 teaspoon vanilla
3 drops lemon extract
4 slices whole wheat bread

METAL BLADE: Add milk powder to a *dry* work bowl. With machine running, gradually pour in milk. Add eggs, vanilla and lemon extract and process only until just mixed. Arrange bread in a shallow pan; pour over the milk mixture and let stand until the bread has absorbed most of the mixture, about 5 minutes. Heat a lightly oiled non-stick frying pan over medium heat. Fry bread until golden brown on both sides and egg mixture has set.

Preparation: 5 minutes
Standing: 5 minutes
Cooking: 5-8 minutes
Protein g/s: 10

Double Wheat Waffles

4-5 waffles

Wheat germ and soy flour give these waffles extra protein value. For a change of pace, top with Ratatouille or Soy Sprout Sauté (see index).

2 eggs, separated
⅓ cup oil
2-3 tablespoons honey
1⅔ cups water
1½ cups whole wheat flour, measured scoop and
    level
¼ cup soy flour, measured scoop and level
2 teaspoons baking powder
½ teaspoon salt
⅔ cup wheat germ
½ cup non-instant, non-fat milk powder

In a measuring cup, stir together egg yolks, oil, honey and water and set aside.

METAL BLADE or PLASTIC MIXING BLADE: Add wheat flour, soy flour, baking powder, wheat germ, milk powder and salt to work bowl and pulse on/off to mix. With machine running, pour in liquid mixture. Stop machine as soon as all the liquid has been added. Pour batter into a medium mixing bowl. Wash and dry work bowl and metal blade.

METAL BLADE: Add egg whites to work bowl; process until stiff but not dry. Fold into batter. Bake in a hot waffle iron according to manufacturer's directions. Thin batter with milk if it gets too thick.

Preparation: 10-15 minutes
Baking: 20-30 minutes
Protein g/s: 4—20.5 per waffle
           5—16.5 per waffle

Desserts

Fruit Nut Squares

16 squares

A moist chewy topping on a shortbread like crust. The processor takes the work out of chopping the prunes and mixing up the dough for the crust!

Crust
¾ cup whole wheat flour, measured scoop and level
2 tablespoons brown sugar, firmly packed
½ cup butter or margarine, cut into 1-inch pieces

Preheat oven to 350°.

METAL BLADE: Add flour and sugar to work bowl. Pulse on/off to mix. Add butter and process until butter is blended into the flour and dough just begins to form into a ball. Turn dough into a 9 x 9-inch baking pan. Press in dough to make an even layer. Bake 16-18 minutes or until lightly browned.

Filling
¼ cup whole wheat flour, measured scoop and level
½ teaspoon baking powder
¼ teaspoon salt
20 pitted dried prunes
¾ cup walnuts
2 eggs
⅓ cup brown sugar, firmly packed
½ teaspoon vanilla extract

METAL BLADE: Add flour, baking powder and salt to work bowl. Pulse on/off to mix. Add prunes and walnuts. Pulse on/off to coarsely chop. Remove from bowl and set aside. Add eggs, sugar and vanilla to work bowl. Process 10 seconds. Stop machine, scrape down sides of bowl. Add reserved flour/fruit mixture to bowl all at once. Combine with 2-4 on/off pulses until just mixed.

Carefully spread filling over hot crust. Return pan to oven and continue baking at 350° 28-30 minutes or until golden brown. Place pan on wire rack to cool completely. Cut into squares. Store in an airtight container at room temperature if to be served in a day or so, or in the refrigerator.

Preparation: 10 minutes
Baking: 45 minutes total time
Protein g/s: 2.5

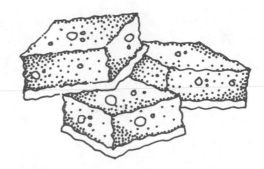

Apple Yogurt Muesli

Serves 1

Muesli, as originally developed by Dr. Bircher-Benner, is a fruit dish with a bit of cereal, milk and nuts. This dish is usually served at the beginning of breakfast or the evening meal, following the Bircher-Benner principle that "the keenest edge shall be taken off the appetite with fresh, raw food, before anything else is eaten." We think muesli makes a delicious snack anytime.

1 tablespoon rolled oats
3 tablespoons hot water
¼ cup low-fat yogurt
1 teaspoon fresh lemon juice
4 whole almonds
1 large apple, halved and cored

In a small dish, pour hot water over oats. Let stand a few minutes to soften, then drain slightly. Stir in yogurt and lemon juice and set aside.

METAL BLADE: Add almonds to work bowl. Pulse on/off until finely grated. Remove from bowl and set aside.

SHREDDING DISC: Cut apple to fit feed tube; shred. Remove shredding disc. With a spatula push apples to the side of the bowl and insert metal blade or plastic mixing blade.

METAL BLADE: Spread apple evenly around the bottom of the bowl and pour in yogurt mixture. Combine with 2-3 on/off pulses. Do not overprocess. Apple shreds should not be chopped. Remove to serving dish, sprinkle on nuts and serve immediately.

Preparation: 5-7 minutes
Protein g/s: 3.5

Fresh Applesauce

1⅓ cups

This uncooked applesauce is an excellent pancake topping. When prepared in advance, the applesauce turns brown, so it's best made just before serving.

2 large Golden Delicious apples, quartered and cored
1 tablespoon lemon juice
1-2 tablespoons honey

METAL BLADE: Add apples, cut into 1-inch pieces, lemon juice, and honey to work bowl. Process until apples are puréed. Stop machine and scrape down sides of bowl occasionally. Serve at once.

Preparation: 2 minutes

Banana Nutty Bars

12 bars

A favorite combination in a not too sweet bar. These taste better if left to sit, well-wrapped, overnight.

1 cup whole wheat flour, measured scoop and level
¼ cup non-instant, non-fat milk powder
½ teaspoon salt
1 teaspoon baking powder
1 teaspoon ground cinnamon
½ teaspoon ground nutmeg
½ cup raisins
⅓ cup peanut butter or
¾ cup peanuts
¼ cup butter or margarine
1 egg
⅓ to ½ cup honey
1 teaspoon vanilla extract
2 medium bananas, ripe, cut into chunks

Preheat oven to 350°. In a medium mixing bowl, stir together whole wheat flour, milk powder, salt, baking powder, cinnamon, nutmeg and raisins. Set aside.

METAL BLADE: Add peanuts, if used; process until smooth and proceed with recipe. Add peanut butter, butter, honey, egg, and vanilla extract to work bowl. Process 10 seconds. Stop machine, scrape down sides of bowl; add banana chunks. Process until smooth. Stop machine, scrape down sides of bowl; add flour mixture all at once. Combine with 4-5 on/off pulses, only until batter is mixed; do not overprocess.

Pour batter into an oiled 9 x 9-inch baking pan. Bake 22 minutes or until a toothpick inserted in the center comes out clean. Remove from oven, cool in pan on wire rack. Cut into bars.

Preparation: 10 minutes
Baking: 22 minutes
Protein g/s: 5.5

Sunflower Seed Carrot Bars

24 bars

Moist bars loaded with sunflower seeds and raisins.

1 *cup whole wheat flour, measured scoop and level*
1 *teaspoon baking powder*
¼ *teaspoon salt*
½ *teaspoon ground cinnamon*
¾ *cup sunflower seeds*
¾ *cup raisins*
2 *medium carrots, peeled*
2 *eggs*
2 *tablespoons oil*
½ *cup honey*
1 *teaspoon vanilla extract*

Preheat oven to 350°.

METAL BLADE: Add flour, baking powder, salt, cinnamon, sunflower seeds and raisins to work bowl. Pulse on/off to mix. Remove to medium mixing bowl and set aside.

SHREDDING DISC: Cut carrots to fit feed tube vertically. Stack and shred. Remove and add to flour mixture. Toss to mix.

METAL BLADE: Add eggs, oil, honey and vanilla to work bowl. Process 10 seconds. Scrape down sides of bowl. Add flour/carrot mixture to bowl all at once. Combine with 3-4 on/off pulses until just mixed. Do not overprocess. Spread batter in a greased 8 x 8-inch baking pan. Bake 30 minutes. Place pan on wire rack; allow to cool. Cut into bars.

Preparation: 10 minutes
Baking: 30 minutes
Protein g/s: 2.5

Carob Nut Bars

16 bars

Moist brownie-like bars.

½ *cup butter or margarine*
¾ *cup honey*
½ *cup carob powder*
¾ *cup whole wheat flour, measured scoop and level*
1 *teaspoon baking powder*
¼ *teaspoon salt*
2 *eggs*
1 *teaspoon vanilla extract*
¾ *cup walnuts*

Preheat oven to 350°. In a small saucepan, melt butter; stir in honey and carob powder. Remove from heat and set aside. Stir together flour, baking powder and salt, set aside.

METAL BLADE: Add eggs and vanilla extract to work bowl. Process 5 seconds. Stop machine, scrape down sides of bowl. With machine running, pour in carob/honey mixture. Process until well-mixed. Scrape down sides of bowl. Turn machine off; remove cover of work bowl. Add the flour mixture all at once. Add walnuts. Combine with 3-4 on/off pulses until mixed and walnuts are coarsely chopped.

Spread batter evenly over the bottom of an oiled 8 x 8-inch baking pan. Bake 31-33 minutes or until a toothpick inserted in the center comes out clean. Remove pan from oven, allow to cool completely in the pan on a wire rack. Cut into bars.

Preparation: 5-8 minutes
Baking: 31-33 minutes
Protein g/s: 2.5

Apfelkuchen Supreme

Serves 8

We enjoy this special occasion dessert because it is high in protein and not too sweet.

⅓ cup walnuts
1¼ cups whole wheat flour, measured scoop and
    level
½ cup light brown sugar, firmly packed
pinch salt
2 teaspoons baking powder
grated rind from ½ fresh lemon
½ cup butter or margarine
3 eggs
2 teaspoons vanilla extract
3-4 drops lemon extract
2-3 Golden or Red Delicious apples
additional margarine for greasing pan
powdered sugar for topping (optional)

Preheat oven to 350°.

METAL BLADE: Add walnuts to work bowl. Pulse on/off until evenly chopped. Remove and set aside. Add flour, brown sugar, salt, baking powder and lemon rind to work bowl. Pulse on/off to mix. Add butter, cut into 1-inch pieces. Pulse on/off until mixture resembles coarse meal. With machine running, add eggs, vanilla extract and lemon extract. Process until well-mixed. Grease bottom of a 9 or 9½-inch springform pan. Using a spatula, spread dough to form an even layer.

Peel and core apples. Slice apples, by hand, into thin wedges. If you are not concerned with perfectly shaped wedges, this can be done using the slicing disc. Stack apple quarters in feed tube horizontally. For even slices, slice 2 quarters at a time with flat side on disc. Starting on the outside, arrange apples over crust in a pin-wheel fashion, overlapping slightly. Repeat to form two concentric circles. Top with walnuts. Bake 20-25 minutes. Allow to cool slightly. Just before serving, dust very lightly with powdered sugar. Serve warm or at room temperature.

Preparation: 10 minutes
Baking: 20-25 minutes
Protein g/s: 6

Sautéed Apples

Serves 4

A simple and excellent topping for pancakes and desserts.

4 cooking apples—Pippin, Granny Smith or Newton
2 tablespoons butter or margarine
2 tablespoons honey
¼ teaspoon cinnamon
¼ cup water

Peel, quarter and core apples.

SLICING DISC: Stack apple quarters in feed tube horizontally. Slice 2 quarters at a time with flat side on disc. Melt butter in a skillet over medium heat. Add apple slices, sauté until they are tender-crisp. Add honey, cinnamon and water and stir to mix. Reduce heat, cook until all the water has evaporated and apples are tender but not mushy.

Preparation: 5 minutes
Cooking: 15-20 minutes

Apple Pie

Serves 8

Only 1-3 tablespoons of honey in this dessert. Do not substitute Delicious apples; the flavor is simply not comparable. A pâté brisée crust is used because it does not absorb moisture as readily as other crusts.

2 recipes Whole Wheat Pâté Brisée Crust (see
    index)
2 pounds tart cooking apples, Pippin, Granny Smith
    or Newtons
1 tablespoon lemon juice
1-3 tablespoons honey
¼ teaspoon salt
½ teaspoon ground cinnamon
1 egg white, beaten
1 egg yolk, beaten

Preheat oven to 375°. Prepare 2 recipes whole wheat pâté brisée crust. Wrap separately in plastic; refrigerate 10-15 minutes while preparing apples. Peel, core and quarter apples.

SLICING DISC: Stack apple wedges in feed tube vertically, slice. Remove to mixing bowl and add lemon juice and honey. Toss to mix. Remove one portion of dough from the refrigerator. Dust lightly with flour and place between two sheets of wax paper. Roll into a circle ⅛-inch thick and 2 inches larger than 10-inch pie plate. Line oiled plate with pastry; trim edge, leaving 1-inch overhang. Prick bottom with a fork. Brush bottom and sides with egg white. Mix together salt and cinnamon. Layer apple mixture into the pastry shell, occasionally adding a sprinkling of salt and cinnamon mixture throughout.

Roll remaining pastry. Place over filling; trim edge, leaving 1-inch overhang. Fold overhang under; bring up over pie plate rim to form a high standup edge; flute. Prick top with a fork to allow steam to escape. Decorate with leftover dough as desired. Brush with egg yolk. Bake 40-50 minutes until crust is golden and apples are tender. Remove to wire rack. Serve warm or cool.

Preparation: 20-30 minutes
Baking: 40-50 minutes
Protein g/s: 4

SLICING DISC: Cut carrots into lengths to fit feed tube vertically, slice. Steam until tender, about 10-15 minutes. Remove from heat, allow to cool slightly.

METAL BLADE: Add carrot slices and orange juice to work bowl. Process until smooth. Add cottage cheese, honey, eggs, salt, and spices to work bowl. Process until well-blended and smooth. Stop machine occasionally to scrape down sides of the bowl.

Lightly butter a 9-inch pie pan. Pour in the carrot cheese mixture. Bake 50 minutes or until center is firm when pan is gently tapped. Place on wire rack to cool. Loosen edges, place in refrigerator until well-chilled.

Preparation: 15 minutes
Baking: 60 minutes
Chilling: 3-4 hours
Protein g/s: 8

Carrot Cheese Pie

Serves 8

A protein rich dessert that's reminiscent of an all time favorite. Use the amount of spice that suits your taste.

5 *medium carrots, pared (about 10 ounces)*
¼ *cup orange juice*
1½ *cups cottage cheese*
¼ *cup plus 2 tablespoons honey*
3 *eggs*
pinch salt
1-1½ *teaspoons ground cinnamon*
¼-½ *teaspoon ground ginger*
¼-½ *teaspoon ground nutmeg*
⅛-¼ *teaspoon ground allspice*
⅛-¼ *teaspoon ground cloves*

Preheat oven to 350°.

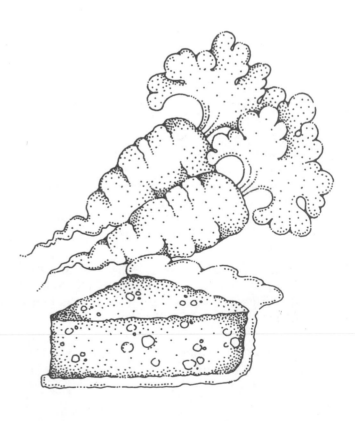

Fresh Apple Cake

Serves 6

Shredded apple makes this spicy cake moist and tender. Serve it warm or cold.

1 *cup whole wheat flour, measured scoop and level*
¾ *teaspoon baking soda*
¾ *teaspoon salt*
⅛ *teaspoon baking powder*
1 *teaspoon ground cinnamon*
½ *teaspoon ground nutmeg*
1 *teaspoon grated lemon peel*
½ *cup walnuts*
1 *medium or large Golden Delicious apple, cored,*
    quartered
¼ *cup butter*
½ *cup honey*
1 *egg*
2 *tablespoons water*
½ *teaspoon vanilla extract*

Preheat oven to 350°.

METAL BLADE: Add whole wheat flour, baking soda, salt, baking powder, cinnamon, nutmeg, lemon peel and walnuts to work bowl. Pulse on/off to mix. Remove metal blade; insert shredding disc.

SHREDDING DISC: Stack apple quarters in feed tube. Shred into flour mixture. Remove to mixing bowl. Toss to mix.

METAL BLADE: Add butter, honey, egg, water and vanilla extract to work bowl. Process 10 seconds. Stop machine, scrape down sides of bowl. Process an additional 15 seconds. Scrape down sides of bowl, add dry ingredients all at once. Combine with 3-4 on/off pulses. Before last on/off, scrape down sides of work bowl. Do not overprocess.

Pour into a greased and floured 8 x 8-inch baking pan. Bake 30-35 minutes or until wooden toothpick inserted in center comes out clean. Cool slightly; serve warm or allow to cool completely.

Preparation: 10 minutes
Baking: 30-35 minutes
Protein g/s: 5.5

Carrot Cake

Serves 6-9

Your processor takes the work out of shredding the carrots for this popular, moist cake. Let the cake stand, well-wrapped, overnight for the flavors to develop.

1 *cup whole wheat flour, measured scoop and level*
2 *teaspoons ground cinnamon*
½ *teaspoon ground nutmeg*
1 *teaspoon salt*
1½ *teaspoons baking soda*
2 *medium carrots, pared*
2 *eggs*
½ *cup oil*
½ *cup honey*
1 *teaspoon vanilla extract*
½ *cup walnuts*

Preheat oven to 350°.

METAL BLADE: Add whole wheat flour, cinnamon, nutmeg, salt and baking soda to work bowl. Pulse on/off to mix. Remove metal blade; insert shredding disc.

SHREDDING DISC: Cut carrots to fit feed tube vertically. Shred into flour mixture. Remove from work bowl, set aside.

METAL BLADE: Add eggs, oil, honey and vanilla extract to work bowl. Process 5 seconds. Stop machine, remove work bowl cover and scrape down sides of bowl. Process an additional 10 seconds. Scrape down sides of bowl. Add dry ingredients all at once. Add walnuts. Combine with 3-4 on/off pulses. Before last on/off, scrape down sides of work bowl. Do not overprocess. Pour into a greased 8 x 8-inch baking pan. Bake 30-35 minutes or until a wooden toothpick inserted in center comes out clean. Cool completely.

Preparation; 10 minutes
Baking: 30-35 minutes
Protein g/s: 6 servings—6.5
              9 servings—4.5

Tropical Uncheese Cake

Serves 8

This high-protein low-fat dessert will keep your guests guessing.

7 graham crackers or 1 cup crumbs
3 tablespoons melted butter
1 block firm tofu, 20-24 ounces, well-drained
4 eggs
½ cup honey
2 tablespoons lemon juice
1 teaspoon grated lemon peel
¼ teaspoon ground cinnamon
1 teaspoon vanilla extract
2 medium bananas, ripe
1 8-ounce can crushed pineapple, well-drained

Preheat oven to 350°.

METAL BLADE: Place crackers, broken into pieces, in the work bowl and process to make fine crumbs. With machine running, pour in melted butter. Pulse on/off until blended. Press crumbs into the bottom of a 9-inch springform pan. Bake 6 minutes. Cool on rack. Reduce oven temperature to 325°.

METAL BLADE: Add tofu, broken into chunks, to the work bowl. Add eggs, honey, lemon juice, lemon peel, cinnamon and vanilla extract. Process until well-mixed. Stop machine, remove work bowl cover and scrape down sides of the bowl. Add bananas, broken into chunks and process until smooth. Scrape down sides of bowl, add pineapple. Pulse on/off only until mixed. Pour into cooled crust. Bake about 1 hour or until center barely jiggles when pan is tapped. Cool on rack. Cover and refrigerate until well-chilled.

Preparation: 15 minutes
Baking: 1 hour, 15 minutes
Chilling: several hours
Protein g/s: 9

Peanut Butter Sandwiches

20 cookies

Homemade peanut butter fills these crisp cookies.

1¼ cups whole wheat flour, measured scoop and level
½ teaspoon baking soda
¼ teaspoon salt
2 tablespoons non-instant, non-fat milk powder
2 cups roasted peanuts or 1 cup smooth peanut butter
½ cup butter, cut into 1-inch pieces
¼ cup brown sugar, firmly packed
1 rounded tablespoon honey

Stir together flour, baking soda, salt and milk powder. Set aside.

METAL BLADE: Add peanuts to work bowl. Process until smooth. Stop machine, remove work bowl cover and scrape down sides as needed. Remove about ½ cup and reserve for filling. Add butter, brown sugar and honey to peanut butter in work bowl. Process until well-mixed. Stop machine, remove work bowl cover and add dry ingredients all at once. Process until just blended. Dough may be slightly crumbly.

Remove dough from bowl. Form into an even oblong 7 inches long and 2½ inches in diameter. Wrap in wax paper and freeze about 2 hours or refrigerate until firm enough to slice. Preheat oven to 350°. Remove dough from freezer.

With a sharp knife, cut half of the oblong into ⅛-inch slices. Place 1½ inches apart on a foil-lined cookie sheet. Place 1 level teaspoon peanut butter in the center of each cookie. Spread to flatten, leaving a ½-inch border. Slice remaining dough and place over peanut butter. Let stand 2-3 minutes to soften slightly. Seal edges by pressing together with fingertips. The tops will crack slightly. Bake 10-11 minutes or until lightly browned. Let stand on sheet 1 minute; remove carefully to racks and allow to cool. Store in airtight container.

Preparation: 10 minutes
Chilling: 2 hours
Baking: 10-11 minutes
Protein g/s: 5

Oat Peanut Butter Crunchies

3 dozen cookies

½ cup butter, cut into 1-inch pieces
¼ cup brown sugar, firmly packed
⅓ cup peanut butter
¼ cup honey
1 egg
1 teaspoon vanilla
¾ cup whole wheat flour, measured scoop and level
½ cup rolled oats
2 tablespoons non-instant, non-fat milk powder
½ teaspoon baking soda
¼ teaspoon salt
¼ cup carob chips

Preheat oven to 350°.

METAL BLADE: Add butter, brown sugar, peanut butter, honey, egg and vanilla to work bowl. Process 5 seconds. Stop machine, remove work bowl cover, scrape down sides of bowl. Process an additional 10 seconds; scrape down sides of bowl.

Stir together whole wheat flour, oats, milk powder, baking soda, salt and carob chips. Add dry ingredients all at once to work bowl. Combine with 3-4 on/off pulses until just mixed. Do not overprocess.

Line cookie sheet with foil. Drop batter by heaping teaspoonfuls onto foil, 2 inches apart. Bake 10 minutes. Remove to wire rack to cool. Store in airtight container.

Preparation: 5-7 minutes
Baking: 10 minutes
Protein g/s: 1.5

Fruit Swirl Cookies

4 dozen cookies

These cookies are best when eaten 1 or 2 days after baking. When stored longer, the filling makes the cookie soft.

4 ounces pitted prunes, about 16, or dried fruit of your choice
2 tablespoons honey
1 tablespoon water
¼ cup sunflower seeds
¼ cup butter or margarine
⅓ cup honey
½ teaspoon vanilla extract
1⅓ cups whole wheat flour, measured scoop and level
½ teaspoon ground cinnamon
¼ teaspoon baking soda
¼ teaspoon salt

METAL BLADE: Add prunes to work bowl and process until finely chopped. Remove to a small bowl, add 2 tablespoons honey, 1 tablespoon water and sunflower seeds. Stir to mix. Set filling aside.

Stir together flour, cinnamon, baking soda and salt. Set aside.

METAL BLADE: Add butter, honey and vanilla extract to work bowl. Process until mixture is smooth. Remove work bowl cover, add flour mixture. Process until well blended.

Divide the dough into two portions. Place one portion between 2 sheets of wax paper and roll to form a 9 x 7-inch rectangle. Spread half the filling over the entire surface of the rectangle. Beginning with the long side, roll up tightly, using the wax paper to lift dough during rolling. Wrap the roll in wax paper and chill in the freezer for at least 1 hour, but no longer than 2 hours. Repeat with second portion of dough.

Arrange oven rack to bake cookes in the upper third of the oven. Preheat to 375°. With a sharp knife cut dough into ¼-inch slices and place on foil-lined cookie sheet. These do not spread. Bake 10 minutes or until they are golden brown. Place on racks to cool. Store in airtight container.

Preparation: 8 minutes
Chilling: 1 hour in the freezer
Baking: 10 minutes
Protein g/s: .5

Oatmeal Refrigerator Cookies

3 dozen cookies

An interesting pattern is produced when the knife slices through the rolled oats. These are crunchy cookies.

1¾ cups whole wheat flour, measured scoop and
　　level
½ teaspoon baking soda
¼ teaspoon salt
1 teaspoon cinnamon
1 tablespoon brown sugar
2 tablespoons non-instant, non-fat milk powder
½ cup rolled oats
¼ cup butter or margarine
½ cup crunchy or creamy peanut butter
⅓ cup honey
1 egg
1 teaspoon vanilla extract

In a mixing bowl, combine flour, baking soda, salt, cinnamon, sugar, milk powder and rolled oats. Set aside.

METAL BLADE: Add butter, peanut butter, honey, egg and vanilla extract to work bowl. Process 10 seconds. Stop machine, remove work bowl cover and scrape down sides of bowl. Process an additional 10 seconds. Remove work bowl cover and add flour mixture all at once. Combine with 3-4 on/off pulses until well-mixed.

Shape into two 5-inch long rolls. Wrap in plastic wrap or wax paper. Chill for several hours or overnight in the refrigerator. Preheat oven to 375°. Remove dough from refrigerator. Using a sharp serrated knife, cut into ¼-inch thick slices. Place ½ inch apart on a foil-lined cookie sheet. These cookies do not spread. Bake 5-8 minutes or until edges are lightly browned.

Preparation: 10 minutes
Baking: 5-8 minutes
Chilling: 3-4 hours
Protein g/s: 2

Oat Fruit Nut Drops

3½ dozen cookies

½ cup walnuts
1 cup rolled oats
¼ cup sunflower seeds
¾ cup plus 1 tablespoon whole wheat flour,
　　measured scoop and level
1 tablespoon soy flour
1 tablespoon non-instant, non-fat milk powder
2 tablespoons rye flour
½ teaspoon baking powder
12 whole pitted dates
2 eggs
¼ cup oil
¼ cup honey
¼ cup milk
½ teaspoon vanilla extract

Adjust oven rack to bake cookies in the upper third of the oven. Preheat to 350°.

METAL BLADE: Add walnuts to work bowl. Pulse on/off until nuts are coarsely chopped. Remove to medium mixing bowl. Stir in oats and sunflower seeds. Add whole wheat flour, soy flour, milk powder, rye flour, and baking powder to work bowl. Pulse on/off to mix. Add dates; pulse on/off until dates are coarsely chopped. Add to walnuts.

Add eggs, oil, honey, milk and vanilla extract to work bowl. Process 10 seconds. Remove work bowl cover, scrape down sides and add dry ingredients all at once. Combine with 3-4 on/off pulses, until just mixed. Do not over-process.

Line cookie sheet with foil. Drop batter by heaping teaspoonfuls onto foil, ½ inch apart. Flatten slightly. These cookies do not spread. Bake 15-17 minutes or until light brown. Remove to wire rack to cool. Store in airtight container.

Preparation: 5 minutes
Baking: 15-17 minutes
Protein g/s: 1.5

Sesame Oat Cookies

4 dozen cookies

1 cup whole wheat flour, measured scoop and level
2 tablespoons non-instant, non-fat milk powder
1¼ cups rolled oats
½ cup sesame seeds
¼ cup currants or raisins
1 teaspoon ground cinnamon
¼ teaspoon salt
¼ cup whole almonds
1 egg
½ cup oil
½ cup honey

Preheat oven to 350°. Stir together flour, milk powder, oats, sesame seeds, currants, cinnamon and salt. Set aside.

METAL BLADE: Add almonds to work bowl. Process until evenly chopped. Remove from bowl and add to flour mixture. Add egg, oil and honey to work bowl. Process 5 seconds. Stop machine, remove work bowl cover and scrape down sides of bowl. Process an additional 10 seconds; scrape down sides of bowl. Add dry ingredients all at once. Combine with 3-4 on/off pulses until just mixed. Do not overprocess.

Line a cookie sheet with foil. Drop batter by heaping teaspoonfuls onto foil, 1 inch apart. Flatten slightly with back of spoon. These cookies do not spread. Bake 9-11 minutes or until edges are lightly browned. Remove to wire rack to cool. Store in airtight container.

Preparation: 7 minutes
Baking: 9-11 minutes
Protein g/s: 1.5

Sunflower Seed Oatmeal Cookies

32 cookies

As cookies go, these are crunchy, extremely nutritious and high in protein.

½ cup butter or safflower margarine
⅔-¾ cup brown sugar
1 egg
1 teaspoon vanilla extract
¾ cup whole wheat flour, measured scoop and level
½ cup soy flour, measured scoop and level
½ teaspoon baking soda
1 cup rolled oats
½ cup sunflower seeds

Preheat oven to 350°.

METAL BLADE: Add butter, cut into 1-inch pieces, sugar, egg and vanilla extract to work bowl. Process 5 seconds. Stop machine and scrape down sides of bowl. Process 10 seconds until well blended and fluffy. Stir together whole wheat flour, soy flour, baking soda, rolled oats and sunflower seeds. Remove cover of work bowl, add flour mixture all at once. Pulse on/off 2-3 times until just mixed. Do not overprocess. Oats and sunflower seeds should remain just about whole.

Line cookie sheet with foil. Drop cookie dough by level tablespoonfuls onto foil, 2 inches apart. Flatten slightly to about 2-inch rounds. These cookies spread only slightly. Bake 10-12 minutes or until lightly browned around the edges. Remove to wire rack to cool. Store in airtight container.

Preparation 5 minutes
Baking: 10-12 minutes
Protein g/s: 2

Almond Rounds

30 cookies

A crunchy, slightly chewy cookie delicately flavored with almond. These cookies travel well.

⅓ cup whole almonds
1¼ cups whole wheat flour, measured scoop and level
1 teaspoon baking powder
pinch salt
⅓ cup butter or margarine
⅓ cup honey
1 teaspoon almond extract
¼ teaspoon vanilla extract
1 egg

Adjust oven rack to bake cookies in the upper third of the oven. Preheat to 350°

METAL BLADE: Add almonds to work bowl. Pulse on/off to finely chop. Add flour, baking powder and salt. Pulse on/off to mix. Add butter, cut into 1-inch pieces; process until mixture resembles coarse meal. Stop machine, pour in honey, almond extract, vanilla extract and egg. Process until well blended. Dough will be soft.

Transfer dough to a sheet of wax paper lightly dusted with flour. Pat the dough into a circle ½-inch thick. Cut into 1½-inch rounds. Gather remaining dough and continue to pat out to ½-inch thick and cut more cookies.

Place rounds on a foil-lined cookie sheet about ½-inch apart. These do not spread. Bake 18-20 minutes or until light brown. Do not overbake or these cookies will become dry. Remove cookies to wire rack to cool completely. Store in an airtight container.

Preparation: 10-15 minutes
Baking: 18-20 minutes
Protein g/s: 1

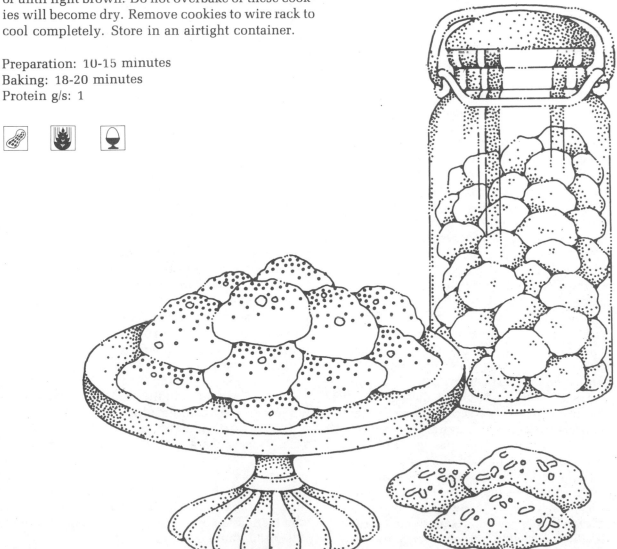

Appendix A—Amino Acids

Protein is found in all plant and animal tissue. Chemically it is made up of 22 amino acids, strung together in different sequences and different numbers depending on the type of protein. Each amino acid consists of a central carbon atom with a hydrogen atom attached, an amino or nitrogen group, and an acid group. Additional atoms (mostly hydrogen, oxygen and carbon) are attached in various patterns. Each variation in pattern constitutes a different amino acid.

It is nitrogen which makes the protein quite distinct from other classes of nutrients, such as fats and carbohydrates. When scientists measure protein, they usually measure nitrogen and use a conversion factor to arrive at the amount of protein present.

Of the twenty-two amino acids, nine cannot be produced in the body. They must be present in the food we eat and are therefore referred to as "essential amino acids." The nine essential amino acids are: tryptophan, phenylalanine, leucine, isoleucine, lysine, valine, threonine, methionine, and cystine and histidine.

Methionine and cystine, the two sulfur-containing amino acids, are usually considered together because cystine is partially convertible into methionine. Sometimes tyrosine, a nonessential amino acid, is paired with phenylalanine because it has the capacity to spare this essential amino acid. The combination of phenylalanine and tyrosine is referred to as "total aromatic amino acids" or TAAA, whereas the combination of the sulfur-containing amino acids is referred to as TSAA. Histidine has been established as essential for infants and may well be for children. It has not yet been established whether or not it is essential for adults.

Traditionally, the egg has been considered the one food which best approximates the ideal balance of essential amino acids needed by the human species. This is why the egg is used as "reference protein," or the food against which the quality of all other proteins is judged. Recently the egg as a standard has been challenged as containing certain essential amino acids in excess of human needs.

However, no alternative food has gained wide acceptance as the "ideal" protein. One difficulty in judging the quality of a plant protein diet against a fairly rigorous standard such as the egg, is that the quality of the protein will in many instances appear to be lower than it really is. This is particularly true of high quality vegetable proteins such as soy products.

It seems reasonable to consider not using a particular food as a standard at all and to base the composition of the "ideal" protein on actual human requirements for individual amino acids. The following table compares the amino acid patterns of the egg and milk with a proposed pattern based on human amino acid requirements in terms of milligrams per gram of protein.

AMINO ACID PATTERNS PROPOSED FOR EVALUATING THE NUTRITIONAL QUALITY OF PROTEINS

(Stated in milligrams per gram of protein contained)

Amino acid	Egg	Milk	Proposed NRC pattern
histidine	24	27	17
isoleucine	66	65	42
leucine	91	100	70
lysine	66	66	51
total sulfur-containing amino acids	55	34	26
total aromatic amino acids	101	100	73
threonine	50	47	35
tryptophan	18	14	11
valine	74	70	48

Source: National Research Council. Committee on Amino Acids. *Improvement of Protein Nutriture*, Washington, D. C.: National Academy of Sciences, 1974.

Proteins approximating the ideal pattern are sometimes referred to as "complete" proteins. This term is often used in a misleading way by people who view the animal sources as "complete" and the vegetable sources as "incomplete" proteins. To the nutritionist, however, an "incomplete" protein is totally lacking in one or more of the essential amino acids, and few foods other than gelatin fall in that category. If animal and vegetable proteins are viewed in terms of usability, which is what is really important, the "complete-incomplete" distinction is largely irrelevant. There is little difference in usability between a soy product such as tofu, and beef.

When the proportion of essential amino acids deviates from the ideal pattern, the one in shortest supply proportionately determines the extent to which all of the others are utilized and is therefore called the limiting amino acid.

When we compute how well the individual amino

acids in a food compare to the egg, or any other standard for that matter, we are computing a theoretical chemical score to predict how a protein should perform biologically, based on the effect of limiting amino acids. This score, in effect, amounts to a percentage of the limiting amino acid in the food compared to the same amino acid in the egg or other standard. When rated according to the egg standard, the chemical score of beef is somewhere around 67-69 because of its fairly low tryptophan content, which is only 67-69% of the tryptophan present in the egg per gram of protein.

It is possible to compute these theoretical values for individual foods or combinations of foods. These values generally correlate well with experimental measurements of protein quality, such as Net Protein Utilization (NPU), which is the percentage of protein consumed that is actually retained and used in the body, and Protein Efficiency Ratio (PER), which is the amount of weight gain in growing laboratory animals per gram of protein consumed.

Chemical or amino acid scores, however, are not always exact predictors of PER and NPU. In some instances these values are far enough apart to cause puzzlement. Possibly the egg, our current reference protein, contains more of some amino acids than we need, thereby making chemical scores for other foods too low. This could be particularly true in the case of some of the legumes (beans, peas, and lentils) which are deficient in the sulfur-containing amino acids, those amino acids which in the egg seem to exceed human requirements. To confound matters further, there is evidence to suggest that estimates based on experimental measurements of proteins on the lower end of the quality scale are far too high—particularly in cases where lysine is the limiting amino acid. A good example of this phenomenon is gluten, a poor quality wheat protein which is extremely low in lysine. It has a chemical score of approximately 26, but its experimentally determined usability is somewhere around 39.

The amount of protein the body can actually use is always less than the total amount of protein in the food, because, in addition to the limiting amino acids, the digestibility of a food limits the availability of specific amino acids, or total protein. If a certain amino acid is concentrated in a less digestible part of the food, less of it will be absorbed.

Protein synthesis occurs in the body continuously. Therefore, for the most part, all essential amino acids should be present in nearly ideal proportions at the same time. But a bit of leeway is provided by a "pool" of amino acids in the small intestine. This "pool" consists chiefly of sloughed off cells from the intestinal lining, which are renewed every few days, but also contains amino acids from protein broken down in the tissues throughout the body and from digestive enzymes which are finally digested themselves. When you ingest a protein food, it is broken down, diluted with amino acids in the pool, and circulated through the bloodstream to the liver and other locations where protein synthesis takes place.[1] However, not a great deal is known about the relative contributions of "pool" amino acids and "food" amino acids to protein synthesis, although synthesis usually exceeds protein intake by a wide margin. What we do know suggests caution in placing too much reliance on this pool, because it has been shown that amino acid patterns in the food consumed are reflected in the blood plasma after digestion when the percentage of protein in the diet is over 10%.[2] This suggests that deficiencies in the amino acid patterns of foods are only partially offset by this amino acid "pool." And recent research indicates that the pool may not be as large as was once thought.[3]

To be on the safe side, we recommend trying to obtain a reasonably good balance of amino acids at each meal, so that they will be in the system in adequate proportion to one another. This is extremely important because tissues and other body proteins are constantly being broken down and rebuilt, and while some amino acids are recycled, others are lost in the feces, urine, sweat, hair, and fingernails, or are sloughed off in dead skin cells. In sum, a continuous supply of essential amino acids is required for maintenance and repair, for growth, and for the regulation of metabolic processes.

In addition to the essential amino acids, the body requires a sufficient amount of nonspecific nitrogen, or protein in the form of the nonessential amino acids, so that it can synthesize those that it needs at any given time.

NOTES

[1]E.S. Nasset, "Amino Acid Homeostasis in the Gut Lumen and Its Nutritional Significance," *World Review of Nutrition and Dietetics* 14 (1972): 132-53.

[2]J.M. McLaughlan, "Nutritional Significance of Alterations in Plasma Amino Acids and Serum Proteins," in National Research Council, Committee on Amino Acids, *Improvement of Protein Nutriture* (Washington, D.C.: National Academy of Sciences, 1974), pp. 89-108.

[3]K.J. Curtis, et al., "Protein Digestion and Absorption in the Rat," *Journal of Physiology* 274 (1978): pp. 409-19.

Appendix B

FOOD AND NUTRITION BOARD, NATIONAL ACADEMY OF SCIENCES—NATIONAL RESEARCH COUNCIL
RECOMMENDED DAILY DIETARY ALLOWANCES,[a] Revised 1980

Designed for the maintenance of good nutrition of practically all healthy people in the U.S.A.

	Age (years)	Weight (kg)	Weight (lb)	Height (cm)	Height (in)	Protein (g)	Fat-Soluble Vitamins: Vitamin A (µg RE)[b]	Vitamin A (IU)	Vitamin D (µg)[c]	Vitamin D (IU)	Vitamin E (mg α-TE)[d]	Vitamin E (IU)	Water-Soluble Vitamins: Vitamin C (mg)	Thiamin (mg)	Riboflavin (mg)	Niacin (mg NE)[e]	Vitamin B-6 (mg)	Folacin[f] (µg)	Vitamin B-12 (µg)	Minerals: Calcium (mg)	Phosphorus (mg)	Magnesium (mg)	Iron (mg)	Zinc (mg)	Iodine (µg)
Infants	0.0-0.5	6	13	60	24	kg × 2.2	420	1400	10	400	3	4	35	0.3	0.4	6	0.3	30	0.58	360	240	50	10	3	40
	0.5-1.0	9	20	71	28	kg × 2.0	400	2000	10	400	4	5	35	0.5	0.6	8	0.6	45	1.5	540	360	70	15	5	50
Children	1-3	13	29	90	35	23	400	2000	10	400	5	7	45	0.7	0.8	9	0.9	100	2.0	800	800	150	15	10	70
	4-6	20	44	112	44	30	500	2500	10	400	6	9	45	0.9	1.0	11	1.3	200	2.5	800	800	200	10	10	90
	7-10	28	62	132	52	34	700	3500	10	400	7	10	45	1.2	1.4	16	1.6	300	3.0	800	800	250	10	10	120
Males	11-14	45	99	157	62	45	1000	5000	10	400	8	12	50	1.4	1.6	18	1.8	400	3.0	1200	1200	350	18	15	150
	15-18	66	145	176	69	56	1000	5000	10	400	10	15	60	1.4	1.7	18	2.0	400	3.0	1200	1200	400	18	15	150
	19-22	70	154	177	70	56	1000	5000	7.5	300	10	15	60	1.5	1.7	19	2.2	400	3.0	800	800	350	10	15	150
	23-50	70	154	178	70	56	1000	5000	5	200	10	15	60	1.4	1.6	18	2.2	400	3.0	800	800	350	10	15	150
	51+	70	154	178	70	56	1000	5000	5	200	10	15	60	1.2	1.4	16	2.2	400	3.0	800	800	350	10	15	150
Females	11-14	46	101	157	62	46	800	4000	10	400	8	12	50	1.1	1.3	15	1.8	400	3.0	1200	1200	300	18	15	150
	15-18	55	120	163	64	46	800	4000	10	400	8	12	60	1.1	1.3	14	2.0	400	3.0	1200	1200	300	18	15	150
	19-22	55	120	163	64	44	800	4000	7.5	300	8	12	60	1.1	1.3	14	2.0	400	3.0	800	800	300	18	15	150
	23-50	55	120	163	64	44	800	4000	5	200	8	12	60	1.0	1.2	13	2.0	400	3.0	800	800	300	18	15	150
	51+	55	120	163	64	44	800	4000	5	200	8	12	60	1.0	1.2	13	2.0	400	3.0	800	800	300	10	15	150
Pregnant						+30	+200	+1000	+5	+200	+2	+3	+20	+0.4	+0.3	+2	+0.6	+400	+1.0	+400	+400	+150	h	+5	+25
Lactating						+20	+400	+2000	+5	+200	+3	+4	+40	+0.5	+0.5	+5	+0.5	+100	+1.0	+400	+400	+150	h	+10	+50

a The allowances are intended to provide for individual variations among most normal persons as they live in the United States under usual environmental stresses. Diets should be based on a variety of common foods in order to provide other nutrients for which human requirements have been less well defined. See text for detailed discussion of allowances and of nutrients not tabulated.

b Retinol equivalents. 1 retinol equivalent = 1 µg retinol or 6 µg β carotene. See text for calculation of vitamin A activity of diets as retinol equivalents.

c As cholecalciferol. 10 µg cholecalciferol = 400 IU of vitamin D.

d α-tocopherol equivalents. 1 mg d-α tocopherol = 1 α-TE. See text for variation in allowances and calculation of vitamin E activity of the diet as α-tocopherol equivalents.

e 1 NE (niacin equivalent) is equal to 1 mg of niacin or 60 mg of dietary tryptophan.

f The folacin allowances refer to dietary sources as determined by *Lactobacillus casei* assay after treatment with enzymes (conjugases) to make polyglutamyl forms of the vitamin available to the test organism.

g The recommended dietary allowance for vitamin B-12 in infants is based on average concentration of the vitamin in human milk. The allowances after weaning are based on energy intake (as recommended by the American Academy of Pediatrics) and consideration of other factors, such as intestinal absorption.

h The increased requirement during pregnancy cannot be met by the iron content of habitual American diets nor by the existing iron stores of many women; therefore the use of 30-60 mg of supplemental iron is recommended. Iron needs during lactation are not substantially different from those of nonpregnant women, but continued supplementation of the mother for 2-3 months after parturition is advisable in order to replenish stores depleted by pregnancy.

Reproduced with equivalents added from: *Recommended Dietary Allowances*, Ninth Edition (1980), with the permission of the National Academy of Sciences, Washington, D.C.

NOTES ON THE NEW UNITS

In the ninth edition of the *Recommended Dietary Allowances*, the allowances for four vitamins, vitamin A, vitamin D, vitamin E, and niacin, are stated in new units of measurement. Because most people have not had time to become familiar with the units and because standard tables of food values will contain information in the old units for some time to come, we have provided approximate equivalents. For niacin, the values using the old and new units are the same, so we did not list them a second time.

VITAMIN A: The allowance for this vitamin was previously expressed in international units (IU). Now it is expressed in micrograms of retinol equivalents (RE). Retinol, or vitamin A, may come from animal or plant sources. If it is obtained from plant sources, it comes in the form of several distinct carotenes. In terms of vitamin A activity, the most active of these is beta carotene, which is converted into retinol at a rate of 50% efficiency. Other carotenes are less active biologically. All are collectively referred to as provitamin A.

If vitamin A is obtained from animal sources, such as milk, eggs, and butter, it has already been converted into retinol for us. In our lacto-ovo-vegetarian diet, roughly 25% of this vitamin is in the form of retinol. Expressed in international units of vitamin A, approximately one half of the adult intake is assumed to be in the form of retinol. For infants, all of the vitamin A required is assumed to be in the form of retinol because milk is the only food consumed. In the adult allowance as expressed in retinol equivalents, 75% is assumed to come in the form of retinol, and 25% is assumed to come from beta carotene.

VITAMIN D: In addition to the vitamin D produced on the surface of the skin on contact with sunshine, there are two distinct dietary forms—cholecalciferol, or vitamin D_3, and ergocalciferol, or vitamin D_2. Cholecalciferol is derived from animal tissues, whereas ergocalciferol is derived from plant sources. Formerly measured in international units (IU), this vitamin is now measured in micrograms of cholecalciferol. Ten micrograms of cholecalciferol are equivalent to 400 IU. The 1980 edition of the *Recommended Dietary Allowances* is the first to contain an adult allowance for this vitamin.

VITAMIN E: Vitamin E activity in food is derived from several distinct tocopherols. Alpha tocopherol is the most biologically active of these substances. Our major sources are vegetable oils and whole grain cereals. Formerly expressed in international units, vitamin E allowances are now stated in milligrams of alpha tocopherol equivalents (αTE). An alpha tocopherol equivalent equals 1 milligram of d-alpha tocopherol and 1.49 IU of naturally occurring alpha tocopherol.

NIACIN: This vitamin has two dietary forms—nicotinic acid (niacin) and nicotinamide (niacinamide). In addition, it can be produced in the body from the amino acid tryptophan. For every 60 milligrams of tryptophan in the diet, enough is diverted to form 1 milligram of niacin. Therefore a niacin equivalent is defined as 1 milligram of niacin in either of the above forms or 60 milligrams of tryptophan.

Acknowledgements

Invaluable technical assistance in the preparation of the nutritional portions of the manuscript was received from members of the University of Hawaii community. We thank, in particular, Professors of Food and Nutritional Science—Dr. Ira J. Lichton for reviewing this portion of the manuscript during the busiest time of the semester; and Dr. Bluebell R. Standal for answering questions on protein quality and for encouraging our early efforts. Many thanks also go to Dr. G. Causey Whittow, Professor of Physiology, for answering our questions on digestive physiology and interpreting conflicting data. The time Barbara Sherrell, graduate student in nutrition, spent in checking the majority of the computations in the nutrition chapter and appendix was greatly appreciated. We are also indebted to Bronwen Solyom and Caroline Payne for ironing out the wrinkles in the initial drafts.

Our thanks go to Joanne Woo, Patrice Whang, Aprielle Chan, Betty Rognstad, Ellen Chapman, Virginia Richardson, and many friends and co-workers who offered recipe suggestions, tried recipes for clarity of directions, and volunteered for taste testing. We also thank Linda McNierney and Paula's mother, Mrs. Paula Kristel, for testing many of our recipes at high altitude.

For their efforts in manuscript review and preparation, thanks to Cj Kuehneman, Grace Ramelb, Holly Alfait Fiocca and Cappy Friedman.

For their support, patience and understanding, special thanks go to Barbara Mussil and Michael McNierney at Johnson Publishing Company.

We also offer thanks and apologies to Noam and others close to us who have shared the joys and frustrations of writing this cookbook.

And finally, to Paul McCarthy, whose idea generated the theme for the book and whose support and constant guidance helped us over the mountain to the completion of this work, our warmest thanks and appreciation.

High Altitude Baking

Yeast Breads

Approximate rising times in this book are for baking at sea level. Yeast grows much more rapidly at high altitudes, so watch carefully to be sure that the rising dough does not expand to more than double its size. No other adjustments are necessary. Baking times, however, may be slightly longer.

Quick Breads and Cakes

The customary adjustments for high altitude are important chiefly for light cakes and other baked goods containing white flour and a substantial amount of sugar. Because we use whole wheat flour and small amounts of brown sugar or honey this is not a problem. A large number of our recipes have been tested at altitudes ranging from 5000 to 6000 feet and have not required adjustments in the amount of baking powder or soda, sugar, and liquids. As with yeast breads, baking times may be slightly longer.

Preparation Times

Preparation times are based on the assumption that ingredients have been laid out beforehand and that the recipes have been read thoroughly. When a recipe is made for the first time, preparation times may be slightly longer.

Subject and Recipe Title Index

Major Ingredient Index

This index lists our recipes by major or distinctive ingredients. It will help you find dishes that can be prepared with foods you have on hand, items that are on special in your supermarket, or vegetables that are plentiful in your garden. This index *excludes* whole wheat flour, butter, margarine, ordinary quantities of eggs, most fluid milk, and all oil except olive oil. Small amounts of honey and brown sugar are also omitted, as are most herbs and seasonings. The arrangement under each ingredient parallels the sequence of recipes in the book.

The Authors

Paula Szilard was born in a German-speaking area of Czechoslovakia and has lived in various parts of Europe and the U.S. Exposure to many local cuisines has interested her in meatless adaptations of traditional dishes. She is presently a science reference librarian at the University of Hawaii in Honolulu.

Juliana J. Woo was born in San Francisco and learned the basics of cooking, especially Chinese, from her mother. As a marathon runner, she finds that a vegetarian diet contributes to her fitness. With an M.A. in public health, she is the director of the Cancer Information Service of Hawaii.